1500

nt

Vüe de la Bourse Royale à LONDRES.

The Sign of the
Golden Grasshopper

Sir Thomas Gresham, 1544
Reprinted with the kind permission of The Mercers' Company, London.

The Sign of the Golden Grasshopper

A Biography of Sir Thomas Gresham

by
Perry E. Gresham
with
Carol Jose

Jameson Books
Ottawa, Illinois

Copyright © 1995 by Perry Epler Gresham

Jameson Books, Inc.
722 Columbus Street
Ottawa, Illinois 61350 USA

Library of Congress Cataloging-in-Publication Data

Gresham, Perry Epler.
    The sign of the golden grasshopper : a biography of Sir Thomas Gresham / by Perry E. Gresham with Carol Jose.
    - -   p.   c.m.
    Includes bibliographical references and index.
    ISBN 0-915463-71-7 (alk. paper)
    1. Gresham, Thomas, Sir, 1519?–1579.   2. Great Britain — History — Tudors, 1485–1603 — Biography.   3. Royal Exchange (London, England) — History.   4. Philanthropists — Great Britain — Biography.   5. Finance, Public — Great Britain — To 1688.   6. Diplomats — Great Britain — Biography.   7. Merchants — Great Britain — Biography.   8. Gresham College — History.   I. Jose, Carol.   II. Title.
DA317.8.G74G74   1994
942.05'092—dc20
[B]   95–9972
                                                                          CIP

Printed in the United States of America

Jameson Books are distributed to the book trade by Login Publishers Consortium, Chicago, Illinois

First Printing

99 98 97 96 95 / 1 2 3 4 5

To Aleece —
Who brought a lilt to my middle years
as we walked the streets of London
in search of Sir Thomas

England

This royal throne of kings, this sceptered isle,
This earth of majesty, this seat of Mars,
This other Eden, demi-paradise,
This fortress built by nature for herself
Against infection and the hand of war;
This happy breed of men, this little world,
This precious stone set in the silver sea
Which serves it in the office of a wall,
Or as a moat defensive to a house,
Against the envy of less happier lands;
This blessed plot, this earth, this realm,
This England!

William Shakespeare
Richard II

Contents

List of Plates

Chronology

DATE	GRESHAM	ENGLAND	EUROPE/WORLD
1519	Thomas Gresham born, 2nd son of wealthy cloth merchant Richard Gresham of Norfolk and Audrey Lynne Gresham.	10th year of reign of Henry VIII and Queen Catherine of Aragon; Princess Mary Tudor is 3.	Charles V, Holy Roman Emperor; François I, king of France; Reformation begins in Europe; Cortez conquers Mexico.
1520–30	Audrey Gresham dies; Richard marries Isabella Taverson; Gresham brothers (Richard, William, John) procure exclusive trading licenses from Cardinal Wolsey.	Henry VIII named Defender of Faith by Pope Leo; meets Mary and Anne Boleyn at Field of Cloth of Gold; begins affairs; death of Cardinal Wolsey.	Field of Cloth of Gold (1520); secret treaty between Henry VIII and Charles V; Diet of Worms; Magellan circumnavigates globe.
1531–43	Thomas Gresham attends Gonville College, Cambridge, then serves eight year apprenticeship; becomes Merchant Adventurer; studies law at Gray's Inn; his father, Richard Gresham, becomes high sheriff of London, is knighted, serves as Lord Mayor of London; his uncle, John Gresham, knighted, serves as high sheriff. Family's wealth, holdings, increase with grants from Henry VIII, profits from trade, purchases of vast estates, monasteries.	Henry VIII divorces Queen Catherine, marries Anne Boleyn; dau. Elizabeth born (1533); Queen Anne Boleyn executed; Henry marries Jane Seymour; son Edward born (1537); Queen Jane dies; Thomas Cromwell executed; Henry marries Anne of Cleves; divorces; marries Catherine Howard, executes her (1542); war against Scotland; suppression of Catholic monasteries.	Pizzaro conquers Peru; Pope Clement VII excommunicates Henry VIII; Ivan the Terrible rules Muscovia; Catherine de Medici of Italy marries Henri, duke of Orleans (later Henri II); Pope Paul III (1535) assigns Inquisition to Holy Office; France and Spain at war; Calvin leads Protestants in Geneva; birth of El Greco (1541); birth of Mary Stuart in Scotland (1542).

DATE	GRESHAM	ENGLAND	EUROPE/WORLD
1544–46	Thomas Gresham marries widow Anne Ferneley Read; birth of son Richard; Sir John Gresham establishes Holt school in Norfolk.	Henry VIII marries Katherine Parr; allies with Charles V, invades France, defeats French armada but loses the *Mary Rose*.	Council of Trent; Treaty of Crépy between France and Spain.
1547–49	Thomas runs family trading enterprises; his brother John knighted at Musselburgh; Sir Richard Gresham, Thomas's father, dies (1549); Thomas cultivates friendship with Northumberland, William Cecil.	Henry VIII dies (1547); Edward VI crowned at age 9; Somerset (Seymour) becomes Protector; *Book of Common Prayer* for Protestants promulgated by Edward VI (1549).	François I of France dies (1547); Henri II becomes king of France; defeat of Schmalkaldic League, annexation of Netherlands by Charles V; Michelangelo begins building St. Peter's in Rome.
1550–52	Thomas becomes King Edward's Royal Agent, moves to Antwerp.	Duke of Northumberland becomes Protector; William Cecil his secretary; Somerset executed (1552).	Pope Julius III; War between Charles V and Henri II; Turkey and Hungary at war.
1553	Birth of Thomas's daughter Anne to his mistress, in Bruges (?); Thomas dismissed by Mary I as Royal Agent, fears for his life; his brother John departs with Muscovy Expedition; sister Elizabeth dies.	Northumberland's son Guilford Dudley marries Lady Jane Grey; Edward VI dies at 16; Jane Grey reigns only 9 days; Mary Tudor crowned Mary I; England returns to Catholicism; Northumberland executed.	Wars in Europe continue.

Date	Gresham	England	Europe/World
1554–57	Thomas to Spain on special mission; his uncle Sir John dies (1556); Thomas ousted again as Mary's Royal Agent in Antwerp, returns to private trading business in England; is recalled to service when Mary I falls into deep foreign debt.	Mary I marries Philip II of Spain (1554); persecution of Protestants; Wyatt's rebellion quelled; Muscovy company chartered; Latimer, Ridley, Cranmer burned at stake; war on France declared by Philip; drains English treasury.	Turks conquer North Africa; Pope Paul IV; Peace of Augsburg; Charles V abdicates in favor of Philip II; Philip brings Spanish Inquisition to Netherlands; Queen of Hungary regent in Netherlands; Livonian War; Portuguese settle in Macao, China.
1558–59	Thomas Gresham knighted by Queen Elizabeth I, becomes Royal Agent and Ambassador to Netherlands; begins building Gresham House in London; writes economic plan for Elizabeth I.	England loses Calais; Mary I dies; Elizabeth Tudor crowned Queen Elizabeth I; Protestants return to power in England; Sir William Cecil becomes Secretary of State.	Mary queen of Scots marries François II of France; Habsburg Valois war ends; Pope Pius IV; Spain controls Italy.
1560–67	Sir Thomas effects recoinage; his brother Sir John dies (1561); Thomas becomes Queen Elizabeth's unofficial financial adviser, arms smuggler, goods procurer, spy; horse–keeper; official Royal Agent and Ambassador to Netherlands; is injured in a fall; son Richard dies (1564); Sir Thomas returns to England; builds England's first paper and gunpowder mills on his estates; begins building of Exchange in London; stepmother Isabella dies.	Cecil negotiates treaty of Edinburgh; Elizabeth I contracts smallpox; great concern over English succession; aids Huguenots; Peace of Troyes between England and France; birth of William Shakespeare.	Maximilian II Holy Roman Emperor; French Huguenot war; Galileo born; Treaty of Edinburgh; Reign of Terror in Russia; Catholic Mary queen of Scots abdicates Scottish throne, son James IV becomes Protestant King of Scotland; uprisings in Antwerp; death of Michelangelo in Italy.

DATE	GRESHAM	ENGLAND	EUROPE/WORLD
1568–72	Exchange completed, opens; Queen Elizabeth visits Gresham House, Exchange, designates it Royal Exchange; Sir Thomas serves Elizabeth as negotiator, host of foreign dignitaries at Gresham House; becomes guardian of Lady Mary Grey; daughter Anne marries Nathaniel Bacon, son of Lord Keeper; Gresham negotiates loan on jewels for Protestant cause; resolves dilemma of Spanish treasure to England's advantage.	Cecil made Baron Burghley, becomes Lord Treasurer; Mary queen of Scots, Duke of Norfolk, and English Catholics plot against Elizabeth; Spanish treasure fleet lands in English waters; Elizabeth considers French marriage alliance; plot revealed, Duke of Norfolk executed; Queen Elizabeth spares Mary; Puritans admonish Parliament.	Peace of St. Germain; Huguenots achieve conditional freedom of worship; Pope Pius VI excommunicates Elizabeth of England; Mary queen of Scots flees to England; St. Bartholomew's Day massacre of Huguenots in Paris (1572).
1573–78	Queen Elizabeth visits Sir Thomas's estate at Mayfield; Lady Elizabeth Neville, niece and heir of Sir Thomas, dies at Gresham House; Sir Thomas retires, writes his will, endows Gresham College in London, leaves bulk of his fortune to Mercers' Company, City of London; Queen Elizabeth visits him at Osterley.	Noted physician Dr. John Caius, of Gonville and Caius College, Cambridge, dies; Queen Elizabeth I forgives Sir Thomas's accounts; Mary queen of Scots remains under house arrest in England.	Drake begins voyage around world; Charles IX of France dies, Henri III becomes king; Philip II, Duke of Alva and Pope continue to plot to put Mary queen of Scots on English throne and return Catholicism to England; death of Titian (1576); birth of Rubens (1577).
1579	Sir Thomas Gresham dies at Gresham House at age 60, is buried with great ceremony at St. Helen's Church in London; his widow, Anne, survives him by seventeen years.	Queen Elizabeth cries upon hearing of Sir Thomas Gresham's death.	Desmond rebellion in Ireland.

Foreword

We all know the law attributed to Sir Thomas Gresham, that bad money drives good money out of circulation, but few of us know anything about this man who was principally responsible for enabling Tudor England of the sixteenth century to balance the royal budgets in spite of spendthrift kings and queens.

The problem was not that England was poor. Her huge exports of wool and woolen cloth to the Continent brought ducats by the millions into the country. Her intrepid merchants ranged even to Muscovy. The problem was that the Tudor monarchs equated show and display with national power; living lavishly was a sign of success. But they often lived on borrowed money, and who would pay the pipers, the merchant bankers of the Low Countries and Germany?

Sir Thomas Gresham, second son of one of the early great English merchant adventurers, followed in his father Richard's footsteps and amassed a fortune of his own. He was also the greatest English financial genius of his time, because he understood the intricacies of international exchange in an era of mercantilism, when a country's wealth was measured by the gold and silver in the royal treasury.

So successful was he that at an early age he inevitably became one of Henry Vlll's chief financial agents in Antwerp and continued to play this role for Henry's successors until his death in 1579. Sir Thomas probably would have preferred to go his own private, prosperous way. Association with the English court was dangerous in an age when intrigues and jealousies could lead to charges of treason and a one-way visit to the block on Tower Hill. And the Tudor monarchs were unruly and sometimes cruel pupils. But Sir Thomas was indispensable. He was also a loyal subject, and a man who spoke the truth even at the risk of royal displeasure.

This is a biography on the grand scale, about villains and heroes. Lavishly written, it takes us back to one of the most interesting epochs in modern history and to one of the principal players in that history. We now know Sir Thomas Gresham for the first time, thanks to the ability of the authors of this biography to make the people of a golden age live again.

Arthur S. Link

Acknowledgments

This book, the fulfillment of a dream, would have been dull without the magic of Carol Jose, whose special touch and months of added research transformed the chronicles of the "old professor" into the living, exciting story of Sir Thomas and his times, and for that I owe her my deepest thanks. This book would have been impossible without the help of Karen Atkinson, who processed my early research and capably managed my Bethany College office so that I had time to consider the life of Sir Thomas Gresham.

Aleece, my wife of two-score years, walked the streets of London with me, patiently waited while I pored over old manuscripts in the British Museum, read our many revisions, and encouraged me to keep on. Nancy and Bob Sandercox, our librarian daughter and her husband, often revived my flagging spirits and plied me with needed reference material. My son Glen and his wife Phyllis inspired us and provided walking guides to Sir Thomas Gresham's London, as well as information on St. Helen's Church, his burial place. Bethany librarian Mary-Bess Halford tapped her network to produce obscure references for us, and the gracious Lady Bath and her librarian Kate Harris generously offered the facilities of Longleat in England for our perusal of Sir Thomas's letters.

Many other friends and colleagues made valuable contributions: Dr. Arthur Link, the George Davis Professor Emeritus of History at Princeton University and Harmsworth Professor Emeritus of History at Oxford University in England and Dr. Edwin J. Feulner, president of The Heritage Foundation, read the early manuscript, lauded our efforts, and wrote the Foreword and the Introduction, respectively. Editing help and encouragement came also from Professor and Mrs. George Spaulding; Dr. Larry Grimes, Gresham Professor of Humanities at Bethany College; Gresham enthusiasts Bob and Justine Grisham of Abilene, Texas; Michael Daly of Atlanta, Georgia; Alison and Anthony Powell and Norman and Pat Bentham of England; and Sir Garfield Todd, former prime minister of Rhodesia, now Zimbabwe. Dale Jose helped Carol retrace the paths and footsteps of Sir Thomas Gresham in England and Belgium; artist Ursula Hartwigs Roka of Vero Beach, Florida, executed the magnificent oil portrait of Sir Thomas from which our cover face is taken, and Irene Joudy Gustavson did our pen and ink reproduction of his grasshopper seal.

The eminent economists Dr. Milton Friedman, Dr. Allan Meltzer, and Dr. Hans Sennholz gave us pertinent advice, helped us articulate Gresham's law, and patiently researched and answered our many complex economic and monetary questions. My dear friend Dr. Robert Preston offered information on Cambridge University; Mr. David Innes and the firm of Strutt & Parker in England kindly opened Titsey Place and its treasures to us; General Christopher Tyler, governor of the Tower of London, and his affable staff of yeoman warders gave valuable insights to the Tudor rulers and to Sir Thomas Gresham and his times.

The curators of the British Museum and Library, the Royal Exchange, the Guildhall Library, the National Gallery, and the Mercers' Company of London all provided us with special and very valuable access that allowed us deep peeks into the lives of Sir Thomas Gresham and his cohorts.

To all of them, and to the many others we might not have named here, our heartfelt thanks.

Authors' Preface

$\mathcal{I}$n the years—nay, decades—spent researching and writing this life of Sir Thomas Gresham, we chose in the writing of it to follow Shakespeare's principle—that the examination and recounting of history need not be dull or overly pedantic. Sir Thomas and his cohorts were vital, lusty human beings, filled with passion, hatred, greed, naïveté, and cunning, and we portray them here as such.

We have carefully studied the paintings and written accounts of those times; we have walked, sailed, and ridden the routes Sir Thomas walked, sailed and rode; we have stood and sat in rooms in which he stood and sat; our dialogue and situations are taken, for the most part, from the written words and expressed feelings of the characters themselves, gleaned from the voluminous correspondence maintained during that period, which we reviewed in the manuscript and reading rooms of the British Museum and Library in London, and in many other locations, and from the scores of biographies and other books written about the Tudor period. We have exercised some latitude in the narration, but only enough to bring color and life to this grand panorama. One character alone bears a fictitious name—Ghislaine, Gresham's mistress, who bore him a daughter. While her real name is probably lost to history (we tried hard, but without success, to unearth it), she did exist, and she was from Bruges, and likely died shortly after the birth of his child.

In these pages, we bring Sir Thomas Gresham and his contemporaries to life again, so that you may come to know him as the vigorous, adventurous, cunning visionary that he was—against the teeming backdrop of opulence, pageantry, intrigue, danger, skulduggery and excitement of the age in which he lived.

We believe Sir Thomas Gresham's story is especially pertinent now, for these are perilous economic times. As it was back in the sixteenth century, the world is again in a state of upheaval and transition, poised on the brink of sweeping financial, political and social change. We can learn a great deal about our own problems from the life and experiences of Sir Thomas Gresham four centuries ago. For as a sage once said, antiquarian biography is simply a magnifying glass applied to a period of history—it brings that period's morals and mores, its problems and solutions, its successes and failures, into clearer focus. What our magnifying glass, applied to the life and times of Sir Thomas Gresham, reveals about him—and about us—is fascinating.

Gresham was a towering figure of the Tudor period, and probably the most neglected star in the great Elizabethan galaxy. It was he who laid the entrepreneurial foundations, and gave Elizabeth I the advice that would later enable her to defeat the Spanish Armada.

His portrait hangs, along with that of his good friend and mentor William Cecil, Baron Burghley, in a place of honor next to Queen Elizabeth I in the National Portrait Gallery in London. They hang together in death as in life, for they were the close-knit triumvirate that managed to keep England solvent and independent during Elizabeth's long, harrowing, and brilliant reign.

Another portrait of Sir Thomas Gresham is in the Rijksmuseum in Amsterdam, along with that of his wife, Anne, for he was a key financial player on the continent of Europe, too. He resided in Antwerp for many years as royal agent to the Tudors, and served as ambassador to the Netherlands for Queen Elizabeth I.

There are those who did, and who might, criticize Thomas Gresham's motives, manner, and methods, and his intent in carrying out his royal duties and personal business ventures. However, few can quarrel with the spectacular results he achieved. Nor can anyone doubt his supreme loyalty to his rulers, and to his native land. But lest we judge him by our standards, we must remember that he lived and acted in accordance with the prevailing mores and morals of his time. The Tudor kings and queens relied upon him, befriended him, rewarded him, and forgave him his few trespasses. Queen Elizabeth I called him friend, and cried openly when he died. The sign of the golden grasshopper marked his success.

We hope this story of his life and times will make readers acutely aware, as Sir Thomas Gresham was, of the virtue of careful fiscal management, and the calamitous result of war, national overspending and the accumulation of national debt.

Perry Epler Gresham

Note: Author and distinguished professor Perry Epler Gresham passed away, a victim of cancer, in September 1994, during the final publication stages of this book. Brilliant, witty and charming—like his illustrious ancestors Perry was a true Renaissance man. He will be sorely missed by all those who were privileged to know him, and call him friend.

Carol Jose

Authors' Notes

e wish to illuminate two items here that are key to understanding this story, and the financial genius of Sir Thomas Gresham.

1. The relative value, in today's money, of the financial terms and issues of the 1500s in which he was a key player;
2. The fundamental monetary principle that became Gresham's Law and why it is attributed to him.

Relative Monetary Values

The authors make no claim to numismatic or fiduciary expertise. Nor is it our intention to create, then attempt to solve, a thorny economic puzzle. But in order to grasp the actual value of amounts referred to in the story, a ratio of £1 in 1550 to £500 today ($900 U.S.) should be imagined, to reveal the true range of responsibilities for national finance that Sir Thomas Gresham assumed during the Tudor period, and to give some relevance to the value of the monies borrowed, repaid and manipulated. Those amounts, stated merely in their sixteenth-century terms, might seem paltry or irrelevant today, until placed in their present value context by the reader. Conversion was not made in the text, but in the end-notes, and the above formula was used for all conversions made there. In most instances, calculations were rounded off to the nearest decimal point in thousands or millions of pounds or dollars.

There are almost as many ways of calculating the present value of a 1550 pound or dollar as there are economists, historians, bankers, statisticians and numismatists to do so. The recognized authorities the authors consulted, including the Bank of England, produced widely differing opinions and approximations, ranging from £1 in 1550 = £222 in 1994, to £1 = £750, depending upon how the problem was approached.

We selected the middle ground. Dr. Allan H. Meltzer, professor of political economy and public policy at Carnegie-Mellon University in Pittsburgh, kindly provided us an update to 1993 of the 1954 Phelps Brown and Hopkins survey, *Seven Centuries of the Prices of Consumables (1420–1954)*. The figure produced from that effort was £1 (1550) = approx. £400 today, based on the parameters of that study.

The median figure of £1 (1550) = £500 (1994) was chosen for use in this book because it is easy to use and remember, is within the realm of reason, and falls closest to the estimated values produced by expert economist Meltzer on the one hand, and a Tudor era expert, historian Jasper Ridley, *The Tudor Age* (p. 200), on the other. An exchange rate of £1 = $1.80 was used to convert pounds to dollars, since it was the prevailing exchange rate at the time our calculations were made. We recognize that it fluctuates daily, and may be higher, or lower, at time of publication.

Gresham's Law

Gresham's Law is better known than the man for whom it is named. Economist Henry Macleod was the one who gave Gresham credit for the law in the 1800s, though its basic concept had been expressed by others much earlier than the sixteenth century.

In his book *The Elements of Political Economy* (London, 1858) Macleod claims that Sir Thomas Gresham has the honor of being the first to discover the *cause and effect* relationship between bad and good currency in concurrent circulation, and was the first to affirm that one was the cause of the other—that is, *at a fixed value or rate of exchange, bad money circulating with good will inevitably drive the good money out of circulation.* That is the basic concept of Gresham's Law.

The dogma was attributed to Gresham by Macleod, (Salter, *Sir Thomas Gresham*, page 37), from a passage Gresham wrote in his famous "five point economic plan" letter to Queen Elizabeth I in 1558, counseling her on the finances of her realm: "It may please Your Majesty to understand," wrote Gresham, "that the first occasion of the fall of the exchange did grow by the King's Majesty, your late Father, in abasing his coin from vi ounces fine to iii ounces fine. Whereupon the Exchange fell from xxvis viiid to xiiis ivd, which was the occasion that all your fine gold was conveyed out of your realm."

Macleod writes, "Now, as he was the first to perceive that a bad and debased currency is the *cause* of the disappearance of the good money, we are doing what is just in calling this great fundamental law of the currency by his name. We may call it **Gresham's Law of the Currency.**" (*Elements of Political Economy*, pp. 476–77.)

According to economist Milton Friedman, in a letter to the authors on 28 April 1994, Gresham's Law is aptly defined in the *Palgrave Dictionary of Political Economy* (1896) and in the *New Palgrave Dictionary* (1987). "It remains a basically correct statement, except that today we would not talk about intrinsic values, nor would we talk about cost of production. We would talk about the market price of the two or more forms of circulatory medium, or their market value for nonmonetary use...."

"Gresham's Law is often misunderstood and therefore misused, especially when it is applied by analogy in nonmonetary contexts, because the requirement that there be a fixed rate of exchange is forgotten." (Milton Friedman and Anna J. Schwartz, *A Monetary History of the United States, 1867–1960*, p. 27, notes.)

Economist Hans F. Sennholz, president of the Foundation for Economic Education, Inc., Irvington, New York, comments in a letter to the authors (15 April 1993): "Please note that Gresham's Law is merely one aspect of price fixing below market prices. If government fixes the price of gasoline below the market price, it will be in short supply. The same is true of gold."

Introduction

ir Thomas Gresham was literally and figuratively a Renaissance man. He became an adviser to the crown, diplomat, spy, royal smuggler, merchant extraordinaire, financial wizard, founder of the Royal Exchange, and farsighted philanthropist during his sixty-year life span.

The first portrait done of him, in 1544, when he was twenty-six, depicts an elegant Elizabethan dressed in doublet, hose, and ruff, looking out at the world with keen, yet wary eyes. By then, Gresham had graduated from Cambridge University, served an eight-year apprenticeship as a merchant adventurer, and read law for a year, before becoming a full-fledged member of his family's trading firm. The Greshams' prominence in the import-export business had not only made them a fortune, but also allowed them to parlay their business acumen and political insight into high positions and substantial holdings. Thomas's father, Sir Richard, a knight of the realm, had also served as lord high sheriff of the Tower of London, and lord high mayor of London.

The family's proximity to power ensured Thomas a front-row seat at the pageant that was England during the Renaissance and Reformation, but it meant that his life and fortune would depend upon the capricious whims of the monarchs he served. Gresham knew firsthand the madness, lust, bloodthirstiness and profligacy of Henry VIII; the kindness and generosity of the boy-king Edward VI; the pathos and zeal of "Bloody" Mary; and the canniness, opulence, tightfistedness, and mercurial genius for statecraft that characterized Elizabeth I. It is a tribute to his luck, ability and perspicacity that Gresham worked well with all of them, helping to put England on the financial footing she needed to hold her own against her European enemies.

Despite his fascinating life and impressive achievements, Gresham's experience as a consummate court politician might seem far removed from the lives of contemporary men and women living in modern democracies. At first glance, it might be hard to imagine how Sir Thomas's life could be relevant to our high-tech world of silicon chips and fax machines, or how his career—financial genius though he was—could shed light on modern economic problems such as the deficit and international trade imbalances.

This story not only convinces us of the relevance of Sir Thomas Gresham's life to our own, but also makes us care about him and his age. Although he was a courtier and servant to the crown, both his personal and professional life seem, in some respects, startlingly relevant to our own. On the human level, Gresham was no stranger to tragedy—his mother died when he was three; he lost the love of his life after the birth of their daughter; and his only son and heir Richard died at barely twenty years of age.

Professionally, Sir Thomas encountered most of the bêtes noires that bedevil those in the business world. Serving as the royal trade representative—often operating at the whim of tyrannous, timorous, vacillating, unreliable monarchs—he knew firsthand what it was to work for impossible bosses. Constantly in danger of imprisonment; once seriously injured in carrying out his duties; he was intimately acquainted with the dangers of a high-stress job. Moreover, his was often a thankless task. In addition to borrowing money for the crown, negotiating international trades, trying to raise exchange rates to favor England, and fobbing off royal creditors, he was assigned additional duties by the Tudors as a diplomat, smuggler, spy, and special envoy. In this capacity, he often transported confidential documents or carried royal jewels, once even escorting Queen Elizabeth's prize new Turkish stallion from Antwerp to London. Shuttling back and forth between those two cities almost constantly—in danger of his life from pirates, brigands and political enemies—he once waited eleven years for the crown to reimburse him for expenses!

Although he may not always have been able to collect on his own behalf, he did an astonishingly good job of borrowing money for England and of discharging his country's debts. In fact, he saved England from bankruptcy at least twice. Once after Henry VIII died, leaving a mountain of debt, crippling interest payments, and a debased currency, Thomas Gresham managed—in record time— to pay creditors what would today be more than several hundred million pounds. After Mary I died, having bled her country dry to pay for her husband Philip's foreign wars, Gresham, as Queen Elizabeth's royal agent, accomplished the same feat.

Meanwhile, he continued to act as CEO of the vast Gresham family trading enterprise, keeping it profitable, and to oversee the many estates and lands he owned.

Many moderns tend to discount such feats of economic wizardry because, they argue, the mercantile age was then in its infancy, and international trade was a far cry from present global markets. Although Gresham was blissfully ignorant of junk bonds, certificates of deposit, money markets, and IRAs—to say nothing of the intricacies of Treasury bonds, the Federal Reserve System, and the Resolution Trust Corporation—he was alarmingly familiar with the major economic issues that we confront today.

Like Sir Thomas Gresham, we struggle to achieve a sound fiscal policy, and like him, we contend with: the dangers of a mounting deficit; the problems of debtor nations, restrictive tariffs, and trade imbalances; the difficulties of establishing free trade; the complexities of conducting fair trade negotiations; and the havoc wrought by devalued currency and wildly fluctuating exchange rates.

Perhaps because the financial issues that Gresham faced are similar to our own, the advice that he gave Elizabeth I upon her accession to the throne seems oddly pertinent today. In a position paper, written in 1558, he advised the twenty-five-year-old queen to recoin the currency to get a better exchange rate, restrict monopolies, curtail foreign debt, pay off existing liabilities, and, most of all, keep good credit with her subjects, for, he warned, they are the ultimate source of any kingdom's wealth.

Indeed, the continuing applicability of the maxim attributed to him as Gresham's Law—that at a fixed exchange rate, bad money drives out good—indicates that his insights are as relevant today as when he first uttered them over four hundred years ago.

Gresham himself, however, used *good money* to attack *bad situations*, drive out inefficiency, mitigate waste, and alleviate poverty. To these ends: he established the Royal Exchange, which he built at his own expense from 1566 to 1568, to enable merchants to conduct business more effectively; endowed Gresham College so that Londoners might receive a better education; and subsidized a number of houses for the poor in order to help alleviate their misery. Farsighted and public-spirited even in his old age, he welcomed the technology of the future, building England's first paper mills on his own estates.

Although the Gresham family's roots had originally been agricultural (Gresham means "grasslands"—hence Sir Thomas's adoption of the golden grasshopper as his symbol in trade), they distinguished themselves at court, as well as in the country and abroad. Like other titans of the English Renaissance—Raleigh, Sidney, and Drake—the Greshams rejoiced in pushing back the boundaries of the known world and in forging ahead into the new.

Sir Thomas Gresham, a remarkable man living in tumultuous times, is inherently interesting, as this lively, well-documented biography shows, and his economic insights are as applicable today as they were in his own time.

Edwin J. Feulner, Jr.

1

A Renaissance Man

The two young kings, astride lavishly caparisoned chargers, faced each other across the wide, grassy plain. The June sunlight flashed off their brilliant gold and silver raiment. On one side of the field it glistened on the massive helmet and armor of Henry VIII of England, and glanced off the lances and maces of the knights and nobles massed behind him. Farther back, it danced along the panes of the miraculous windowed palace that his nimble English glaziers and joiners had somehow managed to erect on that empty field, in less than three months' time. Around the turreted castle were ranged the nearly three thousand white tents of the English king's train. Hundreds of colorful knightly pennants and standards snapped smartly in the breeze. The fleet of swift caravels—merchant ships and warships of the Royal Navy—that had brought King Henry and his entourage across the Channel to this historic meeting, rode quietly at anchor in the harbor.

On the opposite side of the field, additional thousands of graceful pavilions had been erected to house the hordes attending Francis I, king of France. Sumptuously constructed, they presented an almost ephemeral vision with their gauzy draperies and spangled cloth-of-gold canopies. The French king, his garments and armor emblazoned with jewels and gold fleurs-de-lis, held his dancing charger, draped head to hoof in sparkling gold filigree armor, under tight rein. Patiently, he waited for the other man to make a move.

High on a pinnacle, a golden statue of St. Michael presided over the momentous and extravagant spectacle about to unfold below. This royal encounter, which would later include lists and jousting, had been dubbed the Field of Cloth of Gold. The year was 1520.

On the English side, the merchant-adventurers Richard Gresham and his brother John were dazed by the sheer magnitude of the spectacle arrayed before them—a sight of such majesty and grandeur as to be almost incomprehensible. Their merchant vessels *Anne of London* and *Anne of Fowey* were among the ships anchored in the harbor. As gentleman usher extraordinary to the royal household, Richard Gresham, like his brother, had been invited as part of the richly garbed retinue of their friend and patron Cardinal Wolsey, lord high chancellor of England. Wolsey was one of the most powerful and influential officials in Henry VIII's court. The Greshams were honored at the privilege of bearing witness to such an occasion. Richard wished his two sons could have been there to share his honor, but John was a child of barely three, and Thomas a babe of only a year. They were at home in London with their mother and sisters.

This first face-to-face meeting of the two rival monarchs had been meticulously plotted, crafted, and staged by Wolsey, without regard to cost, in hopes that an alliance might bring peace and resolution between the two nations. He envisioned it as the "golden frame of high politics," a show that would strike envy into the hearts of the other European monarchs, especially Charles V, king of Spain and recently named Holy Roman Emperor. Yes, and the Medicis and Pope Leo, too—this would show them all that England was a power not to be lightly dismissed. This would be his moment in the sun, as chess master and ringmaster of the historic event. The festival of meetings, jousting, and knightly tournaments would last a full month or more. The general populace of France, which would pay most dearly for this lavish spectacle out of an already depleted treasury, had been ordered away. They were warned, with threat of hanging, to stay clear of the site at Calais. But such an event was beyond the reach of the power of even a French duc de Berri or a Cardinal Wolsey to regulate.

The public thronged to Calais to watch the arrival of the English court, to gawk at the splendors, to eat, to drink, to glean whatever respite and entertainment were to be had from the tedium and misery of their daily lives. They marveled at the four thousand stalwart men who came with Henry, and the more than a thousand women who attended his queen, Catherine of Aragon. They observed with more than passing interest, for the daughter of the English monarchs—four-year-old Princess Mary Tudor—had already been pledged by her father to their own dauphin and would some day be their queen.

Gaping in wonder, they witnessed the majestic arrival of Cardinal Wolsey with his company of archers and ushers. A scarlet-clad bearer, with an enormous jewel-encrusted gold crucifix held high before him, heralded the lord high chancellor. They wildly applauded their own handsome Champagne-born King Francis and their beloved Queen Claude, and watched them display themselves to advantage at yet another royal extravaganza, this time with the despised English. Maybe this meeting, at last, would mean peace. They could not know that they were witnessing the prelude to disputes and wars that would last another several generations and cost upward of half a million men.

Richard Gresham brushed at the sleeve of his black velvet doublet and absently adjusted the simple gold chain draped across his embroidered vest. He leaned forward in his saddle, restraining his restive mount with a firm hand, watching, waiting for the king's signal. A slender man of medium height and average looks, Gresham's sober black dress and hat, though fashioned from the finest fabric to be found, were devoid of ostentatious decoration, taking nothing away from the court of preening lords and ladies sporting their most costly jewels and finery. In fact, Richard Gresham scarcely rated a second glance. Now, a thrill of anticipation seized him as suddenly all quieted, waiting for King Henry, as the honored visitor, to make the first move.

The earl of Shrewsbury nudged his horse a pace closer to Henry's. "'Tis time," he muttered. "Your Grace should move forward." "That is exactly our intent, milord," replied the king. Henry reached up and dropped the visor of his helmet. Abruptly spurring his mount, he dashed forward at full gallop toward the French king. The great golden plume atop his helmet flowed out behind him in the breeze. A lusty roar went up. "On before!" shouted the English, and swept after their king. At the first move from Henry, Francis too gave spur and his own stallion leapt forward. "Allonsy, pour la France!" The cry rose from a thousand French throats as they galloped forward after King Francis. The duc d'Alençon, husband of Francis's sister Marguerite, the queen of Navarre, rode hard in the place of honor on Francis's right flank, the duc de Berri on his left.

The two massed armies thundered forward, rapidly closing the wide gap. Then, on cue, they reined in and halted. Henry and Francis continued on alone at full gallop, well aware that they were the center of all eyes. Both were young, fit, virile, and equal to the drama of the moment. At the center of the field, they reined in mightily, dead abreast, throwing their great horses to their haunches. In unison, the two monarchs swept off their helmets, then leaned across and ceremoniously embraced. Polite greetings were exchanged as they dismounted and carefully took one another's measure. "A goodly prince," wrote Henry later, taking note of Francis's "stately countenance, merry brown eyes, high nose, and broadness of breast and shoulder." For his part, Francis found Henry, about whom he'd been most curious, to be "a handsome prince, with an honest mien and a pleasant manner, heavyset, with a thick red beard, which looks good on him." Their ceremonial meeting accomplished, the two kings proceeded, arm in arm, to the privacy of a small pavilion.

When their monarchs embraced, a great cheer rose up from both sides. The two retinues were dismissed and set loose to mingle, going from tent to pavilion, all laden with groaning boards of meats and delicacies and refreshments of every kind. There was much toasting and drinking, merriment and entertainment, as the throngs of nobles—French and English—visited back and forth and attempted to communicate.

Richard Gresham, attending Wolsey as the cardinal, and his young acolyte, John Leigh, made the rounds, finding himself often in the company of Sir Thomas Boleyn, the king's ambassador to France, and his two lovely, young daughters, Mary and Anne. They had come to France two years before, to serve at the French king's court. Gresham, caught up in the whirl of social activity, did not notice how the king's eye had lit upon young Mary. His attention was drawn elsewhere. The Greshams were not of the peerage and had never seen such a spectacle, such beauty, such lush extravagance as this. Prosperous, yet thrifty men both, they mentally flinched at what the cost of all this must be. Nevertheless, Richard found himself enjoying the pomp and pageantry, and it stirred in his heart a fierce loyalty to his own—to his king and to England.

From the ranks each day, they watched the two rulers joust and thrust and parry. Francis openly wooed Henry. Henry strutted and preened, laughed and joked, and was gallant to the ladies, especially the Boleyn damsel. He bested all at the lists, rode until his horses dropped from exhaustion, and completely confounded the French. The snobbish, sophisticated French court had expected an untutored country buffoon to sail across the Channel and into their hands. Henry showed them otherwise.

Tudor England might have less than one-sixth the annual income of France, and less than a fifth of France's population, but the English king and his retinue would show a wealth, a pride, and a tenacity that could not be bested. Unlike the French, who were slowly going broke from centuries of war and the excesses of their profligate, party-loving king and court, the English treasury was overflowing, thanks to the frugality—some said stinginess—of Henry's father and predecessor, Henry VII.

Francis I burned to make this lusty, red-bearded Henry VIII his ally. He was resigned to the fact that war between France and Charles V was inevitable, for the lands controlled by France were ever tempting to the Spaniards, and now as emperor, Charles would have the power of other nations at his command as well. If Francis could but win Henry to his side, he would be in a far better position to fight Charles. Now that he had seen for himself in the lists the daring and determination of these English in battle, he believed that with them as his allies, he could win any war.

But the Field of Cloth of Gold, in all its glory, in all its lamentable extravagance, would bring no peace to either nation and no real alliance between Henry and Francis. Henry, mindful that to treat openly with France would rupture his commerce with Spain and Flanders, endangering the lucrative trade of English wool there, talked grandly but committed nothing specific to the French king. Through merchant adventurers like the Greshams, England was sending upward of a hundred thousand pieces of woolen cloth a year, and shiploads of raw wool to boot, over to Flanders, where it enjoyed free entry to the Netherlands. Caravels were sailing twice a year to Antwerp, departing at Michaelmas and Whitsuntide, and florins and livres were pouring into the English treasury on their return.[1] France could offer Henry little in the way of enticement to risk such a profitable enterprise. There was Catherine, too, to consider. A proud and ambitious Spaniard, Henry's queen was firmly against any alliance with France. She wanted England to ally with her cousin Charles V, and she loathed the idea of her precious Mary marrying into the French dynasty one day.

A month prior, upon receiving intelligence of the meeting scheduled between Henry and Francis, Charles V had hastened to England "to visit our dear cousin Queen Catherine." He was young and as yet unmarried, and upon the death of Maximilian I, he had been named Holy Roman Emperor, dashing Henry of England's high hopes for that honor. Though Henry had little use for Emperor Charles, he received him cordially. On the eve of his departure for the Field of Cloth of Gold, Henry had whispered the name of little Mary to the bachelor Charles. Seeking to stack things to his own best advantage and giving no great weight to the fact that he had already solemnly promised his daughter in marriage to the French dauphin, Henry suggested that Charles might want to "tarry for my Mary, and when she is ripe, marry her." Then he gathered his court and sailed for France.

Charles, anxious to avert the entry of Henry into King Francis's coterie, hastened to set sail himself for the Port of Gravelines, where he promptly sent word urging Henry to meet with him there. Henry obliged, and Charles forged a secret alliance with him. Returning to Calais, Henry casually calmed the concerns of the French. "'Tis naught of import that he wanted," he assured Francis. "Charles desired that we promise him my Mary and break her betrothal to your son," he lied, "but we have defended our virtue against this assault, my dearest brother and compatriot, fear not." Privately, his wise minister Bonnivet cautioned the French king, "Do not trust him, Majesty, not for a moment."

The festivities drew to a close with no concrete peace established. As they sailed back across the Channel to England, Richard Gresham remarked to Cardinal Wolsey about the exquisite tapestries that had draped the walls of the French king's pavilion. "Yes, they were exceedingly fine, and you must barter to get me some like ones for Hampton Court, for they will look wondrous well there, and guard the king against the winter's chill of those stone walls."[2] He had hoped the cardinal would ask him this favor, for he and his brothers wanted one from Wolsey in return.

Soon afterward, war was in the air once more in Europe. The love feast in Picardy had sorely gouged the English treasury. The duke of Buckingham, angry over the spectacle that had taken place there with little to show for it, denounced the wasteful cost. Stung, Wolsey accused Buckingham of treason. The duke was arrested and consigned to the Tower of London, that formidable fortress at the mouth of the Thames. The Tower not only was the king's primary residence and seat of power, but also served handily as a prison for his political enemies. Shortly afterward, the outspoken Buckingham was summarily executed. England and the nobles at Henry's court were stunned. If one so powerful as the duke of Buckingham could be dispatched that easily for merely disagreeing with the king and Cardinal Wolsey, then surely no one's head was safe anymore!

Richard and John Gresham, safely under Wolsey's benevolent patronage, traded heavily for the crown, becoming both debtors and creditors on its behalf. Richard delivered to Wolsey the coveted tapestries, which were so costly he had been obliged to ask the cardinal for the money up front, to be advanced to the artisans "for provision of their stuffe."[3] With the tapestries came eight exquisite pieces of cloth of gold for Wolsey to present to King Henry as his New Year's gift, which would place the cardinal even higher in the king's esteem. Richard Gresham then felt secure enough in the service he had rendered to dare to ask Wolsey to obtain for the Greshams an exclusive license to export and import wool and other goods. In return, he offered to forgive a debt the cardinal owed him.

Wolsey was happy to comply. The license was little enough to pay in return for cancellation of his debts to the Greshams, from whom he had borrowed heavily to furnish his elaborate retinue at the Field of Cloth of Gold.

Richard Gresham's star continued to rise. His eyes and ears were invaluable as a source of intelligence from the Low Countries, to which he frequently journeyed on his trading missions, and he soon established himself as the correspondent and confidant of Wolsey on matters of foreign policy there.

In his spacious home on Milk Street in London, at the sign of the golden grasshopper, Richard Gresham's two young sons and their sisters lived in comfort as their father's fortunes grew. Their grasshopper emblem had been proudly displayed in commerce since the early 1400s. Its golden image, painted on an oval wooden sign, swayed gently in the breeze above the door of the shop that comprised the ground floor of their house. Shops were the ground floor of the houses of all tradesmen. Milk Street was in the heart of London's trading district, and the golden grasshopper drew the famous and the mighty of England and other countries to Richard Gresham's door.[4] Already Gresham was a wealthy man, his business acumen was enriching him more every month, and his invaluable services to Wolsey and the king were quickly rewarded with grants of land, purses of gold, and extensive royal patronage. Richard intended that his brood would lack for naught in the way of experience and education. He had a high respect for schooling and was determined that his sons would matriculate at Cambridge, as he had in his own youth.

Thomas, the younger of the two boys, was a curious and precocious child, and his parents gave him free rein to explore the household, the shop, and the world around him. In 1522, when Thomas was little more than a toddler of three, his mother died, plunging the household into grief. The "sweating sickness," a mysterious malignant fever, struck London with ferocity and no warning almost every year, carrying off young and old alike. This time, it left the City taking Richard Gresham's young wife Audrey with it. For a time he assuaged his sorrow by devoting himself to his work and his family. After a while, he took to wife a wealthy young widow, Isabella Taverson.

Isabella assumed domestic management of Richard Gresham's domain, which by that time encompassed not only the large and elegantly appointed town house on Milk Street, but another on Lad Lane in London, and a country seat at Intwood in Norfolk, northeast of London, the area whence the Gresham ancestors had come. Aided by more than a score of servants, nannies, and tutors, Isabella supervised the upbringing of young Thomas, his older brother John, and their sisters Elizabeth and Christiana. Thomas was soon devoted to his cheerful and accomplished stepmother.

In the oak-paneled classroom across from the nursery on the third floor, Thomas studied history, philosophy, and religion under the stern and demanding eye of his tutors. England was prospering and changing its long-held ways. In the previous century, Christopher Columbus and other sea explorers had opened the seas to new markets and initiated friendly commerce with other countries. The result was the emergence of a "middle class" of merchant families like the Greshams. They, and the nobility who were their patrons, no longer had to rely on booty from war to enrich them. The king taxed this new prosperity heavily, but no one complained; they were happy to pay higher taxes to the crown. With lenient trade policies to encourage them, the merchants reaped record profits, and they enjoyed a standard of life never before imagined. By the time the eighteen-year-old Henry VIII assumed the throne in 1509, the long period of destructive territorial wars between the nobles of England had ended, and a new national consciousness had cemented its hold on the country.

Thomas learned from his tutor, James Rodham, that his father's appointment as a merchant adventurer stemmed from the mid-fourteenth century, as an outgrowth of the ancient society of the Merchants of Staple. The guild of the Merchant Adventurers was a closely guarded one, and had its own governor. Whereas most guilds required seven years of apprenticeship, the Merchant Adventurers required eight, with specific standards of performance demanded of both the apprentice and the master who trained him. It would be Thomas Gresham's privilege one day to enter that apprenticeship. Entry into the tightly controlled Merchant Adventurers was difficult and limited.

It was the prerogative of the crown to make appointments to the guild. Made at the behest of the governor of the Merchant Adventurers, these prized appointments went only to a privileged few, mostly the sons of the leading merchants or someone sponsored by one of them. To garner a share in the lucrative trade monopolies controlled by the guild of Merchant Adventurers was well beyond the reach of most merchants. Richard Gresham and his brothers, John and William, were among the fortunate few. As prominent members of the guild, they had become three of the shrewdest and wealthiest merchants in England. Of the three, John was acknowledged to be the sharpest and the best. It was to him that Richard Gresham hoped to apprentice young Thomas one day, for Thomas was showing himself to be bright like his uncle John, and adept at business.

Outside the schoolroom, Thomas and his siblings were privy to the conversations about international affairs that were commonplace in their father's household. There were no newspapers; however, their home on Milk Street was a tiny, world-class learning center for the boys, and Thomas was quick to absorb. He had a gift for analyzing and distilling what he was taught, retaining the essence of what was important, and discarding what was not. He loved to listen to his father's tales about great sea voyages and far-away lands. Since Richard Gresham and his brothers owned several ships, there were always sea captains' maps and charts around. Thomas pored over them, tracing outlines with his small, stubby finger, puzzling out what they meant and where those exotically named places were. The feats of the Portuguese Magellan were often discussed; his daring filled the child's heart with awe and his head with dreams. He vowed that he, too, would sail the seas one day and find new lands for England.

But Richard Gresham had other plans for his younger son. He fully intended that both his sons would follow him in his trade. At the appropriate time, when they had completed their schooling, John, and then Thomas, would be apprenticed and in turn be entered into the fellowship of Merchant Adventurers. His daughters were being schooled in religion, ladylike manners, and the managing of a fine household. In the early evenings, the girls occupied themselves in doing exquisite sewing and embroidery under the watchful eye of their stepmother Isabella.

Although the Reformation had raised its head abroad, England was still dominated by Catholic Rome. In 1521, Pope Leo had named King Henry VIII Defender of the Faith for voicing staunch opposition to the Reformation.[5] Now, it was 1525, and while young Thomas Gresham dutifully studied, and his father sailed back and forth to the Low Countries, staying long away and trading feverishly for Cardinal Wolsey and the crown, gaining profits, rewards, and favor, Henry VIII's court began to reverberate with scandal.

Five years before, young Mary Boleyn had quietly returned to England, and Henry had promptly made her his mistress. Two years later, her younger sister Anne had also returned, her service at the French court completed. Anne was a mere slip of a girl, but possessed of dazzling beauty and accomplished manners. She joined the household of the queen. At first, Henry had taken little notice of Mary's younger sister. Then suddenly, the thirty-five-year-old king's eye had fallen upon her. Immediately, Mary Boleyn had been cast aside, and Henry VIII began a passionate affair with nineteen-year-old Anne Boleyn.

Had Henry desired only a brief liaison, a dalliance with the fresh and lovely dark-eyed maid, the matter would have been simple. But Henry wanted marriage. He passionately longed for Anne to be his wife, and he wanted a legal son and heir—a son Catherine had been unable to give him, a son he was sure Anne Boleyn as his wife would produce.[6] In short, he wanted a church annulment of his marriage to Catherine of Aragon, an idea which she adamantly refused to entertain. To Queen Catherine, it was nothing if not preposterous. Henry VIII was a passionate, strong-willed man. His rage at being frustrated in his desire for Anne was vented upon all who crossed his will, and many paid with their lives for opposing the match.

Catherine, with the church solidly behind her, staunchly stood her ground. For five years, Henry tried every means at his disposal to wrest an annulment from Catherine. He desperately needed the church's sanction to ensure a legitimate marriage to Anne Boleyn, so that the succession of a male heir born to her would not be disputed. The more Henry was thwarted in his quest, the more determined he became to win. When Catherine refused to acquiesce, Henry decided to press the matter on legal grounds, and claimed his marriage to Catherine was null and void from the outset. She had been married briefly to his older brother Arthur, who had died before the union could be consummated. The Book of Leviticus, in the Old Testament, forbade the taking of a brother's widow to wife. Earlier, Henry had sworn the marriage hadn't been consummated in order to receive special dispensation to marry the widowed Catherine. Now, he claimed exactly the opposite, and said he had been duped by Catherine and Arthur.

Wolsey, long accustomed to Henry's penchant for prevarication, was shocked; however, he had little choice but to follow his king's directives. At Henry's insistence, Wolsey went personally to Queen Catherine and begged her to accede quietly and retire to a nunnery. Catherine, outraged, turned on him in fury. "Nay!

What foolishness is this? On that day that Henry takes the holy vows of priesthood—on that day!—shall I retire to a nunnery. Not before." Upon hearing of her husband's charge that she had lain with Arthur, she drew herself up in righteous majesty, coldly denying it. "Have you forgotten, my lord cardinal, that I am a princess of the blood of the Holy Roman Emperor? Do you think my moral fiber is without conscience?" She insisted she had been a virgin "pure, as my mother sent me," when she married Henry, and any claim to the contrary was preposterous. Wolsey backed off before Catherine's angry tirade and fell to his knees before her, head bowed.

Catherine paced her rooms at Hampton Court, her heavy wide skirts rustling across the rough wooden floor, her mind racing. She knew she was in grave danger. Daughter of a king and queen of Spain, cousin of the Holy Roman Emperor, she was not without power. If she gave in and granted Henry an annulment, her little daughter Mary would be declared illegitimate and removed from the line of succession to the throne. At the thought of her beloved daughter being disinherited, Catherine whirled around like a cornered lioness to face Wolsey, fire in her eyes. "Though I be torn limb from limb, or die and come to life again, I am truly married in God's eyes to my husband and lord, Henry, and I would so die before acquiescing to such a thing as you propose!" Wolsey's heart went out to the queen in her predicament, but he dreaded even more the thought of bringing the news of her refusal back to the temperamental Henry and his grasping paramour.[7]

The situation worsened. Within weeks, with rumors traveling the countryside faster than horses at full gallop, the populace of England had rallied to Queen Catherine's beleaguered cause. Henry dared not make an overt move against her. He was forced to send Anne Boleyn to her father's estates outside London for her own safety. Absence served only to make him want her more. Wolsey begged Henry to reconsider, "for England's sake, and for the church, for you are Defender of the Faith." That anguished appeal earned the aging cardinal the lasting enmity of Anne Boleyn.

Richard Gresham knew he had much to fear for his own safety and well-being as word of these developments came to him through Wolsey. His own fate and fortunes were linked to Wolsey's favor at court, and Wolsey was deeply enmeshed in the king's dilemma. Gresham knew this business of Henry and Anne could easily cost Wolsey his head. He needed to seek other sources of support besides Wolsey—and quickly. Thereafter, he endeavored to render even better service to the crown and to cultivate some of the more powerful nobles of Henry's court, like the dukes of Norfolk and Northumberland. He wooed those two worthies by lending them money and buying rare goods for them. Even so, he could not escape his need for Wolsey's immense power and his apparent position of favor with the king.

Francis I and Charles V were at war. Henry, furious because the pope refused him an annulment, would not support Charles, despite the alliance he had signed. As Holy Roman Emperor, Charles staunchly defended the position of the pope and his cousin Catherine in the matter of her marriage. Henry and Catherine, he maintained, were legally married. Outraged, Henry summarily arrested the emperor's ambassadors to his court, and detained some of the emperor's ships. Charles retaliated swiftly. Richard Gresham and his brothers were seized in Flanders, with their ships and goods. Charles would show Henry who was the more powerful! From his dank cell in the dungeons of Antwerp, Richard Gresham managed to bribe a guard to smuggle a note of frantic appeal to Cardinal Wolsey. "We beg Your Grace to intercede with the holy father on our behalf. As you must know, it is vital to England that we, and our ships and goods, be spared."

Crumpling and burning the hastily scribbled note, Wolsey sat and stared into the fire. He knew that what Richard Gresham had written was true. Henry's baiting of the emperor was sheer folly. The English treasury could not bear the loss of its trading fleet, nor was the country ready to wage war against an enemy as powerful as Charles. He sighed, then went to seek out the king and urge him to back away from his bellicose position. That did not sit well with Henry, but he saw the reason in Wolsey's request, and complied. Then the cardinal dispatched an urgent note to the pope, via his ambassador.

Soon, Richard and John Gresham were homeward bound, their ships and goods intact. After more than a month of misery in the stinking dungeons of Flanders, Richard Gresham gave thanks to God for his freedom, but he knew it would not have been possible without Wolsey's intervention. He had made sure there were bolts of fine silks and damasks aplenty in his hold, as gifts for the cardinal, before his ship sailed for England and home.

As the maneuvering in the religious and marital battle of the English monarchs continued, Wolsey began to see his influence with the king slipping. Realizing his days were probably numbered, he called Richard Gresham to him and gave him a sum of money, roughly £1500 sterling "to discharge my indebtedness to you and others, to pay my funeral expenses and pension my servants, and use whatever may be left for alms for the poor and prayer for my soul."[8] Taking the heavy pouch from Wolsey's hand, Richard felt a cold stab of fear and trepidation. Possession of the money would endanger his life, he knew, but he had no other choice. He owed this to Wolsey, and it was little enough in return for favors Wolsey had done him. He looked at his aging patron with deep sorrow and attempted to cheer him. "Be it not so, Your Grace. Fear not—all will come well again with God's help." He felt little assurance at his own words, and hastily continued, "But I shall take and guard this sum for you as you have directed me to do, and I will pray daily for your good health and safety."

Thereafter, Richard and his brothers attempted to distance themselves from Henry's court and avoided the appearance of being intimates of Cardinal Wolsey. King Henry's wrath, they knew, could encompass whole households, along with associates and friends of the offender. And Henry, it was noted, took brutal revenge when opposed.

Meanwhile, the nobles of England and the prelates of Rome adopted a wait-and-see posture. Surely King Henry would give up his hopeless pursuit of an annulment and remarriage. Surely he would tire of Anne Boleyn. But they had not considered Henry's massive ego and his bulldog tenacity. He would not relinquish his objective, or retreat from his position. Finally, in late 1528, he demanded that Cardinal Campeggio, a legate from Rome, be sent by the pope to hear his case against Catherine in a formal trial in London. Campeggio was an English cardinal, and nominally in Henry's power to command. The pope could not refuse Henry's request, though he stalled for as long as possible before he acquiesced to it.

Ten months passed before Henry's case against Catherine came to court. Summer had bloomed in a riot of color that June of 1529, and the boy Thomas Gresham, shielded in his schoolroom, was unaware of the import of the proceedings about to take place in the hall of Blackfriars. There, England's link with Catholicism went on trial, and with it the spiritual and cultural future of Thomas and the English populace. The country held its collective breath, awaiting the outcome. The trial dragged on through the long, steamy summer.

Queen Catherine, after her first impassioned appearance, boycotted the whole affair, calling it "no impartial court for me." She had swept from the courtroom in regal disdain, her train of ladies following in her wake. She demanded that the trial be delayed to allow her to consult with advisers from her native Spain. Her request was coldly denied, and the trial continued without her being present. Henry had persuaded an impressive forty nobles to testify on his behalf. Several quoted purported conversations wherein Arthur had boasted of his sexual conquest of Catherine, saying "I have been this night in the midst of Spain."[9]

In the end, Cardinal Campeggio, on instructions from the pope, adjourned the case without a finding, further postponing it. A stroke of lightning from above couldn't have shaken and infuriated Henry more. The results of that decision would affect Thomas Gresham's life in ways that he could never imagine, as indeed it would the life and future of every Englishman. A deep schism had suddenly yawned open between the Vatican and the king of England, and Cardinal Wolsey sensed that the blame would descend upon his head, which at that moment a furious Anne Boleyn was demanding of Henry.

But Henry still needed the clever Wolsey to help him govern, and to counsel him in ways to thwart the other crowned heads of Europe. However, the idea of one day appropriating the cardinal's vast lands and pensions had not escaped the king's interest, nor Anne's.

As time marched on, his divorce from Catherine preoccupied Henry to the exclusion of almost all else that mattered. England was left to Wolsey and others to govern. The powerful dukes of Suffolk and Norfolk, sensing a vacuum of power, schemed to increase their own. Anne Boleyn chafed and burned to be queen, and as the endless negotiations with the Vatican continued, she nagged Henry incessantly, blaming Wolsey for failure to influence Rome in their favor. Rumors flew that the divorce was costing Henry and the English treasury thousands in gold, and taxes mounted to new heights.

Richard Gresham watched in dismay as alliances and enmities were exchanged with alarming swiftness. He feared for Wolsey, and he feared for himself. He was well aware that men had disappeared into the grim prison at the Tower on the slightest of trumped-up charges and had never returned. No one was safe from the capricious wrath of the king or Anne Boleyn. As was bound to happen sooner or later, Wolsey misstepped and was forced to yield power. His enemies pounced. To save his skin, he ceded York Place, his palatial mansion in London, to the crown, for Anne Boleyn had set her heart on having it. That temporarily placated the royal lovers. They raced through it happily, like two children, exclaiming over its rich furnishings, the magnificent gold and silver plate, the bolts and bolts of costly cloths—of bright satins, crisp taffetas, luxurious damasks, diaphanous silks and lush velvets—all theirs now.[10]

For a few months, as Henry wavered, mollified by York Place and Anne's good humor, Wolsey's fate hung in the balance. At first, he was simply "retired" to exile up country, in his native York. Then he was arrested "for high treason," and all his vast properties and wealth were confiscated by the king. The curtain rang down abruptly on Wolsey's glory, but he would be spared the ignominy of the Tower and the executioner's ax. He fell gravely ill en route to London, and was forced to stop at Leicester. There, Cardinal Wolsey, one of the most powerful figures ever to serve the crown, died alone and virtually penniless. He was buried at Leicester Abbey, in the dead of night, by four monks. There was no state funeral, no parade of mourners to mark his demise. His had been a long, long fall from the pinnacle of power at the Field of Cloth of Gold.

Two days later, Richard Gresham was summoned to the Tower. An armed escort from the king waited outside the door on Milk Street as the master of the house donned his cloak and prepared to leave his family. Isabella and his daughters clung to him, sobbing loudly in their fright. Thomas, pale and sober-faced with fear, bit back his tears and followed his father to the front door of the shop to bid him farewell. All realized what a summons to the Tower could mean. They knew not, nor did Richard Gresham himself, if they'd ever see him again.

2

The King and the Merchant

King Henry was more concerned about confiscating the £1500 that Wolsey had squirreled away than he was about the cardinal's sad demise.[1] The king's agent had questioned Wolsey on his deathbed about the money, and the cardinal had replied: "The money is not mine. I borrowed it from some friends and gave it to them in repayment, plus enough to bury me and to bestow wages upon my servants. But if it be the king's pleasure, let him take this, too, from me." Now, King Henry himself questioned Wolsey's secretary closely. Upon hearing Richard Gresham's name, the king abruptly ended the interview.[2]

Richard Gresham was duly summoned to present himself at the Tower. There, he was called to account for the funds and obliged to swear whether or not the money had indeed been owed to him by Wolsey and given him for the purposes Wolsey had stated. "Yea, Your Majesty, I swear it. But Your Grace is of course welcome to the money or to the accounting for it, if it is Your Majesty's desire." There. The die was cast. Sweating, Gresham remained on one knee, deeply bowed before Henry, and waited tensely for the king's response, certain that his days were over. But Henry, after another long pause during which he carefully considered Gresham's offer, seemed satisfied. He was tempted to take the money—the treasury could certainly use it—but this Richard Gresham was a widely respected man, a canny man with money, and the king had use for him. Looking up, he waved the merchant away, dismissing him mildly. "Leave us now. We shall think upon this matter."

That evening Richard Gresham was set free, and he returned home to Milk Street, none the worse for wear. His family was overjoyed. Isabella commanded the servants to prepare a celebration dinner in honor of the master's return. Thomas's two sisters greeted their father with joy. Young Thomas showed no outward emotion, as befitted one who was at the door of manhood, but that night he fell upon his knees and sent up a fervent prayer of thanks for his father's safe return. Even at his tender age, Thomas realized that his father went often in harm's way in his business, and that in Cardinal Wolsey the family had lost a powerful protector. But to young Thomas, his father and his uncle John were heroes enough, and he spent little time mourning the cardinal's passing from their lives.

The king did not demand that Richard Gresham deliver up the cardinal's purse, nor did he exact any penalty on it. On the contrary, he pressed the Greshams—Richard and John—into rendering more and greater service for the crown.

At Henry's court, onto the divorce scene rode a young Cambridge-educated scholar and theologian, Thomas Cranmer. Cranmer suggested that Henry seek learned opinions from enlightened scholars of the best universities in England and abroad on the matter of his divorce. "Marry," cried Henry, "that man has the right sow by the ear!" He lost no time in dispatching a commission to Cambridge and Oxford. By 1531, the dons of Oxford and Cambridge and authorities at the biggest universities in France and Italy had considered, argued, and ultimately concurred with Henry's position—that his marriage to Catherine was invalid.[3] Whether their decision was the result of learned enlightenment or of political pressure brought to bear by the English king was not revealed, but they unanimously agreed that Henry should be granted an annulment from Catherine of Aragon.

That same year, twelve-year-old Thomas Gresham joined his family in the first row of dignitaries as Richard Gresham, in stately ceremonial cape and robes, was invested as lord high sheriff of London. In this powerful position, his father would exercise great influence in the City and would be privy to many of the secret inner workings of Henry's court. The lord high sheriff was also the chief jailer of the dreaded Tower prison. In that capacity, he was required personally to escort condemned, high-ranking political prisoners to their execution. Executions took place on Tower Hill, the rise just outside the walls of the fortress, or on Tower Green—a small site in the courtyard within the walls, which was reserved for the more private executions of the most controversial, or high-ranking, of Henry's enemies.

Nearly everyone in London would turn out, as for a merry holiday, whenever there was a public execution of some highly placed prisoner on Tower Hill. They also watched with glee the grisly public racking, disemboweling, and drawing and quartering of condemned prisoners. Afterward, the heads and body parts were posted on pikes outside the Tower as an example to all. With Henry continually tightening the clamps on his enemies, Richard Gresham's duties as sheriff would be harrowing.

Less than a month after his father's installation as lord high sheriff, Thomas swung into his saddle and, accompanied by his tutor Rodham, left the house on Milk Street for good. He was off to Cambridge to begin his collegiate studies. With that journey, proud and not a little scared, Thomas Gresham put childhood and the nursery firmly behind him. His older brother John was almost finished with his college term and would soon be at sea, apprenticed to the Merchant Adventurers. So it would be with Thomas in his turn.

After two days of riding, they arrived at Cambridge, which had been a university town for more than three hundred years. Entering the village, Thomas slowed his horse to a walk and grimaced at what he saw. He clapped a hand to his nose, and pinched the nostrils, to blot out the noxious smell. In the dirt streets of the town, garbage was strewn everywhere, and the ripe stench of the heaps of rubble, capped by that of the decaying offal from Slaughterhouse Lane and Butchery Row, overpowered him. In an attempt

21

to escape the horrific odor as quickly as possible, Rodham gave sharp spur to his horse, and Thomas followed suit. Quickly, they galloped through the town, and soon were almost at the wooden doors of Gonville, the college Thomas would attend. The arched stone gateway to nearby Corpus Christi bore the golden arms of Lady Margaret Beaufort, mother of Henry VII and a patroness of Cambridge. Her arms boasted a supporter of yales, those intriguing animals like deer which Thomas had heard about but never seen.[4] Thomas reined in briefly to examine the depiction of them more closely, and then, looking around him, his eyes widened. He could not fathom so much space being devoted to the contemplative beauty of the colleges, with their courtyards and walkways. Tiny Cambridge town was a far cry from the jumble of horses and carts, the cacophony of street hawkers' cries, and the maze of twisted streets and buildings that were the hallmark of bustling London, whose population had soared to nearly seventy thousand in recent years.[5]

Thomas looked around. The towers of King's College, just to the south of Gonville, soared above the grassy backs and reflected on the waters of the Cam, the small tributary from which the town drew its name. The delicately carved stone arches and lacy spires of the imposing chapel reached gracefully heavenward as if in supplication, dwarfing the boy on horseback who stared up at them, mesmerized.

The next morning Thomas bid a brave farewell to his tutor. "See that you attend well to your tasks, for you have yet much to learn," cautioned Rodham sternly. Then, turning his horse, he gave spur and cantered away. Thomas was suddenly quite alone and frightened. Rodham had been with him almost daily since he was a small boy. Squaring his shoulders and holding back tears, he sauntered back into Gonville Hall, outwardly manifesting a bravado he did not feel. But he was curious, nay—eager, to begin this grand new adventure.

Though Cambridge had not the scholastic distinction accorded venerable Oxford, it was a respected center of learning and known for progressive thought. A few decades earlier, the renowned Euro-

pean scholar Erasmus had accepted a professorship there, bringing along with him the bright new light of his thinking. Many of
England's finest parliamentarians and government officials pointed
proudly to Cambridge as their seat of knowledge and philosophic
ideals.

Soon after settling into his spartan lodgings in Gonville,
Thomas encountered John Caius ("Kees") of Norwich, who had
matriculated the previous year. At twenty, Caius was much older
than Thomas and the other students, whose ages averaged somewhere between twelve and fourteen. Caius was a tall, studious
youth, with dark, carelessly trimmed hair, and sallow skin that
showed the marks of an earlier bout with the smallpox. He was
quiet and serious. Thomas, by contrast, was little more than a gre-
garious pup—a leggy, freckle-faced, friendly child with a thatch
of unruly reddish hair that curled about his ears and eyes that were
the startling deep blue of the distant sea.

He was as brash as Caius was reserved. "Hullo," he broached
the laconic Caius, encountering him in the hallway outside chapel.
"I'm Thomas Gresham, up from London. My father studied here,
my brother John is here, and now 'tis my turn. You're lodged at
Gonville too, eh?"

Caius stared at Thomas a full minute in silence, appraising
him, and finally replied, "Yes. Kees, up from Norwich." As unlikely a duo as one could imagine, Caius and Thomas Gresham became
fast friends. Caius then brought into their circle a young acquaintance of his from Norwich, William Framingham. They became
an inseparable trio.

School life for Thomas at Cambridge was centered around
serious, scholarly discussions. All levity was discouraged. Punishment for lapse of attention to the subject at hand was swift, frequent and harsh. Severe beatings with a rod—for the slightest
infractions of the rules, or for failure to maintain proper deco-
rum—were the norm. The short-haired, long-robed young men
of Cambridge quit the classroom only to gather in groups on the
greensward or at the backs, like small flocks of ravens in their long
black gowns and close-fitting caps. There they pursued yet more

scholarly discussion and admired or criticized one another's thoughts. Laughter and games were unheard of. Thomas studied the standard liberal arts curriculum. First came the trivium: grammar, rhetoric, and logic. Then the quadrivium: music, astronomy, geometry, and arithmetic. Reading and writing were conducted mainly in Latin. Thomas was already conversant in Latin as well as English, and he plunged into his studies at Cambridge with great enthusiasm. Like the others, he was beaten occasionally, and punished severely from time to time, but he adapted to the scholastic life, and did well in his studies.

The young men seldom left the college enclave, preferring to remain among their comrades and dons. Thomas, Caius, and Will spent many hours in silent study, or in lively, vocal disagreement about religious theory or the fine nuances of the Greek language. At one point, Caius, devoutly Catholic, asked Thomas: "What are yer thoughts on the Cambridge concurrence with the king on his divorce? Do you think the church will grant him a nullity?"

Thomas was mindful of his family's position and his father's long association with Cardinal Wolsey. However, he was much more open-minded about religion than Caius. He was curious about the Lutheran point of view and wanted to learn more about the religious changes taking place on the Continent. To him, the new religion seemed to offer more freedom of thought and action. However, now, as Thomas considered Caius's question carefully, he decided that his best course would be to avoid stating a personal position on religious or political matters. "I really haven't studied enough, to own to an opinion." He was rewarded with a snort of disgust from his friend. Caius didn't believe for a second that Thomas "hadn't studied enough" about it. Why, the king's desire for an annulment was the most talked-about issue among the students! "So, then I guess you have no thought on the king giving praemunire to the clergy, eh?" he prodded. That fine, which Henry had recently leveled on the priests, was tantamount to a declaration of war against Catholicism. Thomas, his eyes on his book, shook his head in the negative. Caius was thoroughly aggravated by then, and couldn't resist sniping at the younger boy. "Well, certainly your father being high sheriff an' all, he's surely in King Henry's divorce camp, and you with him."

Thomas looked up from his book and his blue eyes bored into Caius's brown ones. "Marry, Kees, I have my thoughts about things, but they stay mine alone." Unperturbed, Thomas returned to his reading. Caius realized he had pressed young Gresham in vain. His friend already knew well how to keep his own counsel.

Thomas learned fiscal responsibility there, too. He received ample pocket money from home each month but rarely spent it in town on new clothes or sweetmeats, as many others did. Under Caius's tutelage, he developed a canny appreciation of the value of money; he had an inborn ability, it seemed, to balance and budget it. As soon as his allowance arrived, he would carefully count it out, designating a small sum to purchase the most basic necessities and another amount to be held aside for books he or Will or Caius might want to buy. The rest was put back and saved "for some time of need." His hoard of coins soon grew to a sizable sum.

Caius was the most conservative of the three in thought and deed. He required little in the way of material goods except his books and a change of clothing. He studied hard, slept little, and spent a great deal of time at chapel. Will Framingham was a careless but brilliant scholar, short and round of stature. He learned easily, and shared well. His goal was a professorship at Cambridge one day.

Thomas had little concern for his own future, which had already been decided—he knew he was destined to be a merchant adventurer like all the men in his family. Caius seemed to be leaning toward becoming a priest or theologian. "Well, you certainly have the mind, and the discipline for it, Kees," Thomas assured him. But the winds of change were already blowing strongly across England, and the scholarly John Caius would soon find himself at odds with King Henry's desires, and the new ideas of the Reformation.

John Caius, who was always addressed as "Kees" by the others, was a brilliant student and often a friend in need to the two younger boys. When Will struggled with a Greek passage, Caius would adeptly translate it for him. When Thomas foundered in the depths of a complex Latin treatise by Erasmus, Caius obligingly helped him translate it into English for better understanding.

One chilly day in November, Thomas came into Caius's tiny cell-like room and flung himself down on the hard wooden stool in the corner. Caius, busy at his small desk stand, looked up from his notes, startled. "I say, Kees, let's you and me and Will read for the Latin plays for this Christmas! I'll bet we can do them better than anyone!" Caius was aghast at the thought of appearing in a play. He never lent his mind, or his body, to dalliance, and the Latin plays, although an integral part of life at Cambridge and certainly within the bounds of his religious beliefs, seemed nothing but pap and frivolity to him.

"Certainly not," he said reprovingly. "We have much more important things to do. There is not time for such foolishness." Thomas's face dropped. He loved drama, craved diversion, and was most anxious to participate in the first real departure from study that had come along. "Kees, you can, you know. You'd be good! Please, consider it, just for me. I really want to do it. You could probably get the part of the bishop—you'd be perfect for it." But Caius would not budge. The most Thomas and Will could do was to get him to coach them in their own parts for the plays, parts they managed to win quite handily, much to Caius's secret pride.

His four years at Cambridge served to expand Thomas's horizons, making of him a man of letters—strong, athletic, and academically well rounded—a fit heir to future Gresham fortunes. His agile body complemented a sharp and inquisitive mind. He was a natural athlete, and soon his horsemanship and ability with the longbow were second to none.[6]

It was during Thomas's student days at Cambridge that Henry VIII's patience with the church snapped. He coldly banished Queen Catherine from court and distanced himself from their daughter, the Princess Mary. The king's actions outraged the women of England and brought a strong rebuke from Pope Clement in Rome, who urged Henry to "put that woman from your bed and return to your wife!" One day Anne Boleyn was actually forced to flee from a mob of angry women who chased her through the streets of London. Furious at the pope's directive, Henry seized ecclesiastical power in England to himself and began open repression of the power of the church. The future of the world turned because the eye of a married king had fallen in lust upon a slip of a girl.

Lord Chancellor Thomas More, saddened and discouraged, resigned his high office. In October 1532, Henry summoned Thomas Cranmer back to England from a mission to Germany and Italy. Cranmer was already married, and a father. Contrary to strict church laws requiring celibacy of priests, Henry was determined to elevate Cranmer to archbishop of Canterbury. Thomas More was consigned to the Tower prison, and another Thomas—Cromwell—stepped into power. Cranmer arrived back in England in January 1533, and "never a man came more reluctant to a bishopric," he would comment later, "than I did to that."[7]

The matter was still not officially resolved when Henry, a short time later, quietly married Anne Boleyn—for she was pregnant. Queen Catherine, cloistered away in quiet exile, dared not mount an open resistance. Henry would not hesitate to execute any and all who opposed him.

At Easter that year, Anne Boleyn appeared openly in public as queen, loaded down with the royal jewels. She had rallied sixty ladies in waiting to her, and none other than the daughter of the duke of Norfolk carried her train. Thomas Cranmer, recently confirmed as the new archbishop of Canterbury, officially declared Henry's marriage to Catherine null and void, proclaiming the king and Anne Boleyn legally married. The English, and the rest of the Christian world, were astonished at Henry's audacity.

Thomas Gresham was summoned home to London for Queen Anne Boleyn's coronation. His father's position as lord high sheriff afforded Thomas a vantage point at the Tower from which to watch the proceedings. A mature but impressionable fourteen-year-old, Thomas was astounded by Anne's coronation, which was staged with fabulous pageantry. In a Venetian spectacle, the new queen, gowned in cloth of gold and draped with sparkling jewels, and surrounded by scores of lavishly dressed ladies in waiting, floated down the Thames in her specially constructed barque. From his vantage point up on the ramparts, Thomas watched the beautiful boats approaching. The glittering royal barge was followed by a flotilla of gaily bedecked craft carrying the court nobles and their ladies.

That night, the fountains and conduits of the City, which had earlier been flushed and cleaned, bubbled and flowed with wine and ale. The celebration lasted two full days and nights. Few gave thought to what the cost of this thrilling spectacle would mean to England's dwindling treasury. King Henry had commanded that the realm celebrate their new queen and his soon-to-be-born heir, and the people were more than happy to oblige.

Caught up as he was in the spectacle, and the beauty of all the pageantry, Thomas was nevertheless uneasy about what the new queen, and the drastic changes that attended her elevation to the throne, might mean for his family, and for England. He thought about Caius back at Cambridge and wondered how he, staunch Catholic and traditionalist that he was, would react to all this. He returned to Cambridge and regaled Caius and Will with tales of all that he had seen and heard. Caius was outraged. He was already distraught over King Henry's divorce, by his blatant taking of a new queen, and by the king's repressive actions against the Catholic church in England. The story of Anne Boleyn's lavish coronation only fueled his sense of anger and futility. But Caius, realizing that the balance of power in England had shifted sharply against the Catholics, wisely kept his counsel, speaking his innermost thoughts on the matter to none except Thomas and Will.

"I've made a decision," he announced quietly, a few weeks later. Thomas pulled his attention from the book he was reading and looked keenly at his friend, afraid he was leaving Cambridge. But Caius merely said, "I've decided to be a physician, instead of a priest." Thomas and Will, delighted, clapped Caius on his thin shoulder, and warmly congratulated him. " 'Tis a fine idea, Caius," said Thomas, "an' there are many who'll bless you for it, I don't

doubt, for surely they need the kind of fine physician you'll be."
"Well, an' if he doesn't talk so long and serious to 'em that they die before," joked Will.

That year, Ivan assumed the throne of Russeland, and Thomas's older brother John sailed away on a long and dangerous expedition to explore establishing trade with Muscovia. Richard Gresham received news that the Spaniards had discovered a new territory, Peru, and had returned with fabulous treasure and several ships loaded with curious goods for their ruler. New frontiers for trade and wealth were opening everywhere, and the elder Gresham brothers were in on the start whenever a new trading prospect appeared.

However, with Henry's marital and religious troubles, and the drain imposed on the treasury by the king's lavish spending, and continual wars, the English were not pursuing exploration in the New World with the same fervor as the Spanish and Portuguese.

In September 1533, Queen Anne Boleyn presented Henry with a feisty, squalling little red-haired mite—another daughter. The king hid his disappointment and dismay, and the babe was christened with solemn ceremony. She was held up before all and proclaimed "the high and mighty princess of England, Elizabeth!" as silver trumpets blew.[8]

The following year, with a single mighty stroke, Henry VIII severed England permanently from its ties with Catholic Rome, and the Vatican. With the promulgation of the Act of Supremacy, he made himself supreme head of the Church of England, eclipsing the pope. The act gave him absolute religious and secular power over his subjects. The response of the Catholics was predictable. During 1534 and 1535 the Greshams witnessed the bloody purge of high-ranking Catholics in England, who died by the cartload—some hanged, drawn, and quartered, their hearts cut out and rubbed in their faces, others chained up for days, perishing in the Tower prison, mired in their own excrement.[9] The king himself, it was said, would have liked to watch the butchery. Henry was showing a new, unbelievably sadistic side to his people. Gentle Thomas More was one of those executed. As lord high sheriff, Richard Gresham watched, with a heavy heart, as the king's dreadful orders were carried out. He saw much, but said little.

In 1535, with the realm in political and religious disarray, and Queen Anne Boleyn expecting her second child, Thomas came down from Cambridge to begin apprenticeship with his uncle, John Gresham. He bid a sad goodbye to Caius and Will, who would remain at Cambridge to continue their studies. His formal schooling finished for the time being, Thomas set out to learn the ways of the sea and the intricacies of international trading under the sharp eye and direction of his uncle John.

Having enacted physical vengeance upon the higher church officials, the greedy King Henry's eye was soon cast upon the rich possessions and properties of the church. Secretary Thomas Cromwell ordered that a commission be convened to survey the value of the Catholic priories and monasteries of England. Richard Gresham was one of seventeen men appointed to that commission, which was ordered to review "the value of the benefices" to the crown.[10]

The commission appraised the vast wealth of the abbeys and monasteries—real property, gold and silver plate, jewels and furnishings. Their report to the crown concluded that the incredible mass of wealth the church owned was being poorly and carelessly managed by the clergy. Henry's treasury at that point was in dire straits. He had been forced to debase the currency by reducing the pure silver in his coins and adding more alloy to them, which caused inflation, unemployment, and poverty to spread throughout his realm. This new report from Cromwell's commission gave him the excuse he needed to seize church properties, turn out the clergy and the nuns, strip the abbeys of their tangible wealth for his own use, and sell off the land and buildings.

Richard and John Gresham snapped up several abbeys and country estates at excellent prices. John purchased a vast country seat in Surrey, near Limpsfield, and Richard bought thousands of acres of former church property in Yorkshire. He was then assessed £2000 in "subsidy" to the crown by the crafty King Henry. It was a substantial, even shocking tax, which Richard Gresham paid without question.[11] "Yea an' I've Wolsey's £1500 out of Gresham's hide after all, and more," chuckled Henry.

Richard Gresham accepted the levy by the king in good spirits. It was a small enough price to pay in return for all he'd gained. The Greshams were enjoying strong favor in the king's eyes, which could bring rewards that would far outweigh the £2000 he had just been forced to pay. Richard Gresham and his brothers were not only willing to give and lend money to the crown; they were able to provide scarce goods and certain great favors to the king and his courtiers on demand. That further raised their esteem in the eyes of the king, which ensured their safety for the moment. Few others could claim such safety in those days.

Before long, with his new queen far advanced in her second pregnancy, Henry's amorous eye was once again roving. This time, it stopped on Lady Jane Seymour, one of the queen's ladies in waiting. Soon King Henry, ever the huntsman, was in hot pursuit of his new quarry. Lady Jane had the good sense to allow herself to be "caught," after mounting a brief resistance that only served to whet the king's desire for her.

Queen Anne happened upon the two one evening, Lady Jane cozily perched on Henry's knee, both giggling like foolish children. Henry paled at the sight of his wife and quickly pushed Jane from his lap. Anne flushed a deep red with rage. "What! Dare you?" she screeched, grabbing the locket Jane was wearing—a gift from Henry. Ripping it sharply and angrily from her rival's neck, she cast it furiously away, leaving a great red welt across Jane's pale skin. Angry, but alarmed for the child Anne carried, Henry tried in vain to calm his wife. Queen Anne launched into a hysterical, screaming tirade at him, tears streaming, the veins on her neck standing out. She slapped at the king, and the Lady Jane, terrified, beat a hasty retreat. That night, Anne Boleyn lost Henry's infant son, the longed-for heir, and by that misfortune her doom was sealed.

That same day, Henry's first wife, Catherine of Aragon, died quietly in exile. She was buried at Peterborough Abbey, with scant ceremony to mark her passing. Their daughter, the Princess Mary, remained cloistered away, distanced by Henry's order from the court and her father. Soothsayers in London made much ado over the coincidence of the deaths of the old queen and the loss of Henry's male heir on the same day, seeing in it the manifestation of the Almighty's displeasure with Henry's actions against the dictums of the church. Word of the queen's terrible misfortune soon spread throughout England.

Furious, Henry turned on Anne in a towering rage. He banished her from his presence and set spies to watch her. Soon, he charged her with "betrayal and high treason," and consigned her to the Tower. Housed in the small apartments that faced the inner courtyard—Tower Green—Anne awaited her trial and sentence. Supervision of her child, the toddler Princess Elizabeth, was given over to Mrs. Ashley, the princess' governess. Anne was tried, found guilty of treason, and sentenced to her death—beheading on Tower Green. Henry was prevailed upon to spare his queen the humiliation of a public execution, but ordered a number of nobles and officials to attend, and bear witness to it. Anne could not help but watch, from the tiny windows of her apartments, as her execution block was readied. In terror of the ax, she begged the king for death by the sword instead. Early on the morning of 19 May 1536, the sheriff was ordered to "clear the Tower of all strangers," an ominous command with which he had become all too familiar.[12] Barely an hour later, in the inner courtyard of the Tower of London, a skilled swordsman severed Queen Anne Boleyn's head from her delicate neck. The Princess Elizabeth, like her half-sister Princess Mary, was motherless.

Within the week, Archbishop Cranmer declared that the king's marriage to Anne Boleyn had been null and void. By the end of the month, Henry VIII's third wife, Jane Seymour, had succeeded Anne Boleyn and Catherine of Aragon as Henry's queen.

Queen Jane, declared but not yet crowned, was quiet and reserved. She tried to avoid all controversy and shunned the limelight. The court considered her plain and dull, but Henry doted on her. Barely a few months following their marriage, Henry promulgated a new Act of Succession. This act barred the Catholic princess Mary from ever reigning, formally declared Princess Elizabeth illegitimate—wags at court had already begun calling her "the little bastard"—and settled succession upon Henry's offspring by this, his third wife.[13] Queen Jane obligingly became pregnant. Henry rejoiced, certain that she would be the queen who would bring forth the male heir he had so long and desperately desired.

It was autumn, and Thomas Gresham stood at the rail of the merchant ship *Anne of Fowey* as she crossed the Channel to England from Flanders. It had been a very good year for the Greshams, and now it promised to be even better. Thomas was returning from his second merchant voyage to Antwerp that year. At eighteen, his skills as a negotiator and trader, and his uncanny sense of the value of currencies and their relative rate of exchange had already been recognized and much praised by his uncle. John Gresham not only touted his nephew's superior trading abilities; he urged his brother Richard to send Thomas back to school soon, to study law. "'Twould not be a bad thing to have a Gresham merchant schooled in the law. Thomas seems the most apt for it. He has a ken for these things." To this Richard readily agreed.

Though Thomas did not need to serve out a full apprenticeship—his father had freed him from service the year before because he had mastered the program so rapidly—he had himself elected to continue. He wanted to learn everything possible about trading from his uncle John, who was the best there was in that perilous game, as Thomas had quickly come to realize. He loved the sea and was not anxious to return to the schoolroom.

Thomas braced himself as the ship dipped, then rose and steadied against the heavy swells. Her hull was laden with precious cargo that would bring the crown, and the Greshams, a tidy profit. They had taken across from England to Antwerp a full load of woolen cloth, and were returning with gold and silver plates and cups, casks of wheat, bolts of velvets and satins, jewels, tapestries, finely woven ropes, Turkish carpets, paintings from Italy, a few spices, and some gold coin. In his own sea chest, Thomas had a beautifully wrought, velvet-covered book of poems, a present for his stepmother Isabella, and bolts of woven sateen cloth and some feminine trinkets as gifts for his sisters.

The ship heeled over slightly in a sudden gust, and Thomas gripped the wooden rail to steady himself. He had grown into a strong, well-proportioned youth, his body set square on thick, sturdy legs. His face was broad of forehead, balanced by a straight, strong nose and firm-lipped mouth. He wore his auburn hair cropped short, and his pointed, close-cut beard—fashionable on the Continent but still an eyebrow raiser in England—was already crusted with sea spray. He drew his heavy woolen cloak closer and peered through the mists toward home, anxious for the pale, chalky cliffs of England to appear on the horizon. He was anxious to reach London, for his father had been elected lord high mayor of London on Michaelmas Day past, and would be knighted by the king and installed as lord mayor only ten days hence, on 18 October.[14] Thomas prayed that following seas and fair weather would speed him home. He planned to take to horse at Dover and ride home, allowing the ship to proceed upriver to London at a slower pace.

In Dover, Thomas at once procured a horse and set off at a gallop in the deepening fog and mist. Hunched low to avoid the tree limbs that drooped across the road here and there, he kept a tight rein, lest his horse trip on a rut and stumble. He hurtled along, the horse's dancing hooves sending red and gold leaves swirling up. Thomas inhaled deeply the welcome smell of the rich, damp earth. Ah, it was good to be in England again! Around midday, he pulled up at a crowded inn set close by the side of the road and quickly dismounted, tossing the reins to a waiting groom. Inside, before the welcome warmth of a roaring fire, he threw back his cloak and called for bread and meat and a tankard of ale. He dispatched his meal quickly, with the relish of hungry youth, making no effort to converse with other diners. He didn't notice the admiring glances the serving wench cast his way. A few coins on the table for the meal, and he was off again at full gallop, his thoughts bent on reaching London before dark. Highwaymen were a threat to the unwary traveler, and though he was armed and strong, he'd be no match for a band of them. Once home, he'd rest and feast. His sole regret was that his brother John, still away on the Muscovy expedition, would not be there to share the grand festivities of their father's honor.

Stopping for a short breather outside the village of Dartford in Kent, Thomas dismounted and let his horse rest and graze for a moment. He looked out across the barren fields, still and brown, awaiting the touch of winter's icy hand. England was in such turmoil now, few knew in which direction it would turn. For just a moment, he felt a pang of longing for his relatively carefree student days at Gonville with Caius and Will.

A few hours later, he was threading his way through the throngs in the streets of London, arriving at last at Milk Street. He turned into the familiar lane, and his heart rose when he spied the familiar golden grasshopper swinging above the door of his family home. His stepmother Isabella greeted him joyously. She was impeccably gowned, as always, this day in creamy linen and deep green taffeta, with bright green sateen plucked out through the slits in her voluminous sleeves. The gable hood covering her hair was stiff with rich embroidery and seed pearls. "Thomas! But you are grown to manhood in such brief time. I believe the sea sets well 'pon your brow."

His sisters, too, awaited him in the luxurious main room, where a blazing fire had been set in the hearth to ward off the evening's chill. He noticed that a new carpet from Turkey graced the wood-planked floor—a luxury that must have cost his father dearly. Few of the floors, even at the royal palaces, could boast such magnificent carpets—they were covered with straw rushes instead. But the house on Milk Street was second to none in London. Fine Flemish tapestries adorned its walls, and the carved oak furnishings were exquisite, fashioned in the latest style.

Thomas stared at his two sisters in astonishment. So recently, it seemed, they'd been his playmates in the nursery. Christiana had blossomed into a lovely, grey-eyed young maid during his absence. She greeted him shyly, and he responded by giving her an exaggerated courtly bent knee, kissing her hand in the style he had learned abroad. He was pleased when she blushed prettily at the compliment, and curtseyed shyly to him in return. As she did, her embroidered French hood, of the new style introduced not long before by Anne Boleyn, and worn only by the most fashionable and daring young women, slipped farther back, revealing a mane of strawberry gold hair. She was dressed in a grey and blue gown, her skin as fair as the creamy pearl brooch that graced her bosom. "Marry, you will be a prize for any husband, sister," he teased her. She would want for nothing as a wife one day, either, for as a Gresham daughter she would go to her husband with a rich dowry of lands and goods.

He turned to his other sister. "And you, Elizabeth? What news have you to welcome your brother home again? Will you soon wed some fine merchant?" The young woman blushed deeply. "Nay, I have not thoughts for marriage, brother, and have no mind to hasten in that regard." Elizabeth was a quiet, religious young woman, with plainer tastes than her younger sister, as her simple dark-blue gown showed. But her gable hood was well made, and about her neck was clasped an intricately fashioned, jeweled cross her father had given her this past New Year. Her brown eyes flashed with intelligence and curiosity. "Well, Thomas, you'll have much to tell us about your voyages and the foreign lands, I trust."

"Truly, that I will." He grinned. Gallantly, he escorted his stepmother to her chair, where she took up her needle and resumed her embroidery. His sisters joined her there, busy at their own frames. Thomas moved over to warm himself by the fire.

"Well, an' I have brought you grande stuffes, ladies all, for dresses and capes that will be envy of the court, yea, and of the queen herself," he announced, pleased at the interest that sparked. "The Lady Gresham, and the daughters of our lord mayor, Sir Richard," he teased, "shall shine as bright as the queen's own jewels at court on the morrow." Thomas smiled broadly, enjoying himself, pleased at being among his family again. "Oh, and there be some small jewels and trinkets in my chest, too, which I doubt not shall please you." Isabella and the girls laughed delightedly. "Let us see, brother, what you've brought," begged Christiana. "Nay, for they came not with me, but will follow in a few days' time." Isabella smiled fondly at her young stepson. "Marry, but the man starves while we blather," she said, rising to call for a servant. "To sup now, ladies, an' you'll talk more with your brother later."

Richard Gresham had quietly entered the room. Dressed in his usual simple black, a soft, close-fitting night cap replaced his outdoor hat. His dark brown eyes lit with pleasure at the sight of his younger son. Going quickly to Thomas, he clasped his hand warmly. "Marry, son, but you've grown a man. I hear naught but good of you from John and the members of the company. Was't a good journey, and profitable?" He turned to his wife. "A cup of mead, that I may celebrate the safe return of my son. Then we'll sup." Isabella again called for a servant to bring warm mead, commanding that dinner await her husband's pleasure.

The two men shared a cup by the fire, and Thomas brought his father up to date on business. "The goods I carried aboard should arrive in London within the week and will please you mightily, father—they came at hard bargaining, but good exchange," he boasted. "Well done, son. We shall go on the morrow to the wharf." Thomas looked forward to that—he enjoyed being in his father's company, and the elder Gresham had much to show him. It was indeed good to be home again!

Early the next morning, Thomas was jolted from slumber by the sudden peal of church bells. Soon all the bells in London were ringing in a great clamor. Jumping from bed, he began pulling on his clothes. Then he heard trumpets sound in the distance, followed by musket fire and the boom of cannon. His heart began to pound. Were they being invaded? He ran to the casement and threw open the window to look. No invasion, surely, for people below were shouting and laughing, cheering, and some were even dancing in the streets. "What goes?" he called. "'Tis a prince!" shouted one of the street revelers. "A prince is born!"

Queen Jane had that night been safely delivered of a boy. Henry at last had his heir. A prince! There was a brusque rap at his door and it opened to admit his father, fully dressed and smiling broadly. "Come, Thomas, dress in your finest, you'll ride in my company today as I make His Grace's announcement of this grand news to all London." His father clapped him on the shoulder. "This is a joyous day for England!"

"From the sound of it, I think London knows already, father." Thomas hastened to dress in his finest gown and join his father for the solemn ceremonial procession through the streets. Only then would the news be official. Outfitted in black velvet and mounted on a fine horse, Thomas followed proudly in his father's train as Richard Gresham, lord mayor of London, in full regalia of his office, accompanied by all his aldermen garbed in their official dress, rode slowly through the streets loudly proclaiming the news, exhorting the throngs to "go and give thanks to God for the birth of our prince!"

Henry was ecstatic. A *Te Deum* of thanksgiving was sung in St. Paul's, attended by the king, the court, and Mayor Richard Gresham and his city officials. The realm went crazy with celebration. Guns sounded day and night. Great bonfires were lit. The city's fountains, and the conduits along Cheapside ran with wine, and sumptuous banquets were staged by the nobles and the wealthy in honor of the newborn prince. The king ordered copious alms to be distributed to the poor, and for the populace, street plays and pageantry abounded.

On 15 October, all the bells of London pealed again, and trumpets once more heralded a great occasion. The nobles of the realm, the ambassadors and foreign dignitaries, and high city officials like Richard and John Gresham, gathered together to attend the solemn and lavish baptism of the new prince of England. The baby's half-sisters—the princesses Mary and Elizabeth—had recently been restored to favor at court at the behest of Queen Jane, and Princess Mary was designated a godmother to her new brother. Princess Elizabeth, barely four, had the honor of bearing the heavy jeweled baptismal chrisom to the archbishop. Its weight necessitated that she be carried, and Edward Seymour, uncle of the new prince, offered to carry the little princess and her jeweled burden in the ceremonial procession.

It was an impressive and lavish ceremony. As soon as Archbishop Cranmer had baptized the prince, naming him Edward, Henry's garter-king-at-arms proclaimed: "God of his almighty and infinite grace give and grant good life and long to the right-high, right-excellent and noble prince, Prince Edward, duke of Cornwall and earl of Chester, most dear and most entirely beloved son to our most dread and gracious lord, King Henry VIII. Largesse, largesse, largesse!"[15] The procession of nobles then bore the heir to the Tudor throne to be blessed by the king and queen. As King Henry received his infant son from his godmother's arms, tears of happiness ran down his face. He beamed at Queen Jane with adoration. "You have given us new life, madam." Jane, still pale and wan from the ordeal of birth, returned her lord's smile and gently offered him her hand. Henry clasped her tiny hand in his enormous paw and reverently kissed it. Seeing that, Thomas Seymour and his elder brother Edward, the child's ambitious uncles, smiled victorious smiles. With this babe, their sister Jane had assured them their place in the sun.

A few days later, Thomas and his family stood by and watched a merry King Henry knight Richard Gresham. The somber, dignified Sir Richard was a stark contrast to the rest of the brightly garbed and jeweled gathering. Yet somehow, though simply and elegantly dressed, sporting no jewels save a massive seal ring and his chain of knighthood, his father exuded an aura of power and command that made the others, in their laces and satins and ruffles, appear garish and overdone.

Thomas vowed he'd adopt for himself his father's manner of dress. Simple black, he realized, threatened no other, allowing the court peacocks to strut about in unmatched finery. There were so many rules of dress at court, it was hard to remember them all. It dawned upon him why his father dressed so. The Greshams were often in the company of the nobility because of all the business they did for the crown. The quiet Richard Gresham, and his increasing power and wealth, passed among them little noticed. Wearing black put him in no danger of breaking the infinitely detailed color codes or the complex rules of dress for men. Also, by not preening, or exhibiting his wealth on his person like the others, Richard Gresham did not attract the sycophants, the dissemblers, and the greedy who hovered about. Most important, he did not engender jealous rivals eager to strip him of his goods and holdings.

However, Richard Gresham was not so conservative that he denied the City the pomp and ceremony of tradition that went with his installation as lord high mayor of London. He had never forgotten the thrill of the Field of Cloth of Gold, and now, in his own moment of glory, he was reminded of the beauty of that great meeting. He smiled as he donned the colorful regalia of his high office, and he revived some of the kingdom's long-buried rituals during the celebration of his installation. Horse guards, halberdiers, and archers preceded the new lord mayor through the streets of London, with trumpeters and drummers lined along the way to announce them. The festivities lasted far into the torchlit night, as all London celebrated with their new knight and lord mayor, Sir Richard Gresham.

King Henry, though seldom far from the side of Queen Jane and the baby prince of late, honored the Greshams by making a brief appearance before the overjoyed crowds, personally to bestow his royal approval on the new lord mayor of London. The crowds cheered and roared with joy at seeing their happy king. Thomas felt a thrill of awe, seeing Henry up close for the first time.

At the mansion on Milk Street, a banquet with an array of the finest foods, wines, and ales to be had was held. Fat purses of alms were taken by liveried Gresham retainers and distributed to the poor throughout the city, largesse from their new lord mayor. Sir Richard Gresham and Lady Isabella had also decreed that all who came to the door at the sign of the golden grasshopper that week would be fed heartily. The tables in the kitchen and scullery groaned under their burden of roasts and sweets and rare fruits.

Then, as abruptly as it had begun, the unrestrained laughter, dancing, and celebrating ceased. A terrified lady in waiting had been ushered into Henry's presence. She had fallen upon her knees before him, weeping. "My lord, I fear I have ill news. My lady queen has fallen grievous ill." Henry and his court physicians rushed to the queen's bedside. Jane lay racked with fever, barely able to move. Henry was shocked at her feeble condition. He sent for Archbishop Cranmer and Secretary Cromwell, the one to pray for the queen's recovery, the other to shore up the raging king, who bellowed like a wounded bull at one and all. Innocent servants were accused of poisoning, overindulgence, or neglect, thrown into prison, tortured and killed, but to no avail. Henry's beloved queen burned with fever and raged in delirium for five days, then died. The king's grief was without bounds. Cromwell wrote, "By the neglect of those about her who suffered her to take cold, and eat such things as her fantasy in sickness called for, the queen is dead."

The English went into deep mourning for their young queen. She lay in state for fifteen days at Hampton Court, gowned in cloth of gold, fully jeweled, crowned in death as she had not been in life. The king then withdrew to Windsor Castle, where Queen Jane Seymour was buried in state. Sir Richard, as lord mayor, attended to the proper obsequies: "Yet shall it please you, your good lordship, that I have caused twelve hundred masses to be said, within the City of London, for the soul of our most gracious queen. And whereas I, the mayor, and the aldermen, together with the commoners, went to Saint Paul's, and there gave thanks for the birth of our prince, I do think, my lord, that when it be convenient, there should now also be masses at St. Paul's for Her Grace's soul." Touched with pity for the growing numbers of poor and homeless in the City, Gresham risked a plea to Henry's generosity in the face of his grief. "My lord, if there be any alms to be given in Her Grace's name, there are many poor people within the City." Signing his name with a flourish, he sanded the letter, sealed it, and dispatched a servant at a gallop to carry it to Henry at Windsor. The servant returned two days later, bearing a heavy pouch of alms from the king. Richard Gresham, his son Thomas beside him, and his retinue following, rode out the next morning to distribute the coins to the poor of London, in memory of their sweet and gentle Queen Jane.

Within weeks, the Greshams gathered again, this time at Windsor, and in more subdued celebration. John Gresham, Sir Richard's brother, was knighted by a grave-faced Henry, whose eyes showed the pain of his recent loss. Sir John Gresham was then installed as lord high sheriff of London with great pomp and ceremony, bringing the City out of deepest mourning to celebrate the ritual with him.

One evening in late November, as the three men dined alone together, Sir Richard shared with his brother and son a project dear to his heart. "I've submitted a design for a bourse, modeled after the one in Antwerp, which I'm sure you've seen." Thomas and Sir John nodded, but made no comment. They continued their meal, awaiting Sir Richard's amplification. "Well, I've asked Cromwell for the court's permission to buy some properties at the site on Lombard Street." Lombard Street was where the merchants of London assembled twice a day—at noon and again at six—every day of the week, in rain, snow, or shine, to trade bills of exchange and conduct their business. Thomas had been there often with his father, and more recently with his uncle. "Sounds a good idea to me," he ventured to comment, "for the merchants would be glad for a place to shelter." His father smiled, pleased that his son approved of the idea. "'Tis a fine plan, brother," agreed Sir John. "You'll have my support at court, and with the merchants on't as well." Sir Richard sat back, well pleased. His brother's influence was strong in both places, and if his plan for a bourse was to have any chance of succeeding, he'd need support from all quarters.

However, to Sir Richard Gresham's chagrin, King Henry never replied to his proposal. He heard, somewhat later, that Cromwell had approved of his idea and had even introduced a bill in Parliament to grant Sir Richard Gresham's proposal for erecting the bourse, but it failed immediately in the House of Commons and never reached the lords.[16] They were annoyed that the merchants had rejected an earlier proposal for a meeting site in Leadenhall, a building admirably suited to their needs. Being resistant to change, the merchants had voted to continue meeting in Lombard Street, which had been the gathering spot for merchants since before anyone could remember.[17]

Not long afterward, the Greshams again petitioned the king,

this time asking him to restore three ancient hospitals of London—St. Mary's, St. Bartholomew's, and St. Thomas's—hospitals which had been taken over by the church and afterward made into residences for priests and canons. Sir Richard asked that the king return them to the City, to be used again for what they had originally been intended—as hospitals "for the relief, comfort, and helping of the poor, sick, blind, aged, not being able to help themselves, and for other miserable people living in the street."[18] That request was strongly seconded by Sir John Gresham, who as lord high sheriff added a plea that the king also return Bethlehem Hospital—popularly known as "Bedlam"—to its former use as an asylum for the insane. This time, the king granted their requests in full, and Thomas was pleased to hear that, for London these days was full of poor and unfortunate souls who needed help.

The holy days of Christmas passed quickly, with the country still in a somber mood. There was little outward celebration. The young prince, though at first rumored to be a weakling, waxed strong and thrived. Henry proudly displayed his son at court, and fussed over him inordinately. The king personally supervised every aspect of the daily routine of his baby prince, planning for and protecting against every possible eventuality. He promulgated strict orders on hygiene to be observed in the care of the prince, and he dictated, writing the orders out in his own hand, the detailed daily routine to be followed by all. Scrupulous cleanliness, which was seldom observed anywhere in England, was the foremost order for everything that surrounded or touched the prince. Failure to comply meant a death sentence for the offender. Henry himself came to the child's apartments frequently to inspect, and to assure himself that his orders were being carried out to the letter.

Meanwhile, Cromwell's agents and Henry's ambassadors began a new project abroad—that of searching out a suitable marital alliance for the widowed king of England. The council had decided that this time Henry would marry for the political and financial benefit of the country, as kings were supposed to do, rather than succumb to lust for some comely maid at his own court. Henry, still despairing over the loss of Queen Jane, offered little resistance to their scheme. The young, pretty, dimpled and appropriately widowed Christine of Milan was considered. So was the far less comely daughter of the duke of Cleves—Anne.

Thomas remained in London until the Feast of Twelfth Night on 6 January 1538. He journeyed briefly to Cambridge, to visit John Caius. Caius, ever the student, was now taking his M.A., and deep into the study of medicine. He greeted Thomas with his usual lack of warmth, but was curious about Thomas's travels abroad. "So, you've been out to see some of the world, eh? And how do you find it, away from England?"

"Ah, 'tis fine, Caius, 'tis fine to see—but finer than ever you can imagine to be home again after a voyage." He told Caius of all he had seen in Antwerp and the Low Countries, and described the strange and wonderful goings-on there. Caius was open in his envy. "Yea, an' I hope to go abroad one day soon, too."

"Marry! Where?"

Caius smiled one of his rare smiles. "To Italy, methinks, to study medicine." Then, without ceremony, "I have sad news to impart. Will Framingham died of the fever this year." Thomas felt shocked disbelief. Will was so young! He had so many plans! For once, Thomas was at a loss for words, and he and Caius sat silently, thinking of their friend. After a bit, they walked slowly across the courtyard to the tiny chapel at Gonville. Kneeling on the hard stone floor, they offered up a prayer for Will. Thomas, who seldom prayed these days, added a prayer for the health of the new prince, whom he felt would be England's only way out of the religious stew Henry had fomented with his marriages and divorces.

Returning to London, Thomas bid his family farewell and headed for Dover and his ship, this time without the company of his uncle John, who remained in London to carry out his duties as the new lord high sheriff.

Sir Richard Gresham soon tired of the petty restraints and squabbles of officialdom and was happy to leave his post in the autumn of 1538 to return to his first love—commerce. Before departing as lord high mayor, however, he made one final effort to interest Cromwell and King Henry in establishing a bourse in London. "The last year, I showed your Lordship a plan that was drawn out to make a Bourse in Lombard Street, for merchants to repair to. I do suppose it will cost about £2000 sterling or more, but shall be very beautiful for the City and an honor to our sovereign lord and king. But, there are certain houses in the street belonging to Sir George Monnocks, and except we may purchase them, the bourse could not be constructed."[19] He asked Cromwell to gain the king's intercession. "It may please your lordship to move the King's Highness to have letters directed to Sir George, willing and also commanding him to cause the said houses to be sold to the mayor and commonality of the City of London, for such price as he did purchase them for, and that he fault not, but to accomplish his Gracious Majesty's commandment. The letter must be sharply written, for Sir George is of no gentle nature." To sweeten the request, Sir Richard promised £1000 out of his own funds toward the construction.[20]

Cromwell was in favor of the bourse, but he and the king were reluctant to tangle with the ungentle nature of Sir George Monnocks, and Gresham's bourse project seemed doomed to failure. At about the same time, Richard Gresham petitioned Cromwell to formally admit his son Thomas to the royal service. "He is a good lad with a fine mind and he has been chosen for his knowledge in the French tongue to attend to certain French lords at Dover, and has served them and Your Grace most well."[21] Cromwell readily agreed to that request, and Thomas began receiving instruction on commissions he should accomplish for the crown, and was initiated by his father and uncle into the manner of rendering financial services to the king, as they themselves had done for many years. Sir Richard, realizing his other son had not inherited the business acumen with which Thomas appeared to have been blessed, was quietly grooming his younger son to take over the family enterprises one day.

Sir John, too, though he had many children of his own, relied on his nephew Thomas more and more for his own family's business needs. Thomas completed his apprenticeship in the Merchant Adventurers, then spent a year at Gray's Inn, reading the law. After that, he returned to sea with the Merchant Adventurers.

Prince Edward grew and thrived, as did the wealth and holdings of the Greshams. Sir Richard and Sir John rendered valuable service to the king, and were suitably rewarded with lands. They continued to borrow and loan money on Henry's behalf, often out of their own pockets. But the treasury of England, sagging under the profligate spending habits of Henry, eluded Cromwell's most determined efforts to shore it up. Henry deliberately skated England again and again across thin ice to the very edge of bankruptcy.

In 1543 Master Thomas Gresham, a polished young gentleman of twenty-four, became a fully licensed mercer and merchant adventurer of England, in service to Henry VIII. It was a day of great celebration. His older brother John was an adventurer and a soldier, but not much of a businessman, and Thomas's accession to the helm of the family business left his father free to retire for longer periods at a time to his mansion at Bethnal Green in London or to his vast country estates, especially his favorite at Intwood in Norfolk.

During the intervening half dozen years, at Henry's volatile court, the dangerous intrigues and plots had continued unabated. Thomas Cromwell had been executed in June of 1540, one more among the many who forfeited their lives for opposing the king's slightest whim, religious or secular. Henry had also married and disposed of two more wives: the first a political union with Anne of Cleves, whom he could not tolerate in his bed and whom he finally divorced; and the next, the lovely Catherine Howard, an empty-headed sprite of a girl whom he adored and lusted for, but who was finally consigned to the Tower for committing adultery. Eventually, like Anne Boleyn, she was beheaded at the execution block on Tower Green. Neither wife had provided Henry with any heirs.

Archbishop Thomas Cranmer continued to serve His Majesty well, and by complying with Henry's every wish managed to avoid the fate his predecessors had suffered.

King Henry, desperate for more funds, was again preparing to debase the currency.[22] It was a move the Greshams knew would bring more inflation, higher interest rates on Henry's foreign debts, and certain disaster to the country's financial future. However, despite his deepening financial difficulties, Henry VIII had managed to resolve some of his pesky territorial problems. Wales had been absorbed, and Catholic uprisings in Scotland and Ireland had been subdued by force, though not without great cost. James V of Scotland had died without a male heir, and Henry had plans to marry his own Prince Edward to James's only daughter, the baby Mary, queen of Scots. Henry hoped to solidify the British Isles before the Scots made a marriage alliance across the sea with Europe. He was certain that a marriage between Edward and Mary would please the Scots. It would also block the Catholic faction, and lessen the danger of Scottish intervention in England's affairs. It was a wise and clever plan. Unfortunately, Henry VIII would not live to accomplish it.

In 1543, the irrepressible fifty-two-year-old king, grossly obese, grey of hair and beard, and often ill, took a sixth wife—the twice-married, twice-widowed Lady Latimer, Katherine Parr. She was only thirty-one, and reputedly betrothed to the dashing cavalier Thomas Seymour, the late Queen Jane's brother and uncle to Prince Edward, but Henry was undeterred. Queen Katherine Parr was soon installed as the new stepmother to his three children. It was an interesting domestic arrangement, but Katherine managed somehow to supersede the petty jealousies and infighting of Henry's brood, and they were fond of her. Each had his or her own faction of followers and detractors. Princess Mary, devoutly Catholic, was then twenty-five; Princess Elizabeth, nominally Protestant, was ten; and Prince Edward, in training as a strongly Protestant future king, was barely six. Leaving his "family" to the tender care of their new stepmother, and under a new alliance with Charles V, Henry prepared to invade France, which was still under the rule of his old nemesis, Francis I.

That same year, Thomas Gresham returned to England from Antwerp after a long spell away, bringing a cargo of gunpowder, cannons, and other war supplies to his king. He tarried at home just long enough to fall in love.

His father's good friend in Suffolk, William Read, had earlier taken a young wife, Anne Ferneley, the daughter of William Ferneley, a country gentleman. Anne was a comely lass—too pretty, some said, to be wed to one as old as Read. In late 1543, word that his friend Read was gravely ill had reached Sir Richard at Intwood. He prevailed upon Thomas to go there and visit Read. "Ride to Suffolk and look you in on William," he wrote his son in London, "and in my stead render his poor wife what assistance you can."

Thomas set out for Suffolk, to oblige his father. On his arrival at the Read estate, he was struck by the rosy-cheeked, well-proportioned young woman presented to him as the lady of the manor. He could scarcely credit that it was she who was Read's "poor wife" and would soon be his widow. He was more than happy to render the lovely Anne Read his assistance, as his father had requested. Soon, Thomas and the engaging Anne were deeply involved. He rode as often as possible to Suffolk to look in on her, as she nursed her husband through his final illness. Anne Read moved with grace and spoke with wit, and Thomas spent hours composing sonnets to her and staring into her liquid eyes, which, like his, were the color of the deep sea in sunlight. Her quick and ready smile enchanted him. She had already provided the aging Read with two young heirs, so Thomas knew she could bear him sons as well.

Their deepening mutual interest did not escape William Read. He sent for his friend Sir Richard, whom he had named overseer of his will, asking him to come to Suffolk for a final visit. "Methinks 'twould be a good match if your Thomas were to take my Anne to wife when I'm gone," he told Sir Richard. "She'll be well provided, as you know, for I'm not a poor man, and she would be a good wife for him. 'Twould appear to be not against their wishes."

The startled Sir Richard made no immediate reply. Thereafter, he watched the two carefully, and realized that his old friend's suggestion was not amiss. Sir Richard had great plans for his younger son, and a match between Thomas and Anne Ferneley Read would fall well into them. She was from good stock and reasonable fortune, without the foolish head of most younger maids. She would be wealthy when Read passed on, and being still young, she and Thomas would bring him many grandchildren.

William Read died at the beginning of 1544. The widowed Anne knew that with her husband's passing she'd be faced with a dreary life, at best. She had few choices. She could return to her father's remote estate, or else enter a nunnery. Or, with luck, she could make a new, and hopefully advantageous, marriage match.

The first two prospects appealed not at all to a young and vivacious woman like Anne Read. She had social ambitions and longed to be in the whirl of London, away from the stifling boredom of the countryside. Marriage was the only way a widow could remain in society. Therefore, knowing her husband's illness was one from which he would not recover, when Fate brought Thomas to her door she had set her cap for the young and handsome scion to the Gresham fortunes. Without appearing to, she quietly wooed him even as her aging husband lay dying. For his part, Thomas had not been a reluctant swain, for he too was ready for marriage and a family, had little time to spend on courtship, and this lovely woman suited his tastes and his needs admirably. Within weeks after Read's death, he approached his father about marrying her.

Sir Richard, out of respect for his friend's memory, insisted they wait a brief but decent interval. Then, at Thomas's urging, he wrote a letter to William Ferneley, Anne's father, telling him what William Read himself had suggested. He made Ferneley a formal proposal for the match. Ferneley was delighted at the prospect of such an excellent second marriage for his widowed daughter. He was well aware of Richard Gresham's vast estates and considerable wealth and the influence at court the Gresham family enjoyed.

Anne blushed as she acquiesced to Sir Richard's formal proposal. "Yea, father, I have met master Thomas Gresham," she allowed modestly, never admitting that she and Thomas had enjoyed far greater intimacy than simply meeting during those long days and evenings of his visits. In fact, she feared she might be with child.

"Thomas and Sir Richard assisted me greatly during William's illness. Thomas is a fair, fine gentleman. Though I be still in mourning for William," she lied sweetly, "I know 'tis better that I wed again. This match would please me greatly."

And so it was arranged. Thomas was happy to set a date to wed quickly. He commanded two enameled gold wedding rings from a Florentine goldsmith. Ornately carved, each was made of two narrow bands set with a ruby and a crystal. So intricate was their design that when released by a secret spring the bands swung apart horizontally, revealing two cunning niches containing tiny, magnificently wrought gold cupids. The Latin inscription "Quod Deus Coniunsit" was engraved on one half, and "Homo Non Seperat" on the other. (Whom God Has Joined, Man Cannot Separate).[23] Anne was enchanted, pleased to learn that her prospective groom had exquisite taste, and more important, the wherewithal to indulge it. She slipped the ring on her finger to try it. The beautifully cut stones caught and reflected the firelight as she held her hand near the flames. "Oh, Thomas, it is lovely. I shall wear it ever for you, my beloved."

Anne was a radiant bride, her headdress embroidered with gold and tiny pearls to complement the rope of pearls that Thomas had presented to her as a wedding gift. She was also wearing a necklace bearing the cross of St. Andrew, set with sapphires the same dark blue as her eyes—a gift from Sir Richard and Lady Isabella.

Sir Richard and Lady Isabella hosted a sumptuous wedding feast at Bethnal Green for the occasion of their younger son's marriage. The great table of the hall was set with the finest plate in chased silver and pewter. It was laden with whole haunches of beef, sides of mutton, pork, every manner of fowl, goose stuffed with dried fruits, turkey, guinea hens, venison, whole roasted fish, oysters, breads, and meat pasties. Every delicacy imaginable was offered. Sweets and savories followed the meats, and everything was offered with flagons of the finest wine and ale. "A Toast! A Toast!" was exclaimed again and again, and cups were raised and clinked together at each new toast, to ward evil spirits away from the joyous festivities.

Dancing followed the feasting. The servants danced in the courtyard and behind the kitchen garden outdoors, to the happy rhythm of a pipe, and Thomas and his bride finally appeared on the gallery, to a great cheer, and tossed coins down to them. Inside, the bridal couple was serenaded by lutes and violins, and they led out the others in dancing the pavane. As darkness fell, the laughing troupe of revelers, bridesmaids, and groomsmen escorted Thomas and Anne Gresham along a flower-strewn hallway to their beautifully decorated wedding chamber.

To commemorate the occasion, his father commissioned a life-size, full-length portrait of Thomas to be painted by Holbein, a favorite of King Henry's.[24] After a brief honeymoon at Intwood, Anne and Thomas set up housekeeping in London. At first, they lived in Sir Richard's mansion on Milk Street, but soon the golden grasshopper marked their own spacious and elegant house and shop in Lombard Street—a gift from Sir Richard and Lady Isabella. There Thomas was close to the gathering place of merchants and could attend their twice daily meetings with ease. The war was not going well for Henry, and his demand for new supplies from Flanders was keeping the Gresham ships busy crossing the waters to Antwerp.

Anne soon informed her husband she was expecting their first child, and Thomas was pleased at the prospect of an heir coming so soon after their wedding. Anne's two young sons by Read were at school in Suffolk, or with their grandfather, and Thomas and Anne rarely saw them. A babe in the house would be a good thing for his wife, with him away at sea so much of the time, Thomas reflected.

Within the year Anne presented Thomas with a fine, healthy son whom they named Richard, after his paternal grandfather. Richard was a happy baby, and Thomas proudly showed his son off to his friends and fellow merchants when they called. His little namesake was the pride of Sir Richard.

That first year of his marriage was a tranquil one for the young merchant Thomas Gresham. He anticipated a prosperous future, and a house filled with children. If, after the second year, Anne began to complain overly much, he paid little heed to it. He had much to occupy his attention in just looking after the business affairs of his family and handling difficult commissions for the crown. King Henry's needs, it seemed, were insatiable. Soon Thomas resumed his trading voyages to the Low Countries, and made handsome profits from the goods he traded. He was determined that his family would be well provided for, and he looked forward to Anne announcing that a second child was in the offing. But more than two years passed, and that news did not come.

John Caius, a full-fledged physician, had returned to England from Padua in time to attend Thomas and Anne's wedding, and he, too, resided in London. Thomas liked to visit Caius at his bachelor quarters and often invited him to join them for dinner at Lombard Street, though the young doctor seldom obliged him. Caius lived a celibate, very Spartan, existence, and seemed shy and uncomfortable around Anne and the child. "He's a strange man, your friend Caius," commented Anne after one of his infrequent visits.

Meanwhile King Henry increased his demands on the Greshams, and on his other merchants, to support and supply him in his battle with Francis I. The war Henry undertook in 1544 was not like the wars of his youth. Nor were Henry, Charles, and Francis any longer the men who had maneuvered so boldly back in 1520. They were now old and decrepit. Instead of charging forth like fiery war horses, they scrabbled and circled one another like three wary crabs.[25] Henry quickly captured Boulogne, then scampered home to await Francis's next move. At the same time, Charles struck the hapless Francis from the south, chopped off a chunk of his realm, then quickly negotiated a peace at Crépy.

Francis finally mounted a retaliation at Henry for the humiliation of Boulogne. He dispatched his fleet for a naval invasion of England. Henry, who prided himself on his own navy, was ready and waiting for Francis at Portsmouth. As was the custom, the Gresham merchant ships, like those of the other merchants, had been commandeered and quickly converted to warships to augment the Royal Navy. When the French fleet was first sighted, the obese King Henry, who had by then grown so stout that even to walk was cumbersome, lumbered aboard his flagship *The Great Harry* to watch the engagement at sea. But the battle that rolled up like a majestic thunderstorm soon departed like a mild summer squall.

The king was hustled ashore for his safety. The once great warrior king could only sit by in a huge chair set up on the dock, as his ships set sail to stand off the enemy. "We'll watch our great ships from here," he boasted, as though it was his own idea, "and our stout men shall send the French invaders to the sea bottom in a trice—ere the sun sets this day." But the French admiral did not like the look of things, especially not the weather to the southwest, so he gave the signal for his fleet to turn and withdraw. At almost that same moment, Henry's greatest warship, the *Mary Rose*, attempting to turn into the wind to hold off the French, became swamped. Her captain had failed to order the lower gun ports closed before turning, and sea water roared into her lower decks. As King Henry watched helplessly from the dock, crying out in horror and anguish, the majestic *Mary Rose* heeled over and in a matter of minutes sank beneath the waves, taking four hundred of his best sailors with her. Fewer than twenty survived. The French, meanwhile, scurried off across the Channel to safe harbor, completely unscathed. So ended the great naval confrontation between the two aging rulers.

Henry's last angry bellow at Francis had bled his treasury nearly dry. Boulogne had cost well over £1 million to win and had returned him only £30,000 in revenue. He had already taxed the people of England to the limit; he knew he could not demand a penny more from them. The cost of living was insupportable. His only choice was to debase once again the coinage, and this he prepared to do, ignoring the howls of outrage from merchants and financiers alike.

During the previous two decades, Henry had steadily reduced the quality of the English coin in both fineness and weight. Initially, he reduced the silver in the pound sterling from ten ounces to nine. Then he debased it further—to only six ounces, and gradually dropped the silver testoon from one hundred ounces of silver to only forty. Now, he reduced the silver in the pound from six ounces to four, adding yet more alloy. Thomas Gresham and the merchant adventurers tried to warn him against such a move, for it would have serious repercussions on trade abroad. Henry's council voiced open alarm at the economic havoc it would wreak throughout the kingdom. But King Henry was determined to proceed. He needed more coin.

No sooner had the debased coins appeared than prices of goods soared, businesses failed, and unemployment climbed sharply—first in London, and then all over England. Soon, the ever-present inflation was galloping out of control, and the country was flooded with poor and homeless. Henry tried to stem the tide by passing laws against poverty and vagrancy, but that was like trying to outlaw the howling wind.[26]

Abroad, especially in Antwerp, England's credit plummeted. The Flemish bankers flatly refused to accept English coin in repayment of Henry's loans, causing a severe drop in the exchange rate, and the interest rates on Henry's desperately needed loans climbed to an exorbitant 13 and sometimes 14 percent. Despite the paucity of money in the treasury and the unfavorable terms he faced in procuring money from abroad, Henry doggedly pursued his war with Francis and his other extravagant plans.

Thomas Gresham and the merchants found themselves pressed to aid the king's causes, to help him borrow new funds, and to parry the Flemish bankers for him. With the value of their money dropping, and Henry's credit diving along with it, theirs became a wretched task. They were forced to lend to the crown themselves in order to meet payments on Henry's debts abroad and preserve England's trading status. Like a ravening wolf, the war consumed money faster than Henry of England and Francis of France could scrape it together. The people of both countries were forced to bear the terrible financial burden that resulted from their rulers' massive egos. Finally, they could hold out no longer.

In June 1546, after two years during which neither side won anything of significance, Henry VIII and Francis I agreed to peace. Though he was forced to return Boulogne to France, Henry wrung from Francis the agreement that France would pay England for it—an amazing two million crowns—which Henry figured (if he could manage to get it in foreign gold) would bolster his ailing treasury. For his part, Thomas Gresham heaved a great sigh of relief. He was more fortunate than most, for his father's shrewd investments and his own success at playing the exchange had kept the Gresham enterprises afloat during the crisis.

Within weeks of signing peace with Francis, Henry lapsed into the half-stupor that signaled his impending end. He knew he must move quickly to protect his only son and successor Edward during the child's minority. He spent whatever hours he could closeted with his wife Katherine and Archbishop Cranmer, the only people he still trusted, though at one point he nearly condemned Katherine herself to the Tower, convinced she was plotting against him.

Together, he and Cranmer carefully drafted a new will. Henry realized that Prince Edward knew little or nothing of the treacherous intrigues that would be quickly and quietly worked against him as soon as his father the king died. At Cranmer's and Queen Katherine's urging, Henry again revamped the Act of Succession. He legally acknowledged his two daughters as successors, designating that first, Prince Edward and his heirs would succeed, then Princess Mary and her heirs, and finally, Princess Elizabeth and her heirs. He named a council of ten to administer a regency for Edward. Then, on 27 January 1547, when Thomas Gresham was twenty-eight years old, King Henry VIII of England gave his last labored gasp, and died.

England had been in Henry VIII's iron grip for thirty-eight long years, and at his hands it had undergone momentous change and enormous upheaval. In the end, the churches and the countryside were in disarray, the treasury was empty, the money for Boulogne was not collected, and all Henry's final schemes had gone awry. This tangled estate would pass to Henry's only live male child out of six marriages—Jane Seymour's Edward, a mere boy of nine.[27]

3

Agent for the Crown

*L*ate in the morning on 19 February 1547, above the green door of the shop below the town house on Lombard Street, the golden grasshopper snapped briskly back and forth in the wind. Inside in her bedroom, with its massive, carved oak four-poster hung with yards of yellow taffeta, Anne Gresham railed at the maids who were helping her dress to attend Edward's coronation procession. It was already near eleven, and they had been at their task for over two hours. Her toilette had been completed, and her long brown hair plaited and dressed.

Now, two maids fussed over the arrangement of her French hood, with its great teardrop pearl in the center, surrounded by smaller ones. They adjusted it carefully, allowing some of her smoothly parted hair to show in front, the dark tresses setting off her fair loveliness. Two other maids worked at fastening the intricate sleeves of Anne's russet overgown and the garters of her pale ivory satin hose. A fifth adjusted the slim woven gold chain, interspersed with jewels, that girded her mistress' waist. Normally, Anne's dress and jewels would have been restricted by the Sumptuary Laws, but because her husband was a landowner of considerable wealth and income, she was, with few exceptions, exempted. The skirt and bodice of her gown were richly embroidered and tucked with bright green thread. Tufts of forest green taffeta were artfully plucked out through slashes in the voluminous upper sleeves. The gown, like her hood, was in the latest fashion, held far out at the sides by a wide farthingale that had been fastened about her waist beneath the skirts. Intricately worked lace ruching from Flanders showed at the square neckline of her fine woolen undergown and peeked from the edges of the sleeves of her blouse. "Haste, now! We shall be late for His Grace's procession! Have a care, fool!" She smacked angrily at a maid who had caught one of her braided tresses in a button of the gown, pulling it loose.

Weary of the tedious process of being dressed, Anne tapped her satin-shod foot in impatience. The king's procession would begin at one, scarcely two hours from now. Fortunately, they had not far to go to their place of honor in the front row near the cross in Cheapside. She leaned forward and stared critically at her face in the polished looking glass. She had the prized milky complexion of the wealthy English, whose skin was never exposed to harsh work or the sun, and the dress she had chosen for this occasion showed her complexion off to great advantage.

Young Richard, already dressed by his governess, was waiting impatiently in the nursery. He had Anne's creamy skin and deep blue eyes, and the sturdy, square-set body of his father. His blond hair was fine and light, so fair that at first glance, without his cap, he appeared bald. His outfit, woven of the finest linen and wool, was fastened with a row of tiny pearl buttons up the front. Pale ivory in color, its long sleeves were padded and tucked at the wide shoulders and delicately embroidered in dark green. He, too, sported a fine lace ruff at his neck and sleeves, and the pleats on the front of his little suit were embroidered in the same dark green as the shoulders. Around his waist was slung a thin leather belt, from which dangled a tiny leather sword in a scabbard—a miniature of his father's, which Thomas had brought his son from his last trading voyage to Antwerp. It was Richard's prized possession, and his governess Marianne could scarcely get it away from him, even to go to sleep.

Thomas, Anne reflected, would probably not even notice how particularly lovely she looked today. Oh, he would take careful note that she was appropriately attired for this occasion, that her dress was expensive and stylish but not too expensive or too stylish, that she sported adequate jewels for her station, and that his son was properly attired and presented, but his attention would be drawn elsewhere, and he'd probably pay her no more than passing notice.

Anne wished her handsome and dashing husband would spend more time in London with his family, but his responsibilities in the trading company and his increased duties for the crown left him little time for his family. He was always going to or coming from Antwerp, it seemed. Even when in London, he was at the Guildhall or the Mercers' Hall or his warehouses, attending to business affairs from early to late. There were meetings with city officials, conferences with his father and uncle, gatherings in Lombard Street to conduct business, dinner with the governor of the Merchant Adventurers. Or else he was closeted with Sir William Cecil, secretary to the protector, or some other high-ranking representative of Edward's court. Thomas Gresham expected his household to run smoothly without his notice, his comforts to be provided for when he arrived home, and few personal demands to be made upon him there. That, after all, was how a good marriage was intended to function.

For her part, Anne enjoyed every material comfort a woman could desire. Her wealthy husband denied her little, except perhaps the affection she longed for, the pleasure of his company, and his personal attention. Their homes were spacious, beautifully and expensively furnished, and staffed with servants who complied with Anne's every command. She had an enviable wardrobe of gowns and jewels, of the sort she had only dreamed about in Suffolk. While the overseeing of her large domestic domain took up much of her time, she still longed for more notice from her husband and often complained bitterly to him about minor household problems, just to command his attention to herself and her world.

She seldom saw her sisters-in-law. Thomas's sister Christiana would soon be wed in a lavish ceremony to Sir John Thynne of Longleat. Thomas liked John, a brilliant and ambitious businessman like himself. However, Anne had little in common with Christiana, and barely knew any of the wives of the other merchant adventurers, for she didn't make friends easily. She was uncomfortable, too, with Thomas's unmarried sister Elizabeth, who lived with Sir Richard and Lady Isabella at Intwood. Elizabeth, who at thirty-three had never married, was far too bookish and worldly for Anne's taste. While routinely surrounded by people and activity in her daily life, Anne Gresham was for the most part a very lonely woman. Much as she had wished it to happen, she had not conceived another child since Richard's difficult birth nearly three years ago.

Richard dashed about the nursery on his chubby little legs, ignoring his governess' admonitions to be still and quiet, lest he dirty his clothes. A cheerful child, he was blessed with the insatiable curiosity and boundless energy of all toddlers. He stopped and preened for his governess, proud of his new green woolen hat with its jaunty yellow feather, which Marianne had just fastened under his chin with a satin ribbon. "Hist, now, I hear someone at the door! 'Tis probably yer grandfather come to see you." The child fairly jumped in excitement. He was anxious for his grandparents to arrive. He understood little of what was going on, but he knew that this day was somehow a special one. He was in new clothes, his grandparents were coming, and a feast was being prepared in the kitchen, its tantalizing smells wafting up to the third floor. Best of all, mama had promised he would go out, wearing his new dark green cloak and hat. That was quite enough to excite him. That a boy not many years older than he would be crowned king of England tomorrow was of no consequence to Richard. He merely wished everyone would hurry, so he could get outdoors. He dashed to the window again and stood on tiptoe, trying vainly to see out, perhaps to catch sight of grandfather and grandmother.

Thomas had left his house on horseback much earlier, accompanied by two grooms. He had agreed to assist the lord mayor and the high sheriff in seeing that all was properly arranged for Edward's state processional through the streets of London on this, the eve of his coronation. It was a cold, blustery day, the pale winter sun only occasionally peeking through its veil of grey clouds. Thomas shivered and drew his thick black woolen cloak, with its dyed collar of curly lamb's wool, closer about him and hoped it wouldn't snow on the procession.

Though outwardly calm, inside he felt the same apprehension others were now feeling. The upheavals attending Henry's death, the recent execution of the duke of Suffolk, and the ascension of the duke of Somerset as protector for the young Edward would surely affect his future, as it would the future of everyone in England, but he had no way of knowing in what way, or to what extent. He had known no other ruler but Henry in his lifetime. He was only vaguely acquainted with the Seymours, the two uncles who were now in firm control of the young prince. Tomorrow, a child of nine would be crowned lord of his future and of the future of England. Thomas shivered again, this time not from the cold.

He knew all too well the precarious financial position Edward had inherited from the free-spending Henry. The kingdom was deep in debt to the bankers of the Low Countries. Henry's funeral and Edward's lavish coronation ceremonies would only run those debts higher. The cost of living in England had continued its rise unabated, and crowds of poor and unemployed clogged the streets of the cities and towns.

Henry had spent more than £2 million on his wars with France and Scotland, and he had been obliged to borrow much of that from foreign merchant bankers, often at onerous interest rates.[1] Sir William Dansell, the crown's agent in Antwerp, was the person responsible for the handling of the king's debts and finances. Occasionally, Thomas's uncle John acted as agent for the king on certain matters in that country. Thomas, too, had accomplished commissions for the crown, but he was still free for the most part to attend to the business of the family. He had his wife's considerable inheritance from Read to manage, as well as the bulk of the Gresham trading interests. Sir Richard, ostensibly in retirement, actually worked long hours every day when he was in London, helping his son direct the family enterprise. The Gresham firm had grown into one of major importance. They had offices and warehouses on both sides of the Channel, commanded numerous merchant vessels, and managed considerable capital and property. Running such an enterprise kept the Gresham men and their trusted factors extremely busy. Lately they had been called upon more and more to assist the crown in its financial difficulties with its creditors.

Foremost among those who lent money to the crowned heads of Europe was the Anton Fugger family of Augsburg, Germany—frequently referred to as the "Medicis of Germany." Without a doubt, the Fuggers (sometimes written "Fokkers") were the wealthiest merchant bankers in the Western world, able to lend over £1.2 million sterling in a single transaction.[2] Thomas was personally acquainted with Anton and Raymond Fugger and had often been their guest at their palatial residence in Antwerp. He had also become close friends with another wealthy merchant banker, Jasper Schetz, at whose magnificent home he often stayed. There were many other wealthy bankers in Antwerp, and in Bruges, some of whom Thomas did not particularly care for, though he was careful to remain on cordial business terms with all.

A port of considerable prominence, Antwerp had grown in recent years into a crowded city—the richest, most bustling hub of commerce on the Continent. It had evolved into a sophisticated international community, with resident ambassadors, representatives, and merchant traders from every country in residence there: English, French, German, Danish, Osterling, Italian, Spanish, Portuguese.

Thomas, under the guidance of his father and uncle, had cut his teeth on commerce in Antwerp during his long apprenticeship. He not only had made valuable contacts in international finance there, but had early developed a wide-ranging view of the conduct of a nation's business. By the time he became a licensed merchant adventurer, he was well versed in how to move with ease in that diverse community.

Though nominally and geographically Flemish, Antwerp was in reality a collective of mini-nations, each preserving its own customs, language, eating habits, dress, and architecture. The inhabitants entertained one another with great frequency at banquets and balls, receptions and pageants. They even occasionally intermarried. Gentlemen and gentlewomen in Antwerp prided themselves on their ability to converse easily in half a dozen or more languages. Latin was the most frequently used, to bridge the gap between the lesser known tongues. Thomas, polished of manner and fluent in Latin, Greek, and French, was welcomed enthusiastically into the eclectic social climate of that vibrant city. He found himself sought after as a guest on his business visits there and in nearby Bruges.[3]

In Antwerp, he spent much of his time at the bourse, the principal gathering place for the practicing merchants of the trade. Thomas paid close and careful attention to how deals were negotiated there. He was quick to notice the effect the rate of exchange of its currency had on all other aspects of a country's economic activity. He also recognized, as most of his countrymen did not, that the value of the nation's currency—its relative rate of exchange—was an especially critical factor in the cost of contracting and repaying debts and bills of exchange.

What Thomas was learning was more critical to England's finances than to his own, for the power of the Greshams was such that Thomas was nearly always able to command the most favorable terms for his own business transactions. His creditworthiness was second to none. The traders, bankers, and moneylenders in Antwerp were always pleased to deal with him. For that reason, he was often able to name his own terms, and he exerted strong influence on prevailing trade practices—not only for his own ships and cargo, but for those of the other English merchant adventurers, too. They looked to Thomas Gresham for leadership in their dealings with foreign buyers and lenders, and they always greeted him cordially and respectfully when they chanced to meet him at the bourse in Antwerp or in Lombard Street in London.

The bourse, located not far from the home of his friend Jasper Schetz, was one of the largest and most imposing buildings in Antwerp, a fitting monument to the growing importance of international trade. Built in the graceful Flemish style, it boasted great

arched, marble-pillared arcades along its spacious interior courtyard, where merchants could stroll in the shade and take the fresh
air while conducting business. Thomas often wished, as had his
father, that there was such a building for the use of the merchants
and bankers in London.

But London today was spending its money on state funerals
and lavish coronations, not buildings for its merchants. Yes, Thomas
reflected sadly, thanks to Henry, his wives, and his wars, the new
king and his advisers would be in for some hard years financially.
He spurred his horse into a trot and made his way back along
Cheapside. He hoped young Edward and his advisers would be
able to avoid war, at least for a while. The country needed some
peaceful time to recover.

Thomas cantered briskly along, quickly covering the distance
between the Tower and Westminster, surveying the route along
which the young king and his entourage would pass this afternoon.[4] The street had been freshly lined with a layer of clean gravel,
and wooden rails had been erected behind the first row of honored spectators to keep the crowds at bay. Thomas kept a sharp
eye out to see that the streets were clear of all debris and that no
beggars or vagabonds were lolling about to disturb the prince's
vista. He glanced up on either side. Banners, cloth-of-gold drapes,
and colorful tapestries hung from windows and balconies, and the
galleries of the buildings along Cheapside were beginning to fill
with fashionably dressed gentry come to watch the grand parade
of their soon-to-be crowned king. Thomas hoped the young king
would survive to reign a long time, and wondered curiously who
his enemies might be.

Henry thought he had wiped out all of Edward's potential enemies by arresting the dukes of Suffolk and Norfolk, and Norfolk's
son, the earl of Surrey, when he learned they were plotting to overthrow him and seize power to return Catholicism to England.
They were condemned to death as traitors. Suffolk and Surrey
were executed just before Henry died. Norfolk, however, survived
because the king was too ill to hold a pen to sign his death warrant. He remained imprisoned in the Tower.

With the powerful duke of Norfolk still alive but rendered impotent, the earl of Hertford, Prince Edward's older Seymour uncle, had moved quickly to alter Henry's will. As Hertford was escorting his grieving nephew Edward to London from Ashridge, where the prince's household had been in residence, his ally Paget had presented to the council the idea of a protectorate for Edward instead of the regency Henry had decreed. The council had agreed, and Hertford was promptly made lord protector for his nephew.[5]

Thomas, his father, and his uncle had all attended the funeral ceremonies, during which King Henry was put to rest beside Queen Jane at Windsor. The very next day, Edward had named his Uncle Hertford duke of Somerset, making him lord treasurer and earl marshal of England. Thomas Seymour, Edward's younger uncle, was named baron of Sudeley and given command of the Royal Navy. Henry's dowager queen, Katherine Parr, was retired with a handsome pension from her stepson. Edward decreed that the thirteen-year-old Princess Elizabeth and her retinue would remain in Katherine Parr's care and reside in her household. The thirty-one-year-old Princess Mary retired with her loyal following of staunch Catholics to her estate in the countryside. Edward had been raised as a Protestant by his father, and was determined that the Catholics would not return to power in England.

Thomas Cranmer remained archbishop of Canterbury and would shortly crown the new king of England. In France, Henry's old rival Francis I had preceded him in death by only a few weeks, and Francis's son, Henri II, succeeded to the French throne. Charles V, the Holy Roman Emperor, was the only one of that once powerful triumvirate still alive. With his defeat of the Protestant Schmalkaldic League, and England and France not in a position to mount a strong opposition, the emperor promptly annexed the Low Countries and placed his sister, the queen of Hungary, as regent over them. Such was the situation Edward faced as he assumed the throne of England.

Thomas, concerned about England's finances, as well as his own, hoped that the new king could somehow be persuaded to suspend the privileges enjoyed by the Hanse merchants, commonly referred to as the "steelyard."[6] These foreign merchants of the Hanseatic League were exempt from many of the restrictions and tariffs placed upon other merchants and enjoyed preferential tariffs over English merchants like the Greshams. The Hanse had been awarded these special privileges back in the twelfth century by Henry II, and they were reconfirmed by Edward IV in the fifteenth century in return for loans the Hanse merchants had made to the crown. Thomas felt it was high time that these special privileges be suspended. The Hanse traded in a variety of commodities, principally herring and woven woolen cloth, woven abroad from raw English wool exported to the Low Countries. Their special tariffs allowed them to reap handsome profits from their trade and afforded them unfair advantage over the English merchants.

The English merchant adventurers had been unable to secure any corresponding privileges from Germany, so there was great hostility between the two groups, which often erupted into violence. It was Thomas's belief that in the absence of reciprocal privileges for English merchants abroad, the advantages enjoyed by the Hanse were detrimental to England's economic well-being.

The political jealousies and rivalries that existed between various merchant factions in England, the uneasy situation with the Hanse merchants, and the fact that he was often required to travel carrying large amounts of cash and valuable jewels on his person made Thomas's life not only highly exciting but very dangerous. He was careful to take excellent security precautions and to keep a low profile. An excellent marksman with a bow and a pistol, he made it a point to remain on good terms with the city officials in both London and Antwerp. To that end, he had offered his services today. Having good political connections always helped. The Gresham ships, warehouses, and holdings were rarely targeted by thieves or vagabonds.

Thomas nudged his horse again and trotted briskly back along the wide street, satisfied that all was in readiness. The conduits that ran along both sides of Cheapside had been flushed and cleaned, and would soon be flowing with wine rather than rainwater. Huge crowds had already begun to gather. Thomas looked about to see if he could spot his parents, or Anne and Richard, but they were not yet at their appointed places. After one more look around, he headed for his own position among the men representing the City—the governor of the Merchant Adventurers, the lord mayor, and the lord high sheriff, with their retinues. He would join Anne and his family later.

Just after one o'clock, Edward appeared in the courtyard of the Tower Palace and mounted his white horse, which was caparisoned in crimson satin and gold damask, sewn lavishly with pearls. The boy king was dressed in a coat of silver trimmed in ermine, and his white velvet cap was so thickly set with diamonds and pearls that it flashed and glistened like a halo about his small blond head. When he emerged from the Tower gate, the crowds, long accustomed to the enormous bulk and imposing presence of Henry, gasped at the sight of this small, dazzling figure perched atop his horse. After a moment of stunned silence, a roar of love and approval rose on all sides. The procession finally began. In front of the king rode his mounted horse guards, hundreds of gaily costumed courtiers, somber-faced clergy, dignified statesmen, and foreign ambassadors. Behind him rode a throng of nobles, regiments of men-at-arms, halberdiers, gentleman ushers, and grooms of the privy chamber.[7]

Cannons boomed, bells pealed, and flowers rained down upon Edward's protective gilded canopy and were tossed in tribute from the audience gathered along Cheapside to watch him pass. Little Richard Gresham danced up and down and squealed aloud with excitement. "Look, look, wave to the king," prodded his mother, lifting him up to give a wave as Edward passed in front of them, almost near enough for them to reach out and touch. Catching sight of the small boy in green waving frantically at him, Edward smiled and raised a hand to return the child's salute. Anne swept the monarch a low curtsey. "Edward! Edward! Long live King Edward! God save the King!" A mighty roar rose from all sides, drowning out the music and the recitals. Edward's small figure seemed even more fragile and vulnerable next to the heavily armored knights astride their huge war horses, who rode alongside, holding aloft the king's canopy. Protector Somerset, resplendent in fur-trimmed deep blue, rode to Edward's left, slightly ahead of him.

At the cross in Cheapside, the procession halted, and Thomas Gresham and his companions bowed low before the king as the mayor stepped forward, fell to his knees, and presented to Edward a purse containing a thousand gold crowns—a tribute from the City of London. It was a purse to which the Greshams had contributed handsomely. Bending down to accept it, Edward sweetly thanked the lord mayor. The purse was so large and heavy that the child king could barely manage to bring himself back upright in his saddle. He turned to his uncle, bewildered. "Why do they give me this?"

"It is the custom of the City, Your Grace, to pay the King's Majesty tribute." The great purse, bulging with coins and much too heavy for Edward to hold, was handed over to the captain of the guard to carry.[8]

After the procession, the exhausted young king slept, tucked up in the same bedchamber in which his father had so recently breathed his last, while the City celebrated far into the night its freedom from Henry, and the promise of a new ruler. The next morning, Edward VI of England was crowned with three crowns: first the gilt circlet of St. Edward; then the enormous crown imperial of the realm, which—too sacred to be altered and too heavy for the child's head to bear—was only held briefly above his head; and finally, a smaller reproduction of the crown imperial, which had hastily been made to fit, was placed upon his head.

At the great banquet in the Tower following the coronation, after all had dined, Lord Dymoke, in full battle armor, galloped his great charger, its hooves clattering loudly against the stone floor, right up to the king on the dais. Holding his sword high, he formally saluted his newly crowned liege lord. Then, turning to face the great banquet hall where amidst the assembled nobles, knights, ambassadors, and officials of every sort, Thomas Gresham sat with his family, Dymoke ceremoniously shouted out the customary challenge: "If there be any manner of man, of whatsoever estate, condition, or degree, that will say and maintain that our Sovereign Lord Edward VI, this day here present, is not the rightful and undoubtful heir to the imperial crown of this realm of England, and that of right he ought not to be crowned king, I say he lies like a false traitor, and that I am ready the same to maintain with him while breath is in my body, either now or at this time, or any other time, whensoever it shall please the King's Highness to appoint. And here upon the same, I cast him my gage!" With that, Dymoke drew off his gauntlet and dramatically flung it to the floor. Then he stared fiercely out over the silent crowd and waited.

Thomas felt a thrill of excitement run through him, and others leaned forward in breathless anticipation. The hall remained silent. No one came forward to pick up the glove. Thus, by ancient tradition, Edward was king of England unchallenged. The assembly stood as one and saluted him. "Edward! Long live King Edward!" The shout rose from a thousand assembled throats, and the garter king of arms stepped forward. The room quieted again. He proclaimed Edward's titles and estate to the hall three times: in Latin, French and English.[9] Edward VI was officially their king.

Shortly after Edward's coronation, Sir Richard and Lady Isabella hosted the lavish wedding of their daughter to Sir John Thynne, scion of Longleat, and yet more honors were bestowed upon the Greshams. Sir John Gresham, Thomas's uncle, who carried the green grasshopper rather than the gold on his seal and sign, was invested in his turn as lord mayor of London. His stately inaugural procession sailed in decorated barges down the Thames to Westminster, returning by land along the traditional route of Cheapside, where the throngs of the City gathered to cheer him.

A few months later, in September 1547, Thomas's older brother John was knighted by Protector Somerset on the field of battle at Musselburgh. There were now two Sir John Greshams in the family. Thomas hoped that one day soon he, too, would serve the crown well enough to achieve the coveted distinction of knighthood.

King Edward continued his studies with his tutor Mr. Cheke,

who confirmed his strong Protestant religious beliefs, and bade the prince concern himself deeply with the religious welfare of his subjects. Meanwhile, his uncles Somerset and Seymour made their private alliances and hatched their separate schemes to gain more political power. Thomas was once again sailing back and forth to Antwerp on trading missions. He heard many rumors, but rarely indulged in discussion of matters at the English court. Through his friendship with William Cecil, Protector Somerset's able young secretary, Thomas became privy to the details of intrigues being worked at Edward's court, but as always, he kept his own counsel. One of the most fascinating tales Cecil told him involved Thomas Seymour, King Edward's younger uncle, brother of the protector.

The dashing bachelor Seymour had already engendered a great deal of court gossip. He had lost Katherine Parr to King Henry, and thereafter had remained a bachelor. He had been in search of an advantageous marriage, it was rumored, to gain the upper hand over his older brother Somerset in the matter of controlling the young king. Thomas had paid suit first to the Princess Mary and was coldly rebuffed by her. Then he had turned his attentions to the young Princess Elizabeth, but was soon hounded off by her protectors, too. By the terms of Henry's will, neither princess could marry without the council's approval and permission. The dissolute Admiral Seymour did not have the backers to achieve his ends with either of Henry's daughters. Realizing that perhaps he had reached too high, Seymour had turned his attention back to the widowed Katherine Parr. To her detriment, the dowager queen Katherine still loved the rogue. King Edward had great affection for his stepmother, who was the only mother he had ever known, and he truly liked his engaging younger uncle. With his stepmother's happiness in mind, Edward had given her permission to marry Thomas Seymour, though by doing so he had earned the deep anger of Protector Seymour.

Lord Admiral Seymour had no sooner married Henry's widow and settled into her household than he began paying unseemly attentions to the teenaged Princess Elizabeth. At first he withdrew discreetly when she rebuffed his advances. Katherine Parr became pregnant, and as her pregnancy advanced, Seymour returned to his earlier objective, and increased his flirtations with the princess. Elizabeth, in the first flush of womanhood, began responding with confused blushes and giggling excitement to Seymour's compliments, coy teasing, and increasingly bold touches.

John Ashley, husband of the princess' tutor, became alarmed and cautioned his wife, who was in charge of Elizabeth's household, to "take heed, for I fear the Lady Elizabeth bears affection for milord admiral." Lady Ashley pooh-poohed her husband, but Elizabeth became visibly excited and appeared love-struck whenever in the company of Seymour, who continued to dally with her at every opportunity.

One night, Seymour was discovered in Elizabeth's room, with the half-dressed princess in his arms.

Thomas was shocked when he heard that. The protector's brother, caught dallying with the princess? 'Twas true, Cecil assured him.

An enormous scandal ensued. Elizabeth was banished in disgrace, and Mrs. Ashley was sent to the Tower prison for not guarding the welfare of her young charge.[10] Seymour pleaded innocent, throwing the blame on Elizabeth and her governess. Edward's concern for his stepmother and her advanced pregnancy was all that saved Admiral Seymour. Then, Katherine Parr and her baby died in childbirth, and the court was once again thrown into mourning. King Edward was despondent over his loss.

The year 1549 found Thomas Seymour trying to work his way back into favor and power with his nephew the king. He lit upon the idea of arranging a marriage for Edward with his cousin Lady Jane Grey, and to that end Seymour made so bold as secretly to propose the match to her parents. "If you'll give me wardship of the girl, I'll see to the match," he promised them. Her ambitious parents were thrilled, and sold Seymour wardship of their daughter for £2000.

Not long after that, late one night Thomas Seymour slipped alone along the passage to the king's apartments in the Tower. His intent, he claimed, was to seek the king out in his chamber without the protector's knowledge, so that he could talk privately with the king about the idea of a marriage with Lady Jane. He didn't know that King Edward had already retired for the night, and that his little dog, which normally slept in the king's chamber, was bedded down that night just outside the doors to his chamber.

As Seymour slipped stealthily along the corridor, and approached the king's rooms, the dog woke and began barking furiously at him.

"Halt! Who goes there!" came the shout from the guards, and suddenly Seymour heard running feet coming toward him from all directions. Shaken and confused, he pulled out his pistol and shot the yapping little animal dead. But by then the guards were upon him. "Treason!" they shouted. "He tried to kill the king! Only the dog saved him." Edward, by then awakened by the uproar, was aghast at the scene, but most of all at the loss of his pet. Seymour was hustled to the Tower prison, where he was formally accused of plotting an attempt on the king's life. He adamantly protested his innocence. His brother the protector did not move on his behalf.

King Edward might have saved Seymour but he was furious at his uncle over all the grief he had caused of late. Not only was there the incident with Princess Elizabeth and the death of his stepmother, but the killing of his beloved pet incensed him to the point that he did not lift a finger on his uncle's behalf. The Lord High Admiral Seymour was tried, convicted of treason, and quickly beheaded.

When word of his execution was brought to Princess Elizabeth in exile at Hatfield, she went deadly white, but said nothing except "on this day died a man of much wit and little judgment."[11]

At about that time Edward's other uncle, Somerset, who had become more and more domineering and dictatorial in his actions as protector, began to fall from grace. Cecil confided to Thomas that he was contemplating moving over into the service of the earl of Warwick, Somerset's arch rival, whose loyalty to the king was unassailable, and whose hard-working public service had long been noted. Soon, Warwick sprang eagerly into the power vacuum left by the Seymours.

It was on a frigid night in February, as Thomas sat warming himself by the fire, that he received an urgent summons to Bethnal Green, for his father had fallen gravely ill. Galloping on horseback from Lombard Street, he arrived barely in time to clasp his father's hand before he expired. Sir Richard's death was a severe blow to Thomas, not only personally—because he had enjoyed a rare closeness with his father—but also professionally, for now the immense responsibility of the gigantic Gresham trading enterprise and family holdings had fallen squarely upon his young shoulders. John, away fighting the Scots, showed little interest in the business. Sir Richard had wisely left the management of the family enterprises to his son Thomas.[12]

Sir Richard left his widow Isabella extremely wealthy, with vast lands and incomes, and provided well for his daughter Elizabeth, who had never married. He also provided well for his older son John and his family. But it was Thomas he designated to prove his will and dispose of his affairs. He left Intwood Hall and other properties to John, and a number of his other estates to Thomas. "I'd like to buy Intwood from you, if you ever decide to part with it," said Thomas, when his brother came home to help him settle their father's estate. "It is my favorite of all father's properties."

"Well, make me an offer for what it's worth, and it's yours," said John affably. Thomas loved the ancestral family estate as much as his father had, but to men like John, a born vagabond, sailor and soldier of fortune, cash was far preferable to land.

Sir Richard Gresham's funeral was an event of great importance in London. Thomas saw to it that the procession to the Guildhall, to the Church of St. Lawrence Jewry, was replete with all the dignity and pageantry the elder Gresham had so loved. As a knight of the realm and former lord mayor, his funeral was attended by those of prominence in Edward's court and in London's government, like Warwick, Cecil, and the lord mayor.

As the solemn procession moved slowly along Cheapside, then down Milk Street past the house where Thomas was born, which was still marked by the sign of the grasshopper, crowds of Londoners lined the streets in respectful silence. Among them were hundreds of Gresham employees and retainers; those who had known Sir Richard Gresham, even if only slightly, and hundreds of the merely curious. At the end of Milk Street, the procession turned and proceeded into the Guildhall Yard. There, in the Church of St. Lawrence Jewry, a moving funeral service was conducted by the bishop. Then with great pomp and formality, Sir Richard was laid to rest in the east wall, next to Thomas's mother Audrey, who had been buried there following her untimely death in 1522.

John Caius was among the mourners. Now a fellow and lecturer at the Royal College of Physicians, he was respected throughout the City for his learned discourse on medicine. At the great reception Thomas hosted in the Guildhall following his father's funeral, he introduced Caius to William Cecil, now the official secretary to the earl of Warwick. Warwick, in attendance as King Edward's representative, extended his condolences to Thomas and to Thomas's brother-in-law Sir John Thynne, designated one of Sir Richard's chief mourners. "I knew your father well," he said to Thomas, "and admired him greatly. I see much of him in you, his son." Thomas was pleased and flattered. The earl of Warwick would be a powerful political ally for Thomas. He vowed to cultivate the earl in the future.

Warwick gained power and respect at court. Bit by bit, under his guidance, King Edward began to make his own decisions. Staunch in his strongly Protestant beliefs, and urged on by the Protestant Warwick, the king outlawed all Catholic ceremony in England. That created the thorny dilemma of Princess Mary's religious observances. How could Edward allow her to continue to hear daily mass, while the rest of his subjects were forbidden by law to do so? Edward held his sister in affection, and she was his successor. He dared not make an overt move against her that might bring the wrath of Charles V, her powerful Catholic relative and staunch defender, down upon his head. England's economic lifeline was tied to the Low Countries, which the emperor now ruled.

Edward was determined to win Mary over to the new faith.

To this end, he attempted to enlist the aid of his other half-sister, Princess Elizabeth. "Our sister is heiress presumptive until I marry and have heirs. 'Tis unthinkable for the country that she continue with her Catholicism. You must help us convince her otherwise." Elizabeth, as a Protestant, listened sympathetically to Edward, but her own position was already precarious enough. She shrewdly avoided any direct involvement over the subject of her sister Mary's religious stand.

As soon as Edward had issued his decree against the practice of Catholicism, the Catholics in Norfolk rebelled. Edward was forced to send troops, headed by Warwick, to quell them. Thomas Gresham was staying at Intwood Hall at the time, and he invited the earl and his retinue, which included his secretary William Cecil, to stay there as his guests. Warwick and Cecil were pleased to accept Gresham's hospitality for a brief stay.[13] The bond between Thomas and Cecil was strengthened even more during that visit. Cecil had much in common with the intelligent young merchant prince Gresham. As they rode away at the head of their victorious troop, Warwick commented favorably on how they had been received and entertained by young Gresham. "Yea, and that one has a canny mind for finance, and can do us much good service in the future, your Grace," Cecil was quick to point out.

In Flanders, the great debts Henry had accumulated were coming due, and the English treasury had not the wherewithal to pay. In May of that year, the council wrote sharply to Sir William Dansell, the king's royal agent in Antwerp. His administration of the king's finances was lacking, they claimed, and he was derelict in his duty. There was the issue of £40,000 annual interest on the late King Henry's bonds.[14] The council was furious at what it faced, suspecting Dansell had made some deals to his own advantage and had siphoned off the crown's money to unexplained uses. The council demanded he reply at once, "for we cannot conjecture how to excuse you, but you have done His Highness marvelous evil service." Dansell wrote a long reply defending himself, claiming that for the transactions of which the council complained, he was in no way to blame. Dansell's protestations were ignored, and the council insisted he give it a full and immediate accounting. It received no response.[15]

Meanwhile, Edward continued to struggle with Princess Mary's religious recalcitrance. She flaunted her continued practice of Catholicism until she was finally summoned before the council and formally rebuked by it. When the Emperor Charles V got wind of that, he dispatched an ambassador to Edward and his council to deliver a strong ultimatum: If the Princess Mary were forbidden by her brother to hear mass, Charles would declare war on England. Edward wrote in his journal, "The emperor's ambassador came with a short message from his master of war, if I would not suffer his cousin the princess to use her mass. To this no answer was given at this time."[16] A far different gauntlet had been flung down before Edward and his court, but neither Edward, nor anyone in England, bent to pick it up. They simply could not, at this time, afford another war.

As winter gave way to spring in 1550, events remained at a standoff between King Edward and Princess Mary. Edward suffered greatly over Mary's resistance to him. His entreaties, then his commands, were to no avail. Finally, a compromise was reached. Publicly, the king and council saved face by announcing that the princess was bound, as were all his subjects, by the king's commands. Privately, the ambassadors assured Charles, Mary would continue to hear daily mass.

The earl of Warwick was ever with the king "like a father to His Majesty" some said.[17] Cecil's influence and power at court rose along with his new master's. The close-mouthed Thomas Gresham became the only confidant Cecil felt he could trust. The king might have temporarily allayed his religious problems, but the financial ones facing England were monstrous and menacing.

In April of 1551, exasperated at his failure to resolve their financial crisis with the Antwerp lenders, the king's ministers formally recalled Dansell, revoking his office of agent "by reason of his slackness." They ordered him to return to London immediately to give an account of himself and his financial transactions. Dansell delayed his return for almost a year. In truth, he was lit-

tle to blame, for Henry had debased the currency and missed making payments to such an extent that his agents were obliged to
borrow on unfavorable terms. Dansell, in his reply to the first letter of 1549, had written, "I take God to witness that if I had 40,000
lives, and could have spent them all, I could not have done more
in this matter than I did."[18]

With the firing of Dansell, the king and his council were without a royal agent in the Low Countries. Beset by the financial tangle facing them, they decided to call in several merchants and
consult with them on how to resolve their dilemma. Thomas
received the summons as he sat at dinner with his family. The servants were agog. It was not often that a royal messenger in full livery appeared at their door. "What does it mean?" Anne asked her
husband anxiously.

"I do not know. I have been asked, or rather commanded, to
appear before His Majesty and the council tomorrow at one of the
clock." Rising, he called for his horse to be saddled, and, pulling
on his cloak, trotted off to consult with his uncle John about this
most unexpected command.

The next day, Thomas Gresham bowed low before King
Edward, Warwick, Somerset, and the Council of Lords. "We have
asked you to attend upon us here, Mr. Gresham," began the lord
high treasurer, "as we have the several of other merchants come
afore you this day, to give us your best opinion on a weighty matter concerning His Majesty's financial affairs in Antwerp, of which
you have some knowledge." Thomas, kneeling before the lords,
head bowed, said nothing, waiting for the treasurer to continue.
Somerset then detailed the king's monetary problems, particularly
the crushing interest owed on Henry's debts, of which Thomas
was already aware. "Now therefore, we wish you to take the room
in hand and advise us, to your best knowledge, in what way, and
with the least cost, His Majesty may discharge his debts to the
bankers in the Low Countries. You may rise."

Word of Dansell's dismissal had come to him, of course, and
although the Greshams had in many ways acted in the capacity of
financial agents to the crown on various matters during the past

twenty years, none of them had ever held the official title of royal agent. Thomas was aware of Dansell's attempt to throw the blame for the loans contracted at high interest onto him, among others. He knew he had to tread carefully, but this was also a big opportunity for young Thomas Gresham, and he was quick to see it and anxious to seize it. For the lords to call upon him to render an opinion before council on such a matter was not only highly unusual; it was a formidable honor. It meant he had the respect and confidence of the privy council and the king, and enjoyed a reputation as one of the most knowledgeable merchants in the kingdom.

Thomas tried not to let any of this cloud his mind as he rose and carefully considered his reply. He knew that his credibility with the king, along with his possible appointment as royal agent, hung in the balance. However, as one who always spoke his mind, he knew that some bold moves would be required to solve the king's financial dilemma, and risk might not sit well with the lords. He had been well schooled by his father and uncle; his court manners were impeccable. He knew how to bow gracefully before his betters, but when Thomas Gresham spoke out on matters of business and finance, it was with authority and knowledge, and he bowed to none on that.

Thomas cleared his throat, took a deep breath, and respectfully addressed the king and council: "Milords, I would make bold to allow there is much that can be done to relieve His Majesty's affairs, and it would please my heart and bring honor my poor name to offer my humble services. I am indeed honored to be asked to do what I might in service to my liege lord, to try to advise how to bring His Grace out of these his debts, at the least cost to England. I would propose milords several ways in which to do that." The lords were listening intently. Their interest had perked at the words "out of these debts." "Continue, Mr. Gresham," encouraged Warwick.

Thomas was sure then that it was Warwick who had put his name forward to be included, mayhap at Cecil's prompting. He therefore addressed his next remarks toward where the earl and his secretary were sitting. "I would most humbly suggest that His Most Gracious Majesty might approach the problem on several fronts, having to do with cautious management of the rate of exchange to His Majesty's best advantage. I would also beseech and humbly beg that His Grace consider a recoinage, which could serve to bring the value of our coin and currency upward against foreign coin. The debased coinage serves us ill in our dealings abroad. These are some ways that would serve His Grace marvelous well in reducing the amount of interest paid out to the lenders, so that they be sooner paid and render His Grace free of care in these troubling matters."

The assembled lords, who understood little or nothing of the intricacies of foreign exchange, were by this time muttering to one another in boredom. But Warwick, Cecil, and the king were listening closely to Gresham, and Cecil was carefully taking notes. Gresham concluded, "I would, with all my humble endeavor and God's guidance, seek with utmost diligence, should His Grace and Your Lordships desire to avail of my poor services, to endeavor to bring His Grace the king fully free of debt in the space of but two or three years, if he shall acquire no wars, nor suffer any great debt to increase in that time." The audacity of Gresham's bold declaration brought a gasp of surprise from some, and louder murmurs ran through the assembled Council.

Thomas fell silent and awaited their pleasure. Seeing he had finished, Warwick thanked him graciously, and Thomas slowly and gracefully bowed himself out. Only when the great double doors of the chamber had closed did he allow himself a small sigh of relief, and not until he was away did he wipe the nervous perspiration from his brow. But though he was aware of the high debts the king had inherited and the insupportable interest payments with which Edward was saddled, Thomas was not aware of the deep revulsion the council felt toward the custom the lenders had used with Henry and others—that is, forcing them to buy a large and valuable jewel, or other overpriced commodities, as a precondition of initiating, renewing or carrying over a loan. Dansell's predecessor Vaughan had recorded, during Henry's reign, a loan of 600,000 ducats, which, he wrote, was promised the king if "the King's Majesty will please take a jewel with it, priced at 100,000 ducats, which it is certainly worth. It is a great point diamond, set about with many other point diamonds, like a rose [the Tudor symbol]."

This condition imposed by the moneylenders was one of long-standing, and it had grown almost into a custom.[19] However, Edward's ministers, facing an impoverished country, unable even to meet the required annual budget, balked at the idea. They considered it tantamount to extortion by the bankers and had resolved among themselves to refuse any attempt by the crown's creditors to continue it. In truth, most of them still viewed the lending—"renting" they called it—of money as sinful and the charging of any interest as usury.

For the next several months the king and council were engaged with other pressing matters, and Thomas heard nothing more on the king's finances, or the position of royal agent. Everyone had disappeared from London. The sweating sickness had struck again, forcing the king and his nobles to scurry off to their various country estates. Visiting Caius at his new abode in the close of St. Bartholomew's Hospital, Thomas was advised by him to "quit the City as quickly as possible, and your family with you, until this danger has passed."

Thomas took Anne, Richard and the servants to Norfolk, to Intwood Hall. He wandered through its many spacious rooms, his mind filled with thoughts of his father, for Intwood had been Sir Richard's favorite residence. Anne, unhappy with the furnishings and the somewhat run-down condition of the stately old mansion, complained ceaselessly. She hated being isolated in the country-side, and she hated Intwood. One afternoon, to escape her harangues, Thomas retreated to the back garden and sat there qui-etly, staring up at the carved stone escutcheon atop the archway at its entrance. His father's initials, "R.G.," encircled a grasshop-per, below which was represented the senior Gresham's coat of arms. His father's mark was also carved rather fancifully over the doorway leading to the kitchen. Yes, Thomas reflected, his father had served his country well, and had left his mark not only on Intwood Hall, but upon England, too.

Drowsing there in the midday sun, Thomas let his mind drift. He thought about his own son, about life and mortality. He was in his thirty-third year, strong and healthy of physique, thanks be. Though not particularly religious, he leaned more to the Protestant thinking of the new king than to the Catholic faith in which he had been raised in childhood. He could count himself a fortunate man. He had a good wife and a six-year-old son to follow in his footsteps. He had hoped for more children, but Anne had not conceived another since Richard. He was wealthy and successful in business and property in his own right, and he had acquired even more wealth and property by his marriage and in the inheritance he received from his father. He routinely bore responsibilities that would overwhelm most thirty-three-year-old men. Still, he couldn't help but wonder if, in the lifetime left to him, he would ever succeed in accomplishing anything worthy enough to leave his mark upon his beloved England.

When the danger of the sickness seemed past, Thomas gathered up his family and returned to London. Thousands in the teeming city, they learned, had perished during their absence. Edward and his court had returned, too, and Thomas learned from Cecil that the earl of Warwick would be elevated to duke of Northumberland by Edward on 11 October. In that same investiture ceremony, the king intended to bestow knighthood upon William Cecil and make the earl of Dorset—Warwick's friend and father of the king's cousin Lady Jane Grey—the new duke of Suffolk. Warwick's faction was reaping the king's reward. Somerset realized he had been eclipsed, and his days of influence were ended. Since Thomas Seymour's death, no one had dared advance the idea of a marriage between the king and the young and lovely Lady Jane Grey, and none except Cranmer knew that Henry's secret plan had been to marry Edward to Mary, queen of Scots. With such an eligible prince to dangle as a marriage prospect, Warwick had his own thoughts—perhaps a marriage alliance with France, to cement relations there once and for all. The religious issue, though, would be a formidable problem with any of the Catholic nations.

Thomas was invited by Cecil to attend the investiture ceremony, and he was pleased and proud to witness that great moment when knighthood was bestowed upon his friend William Cecil. He wondered once again if that day would ever come for him.

In December, Thomas was called into service to Edward VI as the new royal agent in Antwerp. He was jubilant. "You must pack quickly and make ready," he informed Anne, "for we remove to Antwerp in January. You need not worry about a house—we will abide with my friend Jasper Schetz at his home." Anne was apprehensive, but excited. She had never been out of England, and the prospect of moving to a foreign land was a daunting one. There was so much to do! Hastily she called the servants together and began issuing orders.

Jasper Schetz, the wealthy merchant banker of Antwerp, was delighted to hear that his English friend Thomas Gresham was coming to Antwerp to live. Stout and imposing of figure, with a bushy beard and well-fed waist, Schetz was no ordinary middle-class merchant banker. He held numerous lordships, was official factor for Emperor Charles V, and was also the treasurer general of the Low Countries. Nor was the Schetz home a humble abode into which Thomas Gresham would move his family. It was more a palace than a mansion. When he received the news of Gresham's impending arrival with his family, Jasper Schetz promptly set aside an apartment of twelve rooms for Thomas and Anne Gresham's use. Thomas counted the whole Schetz family—three brothers in all—as his closest friends in Antwerp. He knew that Anne and Richard would be safe and well cared for by them and would not be alone during his absences, which was important, for he would be required to leave them often—to travel back to England in the performance of his duties.

While Anne tended to packing and closing the house on Lombard Street, Thomas quickly put his extensive business affairs in London in order. He appointed John Eliot, his cousin's husband, as his London factor—Eliot would be his agent, to oversee business affairs in London and to administer his numerous properties in England—and Thomas put at his command an adequate and trusted staff. By early January, Thomas felt he had things well enough settled that he could safely take his leave of England.

At Dover, he and Anne and Richard boarded his ship the *Anne of London*, whose holds were heavily loaded with trading goods. There was barely room enough left for the few belongings Anne felt she must have with her. On a bleak and frigid January day, with a fierce north wind kicking up the waves, they cast off from Dover and set sail for Antwerp. Anne, her face hidden by the deep hood of her fur-trimmed cloak, hung on at the rail and wept bitter tears of fright and loss as the shores of her homeland receded from view.

Young Richard stood the crossing well, asking endless questions of his amused and indulgent father, tugging him by the hand as they explored the ship together. But Anne remained in her tiny cabin, dreadfully seasick, for most of the two turbulent days of the journey. Wan and miserable, she barely managed the amenities of greeting when at last they arrived at the home of Jasper Schetz. She excused herself and withdrew immediately to her rooms, where she remained closeted for the next several days. Jasper's wife sent trays of exotic fruits and steaming herb tisanes to cheer her guest, but Anne was not a happy settler in this new land and did not respond favorably to her hostess's ministrations in her behalf.

Thomas threw himself into his work as royal agent with zest and enthusiasm. He would show his benefactors Northumberland and Cecil that their faith in him was not misplaced.[20] There were immediate problems to solve, and trade deals to negotiate with Schetz and the Fuggers. But busy as he was in those first weeks, he didn't lose sight of his long-range goal, which was to get England, and King Edward, out from under the yoke of foreign debt as quickly as he could. To accomplish that, he was not afraid to make bold moves where necessary.

Antwerp was his turf as much as London had been. He listened carefully, watched, and spent long evening hours deep in thought, devising plans and strategies. Every day he went to the bourse to oversee the conduct of his own extensive business affairs, which he now placed in the hands of his capable Antwerp factor, Richard Clough. When at the bourse, Thomas kept a close watch on the rate of exchange.

As he plunged into his new duties, working from early to late with never a day off, it did not occur to Thomas that he was neglecting his family, or that his wife might be frightened, unhappy, or lonely in a foreign land, where she understood little, was housed among strangers, and spoke no language save English. In fact, his family rarely entered his thoughts. He was too preoccupied with the monumental task that faced him.

4

"You Have Served a King"

Thomas, locked in his library, studied the council's letter again by the light of his guttering candle. It was close to midnight. Anne and young Richard had long been asleep, Anne in her room, which adjoined his own bedroom across the wide hall from the library, and Richard and his governess in rooms just down the corridor from Anne's spacious sitting room. He paused for a moment, thinking of his wife. Though their apartments were exceedingly fine and comfortable, Anne was not happy in Antwerp. She resented living under another's roof. She wanted her own home, and had nagged Thomas almost from the first week to find a house for them in Antwerp. "I cannot even speak to these people—they barely understand our tongue, and I certainly can't comprehend theirs."

"I have not the time in this moment to search out a house," he had told her the week before, "but soon I shall look unto it." He knew that by now his wife's patience was wearing thin, but for the moment, it was all he could handle, and more, to orient himself to his new position and its requirements, which were considerable. With a small sigh of frustration, he turned his attention back to the instructions in the letter from the king's council.

"Marry, for your first proceedings, this we would should be done.... Take the £10,000 at 7 percent for six months, and with part of it, pay what must be paid the last of this month—pay the

Schetz brothers £3,000. You should have about £5,000 left toward other interest, except Hoby needs some money for munitions purchases, so you may have to give him some funds, but keep at least £5,000 for payments coming due later."

Thomas noted ruefully that Hoby's portion was not included in any of the totals, which meant he would probably have to advance Sir Philip some funds himself, for giving the king's ordnance master a "loan" to purchase necessities would only incur another obligation that would be difficult to meet. The letter continued: "Having made these payments we want you to make a speedy repair home to England, so that we can confer with you in confidence. We must discuss the matter of the bell metal. For the which, seeing the Schetz's have desired a month's day to give answer, we doubt not but if you will hasten to return, and then the king may wish you to also go to France on your return journey, but you must be back in Flanders in time for the answer from Schetz."

Contemplating that, Thomas groaned aloud. England, France and back in a month. It would be almost impossible to cover such distance in so little time! But Thomas knew he had no choice. This was not a suggestion, it was an order. Serving the king's majesty at a salary of only twenty shillings a day, he realized, would leave him little time for other matters, and it would certainly not enrich him.[1] He'd be fortunate if he could contrive to be reimbursed by the crown for out-of-pocket expenses incurred on its behalf. It was fortunate his own business interests, his wife's dower properties, and the income from the lands he himself had inherited provided him with the funds for the kind of financial outlay that would be required in order to accomplish His Majesty's wishes. His personal fortune, he reflected wryly, was probably one of the main reasons he had been chosen as royal agent.

The letter concluded, "And thus deferring answer of the rest until your return, we wish you good success in the service of the King's Majesty. From Westminster, 24 February 1551. If convenient, please make Mr. Hoby privy to this letter." Signed, "Your Loving Friends, Northumberland; J. Bedford; E. Clinton; T. Darcye; W. Cecill."[2]

Having reread the long missive for the third time, Thomas at last threw it down and got up from his desk, stretching. Deep in thought, he walked the length of the huge room, carrying his candle, occasionally stopping to hold it close enough to study the portraits of the Schetz ancestors ranged along one wall. He thought carefully. He knew he had little time left to make the arrangements regarding the most urgent matters, and yet prepare for his journey back to London, then to France. He did not know then that this was only the first of many such round trips he would make that year. He wasn't pleased at the suggestions the privy council had made, either. He had somehow to convince the council and the lord high treasurer to pay the Fuggers some substantial amount, and soon, if the king were to retain credit with them for future needs. Finally he snuffed the candles and found his bed.

Ignoring Anne's grumbling that he could not possibly be making a trip back to England already and leaving her and Richard "alone among all these strangers," Thomas set out for England as quickly as he could make the arrangements. During March of that year, the Fuggers received two substantial payments, sent by Thomas for King Edward's debts: one to pay a £64,000 loan in full, and, that done, Thomas was able to convince the council to scrape together enough to pay off the debt of £14,000 in full on 30 April, instead of making the partial payment of only £5000 they had proposed.[3]

Then he returned again to Flanders, by way of France. He had been instructed by His Majesty and Northumberland to meet with Barnaby Fitzpatrick, Edward's childhood friend, whom the king had sent to the French court, to remit him some needed funds and give him some special instructions His Majesty would trust to no other agent except Thomas Gresham. Northumberland and King Edward wanted a private assessment by Fitzpatrick on the daughter of Henri II, and his thoughts on a possible alliance between France and England through a marriage of Edward with Princess Elisabeth of France. This they wanted done secretly, before making approaches through official channels.

It was on that trip that Thomas realized the benefit of travel-

ing to London personally to present his case and conduct his negotiations with Northumberland, the king, and the council. His ability to parry their questions and argue his case then and there
brought far better results than any letter would have done. It also
impressed upon the nobles of the council that Thomas Gresham
took his new responsibilities seriously, raising him higher in the
esteem of the king and Northumberland. In private, Cecil was
able to regale him with the latest court intrigues and impart the
best gossip, of a nature so sensitive, it could not be put in writing.
Thomas resolved that, even though it would take a heavy toll upon
his energies and his time, he'd conduct his business with the crown
in person as often as humanly possible, and do as little as he could
by post or agents.

Home in Antwerp once again, Thomas reflected with pleasure on the way his transactions at court and in France had proceeded. His visit to England had also afforded him the opportunity
to visit John Caius, and to confer with his factor John Eliot about
the progress of businesses and the needs of his properties.

Barnaby Fitzpatrick had been delighted to meet him in Paris
and he had wined and dined Thomas, showed him about the capital city of France and its environs, and introduced him to some
highly placed and influential courtiers. Thomas had enjoyed the
charm and sophistication of Paris, and had taken time to see the
beautiful castles Henri and his father had constructed on the banks
of the river Loire, at some distance from the city. He had returned
to Antwerp by way of Bruges, arriving home in fine fettle.

The payments he had negotiated had restored King Edward's
credit with the Fuggers, a substantial accomplishment for Thomas
so soon after his appointment to the office of royal agent. He knew
that his own credibility as royal agent hinged upon his ability to
negotiate credit—as well as payment delays—for the king when
most critically needed, yet maintain good terms with bankers like
the Fuggers. He also knew that news of the payments would circulate quickly in Antwerp and would bring him, and England, new
respect in the financial community.

In May, the council wrote that it was only paying the Fuggers

£5000 on the £45,000 still outstanding, instructing Thomas he must be patient with the council and get the Fuggers to "put over the rest according to the old interest, 14 percent." To this the Fuggers had no objection, since they had just been paid such large sums from King Edward.

The duke of Northumberland's influence on the king had become profound. He seemed to have found just the right combination of attitudes and behavior to retain Edward's attention and esteem, and without appearing to be as powerful as he was, Northumberland gradually became the virtual dictator of government policy in England. That Thomas had Northumberland and Cecil solidly in his corner allowed him leeway to employ measures in his negotiations that would have been denied to others and accorded him tremendous power in the management of the king's financial affairs abroad. He corresponded freely and liberally with Northumberland and Cecil, and it was none other than Northumberland who carried Thomas Gresham's recommendations to the king and council for their stamp of approval. Securing Northumberland's own approval was the all-important first step. Thomas was astute enough to recognize, and diligently follow, that chain of command approach—via Cecil and a handful of other influential nobles to Northumberland, thence to the council and King Edward.

In May, the French ambassador wrote to King Henri II his assessment of King Edward, for Henri had asked that the young English king be viewed as a candidate for his daughter's hand. The ambassador's correspondence was intercepted by Northumberland, who had spies everywhere and he read the letter with great interest and relish. The ambassador reported that in the area of religion, England was going "from bad to worse," given the latest Protestant reforms, which outlawed all vestiges of Catholic practice that remained. On one point, he emphasized to his liege, all classes of Englishmen seemed to agree, in that "whether of the old or the new religion, detestation of the pope [Julius III] is so great that no one in England can bear to hear him mentioned." He described King Edward as "handsome, affable, of becoming stature, seems to be liberal, is beginning to interest himself with public business and in bodily exercises, literary studies and knowledge of languages, surpassing his contemporaries and the standards of his age."[4] The ambassador concluded his long report with a positive assessment of the military and parliamentary systems in place in England, and with assurances to his lord that, despite the problems with which it was beset, the English government seemed unlikely to fall, "for the people love their king and put up with anything to retain him."[5]

Northumberland fervently hoped that marriage negotiations between Edward and Princess Elisabeth would proceed well, for a French alliance was the one he favored most. It would cement the English hold on Calais, a vital port.

Then the sweating sickness invaded London again, and the king was forced to flee the city. It claimed the life of the young duke of Suffolk, one of Edward's close companions, and plunged the whole court into mourning. Edward wrote in his journal: "Came the sweat into London, which was more vehement than the old sweat. For if one took cold, he died within three hours, and if he 'scaped, it held him but nine hours, or ten at the most. Also, if he slept the first six hours, as he should be very desirous to do, then he raved, and should die raving. It grew so much, that I removed to Hampton Court, with a very few with me."[6] John Caius had become one of the court physicians to Edward, and he scrawled a note to Thomas to warn him away from London. Thomas took his friend's advice and repaired straight to Hampton Court, where he arrived in time to attend Edward's investiture into the Order of St. Michael on 16 July. This was a prelude to official marriage negotiations with the French. Carloix, secretary to the French king's envoy Vielleville, reported, "King Edward looked like an angel in human form, for it is impossible to imagine a more beautiful face and figure, set off by the brilliance of jewels and robes, and a mass of diamonds, rubies, and pearls, emeralds and sapphires—they made the whole room look as if lit up."[7] The solemn investiture was a sight and a ceremony that dazzled the eyes of all in attendance. It was so beautiful, and so moving, that Thomas and many others there found themselves wiping away tears at its completion.

The king had grown, at fourteen, into a handsome specimen of young manhood, Thomas noted, taking almost fatherly pride in his young king. But by the time the ceremony and the feast, and the lengthy entertainments that followed it, had ended, Edward was looking somewhat pale and obviously tired. However, within a few days, the protracted haggling over the French princess' dowry had been concluded and the conditions of the betrothal had been agreed upon. The Spanish ambassador reported to Emperor Charles V that to his eye, the English king had become thin and looked a little frail.

Edward's uncle, the former protector Somerset, had been quietly arrested in October of 1551. He was accused of a plot to have Northumberland and other nobles murdered, and his own third daughter, Lady Jane Seymour (who had been named after Edward's late mother), betrothed to the king. Somerset denied everything; nevertheless, in December he went on trial. It was not an easy matter, for the council was aware that Somerset had great support from the people, who felt that even if the aging duke may have acted improperly at times, he was innocent of being a traitor to his nephew. Though subsequently acquitting him of the charge of treason, the council instead convicted him of felonious intent, a crime for which the only penalty was also death. The lord treasurer stood and pronounced the grim sentence upon the king's uncle. Seven weeks passed. Somerset's situation was being debated throughout England, and the nobles waited to see if the king would grant his uncle clemency.

King Edward, doubtless influenced by Northumberland, did not act on behalf of his uncle, and the sentence was carried out on 22 January 1552. With his last rival removed, Northumberland was without opposition to his enormous power.

In the performance of his duties as royal agent that first year, Thomas Gresham found himself traveling back and forth to England at least once a month, and sometimes more often. "I trust," he complained to Anne, "I'm little better in this than the king's post." Indeed, he often traveled the same route as the post, going by fast horse from Antwerp to Bruges, Bruges to Nieuport, then via Dunkirk to Calais, where he took ship to Dover and thence to Gravesend and up the Thames to the Tower docks, arriving on the fourth or fifth day. Occasionally, if he tarried a day or two in Bruges on the way, he'd board ship at Dunkirk instead of Calais.[8] Sometimes, he'd leave the ship at Dover and proceed by horseback to London along the King's Highway, in order to make better time.

By any route, it was a grueling trip, and not without great personal danger attached to it. Often he carried large sums of cash, bonds, gold bullion, silver, or jewels for the king, and sometimes valuable documents that Northumberland wanted seen by no other eyes. Thomas resorted to employing spies, bodyguards and agents at all stages of his route, to watch over him and the goods he carried. Wherever he went, he traveled well armed and well guarded, but the danger still lurked—there were many who would like to get their hands on the valuables and state secrets Thomas Gresham carried on those trips. He had to remain ever alert.

He had not yet found a house for his family, but in Antwerp, where he was not subject to the severe restrictions of the Sumptuary Laws that governed England, Thomas began to acquire a store of the kind of valuable household plate, tapestries and furnishings that were denied to those not of the peerage in England. Anne was pleased, and temporarily mollified, by these novel indicators of her new status. Thomas felt he needed the perquisites which would enable him to receive and entertain the king's creditors in the lavish manner to which they were accustomed. They were frequently entertained by the representatives of other royal houses, but Thomas's predecessor, Dansell, had not attended overly much to such duties on behalf of the English king. However, Thomas felt it was important to woo the king's creditors in every manner possible. He wanted to ensure that his requests for funds on behalf of his lord would receive the most immediate consideration and the most advantageous terms for the English king.

To that end, in the spring of 1552 he hosted a great banquet to honor all the king's creditors, most especially the Fuggers, and his hosts, Schetz brothers. The banquet was such a success, it gained Thomas Gresham considerable renown in Antwerp. The twenty-four guests who received the coveted gold-bordered folio invitations, sealed with the golden grasshopper seal, arrived at the Schetz mansion on the appointed evening in their litters, decked out in their finest velvets, satins, and jewels. There, they were announced by Schetz's liveried servants, greeted by Thomas and Anne, and escorted to the great dining hall.

The long, heavily carved oak table could seat forty with ease, which afforded the two dozen honored guests ample room to enjoy the elaborate meal. The table covers were of exquisite linen and lace, crafted by the best local weavers. Each place boasted a large, elegantly wrought silver spoon and a fine blown-glass drinking cup from Venice, each cup of a different hue, all rimmed with silver. They ate from shallow silver basins in varying sizes, each engraved with the Gresham grasshopper, and the initials TG. Servants poured the best French wines and English ales from enormous pewter flagons, refilling a cup or glass as soon as a guest had drunk from it. In a corner of the room, a lute player strummed his instrument and sang softly.

The guests' jewels glittered in the light of the hundreds of candles in filigree holders that lit the huge hall and were placed along the banquet table. At each place—an almost unheard of extravagance—was a finely wrought silver-handled knife for the guests to cut and spear their meat. These, too, bore the Gresham grasshopper crest, and a like knife, bearing each guest's personal crest or seal, was presented as a "favor"at their place—the traditional small gift from the host to his guests as a memento of the evening.[9]

Mimes, masques, and jugglers entertained as the diners enjoyed each course of the lengthy meal. Between the nine courses, as the surfeited diners relaxed and chatted, colorful pageants were staged. There was ample time to stage such events, since the kitchen was at some distance from the dining hall. The Gresham banquet continued for more than six hours. Extravagantly large bowls of the finest English honey and fresh-churned Flemish butter—expensive delicacies both—graced the table, and Thomas and Anne urged their guests to help themselves at will.

The dinner opened with delicate prawn-filled pastries baked in the shape of castles and swans. The guests exclaimed over the charming presentation. Then heaping platters of oysters, boiled eggs, and whole fish were laid the length of the massive table by the servers. After the fish course came soup and fowl: roast whole capons and fat geese stuffed with fragrant dried fruits, nuts, and onions, and along with those came great tureens of beef brawn soup. In the English tradition, Thomas offered his guests meats in a quantity and variety seldom seen at even the richest tables in Antwerp. Spit-roasted haunches of beef, mutton, and veal came out on great pewter platters, and the carvers employed jeweled daggers to carve off chunks of meat for each guest. The roasted meats were quickly followed by stewed rabbits, baked partridges, pheasant, and other small game birds and wild fowl, all fancifully decorated. The guests used chunks of the fragrant, freshly baked wheat and rye bread to lift the meat and game to their mouths and to mop their basins clean of flavorful sauces and juices. They spooned up vegetables to wash down the meat—creamed leeks, boiled turnips, carrots, and parsnips—and drank prodigious quantities of wine and ale.

Throughout, servants offered basins and drying cloths, and poured rose water for the guests to wash away the grease from their fingers. Then at a signal from Thomas, the musicians struck up and thirty handsome young menservants entered in a procession, all colorfully dressed and turbaned in the Turkish manner. The first bore flaming torches, the next tumbled and danced about with sparkling curved scimitars, and the others bore aloft flaming trays of sweet puddings and pastries, all ethereally decorated with spun sugar, which they deferentially served to the guests, bowing low as they offered them. With the sweets, they poured cups of mead—warmed ale liberally laced with more of the expensive honey—or sweet wines and port. The guests, impressed as Thomas had intended them to be at such an extraordinary presentation, clapped their hands in delight, showering compliments on their host and hostess.

Anne, lovely in a modish green gown her French dressmaker had fashioned, touched the brilliant emerald and diamond brooch at the low neckline of her gown and smiled thinly at her guests' enjoyment. She knew that after this night her husband's stature and success in Antwerp were ensured. If only she could feel happy for him! But she wanted nothing more than to leave this place and these people whom she detested, and return to her home in England.

After the puddings the servants brought in great montages of fresh fruit. Many varieties were available at the local markets, but the rarer fruits—fresh figs, damsons, oranges, and dates—had all been brought in by the Gresham ships for the occasion. The banquet concluded with delicate savories, then a variety of French, Flemish, and English cheeses, nuts, and more entertainments, lasting into the early morning hours.

The departing guests climbed sleepily into their litters, agreeing that it had been by far the most elegant and delightful evening they had ever enjoyed. Gossip over the hospitality they had received at the home of Edward VI's royal agent flew throughout Antwerp the following day. Thomas smiled in glee when the word filtered back to him. Jasper Schetz clapped his friend heartily on the shoulder. "You are a great success here, Thomas. You serve your king well, which reflects well upon my poor household. Proud I am, and the envy of all Antwerp, to be your friend and host." Not long afterward, Thomas commissioned a young artist to paint a huge scene depicting that great banquet, and his guests, which when finished he ordered placed on the wall behind his desk.[10]

In April 1552, Thomas received some disquieting news from Northumberland. "The king has fallen ill of a sudden. He has suffered a combination of measles and smallpox. It was in truth a sickness that most certainly might have killed him, but we are pleased to tell you that with the strength of youth he managed to throw it off, and in a fortnight was well again."

Thomas hastened to England to see for himself how Edward

was doing, for the rumor of the English king's illness had reached Flanders and was playing havoc with the exchange rates. It had also diminished the willingness of the moneylenders to negotiate new loans. Edward had no heirs, and the Catholic Princess Mary, herself unmarried, stood to succeed him. Northumberland informed Thomas in one of their private chats that Edward's relations with Princess Mary had become seriously strained. "I've little use for Her Catholic Highness," he said cynically, "and I'll be glad when Our Gracious Majesty King Edward is married and has an heir of his own to remove her from the succession."

"What news of the suit with the French?" Thomas wanted to know. "The king's marriage with the French princess might be concluded soon," answered Northumberland, "when he is fit again, and for all, it can't be soon enough."

King Edward, estranged from his Catholic half-sister Mary, was more cordial to his other half-sister, nineteen-year-old Princess Elizabeth. Elizabeth, a feisty redhead like her father, had grown almost as comely as her mother Anne Boleyn had been at her age. When Edward first became ill, Elizabeth had ridden in state to his bedside. However, it was a shorter visit than planned, for after only a day or two, in fear of catching the pox or her brother's measles, the princess withdrew to the safety of her own residence at Hatfield, and there she remained.

In early August 1552, Thomas rendered a written accounting of his labors from 1 March to 27 July of that year, in which he reckoned he had made payments on Edward's debts of more than £106,000. The funds to pay those debts had been borrowed for the king by Thomas from various Antwerp moneylenders. His expenses, including eight trips back and forth to England during that period, were billed to the crown at £102, and the last item, noted separately, included the bill for the great banquet: "for a supper and a banckett that I made to the Fugger, and to the Schetz, and other that I have had to do withall for Your Majesty, since Your Highness has committed this great charge unto me—£26."[11]

Thomas had been inordinately successful as the king's agent up to that point, and his personal life, too, was proceeding in comfortable fashion. His son Richard, at seven, was growing fast, and doing acceptably well in his studies. It was Thomas's desire that his son's future would follow much the same path as his own. Richard would be sent back to England in due course to study at Cambridge, then be apprenticed to the Merchant Adventurers. Anne had not shown signs of quickening with another babe, and Thomas had resigned himself to the probability that she would bear him no more children. She was not a happy woman in Antwerp, and she let him know that at every opportunity.

They had recently quarreled, and now guilt flooded him. He had found a lovely young mistress in Bruges who was much more amenable to him than his unhappy, nagging wife, and Ghislaine left him with little energy or desire for Anne. He rarely even dined with his wife or son anymore—he ate with Jasper or from a tray brought to his study, unless they had guests, and Anne was usually long asleep before he found his own bed at night.

A few months before, he had gone to Bruges on an errand for Jasper Schetz. There, he had called upon a gentleman to whom Schetz had referred him with a letter of introduction, and in the course of the meeting the banker had introduced his daughter. Her appearance had taken Thomas's breath away. She was fresh and exquisite of face, barely nineteen years old. Small in stature and slim of build, she had long dark hair and grey cat's eyes, with the smile and voice of an angel. He had been mesmerized by her, and was immediately his most courtly self. Things had proceeded from there, and before a month had passed, Ghislaine was his mistress.

Now, Thomas had her set up in a luxuriously appointed little house on one of the tiny, cobbled streets of Bruges, with a garden in back that overlooked a quiet canal. He had settled a generous monthly allowance upon her, which was administered by the discreet Richard Clough. Marriage was out of the question. Thomas had no intention of divorcing his wife, who was his legal mate and mother of his only son. He was content for Ghislaine to remain as his mistress, though he knew he had outraged her father with that arrangement, and her father had disinherited her. But no matter. Thomas adored her, and fortunately he had the wherewithal to take care of her. She would want for nothing. He looked forward eagerly to the little time he could eke out to be with her when he passed through Bruges on his frequent trips to England. Their liaison had been nothing short of idyllic these past months. But now he had much to concern him.

Ghislaine had recently informed him, with shy blushes, that she was expecting his child, and though he was secretly delighted at the prospect, he scarcely knew how he would deal with that matter when the time came. He dreaded what Anne might do if she found out. He intended to give the baby his name when it was born and acknowledge it, and Anne would have to accept that. He shuddered to imagine the scene that would create.

"Prithee, wife," he began, touching Anne's shoulder gently in remorse, wanting to reconcile her anger at him this night. But she went rigid at his touch, and cried the louder. Contrarily, anger flared in him at that. Dare she refuse him! She had not the right to deny her husband. He should beat her, ungrateful wench! It would be what she deserved, with her wretched tongue and willful ways! It was no wonder he sought another's bed—one who welcomed him with smiles and open arms, and not this eternal coldness he got from his wife. But Thomas hadn't the energy for such scenes. Besides, he carried within him the knowledge that he had wronged her with Ghislaine. Chagrined, he sighed, got up and donned his night robe, and crept out. All desire for Anne was gone, and he was glad to return to the peaceful haven of his own rooms. It was the last time he would seek her bed, only to feel her anger, he vowed.

Anne Gresham tossed sleeplessly in the big bed after her husband left. She was a lost pilgrim in an alien land, and she stubbornly refused to bend to her husband's will. She was miserable, without quite knowing why, spending every day mourning for her home on Lombard Street. She had even once hinted to her husband that he should allow her and the boy to return there to spend a month or two, or to go stay with his sister Christiana and her husband John Thynne. Thomas had not given any indication that he had noticed the hints. A great wave of despair washed over her. She could not, would not, live here much longer among these strangers! If he would not send her home, she'd go herself, she vowed. That was but a foolish thought, she well knew. She could not go alone, without his permission. If she left her husband, none would dare take her in. She had no reason to leave him, really. But she felt married to a ghost. He was there, but not there. The long, sleepless night offered few answers to Thomas Gresham's unhappy wife.

Thomas, too, tossed in his bed in his own spacious bedroom. He had noted his wife's wish to return to England, as he noted everything. He saw how she chafed at life at the Schetz's, how little interest she took in the social whirl of the city. He had ordered her fashionable gowns and jewels aplenty; she had use of a litter and servants to carry it, for visits and shopping in the city—even her own liveried footman—enough to turn the head of any woman. But Anne seldom used it, never thanked him, and barely glanced at the lavish gifts he gave her.

Thomas was not unsympathetic to her loneliness and sense of alienation. His guilt over Ghislaine certainly caused him to accept her bitterness toward him more than he would have otherwise, but deep down he felt little pity for his wife's unhappy state. Everyone around her, especially Jasper Schetz's wife and sisters-in-law, had tried to help her adapt to her new home, but she had turned coldly away from them all, refusing to take part in their lives or to show any interest in them, or in Antwerp. She hated "foreigners." This infuriated Thomas. Anne had a life of wealth, ease, and comfort, and should be grateful for all she enjoyed. Still . . . a visit home might help things. Perhaps he would send them back for a visit at Michaelmas, Thomas thought, and allow them to remain until after Twelfth Night. If possible, he could join them at Christmastide. That settled in his mind, he fell into a deep, almost dreamless sleep.

The next day Thomas's horse picked his way carefully along the rain-slick streets of Antwerp. Thomas pulled the hood of his cloak forward to keep the rain off his face and drew the garment

closer about him. He could smell summer in the damp streets—
a sweet, decaying scent of rotting, overripe fruit and bruised flower
blossoms. He could just make out the bell tower of the bourse
ahead, for the wind off the water was blowing the cold rain across
the road in great slanting grey curtains. Anne was lucky she could
snuggle in the dry warmth of her bed for as long as she wished
each day, without a care.

Thomas's mind was full as he rode slowly along. He had been
paying close attention all year to the activities of the Hanse merchants and to the fluctuations of the exchange. He knew he had
to keep the exchange value of English currency at as high a rate
as possible in order to profit by it, and to pay off the king's debts
at the best rate, but the failure of the king and Northumberland
to control the Hanse merchants adversely affected the exchange
rate and was a source of great frustration to Thomas. No matter.
He'd take that up again when he returned to England.

In mid-August he headed back to England and at the end of
the month returned to Antwerp with instructions to persuade the
Fuggers and Schetz to postpone payment of the debt of £56,000
the king owed them—£44,000 to the Fuggers, £12,000 to Schetz—
which debts were now due. Schetz and the Fuggers agreed to wait
for their money, but told Thomas the terms of the loan had to be
altered, to give them recompense for the extension of credit. They
demanded, as had been the custom, that the king buy jewels or
merchandise to cement the extension. Innocently, Gresham hastened back to England once more to lay those terms before the
king and council. He was stunned at their reaction. They adamantly
refused to comply, became incensed at him, and berated him at
length. Before it was over, they almost fired him as agent. They
would agree to nothing except the prolongation of payment on
the original terms, with nothing added for the renewal.

Dejected, smarting, Thomas returned to the Low Countries,
authorized only to conciliate the matter and seek the friendly
approval of the king's creditors, who, Thomas knew, would be
most unhappy with that proposal. He, too, was unhappy at the
failure of the English council to see that by taking such a rigid

100

stand they were harming the king's credit and putting the royal agent in an untenable position with his host and most important creditor. Frustrated and angry by the time he reached Antwerp, Thomas greeted his family brusquely, then closeted himself in the library. He was glad that Jasper Schetz and the Fuggers were in Brussels, and not expected back for at least another day. He paced back and forth in agitation. Both his personal word and his honor with his business associates here were at stake, and the council had played him badly, he felt. He could not let that insult to his dignity pass. He had no choice now but to resign as royal agent.

Resolutely, he sat down at his desk and opened a drawer.[12] Drawing out a clean sheet of paper, he took quill pen in hand and began a letter to Northumberland:

> The very love and obedience I owe you allows me to write you, without fear, of what is on my mind, for this matter touches the King's Majesty's honor and credit, which I am bound by my oath to maintain and keep. It is no small grief to me that, in my time as His Majesty's agent, any foreign lenders should be forced to go without payment against their will, and this must in future be otherwise managed, or else in the end, the dishonesty of this matter shall hereafter be laid upon my neck, especially should anything happen to you or Lord Pembroke, recognizing that we're all mortal.

Thomas sat back and stared into space, unseeing, as he collected his thoughts. Then, dipping into the inkwell, he scribbled furiously again. He was determined this time to speak his mind to Northumberland, regardless of the consequences. He briefly reiterated what had taken place with the council and expressed his surprise that the council had failed to inform him of their new position on the taking of jewels or merchandise in renegotiating their debts, "which matter did not a little abash me, considering how things had up to now proceeded."

He harked back to how it had been with his predecessors:

And so it has been ever since in the taking of wares, when the King's Majesty made any prolongation of paying the debt, until the charge was committed to me. I exercised my personal power to the utmost to get His Majesty a loan of £20,000 without his taking of any jewels or merchandise, as Your Grace well knows, and to be plain with Your Grace about it, I had to give my own personal word that this money would be paid on the stated date, or else I could never have succeeded, and the King's Majesty would not have had the money.

To be frank with Your Grace, if there is no other way that can be found for payment of His Majesty's debts except to force men from time to time to prolong them, I must tell you that the end of the matter shall be neither honorable nor profitable to His Highness.

Therefore, if the matter cannot be otherwise resolved immediately, this letter is to most humbly ask Your Grace that I be relieved of my office of agency. Otherwise, I foresee no result except shame and discredit, which would be the undoing of all I have worked to achieve in my life to now—but that is a small matter indeed—what is far more important is that the King's Majesty's honor and credit not be besmirched by these actions, especially here in foreign lands, where now his credit is better than the emperor's, which I pray God will continue. At present, the emperor must pay 16 percent interest and still cannot get funds. As soon as I receive a reply from the Fuggers and Schetz' on this matter at hand, I will at once repair to England with it and lay it before the court, trusting that I shall succeed in accomplishing the wishes of the king and council. If my poor and simple advice that follows will but be heard and heeded, I believe that in just two years' time I can bring the King's Majesty completely out of debt, may God grant me enough life to see that day.

Having leapt over the first hurdle, Thomas found his thoughts tumbling forth. His pen squeaked and scratched to keep up with them, galloping effortlessly through words and pages, pausing only to dip more ink from the well or seek a new sheet of paper as he laid his financial plan for King Edward before Northumberland.

> To accomplish this, my request to you and His Majesty is that you allocate me weekly £1200 or £1300, to be received by one very trusted, specially appointed agent, so that it remains a secret. I shall use that money here in Antwerp, where every day I will take up £200 or £300 sterling by exchange. Thus, for such small amounts, it won't be noticed, nor will it be enough to make the exchange rate fall, for it will be done in my name. I would expect, by the end of a year, to have saved the King's Majesty £20,000 in the payment of his debts and at that time would give up my trade and devote all my time to the service of His Majesty, so that I may serve His Majesty's needs better. By this method, and another that follows, in two years things will be accomplished according to my plan. Then you will not have to go to others such as the Merchant Adventurers, the Staplers, or foreign merchants, for funds.
> I beg His Majesty also to make a staple of lead and take all the lead in the realm into his own hands, prohibiting the exportation of any for five years. This will cause the price of lead to rise in Antwerp, at which point we might feed what they need to them from time to time, and profitably. Thus His Majesty can keep his treasure in his own realm and extricate himself from the debt into which his father and the late duke of Somerset have plunged him, and with that Your Grace shall do His Majesty such great service as never any duke did in England, to the renown of your house forever.

Thomas then turned to giving the duke the latest intelligence on the emperor's movements, and whatever tidbits of news from Antwerp and the local gossip he thought might please or amuse His Grace. The long missive finished at last, Thomas signed it with a great flourish, then sanded, rolled, and sealed it, ready for his trusted messenger Francis de Tomazo to set out with on the morrow.[13]

Northumberland, dismayed at the prospect of his trusted agent Gresham resigning his post as royal agent, convinced the council to accept part of the proposal the letter contained. They purchased the jewel to renew the loan one more time, but instructed Thomas to make the bankers understand this would be the last time, and in future their good credit would have to stand on its own for renewals. They refused to go along with making a staple of lead, but they did allocate the £1200 weekly that he had requested, ordering the treasurer of the mints to remit the payments to him. However, that lasted for only eight weeks. Then, without explanation, the payments stopped.

Undeterred, Thomas continued devising schemes and making suggestions in his frequent long letters to Northumberland and the king's privy council on how best to use the exchange to the king's advantage. He had to go into great detail about the system of commodities, prices, and exchange rates in these letters, because the nature of how such matters went was not well understood by those gentlemen. That they accepted—nay, welcomed—Gresham's frequent advice and explanations was amazing even to him, but Thomas believed deeply in his mission and in what he was trying to accomplish for Edward, and no effort or risk was too great to undertake in that endeavor.

His second year as Edward's royal agent to the Low Countries was drawing to a close, and by his own estimation Thomas had traveled back and forth from Antwerp to England no fewer than forty times. Despite setbacks and disappointments, he had enjoyed considerable success in handling the king's affairs, making slow but deliberate progress in pulling His Majesty up from the morass of debt. The king, to show his appreciation for the service Thomas was rendering to the crown, rewarded him with the grant of Westacre Priory in Norfolk, an imposing structure of considerable value.[14]

But by late October 1552, insistent rumors began to circulate that King Edward was seriously ill.[15] The duke of Northumberland, taking breakfast with the king, noticed that Edward did not look at all well, though the young man never complained. No English physician would dare admit a monarch was seriously ill, and one's impending death was never mentioned—it was an offense punishable by death for the physician. But Northumberland had become alarmed at the king's paleness, and he knew something was gravely amiss with Edward. Quietly, he summoned the celebrated Italian physician Girolamo Cardano to come to England. Cardano, a rotund little man, fussily examined the king and spent several months observing Edward, casting his horoscope and forming a diagnosis. He observed to Caius, " 'Tis sad. This boy king has so much charm and promise, but alas, there is a sign of death in his face, death that will come too soon."[16]

But although the eminent doctors might agree among themselves that the king was gravely ill, Caius warned Cardano that at the court of the English he was in a terrible quandary. "You cannot, on pain of death, reveal to the council, or any living person, that which we know—that His Majesty is seriously ill and likely to die before too long." Frightened, Cardano decided to cast a false horoscope to the council. He would warn them against unduly tiring their young king, and then quickly take his leave and return to safety in Italy. "I saw some omens," he reported. "Omens of great alarm and upset. I fear there will be sickness for His Majesty, but he will recover each time and live for at least another two decades," he lied, and promptly left England.[17]

Toward the end of 1552, King Edward asked Thomas Gresham to undertake a delicate diplomatic mission for him. Thomas was extremely honored and flattered at this expression of high trust from the king himself. Thomas was to arrange to meet socially with the emperor's ambassador in Antwerp and to sound him out as delicately as possible to discover what the emperor's present and future plans were in relation to England. This Thomas managed to accomplish without too much difficulty. As a result of their conversation, the ambassador wrote the regent to inquire about Gresham.

As soon as he heard that from Schetz, Thomas reported it to Northumberland. "The regent herself," he wrote, "made inquiry about me of my friend Jasper Schetz. She asked him what manner of man I am, and whether I am a man of honesty and credit, and if I were to be trusted. Schetz informed her that I have been staying at his own house for eight years and he knew me to be a right honest man, making more of me to Her Grace than I am worthy of. She commanded Schetz to ask me why I had opened the discussion with the ambassador. I had explained well enough to my friend, thus he to Her Grace, so that all progressed to our advantage, and Her Grace, as a token of friendship, sent to me through her treasurer, Monsieur Longine, several letters intercepted from Her Majesty Mary, queen of Scotland, to His Majesty Henri II, king of France." Thomas posted the letter and then headed for England himself, carrying the important letters from the Scottish queen, for he wanted to tell Northumberland in person that Longine had informally opened a proposal to Thomas for a closer alliance between England and the Low Countries through a union between King Edward and the daughter of Charles V.

He arrived in England, this time with his family, prepared to spend that year's holidays at home. He had visited Ghislaine in Bruges a week before departing and assured himself all was well with her, since she was now well along in her pregnancy. He had held her close as she bid him a tearful farewell, and had given her a beautiful sapphire and emerald pendant fashioned in the shape of a bird, as his New Year gift, as well as yards of cloth for new gowns and money for necessaries for the babe, which was due early in the year. Then he returned to Antwerp to collect his family and sail home to England. Anne was radiant and stood the rough crossing well. She was so happy to be going home again for a visit she could have withstood any hardship with ease.

Thomas had ordered the Lombard Street house opened and readied for them. Once they were settled there he was able to renew social acquaintance with old friends and business associates. Anne, ecstatic to be back on English soil, was the picture of wifely contentment. Secretly, she vowed not to return to Antwerp with Thomas after the holidays. She would feign illness, pregnancy—anything—to remain in England. She had missed it so!

The Greshams entertained lavishly that year. Thomas visited with his uncle, his sisters, and his friend John Caius. Caius was still one of Edward's court physicians. "I am so busy, I scarce have time to sleep or eat any more," Caius complained, but said nothing to Thomas about the state of the king's health, and Thomas did not openly ask. Caius was most interested to hear of Thomas's adventures in Antwerp. Thomas noticed that his friend was becoming very eccentric in his behavior, and was dismayed that Caius looked almost unkempt. "Take you no wife?" he teased. "I trust, Kees, you need a good woman to warm your bed, keep your clothes, and put meat on your skinny bones." Caius protested that he had a woman for a servant who came in by day to cook and clean for him. "'Tis all I need, Thomas. Women do naught but meddle and muddle life." He looked nervously about the room as though a woman might somehow enter and muddle his world at any moment. Thomas agreed. "Aye, well I know. Mine own Anne is not an easy woman to bear, certainly, but she is a good wife who has given me a fine son, and keeps my house in good order. A woman of sense is a bargain to be held dearly, though her tongue be sharp." Then he thought of Ghislaine and the child she was expecting, and almost sought his friend's advice in the matter, but then changed his mind. No, he would deal with that problem himself. Instead, Thomas turned the talk to the book Caius had just completed about treatment of the sweating sickness.[18]

For his New Year's gift, Thomas presented the king with a pair of very rare silk hose from Spain, which he had procured through his factor in Seville. The gift was a great success with the king, who thanked Gresham profusely for it, noting that "King Henry VIII did wear only cloth hose, or hose cut of taffeta, unless by great chance a pair of silk stockings like this came from Spain."[19] The king and council wanted Thomas to maintain his newly formed liaison with Longine and the emperor's ambassador when he returned to Antwerp and to record and include details of any visits or conversations with them in his reports to Northumberland. Thomas had already established a large network of paid agents, for his trading business took his ships and men to every country. They in turn provided him with reports and intelligence from faraway places, which information, passed on by Thomas, was invaluable to Northumberland and the king.

Thomas felt extremely fortunate in that he had few enemies at court. However, one of his enemies, Gardiner, the Catholic bishop of Winchester, was extremely powerful, and that worry nagged at him should Princess Mary ever come to power in England. Fortunately for Thomas, Gardiner was very much out of favor at the moment, so his acrid comments and accusations against Gresham, whom he styled "a foul usurer," were seldom heeded. However, Thomas knew he had to tread very carefully where Gardiner was concerned—especially since Gardiner still had the ear and sympathy of Princess Mary, and she was still the heiress presumptive. He'd need to watch his back on that one.

After the holidays, Anne was persuaded by Thomas to return to Antwerp with him, but it was not accomplished without harsh words between them. Anne did not back down before her angry husband. She spoke her mind about Thomas's preoccupation with "His Majesty's affairs to the detriment of your own," and about her unhappiness living in "the home of those strangers." Her persistence in referring to his dear friends the Schetzes as "those strangers" annoyed Thomas, but he held his temper in check. Some of her complaints, he realized, were not without merit. Ultimately, to placate her, he vowed he would, upon their return to Antwerp, look seriously into buying a home for them there. Anne then relented and agreed to go back with him. Thomas was deeply relieved to have surmounted this latest domestic crisis. His marriage was very important to him. He admired his lovely young wife and hated to see her so unhappy all the time. He'd return to visiting her bed when they were back in Antwerp, he decided. Maybe this time it would do some good. Besides, at thirty-four, he was still young and lusty. Ghislaine was far along in her pregnancy and, denied access to both women, Thomas realized he missed the conjugal intimacy he had once shared with Anne.

At the end of January 1553, King Edward fell seriously ill and was bedridden for almost a month. Thomas, unaware of the gravity of his monarch's illness, toiled mightily to discharge all of the king's foreign debts, a feat he had already managed to accomplish, albeit only briefly, on two occasions in the past. Northumberland and the privy council were astonished at the progress Gresham had made in ameliorating the king's foreign debt problem in such a short space of time.

In mid-February, Ghislaine bore him a healthy daughter. Thomas was overjoyed, and in what was perhaps a flash of inspiration named the child Marie-Anne. Barely a month later, Ghislaine perished of childbed fever, and the grief-stricken Thomas was forced to break the news of his infant daughter to his wife. Anne, though stunned and infuriated at the news her husband brought her, had the good sense to accept the child. She took the little mite into her home, and called the baby by its second name, Anne, after herself. She was secretly overjoyed to learn that the child's mother had died, removing her from competition for the affections of her husband.

The advent of the baby and the full realization of the extent of her husband's association with its mother shocked and awakened Anne Gresham to the ease with which her handsome and wealthy young husband could stray from her bed and find solace elsewhere, a not unusual situation in the society in which they lived, and Anne knew that. It happened all the time, in fact. King Henry VIII, she knew had, despite six wives, sired a base-born son by his mistress Bessie Blount, and had acknowledged the boy and named him duke of Richmond. And many other powerful men had children born "on the other side of the bed," as the saying went. So Anne held her tongue in check, concealing her deep anger. She bent her efforts more to pleasing her husband, and fully accepted his child. In truth, she had longed for another child but had been unable to conceive one. Richard was now in the hands of his tutors, and this new baby daughter was like a heaven-sent gift to the lonely Anne. In England, she could claim the baby as her own, and none would dare dispute it. She could lavish a mother's affection and love on this child of her husband's without fear of anyone back there knowing she had been displaced briefly by a younger, prettier rival.

Thomas, relieved that Anne would be compliant in this delicate matter, threw himself back into his work with great energy. It provided an antidote to the deep and painful grief he felt over the loss of Ghislaine. He looked earnestly for a house and finally found one on Long New Street. He moved his family there, installing a full staff of servants and a nurse for his daughter.

At about that time, to accomplish full remission of the king's debts, he decided to force the Merchant Adventurers to loan money to the crown by detaining their fully loaded ships when they were ready to sail. To obtain release of their trade goods and ships they were required to pledge their bills of exchange for merchandise to repay King Edward's debts, money to be repaid them in London at a fixed date and rate of exchange, which Thomas himself set to the crown's advantage.

This high-handed abuse of power on his part infuriated his fellow merchant adventurers and brought Thomas no small amount of grief—especially from his uncle Sir John, who rode to London from his country manor at Titsey to deliver his nephew a scathing dressing-down. It was the first time the uncle and nephew ever had a falling out, and it distressed Thomas mightily to have his uncle so angry at him. However, he was more concerned with England's financial health than with the profits or goodwill of his uncle or the Merchant Adventurers.

"My uncle, Sir John Gresham," he told Northumberland, "stormed at me for setting the price of the exchange and said that it lies now with me to do something to redeem myself with the merchants of this realm, to regain my good name with them. It is no wonder he storms, for he had bought £4000 in wool.[20] I assure Your Grace we had some serious words and were on the verge of a permanent falling-out, but before we parted, we drank to one another again." Northumberland was relieved to learn that Thomas had averted a serious family rift with his uncle, for the wealthy and powerful Sir John Gresham was not one he wished to alienate.

Thomas tried to take that opportunity to use his case against the Hanse merchants as a way to placate the English Merchant Adventurers and his uncle. He again advanced a plea to Northumberland and the council to put a stop to the privileges enjoyed by the Hanse Steelyard merchants. They had been wreaking havoc with the exchange rate of currency in London, he reported to Northumberland, and Thomas had to resort to some heavy-handed methods with them in order to preserve the value of the currency so that he could discharge the king's debts. "They are not worthy to be called merchants," Thomas fumed to the council, "for they behave no better than a shoemaker or minstrel. They lack the discipline of long apprenticeship required of our own merchants. The Hanse, for lack of experience and knowledge, have been, and are, one of the main causes of the fall of the exchange rate, and also have damaged the reputation of our goods and our merchants."[21] The council took Thomas's complaint and recommendation under advisement, but did not act.

Scarcely a week later, Thomas received the tragic news that his sister Elizabeth had died suddenly from a fever. He hastened to Longleat to console his remaining sister, Christiana, and his stepmother, Isabella. Elizabeth had spent her life caring for her stepmother and looking after Christiana's growing brood. Had King Edward not outlawed Catholicism, Thomas reflected sadly, Elizabeth, a gentle and studious woman, would probably have entered a convent. As it was, she had expressed a strong desire to remain single, and her father Sir Richard, who doted on his elder daughter, had given in to those wishes and allowed her to remain unmarried and to live at Intwood with them.

Thomas was so busy traveling back and forth, attending to business, he had little time to grieve. Death was commonplace, it struck without warning, and Thomas had learned early, with the loss of his mother, to accept it.

In April 1553, elated by the success of his daring, if disputed, financial moves, Thomas wrote Northumberland from Antwerp, "The exchange here remains at nineteen shillings eight pence" (a rise of more than three shillings from the sixteen shillings it was when he assumed his post), a rise he had achieved through adept management of the king's credit, enabling him to discharge all the rest of the king's debts at the higher exchange rate. That brought more money to England, more profit to its trade, and raised the crown's credit abroad to a higher level than it had ever enjoyed.[22]

Thomas then undertook to explain some basic economic principles to Northumberland. "As the exchange rises, so the [cost of] commodities in England will fall, and as the exchange falls, so the commodities rise. And also, if the exchange rises, our gold and silver will stay in our realm and other realms will bring in gold and silver to our benefit, as heretofore they have done."

Thomas Gresham had also become feared and respected by all the bankers and merchants in Flanders. Later that month, he told the privy council: "I perceive you are now through with the Staplers for £25,000 and with the Merchant-Adventurers for £36,164, and I trust that you have given them 23 shillings 4 pence for every pound sterling, for without doubt the exchange will rise if you did so, and now is not likely ever to fall again. I have so plagued the Hanse and other foreigners that from now on they will beware of meddling with the exchange in London. As for our own merchants, I have put them in such fear that they dare not meddle, which I would be aware of immediately, since I have the brokers of the exchange in my command and confidence. So that there is never a bourse but that I have a note on what money is exchanged, whether by foreigners or Englishmen, so I expect the exchange to stay where it is."[23]

But by the time Thomas's letter reached him, Northumberland had much more on his mind than finances. He knew that although the king seemed to have rallied for the moment, the fifteen-year-old Edward's life was ebbing away, and with it would go his own seat of power and influence, along with Protestantism in England. If the king died without revoking Henry VIII's will, Princess Mary would succeed to the throne. With Mary as queen, England would most certainly become Catholic again, and his own days without a doubt would be numbered.

During the days that followed, Northumberland endeavored to reinstate himself in Princess Mary's good graces, while he plotted to remove her, and Princess Elizabeth, from the succession. Northumberland's plan was simple, feasible, and self-serving:

First, he would marry his youngest son Dudley to the Lady Jane Grey, daughter of his ally Suffolk. Lady Jane was the granddaughter of Henry VIII's sister, and a great-granddaughter of Henry VII. Therefore, if Northumberland could somehow convince Edward and the council to write a new Act of Succession, excluding Mary and Elizabeth by the illegitimacy of the marriage of their mothers to Henry VIII; Lady Jane's unquestionable blood relationship to the crown would make her Edward's legal, and most logical, successor. Adding to the strength of his case, Lady Jane and his son Dudley were firmly Protestant. He could also present the powerful argument that with Lady Jane as queen, his own Protestant son, and not some foreign Catholic prince, would be England's king. Northumberland's continued power, and that of the Protestants, would be ensured. Northumberland was convinced that King Edward and the council would go along with him in this. They did not want the Catholics back on the throne, either.

But Northumberland had not counted on resistance from within his own ranks. At just over fifteen years of age, Lady Jane Grey was a young woman of high intelligence and remarkable frankness. "I will not marry Guilford Dudley, never!" she declared vehemently. "He is spoilt, self-serving and most unattractive. I detest him." Northumberland and Suffolk, furious that this slip of a girl dared challenge their plans, ordered her to comply. Her mother screamed at her and yanked the girl's hair, smacking her repeatedly in rage. Jane again stubbornly refused, whereupon she was whipped soundly until, sobbing, she agreed to obey her father's orders and marry Dudley.

The lavish wedding of Lady Jane Grey and Guilford Dudley took place in May. Unfortunately, since the execution of Somerset, the English populace had distilled its frustration into a hearty dislike of Northumberland. Now, they openly resented his thinly veiled grasp for power. They were incensed by such a callous display of frivolity as this wedding, while their beloved young king lay abed, gravely ill. The newlyweds themselves made little attempt to conceal their intense dislike of each other from their families or the public. But Northumberland and Suffolk cared not a whit about the happiness, or lack thereof, of their newly joined youngsters. A matter of far greater importance—the crown of England—was at stake.[24]

Shortly after the nuptials, Northumberland realized he must soon risk approaching Edward about overturning Henry VIII's will. To do so, he would have to refer openly to the possibility of the young king's impending demise, a perilous undertaking, punishable by death. Northumberland felt he had enough power with the king, and enough at stake himself, to risk such a move. King Edward at first resisted the idea of disinheriting his half-sisters, but then was convinced by Northumberland on the strength of what it might do to England to have a Catholic like Mary succeed Edward. To discredit Elizabeth, who was Protestant, and a favorite of Edward's, Northumberland pointed out to the king what might happen should she later marry a Catholic prince. There were few Protestant princes in Europe for Elizabeth to marry. There would be no such concern with the heirs of Lady Jane, he assured Edward, for she was already married to the duke's own son, a staunch Protestant.

Finally convinced of the feasibility of Northumberland's plan, Edward reluctantly agreed and although he had grown very weak he drafted, in his own hand, his device for the succession at his death. He moved the crown, and the succession, over to Suffolk's line, decreeing that first in line of succession would be "the Lady Frances's (Lady Jane's mother) heirs males" and second "the Lady Jane and her heirs males" and then "the Lady Katherine's (Jane's sister) heirs males." He then wrote a second draft, for Northumberland had at last convinced Edward to put into writing that his half-sisters could not succeed because of Mary's avowed Catholicism and Elizabeth's purported illegitimacy.

King Edward wrote that should there be no heirs from the Lady Frances Brandon's line, the crown should pass over to the descendants of Frances Brandon's sister, the Lady Margaret, also a Protestant.[25] That done, the lords of the privy council were summoned to Edward's bedside, shown the device of the king in his presence, and on the spot were sworn to uphold it upon King

Edward's death. The new Act of Succession was carefully kept secret from the public.[26]

Thomas had come to London in late May for the wedding of Northumberland's son to the Lady Jane Grey, and in June he was escorted by Northumberland for a brief visit with the bedridden king. Edward, who had deep respect and affection for Thomas Gresham, thanked him once again for the marvelous gift of silk hose Gresham had presented him at New Year, and commended him for his loyal services to the crown as royal agent for the past two years. The king bestowed upon Thomas several properties whose income was worth over £100 a year, saying, "You have done well. Hereafter we will reward you better. You shall know that you have served a king."[27] Thomas Gresham was the last person to see the king in an official capacity. Three weeks later, Edward VI of England was dead.[28]

King Henry VIII (1491–1547). *Reprinted by courtesy of the National Portrait Gallery, London.*

Queen Catherine of Aragon (1486(?)–1536). Mother of Mary I.
Reprinted by courtesy of the National Portrait Gallery, London.

Queen Anne Boleyn (1505–1536). Mother of Elizabeth I. *Reprinted by courtesy of the National Portrait Gallery, London.*

Queen Jane Seymour (1509(?)–1537). Mother of Edward VI.
Reprinted by courtesy of the National Portrait Gallery, London.

Mary I (1516–1558). *Reprinted by courtesy of the National Portrait
Gallery, London. (Presented to the National Portrait Gallery by Richard
Burton and Elizabeth Taylor.)*

William Cecil, Baron Burghley (1520–1598). *Reprinted by courtesy of the National Portrait Gallery, London.*

King Edward VI (1537–1553). *Reprinted with the kind permission of Lord Braybrooke, Audley End House, and the English Heritage library.*

Lady Jane Grey Dudley (1537–1554). Queen of England for nine days in 1553. *Reprinted by courtesy of the National Portrait Gallery, London.*

Mary queen of Scots (1542–1587). Mother of James VI of Scotland, who became James I of England in 1603. *Reprinted by courtesy of the National Portrait Gallery, London.*

Queen Elizabeth I (1533–1603). *Reprinted by courtesy of the National Portrait Gallery, London.*

Anne Ferneley Read Gresham (d. 1596), wife of Sir Thomas Gresham. *Reprinted courtesy of the Rijksmuseum Foundation, Amsterdam.*

Queen Elizabeth I opening the Royal Exchange. *By Richard Beavis (1824–96), Guildhall Art Gallery, Corporation of London/Bridgeman Art Library, London.*

5

A Queen's Pawn

T he Princess Mary, daughter of Queen Catherine, is the rightful heir." Lady Jane Grey drew herself up, chin high and eyes blazing. The petite red-haired girl bravely faced the four ranged before her.

"Silence!" thundered her father. Jane jumped slightly in fear, her pale skin going chalky white, but she held her ground. Her mother took a step forward menacingly, arm raised to strike, as was her habit whenever her daughter resisted their demands. "Hist, woman!" Northumberland stayed the Lady Frances with a glare. "Would you strike your queen?" He fell to his knees before his daughter-in-law, motioning his son to do the same. Lord Guilford Dudley, though his thin lips twisted in a sneer, dared not defy his powerful father. Reluctantly, he bent his knee to his wife. Seeing this, her parents, too, went slowly to their knees before their daughter.

"I say again, Milady Queen," Northumberland stated patiently, but with a hint of threat in his voice, "will you accept the crown of England, to which your cousin, the late King Edward VI has named you heir, and for whose bidding the nobles of England declared their will and support to him, and to you as their queen, at his deathbed?"

The girl was terrified. She did not want any part of this responsibility they were bent on thrusting upon her. It was bad enough they had forced her to marry the arrogant snake who now knelt before her in false deference. It was false deference from all of them, she well knew. If she complied, as soon as she said "yea" they would take control of her life again and force her to do their bidding. This time, she knew, more than wedding vows were at stake. With Northumberland's audacious move their very lives had been placed at risk. Jane remained silent, biding her time, pacing anxiously back and forth, her wide amber skirts rustling as they trailed the floor, her gaze fixed on the narrow, leaded windows of the hall.

"Please, God," she prayed inwardly, "give me a sign. Help me to know what to do." Then she stopped still and waited in submission, head bowed, hoping for a sign—thunder, lightning, something—from above that would show her what she must do. There were only silence and the quiet breathing of the four who awaited her word. Finally, she raised her head and her grey eyes locked with Northumberland's cold blue ones. "I accept the crown of England, as my cousin, the king now dead, has decreed."

Northumberland bowed again, permitting himself a small smile of victory. With Jane's acceptance, he and her father Suffolk had won. England would remain Protestant, and he, Northumberland, would be the most powerful noble in the realm. The council had sworn to uphold Edward's will and his new Act of Succession.

Even now, Northumberland's two eldest sons were riding hard to intercept Princess Mary, who was en route from Hertfordshire to her ailing brother's bedside, or so she thought. Northumberland had not sent word to Mary that King Edward was dead, merely that her brother was gravely ill. His sons would catch Mary on the road and arrest her and all her party of strong supporters. With them imprisoned, there would be no opposition to mar the coronation of Lady Jane and the naming of his son Dudley as king. Once Dudley was crowned king, the willful Queen Jane could be controlled easily enough.

But even as Northumberland savored his victory, an officer in the palace guard who was loyal to Mary clattered into her goldsmith's tiny shop in Hoddesdon and breathlessly revealed the plans he had overheard. Minutes later, the goldsmith was galloping hard, cloak billowing out behind him, to warn Mary of what had happened.

"Majesty!" he gasped out, reining in hard before the startled princess and her party, blocking their way. "Stop! You must turn back!" Trotting closer, he leaned over to speak low to the princess. Out of breath from his urgent ride, his news came in staccato bursts. "Majesty. Sad news to impart. Must in haste. Our sovereign king. Your brother. Dead, God rest his soul." He hastily made the sign of the cross, and Mary's courtiers, murmuring in stunned shock, quickly followed suit. "Duke of Northumberland sends riders," he panted. "Now! He'll arrest you. All. Place Lady Jane Grey and Guilford Dudley on the throne."

At that, Mary's eyes widened in fright, and she went deathly pale. Murmuring in outrage, her courtiers drew their swords threateningly. The goldsmith had at last retrieved his breath. "'Tis so, Your Grace, I swear to't! They did coerce His Majesty your brother to write so afore he died." Mary's shock was evident, but there was not time to waste on grief, nor to allow the impact of such news to sink in. "Ride hard away," the goldsmith implored them, "for Your Highness's life is in grave danger! Even now Northumberland's men ride this road to arrest you! Away, at once!" A gasp escaped Mary's tight lips, but her rigid training quickly took over. She had been witness almost from birth to crises in which her very life was pawn. "Well done," she said to the goldsmith. "You have served us, and will be well rewarded." Wasting no more time, she wheeled her mount, and they fled at full gallop for Newmarket and the coast.[1]

In London, Northumberland paced the cool stone halls of the Tower, anxious for the news that Mary was in custody and no longer a threat. He did not know that his prey had already eluded him. Worse, the Catholics were hard at work, and the people of England had begun flocking to Catherine of Aragon's daughter in fealty, for they hated Northumberland and his son Dudley and were not fully convinced that the new religion Henry and his son had foisted upon them was indeed the true faith.

119

Northumberland and Dudley also had their hands full trying to control Queen Jane. Northumberland was headed for a meeting with her to make their plans for a speedy coronation of the couple. He knew he must quickly solidify Jane and Dudley as England's new king and queen in the minds of the people. But Jane wasn't cooperating, and Northumberland was fast losing patience with her. "No, Guilford Dudley, you shall not be king," Jane declared vehemently, her disdain for her husband clear in her tone. "What! You would deny your husband his place at your side?" Northumberland could not believe what he had just heard. Dudley's jaw, too, dropped in astonishment. Jane smiled thinly at her father-in-law. "Nay, by my side he shall be, Milord, though as duke, and not king. Never king." Dudley stepped forward, ready to beat his wife into submission, as her father had done. It was a task he would relish. But Northumberland stopped him. "Milady queen knows not her mind yet," he said with silky conciliation. "She will think better of this when she has rested."

But none of their threats, recriminations, or demands could budge the stubborn Jane. "I shall never, unless Parliament orders it, make Guilford Dudley king." She knew she was on safe ground there, for Parliament had no love for Northumberland or his wastrel son. "Then my son shall no longer sleep in this castle," cried the duchess of Northumberland. "He shall not keep the bed of such an undutiful wife."

"Nay, madam." Queen Jane spoke with regal authority for the first time. "Your son shall remain in this place, for that is as I will it. I protest not your wish to have him sleep away from me, for I have neither need nor want of him in my bed. But before my subjects my lawful husband shall appear by my side, and so I command it." The duchess, sputtering furiously, could do nothing except curtsey and take her leave of the queen. Northumberland's hands itched with the urge to strangle his young daughter-in-law.

Later that day, when the duchess attempted to leave the castle, taking her son with her, the palace guards allowed the duchess through, then swiftly crossed their halberds in front of Dudley, barring his exit, "on order of the queen." Jane had won the first round.[2]

Meanwhile, the messenger bearing the tragic news of King Edward's death and Lady Jane Grey's accession had arrived in Antwerp. Thomas grieved deeply for the young king who had treated him so kindly and trusted in him so well. At the same time, he knew that he was in grave danger. He knew that his fate now hung in the balance along with Northumberland's, for he wasn't sure the people would accept Lady Jane and Northumberland's son. Word had come to him via his spies of the forces flocking to Mary's cause. And Mary was fiercely a Catholic, determined to revenge her mother.

Northumberland's life, and most certainly his own as well, depended upon the people of England accepting Jane Grey as their rightful queen. Thomas was also well aware of the capricious nature of the English and their rulers, so it was by no means a foregone conclusion that Edward's will and act would be upheld.

The hapless Queen Jane's reign lasted only nine days. The nobility, the gentry, and the people, angry and distrustful of Northumberland's motives, shifted their allegiance to the support of the daughter of Henry's first queen, Catherine of Aragon. In early July, Mary came out of hiding with an army at her back. Northumberland, designated by the fearful council to head the opposition army, rode out with his sons and his troops to vanquish Mary and her troops. To his dismay his own forces rapidly deserted him and went over to Mary's side. Even the general populace was sullenly resistant to his entreaties in behalf of their dead king, and he could garner no support among them. Within days, Northumberland was forced to surrender to Mary. On 19 July 1553, the thirty-seven-year-old daughter of Henry VIII and Catherine of Aragon, entering London in triumph, was proclaimed queen of England. Queen Jane, Guilford Dudley, Northumberland, Suffolk, and Archbishop Thomas Cranmer were immediately arrested, thrown into the Tower prison, and sentenced to death.[3]

"We must prepare for the worst," Thomas told his wife, as he paced up and down before her in her sitting room. The terrible news of Northumberland's fall from power had just reached him by official dispatch. "They have arrested Queen Jane and Northumberland and condemned them to death. 'Tis well known Northumberland was my patron and benefactor and that it was largely by his hand I came to this position. 'Tis known I am of the Protestant sympathy. I expect the queen will order my own arrest betimes. Perhaps 'twill mean the death sentence for me, too. If not, then imprisonment in the Tower, or worse." Anne, wide-eyed with fright, cried out helplessly, "Oh, husband! Can't you plead with milady queen? You have done nothing against England save serve your king, her own brother! Why would Her Grace wish you harmed?"

"A man is judged by his associations, and I have long corresponded with Cecil and His Grace Northumberland, may God have mercy on him! 'Twill be difficult to prove I knew naught of his plot to seize the throne." Thomas fell silent, thinking of the fate his patron and benefactor would soon meet. Perhaps soon his own fate, too, for all he knew. He wondered about Cecil. He had heard no word of Cecil's arrest, or of his friend's being barred from royal service by the new queen. He hoped that Cecil would not meet Northumberland's terrible fate.

Briefly, Thomas contemplated taking flight with his family—exile in Italy or Germany, where he was sure the Fuggers would offer him assistance. But he quickly abandoned that. He couldn't live as a fugitive—it went against every fiber of his being. If he turned tail and fled, it would be a certainty that a death sentence would be passed upon his head, and all his lands and properties would be forfeit. He couldn't condemn his wife and children to such a fate. He wasn't sure he could protect them from it, either, but he had to chance it. He must stay put and await a move from Mary and her envoys.

Leaving his distraught wife, he went to his friend Jasper Schetz. There, he outlined what he wanted Schetz to do in the event he was arrested. He placed enough funds in Schetz's safekeeping to maintain his family in comfort in Flanders, should he not return. He doubted that Mary would reach so far as to arrest his wife and children. They were no threat to the crown and knew nothing of the realm's affairs. That done, he settled in to wait for word or a messenger from London.

It was not long in coming. Queen Mary promptly released the Tower's two most celebrated prisoners—the Catholic duke of Norfolk and Bishop Gardiner of Winchester. As they knelt before her, Mary wept over them and acclaimed them martyrs for their religion. Gardiner was restored to power and named archbishop of Canterbury, replacing the condemned Cranmer. He immediately opened a campaign to eradicate all their Protestant enemies. Thomas Gresham's name was high on that list.

However, Queen Mary was not interested in exacting revenge. She extended clemency to most of the council members who recanted their Protestant leanings. She reinstated them to their positions when they claimed they had signed her brother's deathbed device under duress. Sir William Cecil, who had been Northumberland's secretary, managed to land on his feet, and remained in the queen's service as an adviser. Like her sister Elizabeth, Mary had a strong respect for Cecil. She welcomed him to her service, calling him "an honest man."[4]

Northumberland, though, was sentenced to death, along with two of his closest henchmen. Surprisingly, the death sentences of Suffolk, Lady Jane Grey, and Guilford Dudley were stayed. They were permitted to live, but remained prisoners in the Tower. Queen Mary realized that Jane Grey had been little more than a victim of her elders. Jane was separated from Guilford Dudley, and given a room in the small apartments of the Tower, where she lived in relative comfort with her maid, some books, and writing materials. Archbishop Cranmer recanted his Protestant beliefs under torture, and also escaped death.

Thomas Gresham was summarily dismissed from his position as royal agent, but nothing more happened. Quietly, he returned to his private business interests in Antwerp. Queen Mary was concerned more with returning Catholicism to England and organizing her government than with persecuting civil servants like the Greshams.

However, Thomas knew that Gardiner was of another mind. The bishop detested everything that men like Thomas Gresham represented. Thomas knew that Bishop Gardiner was bent on destroying him, and other wealthy merchants like him, and Gardiner had Paulet, the powerful marquess of Winchester, in his corner. It was only a matter of time.

At first, the queen and her council attempted to deal directly with the Fuggers on matters financial, but soon they had to rely on Thomas's inept predecessor Dansell to help them. They appointed another agent, Sir Christopher Dauntsey, to help Dansell in Flanders.

Anticipating being ordered home, Thomas packed up all his belongings and put them on a ship for England, consigned to John Eliot, who had been instructed to prepare the house on Lombard Street for its owners' return. He reinstalled his family in the apartments at Jasper Schetz's home. He was certain he'd be summoned to England any minute to face trial, and he wanted his family to remain in Flanders, under the protection of Jasper Schetz. His mood was as foul as the weather in Antwerp.

The next day, his grave-faced factor, Richard Clough, came to him. "I'm afraid I've terrible news, master Gresham," he said. The ship carrying the Gresham's household possessions—all the lovely things they had amassed in Antwerp—had gone down in the storm off Flanders, taking nearly everything they owned with it. Devastated, Anne wept for days. "'Tis an evil omen. All we own, even our lives, will be forfeit!"

Thomas was sunk in gloom. His life and fortunes were at their lowest ebb. Perhaps he should chance sending a letter to the council before he was ordered back to England. He was certain that the council members held him, and his financial abilities, in high esteem. Perchance they'd bring his letter to Mary's attention. The queen might then take pity on him, forgive him, and allow him to resume his private trade in peace. It was worth a try. He had nothing more to lose.

As Thomas was laboring over his letter to the council, someone who had been long away arrived at court in England. It was a man Thomas knew well, a man high in Queen Mary's favor. Sir John Leigh was a Catholic knight whom Mary had known since childhood. He held her complete confidence and was accorded immediate access to her upon his return to England. Sir John had spent the last few years in voluntary exile in Italy and France, traveling frequently through Antwerp, where he had become close friends with young Thomas Gresham.

In his youth, Sir John had served as a squire in the household of Cardinal Wolsey, and during that period had become good friends with Sir Richard Gresham and Lady Isabella.

Reinstalled at court, John Leigh quickly became privy to the meetings of the new queen's council. There he doubtless heard Gardiner's strident demands that Thomas Gresham be arrested and condemned for treason because of his close association with Northumberland. Sir John Leigh's ears perked up at that mention of Gresham's name. He had taken rather a paternal interest in the young merchant during his visits to Antwerp and had great admiration for his business acumen. Sir John, whose own large fortune and high connections were ample, told the council that "'twould be a pity to waste such talent, which, I trust, has never been used to the crown's disadvantage."

However, Gardiner would not be deterred in his pursuit of Gresham's head. Sir John Leigh realized that Gardiner's dislike of Gresham was a deep and personal one, and that it would be difficult to turn him from exacting his revenge on Sir Richard's son. Sir John decided upon another tack. As quietly as he could, he intervened with Mary herself in Thomas Gresham's favor. The queen deeply respected Leigh and almost always followed his advice. She agreed to spare the merchant's life, on his recommendation, though she could not, she cautioned, countenance a Protestant to serve as her official royal agent abroad.[5]

Sir John dared not dispute her on that. "In truth, Your Grace has reason. But I would advise you, Your Grace, to keep your counsel on this and maintain the gentleman's confidence, for Thomas Gresham is wise in money matters and has great power and respect with the bankers in Flanders. Your Grace might have need of his abilities one day." Mary listened carefully to Leigh. After the costly struggle to retrieve her crown, the financial status of her realm was now one of the most pressing problems with which she was faced, and she conferred almost daily with Cecil and the council about it.

The French ambassador to Mary's court wrote to the French king, "The communications of Sir John Leigh must be of greater value than any which others can furnish, from his opportunities of access to Mary, with whom he is most familiar." While Leigh was negotiating with the queen in his young friend's favor, Thomas's long letter, detailing his service to the crown and his personal sacrifices in that pursuit, was delivered to the council. It arrived at court on the very day that Northumberland mounted the scaffold at the Tower and paid with his life for his lust for power.

In opening his long pleading to the council, Thomas reiterated the circumstances which had brought him to serve King Edward as royal agent. He reminded them of how great the king's debt had been then—£260,000 Flemish—and how high the rate of interest on the debt had become, amounting to £40,000 a year.[6] And, he reminded them, "before I came to serve, there was no other way devised to bring the king out of debt but to transport the treasure out of the realm, or else, by way of exchange, by great abasing of the exchange." He reminded them that he had succeeded in eliminating the practice of paying with the purchase of jewels or merchandise to renew a loan.

> When I came to office, I found the means, without charge to the king or hindrance of any other, to discharge the king's entire debts, as they grew due, at better than twenty shillings to the pound, whereby the King's Majesty—and now the queen—has been saved 100,000 marks clear. And because the exchange was raised from 16 to 22 shillings, where it still remains, all foreign commodities fell in value and were sold at the lower value, to the enrichment of the subjects of the realm in their commodities, in a brief period of time, more than 3 or 400,000 pounds.

Also, by raising the exchange rate to the level I did, whereas before the gold and silver were flowing out of the realm because of the drop in exchange value, now they are flowing into our coffers again by the raising of the exchange rate. For there has come lately more than £100,000 into the realm, and more every day. When I took this office, the King's Majesty's credit overseas was limited, and before his death his credit was so good with both the foreign bankers and his own merchants that he could have any sum of money he desired. Whereby his enemies began to fear him, for the commodities of his realm and his power among princes was not known before. Which credit the Queen's Highness can still obtain, if she is in need of money on this present day.

Also, in order to work the matter of the raising of the exchange in secrecy, I used my personal credit with my own assets and friends, to prevent foreign and English merchants from thwarting my purposes, so that when the exchange fell, to raise it again I bore a risk of my own monies of (as the King's Majesty and his council well knew) £200,000 or £300,000! And this was done many times over. Besides that there was the credit of £55,000, which I took by exchange in my own name, without using the king's name, as in my account and letters that I sent to His Majesty will show. To serve in the capacity of agent, I not only left the realm, with my wife and family, and abandoned my business and trade from which I made my living, and for more than two years, but also made sixty trips back and forth during that time, at the king's sending. I also had, on an infinite number of occasions, to write long documents and accounts to the king and his council, which had to be in my hand only, to avoid mistrust in such a dangerous business, until I had clearly discharged all of the aforesaid debt and delivered all the bonds clear, to the great benefit of the realm, and to the profit of the queen. For had the debt been left as it was growing, and deferred at interest another three to five years, Her Majesty would have found herself in debt of £1,500,000 at the least. Which (God be praised!) is not the case, and therefore she has not care of such debts on this day.[7]

Thomas then related to the council his final interview with King Edward, the lands with which Edward had endowed him, and the promises of future rewards the king had made, in gratitude for how well Thomas had served him.

> Finally, if upon consideration of all I have listed here of my service (which is all true), you find this meet to be shown to the queen, and it shall be Her Grace's pleasure to accept them (also that I may have access to Her Highness thereby), I will continue to do Her Grace as good and profitable service, for her and for her realm, as the service I rendered to her brother was. Nonetheless, I see that those who served before me, who brought the king into debt and took wares and jewels to the king's great loss, are esteemed and preferred for their evil service, whereas I myself am discountenanced and out of favor. It grieves me greatly that my diligence and good service to bring the King and Queen's Highness out of debt clear are so little valued. I ask only that Her Majesty take part in the understanding of the service I have rendered, which is all I require.

Gresham concluded the letter by describing the loss of his ship and his family's possessions in the disaster at sea. "And now, God help poor Gresham!" he wrote dramatically in closing, a man in despair not only of his fortunes, but of his life and future.

Gresham was summoned home to England in September. The order seemed ominous to Thomas when he received it, and it was with great trepidation that he made ready to sail home to England, leaving his family behind under the protection of the Schetz brothers in Antwerp.

However, when he arrived back in England in late September, nothing happened. Cecil told him his letter had been received at court, but no action had been taken on it as yet. He assured Thomas that he himself had spoken favorably of him to the queen, as had others in strong positions. Thomas thanked him and quietly took up residence once again in Lombard Street, at the sign of the golden grasshopper. He then sent a formal message to Her Majesty and the council informing them that he had arrived and that he awaited their pleasure.

For the next two months, Thomas spent his days with John Eliot, handling his business and personal affairs, and was soon fully occupied with managing his private trade. The days flew by. He sent encouraging messages to Anne in Antwerp, reassuring her and asking after the children. In late October, he sent word that she should begin preparations to return to England. The storm that accompanied Mary's succession seemed to have passed him by, thanks be to God.

Eventually, he learned from Cecil all that had happened while he was yet in Antwerp. He paled at how close he had come to being arrested and executed. He also learned that it was Sir John Leigh who was his benefactor at court, and who had personally intervened with the queen in his behalf.

Thomas breathed a prayer of thanks for that good man. Nevertheless, Cecil cautioned, Gardiner remained extremely powerful at court, and Paulet had been named lord high treasurer. Thomas had two very powerful enemies now, and he was on a tightrope. At this moment he owed his very life to Sir John Leigh. However, as long as Gardiner and Paulet lived, the balance could be tipped at any time. Thomas decided that his most prudent move would be to stay as far away from any contact with the court as he could, tending quietly to his own affairs. He'd attract as little notice as possible. Let Dansell and Dauntsey worry about the queen's finances.

But around the first of November, the summons Thomas feared most arrived by court messenger. As he broke the royal seal and read the message, fear and dread snaked through him and congealed in his innards. He was ordered "to present himself immediately before Her Majesty's council."

Thomas dressed carefully, wearing his usual black with almost no adornment, and mentally rehearsed again and again what his responses would be if they charged him with treason. Often a man's life hung on the first words he spoke after being so charged. He set out for court with his mind in a whirl.

Thomas need not have worried. The last thing on the minds of the council and Queen Mary was that he should come to harm, or be charged with treason. Dauntsey and Dansell had made a mess of things in Antwerp, and the queen was in dire financial straits. The interest rate on her loans abroad had soared as soon as Thomas Gresham left his post, and Dansell and Dauntsey were unable to accomplish the slightest improvement. After only a few months, the queen found herself on the verge of bankruptcy.

Desperate, she had ordered the council to send for Gresham. "He shall serve us as he served our brother before us."

"What? A Protestant usurer serve the crown? Never!" cried Gardiner. Mary turned on him. "Silence!" He subsided.

"I understand the archbishop's feelings," said the queen more gently, in an attempt to placate him, "but Thomas Gresham's past religious leanings are of no consequence in matters this serious. Our realm is at the brink of fiscal disaster! Gresham's loyalty to us is without question, as this his letter, and his actions, have shown." She waved Thomas's letter at Gardiner and Paulet. Cecil hid a smile. "This man," she reminded them, "has not fled, but has returned to us, sending word to us that he be ever ready to serve us, and only awaits our pleasure. Is that not proof of his devotion to us?"

Paulet and Gardiner could think of no ready charge that would turn Mary from her decision. "In truth," she continued, fixing them with a stern look, "Sir John Leigh has given us advice far better than yours! He advised us to spare Gresham and keep his confidence, while you cost us dearly with your choice of agents."

With that, Paulet and Gardiner became aware of the identity of Thomas Gresham's powerful ally, and knew they could not oppose anyone as close to the queen as Sir John Leigh. They also knew what a disaster Dauntsey and Dansell had proved to be, and

that misfortune fell squarely on their heads, for they had personally advanced those two to the queen. They counted themselves
lucky the queen did not order them punished because of it. Very
well, let this Gresham get them out of trouble with the queen.
There was always time. They'd make him pay, eventually.

Thus, scarcely four months after Mary was proclaimed queen,
Thomas Gresham was once again named to the post of the crown's
royal agent in Antwerp. The situation was so precarious Mary
ordered him to repair "in post haste" to that city. He arrived there,
to be reunited with his wife and children, on 6 November.

A few days later he sent a letter to the privy council, outlining
the situation as he found it. Not wishing to raise Gardiner's hackles, he dealt lightly with Dansell's errors, saying "he has not before
had handling of such weighty affairs, and in this, for my part, I
judge he has done his best."

But however lightly and prudently he endeavored to excuse it,
Thomas found to his utter dismay that Dansell and Dauntsey had
managed in that brief period to botch everything Thomas had spent
years building. Through failure to negotiate properly the queen's
bonds, their bargains were costing England thousands of pounds
more in interest every month than Mary should have been liable
to pay. Thomas, inwardly appalled, endeavored to reassure the
queen and council as best he could. His main worry, he said, was
that "this matter has been very openly handled, and marvelously
indiscreetly. The Queen's Majesty and Your Honors cannot hope
to procure money for less than 13 or 14 percent now, and the word
of that is all over the city." However, he advised them, "if Your
Honors will forbear borrowing for a month or two, I do not doubt
but that I can bring what you wish to pass according to your heart's
desire, and to accomplish all my plans accordingly."[8]

Anne Gresham was furious that her husband had accepted the
queen's commission to serve as royal agent in Antwerp again. "You
allow them to treat you so!" she stormed at him. "We have lost all
once. Is that not enough? Now we are obliged to risk all again!"
Deep down, she knew she should be grateful that her husband's
life had been spared. She knew he had been in grave danger, and

she was truly fond of him, and glad he had been spared. She also realized he had no choice but to accept the queen's command. Still, in her frustration at being consigned to Antwerp yet again, she berated him. She could not bear the thought that she had been so close to returning to England! Now that hope was dashed, and for how long heaven only knew. She railed at Thomas morning and night, but he proved impervious to her anger. He had more weighty affairs on his mind than a wife's complaints.

He departed early for and returned late from the bourse, where more than five thousand traders from all the European nations now met and exchanged bills. Seldom were there fewer than five hundred ships docked or riding at anchor in Antwerp's harbor.[9] Flanders, and all Europe, were booming markets for trade, and Gresham's mind and time were taken up with rates of exchange and levels of trade. His meetings and negotiations with bankers like Lazarus Tucker and the Fuggers went on far into the night.

Anne, thoroughly vexed, took her fury out on everyone around her. She boxed young Richard smartly about the ears, for he was growing to be much like his father. She criticized and threatened the tutor, the governess, the servants. She coldly snubbed Mrs. Schetz. Her only consolation was the presence of the baby Anne, who was just beginning to creep about and stand. She was an adorable child, dimpled and sweet-natured, and Anne doted on her, though her mind darkened whenever she dwelled on her husband's affair with Anne's true mother; at those times a deep depression came over her, leaving her sad and listless.

Thomas, meanwhile, was having his own vexation with Lazarus Tucker, a man he had never liked or trusted. When Thomas Gresham was dismissed by the queen as agent, the wily Tucker had quickly seized his chance to profit from it. Gresham had known the bourse down to the last farthing and had watched and controlled the exchange like a hawk. His personal power and influence was so strong in Antwerp, especially with the Schetz brothers behind him, that no one dared attempt to take advantage of him in a deal. He was as careful of the crown's money as he was of his own—perhaps even more so, since he had often procured loans for King Edward by using his own fortune and his personal guarantee to back the transaction. None of the moneylenders cared to try to cheat him. His business was too valuable to them, as was his strong influence with the Merchant Adventurers. Nor did they dare offer him bribes or personal gains to milk a bit more from their deals with the English crown. No, they had great respect for Thomas Gresham, and he commanded their immediate attention and their best terms.

Dansell and Dauntsey, however, had been a different story. They had pushed Dansell around before. Dauntsey was a mere babe in the woods where financial matters of such magnitude were concerned. Lazarus Tucker had been the first to see an advantage and moved quickly to exploit it. He had borrowed vast sums himself, on his own good credit, at 10 percent, then loaned the same monies to the queen of England's new agents at 13 percent. The others, when they saw that Dauntsey had not the brazen fortitude, nor the personal power, to stand up to Tucker as Gresham had, soon followed his lead, for Tucker had a big mouth, bragging all over Antwerp about the advantageous deals he had struck with the English queen's new agents.

It was with trepidation and dismay that Lazarus Tucker greeted the return of Thomas Gresham to Antwerp. He, as the others, thought Thomas had been sent back home to disgrace, possibly execution. Now, to see him back as before meant their newfound advantages would be lost. Despite Thomas's demands, then threats, Tucker remained adamant that the high interest loans already made to the English queen would remain in force, and Thomas found he could do little to change what was past. "But I warn you, Lazarus," said Thomas, fixing the banker with a look that Tucker could not possibly misinterpret and that sent a chill along the moneylender's bones, "that you'll guard your tongue from this day forward when speaking of my most gracious Queen's Majesty, and treat her right in her needs, for you have me and mine to answer to now, not Dansell and Dauntsey."

Thomas's initial instructions from Mary and the council that November were to borrow £50,000 for a year, at the rate of 11 or

12 percent, under the queen's bond. He was further instructed to ship, in the greatest secrecy, in gold or silver coin all sums he borrowed or any surplus gained by the exchange rate. He could send up to £1000 by ship to London or Ipswich, or up to £3000 over land to Calais, which the English still held. As agent, he would be paid the usual salary of 20 shillings (approximately £1) a day, and Mary promised that he'd be reimbursed by the crown for all expenses such as messengers, letters, and the shipment of treasure.[10]

The shipping of gold out of Antwerp, as out of most countries, was forbidden by law of Emperor Charles and the regent, so was undertaken only at great personal and national risk. The customs house officers were strict in their scrutiny of all shipments leaving Antwerp. The danger of trying to smuggle gold out as the queen and council had ordered him to do presented Thomas with a stimulating challenge, which always got the adrenaline surging through his veins. He loved being confronted with a seemingly insurmountable problem and liked nothing more than the intricacies of solving it. How to smuggle the gold out of Antwerp and across to England interested him more as a logistical puzzle to be solved than as a legal question for his conscience to weigh. He was, after all, obeying direct orders from the queen and council.

At first he proposed sending the gold and silver out concealed in bags of pepper from the Spice Islands. Also, he decided, he'd try to send £20,000 or £30,000 worth at a time with Sir John Mason, the queen's ambassador to the court at Brussels, whenever he traveled back to London to confer with the queen. An ambassador's baggage, by long tradition, passed without customs examination. The council agreed to those methods, but then Thomas decided against the pepper shipments. "It would require purchase of too much pepper, for one thing, and would increase the weight of the bags too much, which would arouse suspicion. Therefore, my mind is now altered, and I would like a commission to buy arms—a thousand demilances harness, which will not only serve my purpose better, but will be of more advantage to our realm. The queen's stuff shall be packed in harness, in great dray vats, but I also require permission to ship larger amounts. I request to put in every dray vat £3000 and to put on every wagon I send three vats (£9000), in order to save costs on hiring of wagons and men. It will of course be done as you wish, but to encourage Your Honors, I did convey the value of £100,000 this way in my own name in one year and was never touched."[11]

Meanwhile, Anne's dissatisfaction was having a deleterious effect on his domestic life. In an attempt to appease her, he wrote the queen in early December, requesting permission to take a brief leave over Christmas to return with his family to London, "for there is nothing to be done at Antwerp during the holidays, nor for the ten days following." Mary gladly gave her permission, but then diplomatic matters became so pressing between the queen and the emperor, Charles V, that she was unable to spare Thomas, and, to Anne's chagrin, they remained in Antwerp until early March.

Queen Mary, anxious to secure the Catholic succession, was negotiating marriage. Though she was personally disinclined to marry, she knew that at her age she would have to do it, and quickly produce an heir, if there were to be any hope of preventing her Protestant half-sister Elizabeth from succeeding her, and returning Protestantism to England. Mary finally agreed to Ambassador Renard's suggestion that she marry Philip of Spain, son and heir to the Holy Roman Emperor, Charles V, her own distant cousin. Philip was eleven years her junior, but the marriage would form an alliance between England and powerful Spain, her mother's country, and would put England in alliance with the powerful Catholic emperor. Mary was not aware that her father, Henry VIII, had once offered her as a bride to Charles himself.

Charles V, seeing the match as a great opportunity, agreed with alacrity and gave his assistance in every way to equip Mary for war. With England's help and her added treasury that would fall under his son Philip's direction as king of England, the emperor might soon have France and Scotland under his thumb, too. Charles was delighted to grant Thomas Gresham's requested official license "to export gunpowder, military stores, ropes, and other necessaries"—basically an open passport—into which Thomas slyly packed all the gold he could ship.[12]

Thomas bribed the captain of the Flemish guard at Gravelines and sent him, and all the Flemish customs officials, bolts of fine cloth for New Year gifts in 1554. He notified the British ambassador John Mason of what he had done. "Milord, because of this small gift, at all times of night the gates of the town will be open to my servants when they come to you with treasure." Thus more and more gold was sent to Mason by Gresham, and spirited out to England by the ambassador.

The system of bribing officials with gifts and banquets was commonplace in all European governments, and Gresham was quick to use it to the queen's full advantage to accomplish more easily his assigned mission. It is doubtful that his conscience was much bothered by the illegal means he was forced to pursue under orders from Mary and the council. Such chicanery was normal, and far more drinking, gambling, and bribery went on among the representatives of other governments and nations than Thomas attempted for England's benefit.

Thomas himself drank little and refused to accept bribes in the conduct of his affairs for the crown, so there was little the moneylenders could do with him and nothing they could grasp to hold over his head. He entertained lavishly and sent gifts of rare goods to the crown's creditors. Happily, except for those few still stubbornly held by Tucker, the interest rates on the queen's loans came down almost as soon as Thomas Gresham resumed his position as her royal agent in Flanders.

In March 1554, with Mary's affairs in the Low Countries proceeding well and her marriage contract with Philip of Spain ensured, Thomas escorted Anne and the children back to England for a visit. High winds pitched and pounded their little ship all the way, and Anne and little Anne were wretchedly seasick. Once she set foot on English soil again, Anne turned to Thomas and declared with finality, "I am home at last, and marry, I shall never leave England again!" For Thomas, such thoughts and declarations seemed little more than idle dreaming—but Anne meant every word of what she said.

Thomas had no sooner deposited his family at Lombard Street

than a royal messenger galloped up. He broke the impressive seal and read the royal summons. Minutes later, he was himself riding hard to present himself before the queen. Mary looked the best he had ever seen her. In fact, she seemed positively radiant. He murmured his sincere compliments. The queen blushed, pleased, and smiled at him. "You have done well for us," she complimented him in return, "and we are pleased with your services. Now, it is our wish and command that you return to Antwerp as quickly as you can." Thomas, startled, looked up at her in dismay. "There, you will receive our special orders from the emperor. Then you will proceed on a mission to Spain. It is our express wish that you arrange to arrive in Spain in time to talk privately with Prince Philip and carry out our orders and desires, which you will learn from his hand. You must meet with him before he departs there to come hither to England for our wedding."

Thomas hesitated, then bowed deeply and dared speak. "Yes, Your Majesty, it shall be done as you desire. However, Majesty, I humbly beg a small leave first—that I may settle my family here again ere I depart from them on such a long mission away." The queen reluctantly gave her permission for him to remain two months in England before departing.

Mary's attention was at that moment fully occupied elsewhere, for the Protestants, at the prospect of her marriage to a foreign Catholic prince—a detested Spaniard at that—had developed a plot, hatched by Suffolk and some of Northumberland's former supporters, to overthrow Mary and put her sister Elizabeth on the throne. Several Protestant revolts broke out simultaneously in different parts of the kingdom, but only the uprising in Kent, led by Thomas Wyatt, generated enough steam to be a threat. Troops rode out, and Wyatt and his followers were quickly surrounded and subdued. Mary realized she'd had a very narrow escape.

This time, she exacted revenge. Wyatt, Suffolk, Guilford Dudley, and the other leaders of the rebellion were promptly beheaded. Princess Elizabeth, too, was arrested and thrown in the Tower, consigned to the same apartments in which her mother, Queen Anne Boleyn, had spent her final days. Daily, the beleaguered young princess walked along the same forbidding parapets her mother had, to exercise and take the air. From high on the ramparts, she looked out over the river Thames, and then along the other side, the City of London. Only twenty-two, she wondered if she'd live, or if she'd be doomed to her mother's fate—to end her life here, in disgrace—a sacrificial lamb of the Protestant cause, falling helplessly beneath the headsman's ax.

But despite their most vigorous efforts, the Catholic faction could not produce proof for Mary that her half-sister had been directly involved in the rebellions, or had in any way encouraged them. Gardiner and Paulet urged the queen to execute Elizabeth anyway, and eliminate the threat to future succession, but Mary could not bring herself to sign a death warrant for her own sister. Elizabeth, through rigid self-discipline, had managed to keep a cool head throughout her terrible ordeal, as hundreds around her were sacrificed. She had maintained her innocence, and her silence.

Eventually, Mary ordered her half-sister released, for she had no substantial proof that Elizabeth was implicated in any plot against the queen. Gardiner and Paulet, furious, continued searching for other ways to implicate the Protestant princess, so they could rid themselves of her.

Meanwhile, they had been steadily lobbying to eliminate another innocent—the erstwhile Protestant queen Jane Grey. When news of Wyatt's rebellion reached Antwerp, there was panic on the exchange, threatening the queen's newly won credit. The emperor, outraged, declared that his son and heir Philip, Mary's intended husband, would not be permitted to come to England unless all danger of Protestant revolt had been removed. Jane Grey was the symbol of the heart of Protestantism in England. Though she had lived quietly in her rooms at the Tower, and was completely innocent of any complicity in the uprisings or the Wyatt rebellion, Gardiner, Paulet, and the council convinced the queen that as long as Jane lived, the Protestant uprisings would continue. Elizabeth might be spared, they told her, but Jane must go. This time, Gardiner and Paulet prevailed.

With Queen Mary's reluctant consent, her seventeen-year-old

cousin's death sentence was reinstated, and quickly carried out. Jane Grey, instead of Elizabeth, walked the short and narrow traitor's path to the execution block in the inside courtyard—Tower Green—where she was beheaded. Like the two young Tudor queens before her—Anne Boleyn and Catherine Howard—Jane Grey's headless body was thrown without ceremony into an unmarked, shallow grave in the courtyard. It was the ultimate disgrace in death.

It was late in April when Thomas set out again for Antwerp. He bore with him very secret despatches to the emperor from Renard, the emperor's ambassador to the English court. That Charles and Mary together were conniving was evident in the letters Gresham carried, one of which, from Mary, begged the emperor to give Gresham another passport for exporting military supplies from Antwerp to England. Renard had endorsed Mary's urgent request, saying, "I could not refuse her, for reasons well known to Your Majesty."

Ten days later, Thomas left Antwerp aboard a merchant ship bound for Spain. He was well armed, for he carried on him bills of exchange for 320,000 ducats he had borrowed from the Fuggers, Schetz, and various other merchant bankers in Antwerp, payable at various trade fairs in Spain.[13] To buy, sell, and loan via bills of exchange was the most convenient and common way for merchants and bankers to handle the international transfer and exchange of money for their goods.[14] Once in Spain, Thomas was to convert the bills of exchange to gold at the various fairs where merchants showed and sold their wares, and through playing the exchange and shrewd borrowing and bargaining, he hoped he could add enough to make up 500,000 ducats in gold.

Spain was richer in gold than any other country, for gold was flowing into Spanish coffers from its conquests in the New World. Thomas was instructed to ship the treasure from Spain to England aboard the fleet of ships taking Prince Philip to his wedding. He was to risk no more than £5000 on any one ship.[15]

"Prince Philip? But, sir, he is not here—he has already sailed for England and his wedding," he was informed when he presented himself at the palace. "What? But he was not to leave for another week!" Thomas could not believe his ill luck. "The winds were favorable, and my son wished to hasten to his bride," said the emperor's wife, receiving Thomas graciously. "We are sorry you missed him, but we extend you our hospitality on his behalf, and urge you to enjoy your visit to our fair country."

Frustrated and upset, Thomas was left with the task of procuring a fortune in gold and silver at the Spanish fairs, with no way adroitly to remove it from Spain. He made the exchange of the bills to gold and managed the exchange well enough to gain the additional monies, though not without some difficulty. He had been unable to convince the preoccupied Queen Mary and the council first to get a passport from Charles V for him to remove that much gold out of Spain. They were busy with the aftermath of the rebellion and were sure the emperor would hardly object if the gold went out with his own son to his marriage.

Having missed the prince, Gresham's lack of a passport for the gold presented a thorny problem. He could not legally remove the gold from Spain, and it was far too risky to smuggle it out. Getting the necessary permissions would take months, leaving him stranded in Spain the whole time—a place he had no desire to be. Thomas fumed and plotted, but no easy solution presented itself. Finally, in desperation, he requested an audience with the emperor's wife, the Spanish queen. She listened kindly to the representative of her son's bride-to-be, then told him to put his request in writing and she would forward it to the emperor, via her own ambassador. The ambassador, she informed him, was not due to arrive at the Spanish court from Flanders for another week, at least.

Privately, the Spanish queen was hardly pleased at Thomas Gresham's request. She, like other rulers in Europe, was loath to see so much treasure leave her country, even for her son's new territory. Exportation of so large an amount of gold would undoubtedly place a serious strain on the Spanish treasury. In fact, the Bank of Seville, on learning the gold was to leave Spain, balked at paying it out. However, with the marriage of her son Philip and the

English queen looming, the queen dared not deny Thomas's request without consulting her husband, who was then in Brussels.

Thomas had no choice but to cool his heels and await the ambassador's return. Annoyed, he wrote sharply to the council, "I do give my attendance and shall then follow with him to Brussels, 'til I have obtained the emperor's passport. For without His Majesty's license, there will be no gold nor silver suffered to be carried out of Spain, which should have been taken care of first, as I advised Your Honors in the beginning of this matter."[16]

After a long, wearying journey, over rough seas, from Spain to Flanders, Thomas was able, with the ambassador's help, quickly to obtain the emperor's passport. Taking a fast post horse to Calais, he proceeded by ship to England for the required signature of the English queen on the passport, snatched two brief days with his family while waiting for Mary to sign and return the passport to him, and in June 1554 was once again on the high seas, bound for Spain.

He reached Spanish soil again at about the same time in July that Queen Mary of England and Prince Philip of Spain were married in London.

It was a marriage that the people of England both feared and detested. Charles V had little of England's interest at heart when he contracted the marriage to her Catholic queen. Soon after the wedding festivities, England became little more than a vassal state to Spain and the Holy Roman Emperor.

Through his careful attention to his duties as royal agent, and the advantages he procured for her, Thomas Gresham had earned Queen Mary's complete personal trust. She not only treated him with great friendship, but wrote him personally to ask his advice on certain matters or to give him instructions. Her ministers, on the other hand, treated him with cool formality, and Paulet and Gardiner never ceased in their efforts to have him discredited.

For his part, Thomas was always careful, in his replies to Mary, to keep her abreast of such foreign intelligence as he could. Her husband Philip had not been made king, but was only king consort of England. The council had staunchly refused to allow the queen to crown her husband king of England, the ripe plum he and the emperor thought they'd reap from the marriage. Queen Mary was besotted with her young bridegroom from the outset, but rarely had the pleasure of his company.

Deeply religious, having preserved her virginity into late middle age, Mary could hardly have been an appealing bedmate for the lusty young prince, but his effect on her was amazing. She openly doted on him, and tended to follow him, and his advice, blindly.

Now the Protestants found themselves in worse straits than ever. Philip had fully supported the dreadful methods of the Inquisition in Spain, and now he encouraged his new wife relentlessly to persecute and exterminate the Protestants in England. Mary accepted whatever Philip wished, and Philip wished cruelty and death for the nonbelievers. Mary gave free rein to his religious zeal. Great fires were lit, and hundreds of "heretics" were burned at the stake during late 1554 and early 1555, while Thomas was in Spain conducting business for the queen and her new consort. Fortunately, probably due to his favor with the queen and his service to Philip, his own family was untouched.

As women and children, even small babies, were flung mercilessly into the flames, or cast alive into great vats of boiling oil, the people of England became incensed at the excesses, and their hatred for Philip of Spain festered and grew. Although Thomas had never embraced Catholicism, he knew that his life depended on not ever allowing his Protestant leanings to show in public. Even Princess Elizabeth, to guard her life after Jane Grey's execution, prudently made a show of returning to Catholicism.

Thomas returned to Antwerp in the spring of 1555, and soon heard rumors that Queen Mary was pregnant. There was great rejoicing in the Low Countries over the prospect of a Catholic heir to the English throne. Both England and the Continent remained abuzz with the news as Thomas went about his business of procuring loans, paying off bonds, and shipping war supplies back to England. Early in May, news came to Antwerp that Queen Mary had safely been delivered of a prince.

Gresham wrote to the council to describe the celebration in Antwerp that had greeted those tidings: "It may please your most honorable lordships ... that as of the second of this month here came news along the seas by men of this country that the Queen's Majesty was brought abed of a young prince the last of April, and the regent, being in town, did at seven o'clock order the great bell to ring at the cathedral to give all men to understand that the news was true. And on the second day after receiving the news, all the queen's merchants here, according to their bounded duty, caused our English ships to fire their guns with such joy and triumph as could be devised, in the presence of the regent and all her nobles and gentlewomen. Whereupon, the regent gave our mariners one hundred crowns for drinks. Trusting in God that this news be true, for I, nor any other of our nation have had any official notification thereof."[17]

Like everyone in Antwerp, Mary herself had somehow been deluded into thinking she was pregnant, and the court had been duly staffed with "midwives, nurses, physicians, and rockers." But England was to be denied its prince. The queen's "pregnancy," as it turned out, was nothing more than a mirage.

By mid-June of that year, Gresham, traveling back and forth to Antwerp regularly, had submitted to the council nine paid and canceled bonds, to be "sent to the lord treasurer to be laid up in the queen's treasury, and to deliver the City's bonds to the lord mayor." Thomas had often been obliged in Edward's reign, as he now was in Mary's, to secure the seal of the City of London, as well as the queen's own seal, on certain bonds before the money-lenders would release the funds to him. Fortunately, since he, and before him his father and uncle, had kept their friendships and influence with the City officials strong, he was able to secure such bonds from the City without much difficulty.

In August, tired of cooling his heels in England, and convinced his wife was probably either too old or too infirm to conceive, Philip prepared to leave the distraught Mary and sail to the Netherlands. He would attend to the affairs of Charles V, who was in failing health, and take a hand in the war his father was waging. The queen stormed and wept at the prospect of his leaving. Philip, to console her, promised that he would return in six weeks. But Mary was not a foolish girl; she was a woman of great wisdom and sensibility. She read otherwise in her husband's eyes. No sooner had he departed than she flew into a great rage. Sweeping across the room, the ends of her dressing hood flying out behind her, she turned her husband's portrait to the wall, then in a most unroyal act, fell upon her great empty bed and cried her heart out for the husband she adored but could not hold, and the child she would never have.

When at last she arose from her grieving, the Tudor temper was in evidence. Queen Mary's outlet for her frustration and the denial of her dream became the persecution of the Protestants, and she went at it even more fiercely than Philip had. Eventually, it earned her the nickname "Bloody Mary." Thomas Cranmer, her father's archbishop, was one of the many thousands she consigned to the flames as heretics.[18]

Meanwhile, the world trade routes continued to expand. At about that time, Thomas's older brother, Sir John Gresham, arrived back in England from another long expedition to Muscovia (Moscow). He had been away for years, and was appalled at the conditions he encountered in England upon his return.

He and his fellow merchant adventurers cautiously approached the queen to request a charter for the Muscovy Company they had formed in 1553 to explore trade possibilities with Cathay (China), Muscovia, and Russeland. The first expedition had been a disastrous one—they had lost two ships out of three—but the end result had yielded success. Chancellor, leader of the group aboard the third ship, had pushed on to Muscovia, and there had been accorded an audience with Tsar Ivan. He had managed to negotiate some favorable trade concessions between England and the tsar's territories. "This, Your Grace, will give England a great market for woolen cloth and kerseys, and will obtain for our use all the tar, ropes, timber, and other such that our Royal Navy should ever need," Chancellor assured Mary.

The queen was pleased at that news, and granted Chancellor and his friends a trade monopoly for the Muscovy Company. Sir

John Gresham's name was prominent on the list of assistants of the company, and Thomas gladly bought a share in the endeavor, though he ventured not as much capital in it as his brother did. The Muscovy Company was chartered as a joint-stock venture, with the explorer Sebastian Cabot as governor for life. Cabot would be assisted by an advisory court of four consuls and twenty-four assistants.[19] Each share was subscribed at a price of approximately £25, and the £6000 of initial capital raised was used to buy and outfit three new ships, which, when ready, were promptly sent out with goods on the first trading mission to Ivan's court at Muscovia.

In September, Thomas sailed back to England for a brief sojourn with his family. The children greeted him happily, but Anne had grown distant again during his long absences on the queen's business. A Protestant, she was sunk in gloom over the present state of affairs in England, and feared daily for their lives. She blamed everything on Thomas, and barely tolerated his presence at the house on Lombard Street, withdrawing from him with a wintry smile whenever he approached her.

Thomas was delighted to encounter his brother once again, and he spent time visiting with him and his wife, Frances, whose little daughter Elizabeth was a special favorite of his. He'd take little Anne with him whenever he could, for under her mother's dark influence she was becoming much too serious a child.

John Gresham had only the one child, but his sister Christiana and her husband Sir John Thynne had been blessed with several sons. Although he wished he and Anne might have had more, Thomas was grateful for his own two healthy, lively children.

Richard at eleven was a bright young lad, sturdily built, with a thick mop of curly auburn hair and a piercing, clever look in his eyes, which sparkled with the same deep blue as his parents' eyes. Initially, he was shy and fearful of his father, whom he barely knew. Thomas occasionally took Richard along with him to the Gresham warehouses and offices when he went to consult with John Eliot, and there he allowed the boy to watch the loading and unloading of the wagons and drays, with the horses braying and the men shouting. Richard was enthralled by the clank of metal and the jingle of harness, as the men and wagons came and went to the wharfs, bringing goods to and from his father's ships. It was exciting to be there, and difficult to imagine that it would all be his one day.

"So," said Thomas, as they walked along Lad Lane to the Guildhall one day, "You progress well with your studies, I trust?" The boy nodded shyly and mumbled, "Yes, father." Thomas rewarded his son with one of his rare smiles. "Good. You must apply yourself with diligence, for you're almost ready to be off to Cambridge, eh? Like all the Gresham men." Richard did not fail to note his father's use of the word "men." He drew himself up taller. "Yes, father. When do I go?"

"Probably in a year or so, I doubt not. Then, after university, you'll take up apprenticeship with the Merchant Adventurers. I'll speak with my uncle and with Doctor Caius this very week about it."

Richard's heart leapt with joy and excitement. He thought his father, always so busy and harried, had forgotten he existed. He almost never came home any more, and mother rarely mentioned father, except in anger. He had stopped asking her about him long ago. Bound to his tutor by day, and to his mother's cold silence or her endless litany of complaints against his father at night, Richard had wondered if he'd ever go to Cambridge, or off to sea as father had. But now he had his answer. He would follow in father's footsteps, and within the year. Life was not so bad after all.

Little Anne was a charming toddler. He ordered that the governess should bring Anne to him each evening before he supped whenever he was in London, and when the child appeared, serious in her pleated white frock with its blue ribbons, he would swing her up close and bury his face in her neck, breathing in the delightful smell of her perfumed dark curls. His beard tickled her, and she'd invariably break into giggles and tug playfully at it. Thomas was extremely reticent in his emotions, seldom giving way to them, and it was only with his children that he occasionally dropped his sober look and serious reserve and only with little Anne that he ever teased and laughed. She was the image of her mother, and she brought warmth and joy to his weary heart.

Anne, watching them, could not help but smile. She stared intently at her handsome husband, then sighed in exasperated resignation. The flesh and blood mistress of a few years past was no longer a threat, she knew, but two others now replaced her, two so strong that Anne could not possibly vanquish them. Her thirty-seven-year-old husband, a man in the prime of life, was in thrall to twin aphrodisiacs: the exercise of awesome personal power and the accumulation of vast personal wealth. How could she possibly compete against them?

The queen was well pleased with Thomas Gresham's service to the crown, and she rewarded him with the priory of Massingham in Norfolk, and the manors of Langham, Merston, and Combes, thereby adding about £200 a year to his already considerable annual income.[20] That autumn, Thomas was once again in Antwerp and was present when Charles V abdicated in favor of his son Philip. The regent abdicated on the same day in favor of the duke of Savoy, one of Philip's most trusted generals. Philip's haughty manner and warlike nature, and his insistence on stamping out the Protestant influence in Europe immediately raised the hackles of the Flemish people he came to govern upon his father's retirement. He continued the emperor's war with France, dragging England into it, and Thomas was kept busy borrowing funds and shipping munitions. King Philip dipped deeply into the English treasury, with the full support of his doting wife.

That December, Thomas braved the icy winds and wintry seas to return again to England and spend the Christmas season with his family. He found no warmth at his Lombard Street hearth after the long, cold voyage. Anne greeted him with characteristic coolness and not a little sarcasm. Less than a week later, Thomas found he was unable to rise from his bed—he was afflicted with a hot, burning ague, a fever that continued unabated for days, leaving him weak and listless. It was Christmas week before he felt well enough to move from his bed, even to go to his desk. That illness, he noted in a letter to the queen on 23 December, prevented him from carrying out a meeting she had arranged for him with Paget, the bishop of Ely, and Sir William Peter, in order to resolve some of her financial problems, "which, as yet, by the reason of my continual sickness, I have not done," he regretfully informed her.

He decided to include for Mary's enlightenment an abstract of all debts owed in Antwerp at the end of that year, which amounted to some £148,526,[21] and an accounting of all monies he had borrowed and paid for her recently, requesting that she audit his accounts, and closing "that I may know your further pleasure therein: wherein I shall most reverently follow Your Majesty's order, wheresoever it shall stand with Your Grace's pleasure to appoint me, so that it shall stand with Your Majesty's honor and credit, and for the profit of Your Majesty and the realm. I shall pray to God to give me grace and fortune, that my service may always be acceptable to Your Highness." Dipping his quill, he signed with a flourish, "Thomas Gresham, mercer," and addressed it boldly "To the Queen's Most Excellent Majesty," affixing his wax seal to close it. He entrusted it to John Eliot to deliver to Hampton Court, where the queen was spending the holidays.[22]

The seriousness of her husband's sudden illness had given Anne a fright. Pleased to see him recovering, she fussed over him and brought possets and tisanes to him with her own hands, suffused with happiness that he was confined to home, and she had him to herself. The children and the servants were amazed at the change in her. She took great care with her dress and drove the maids to distraction, demanding that her hair be arranged just so before visiting with her husband in his sitting room. In fact, she was almost cheerful that Christmas. During his recovery, Anne and Thomas talked of many things as she sat with him—the children, the state of England's economy, Thomas's increasing stature with the crown, the needs of their various manors and estates. Bit by bit, the frosty climate between them thawed, to Thomas's great relief.

Thomas was also glad to be able to spend some time with his friends Cecil and Caius again. Cecil was firmly entrenched in the queen's favor. The eminent physician Caius, concerned over his friend Thomas's illness, visited the Lombard Street house. Caius had recently been elected president of the College of Physicians and was a respected court physician to the queen. Having the country under a Catholic ruler again was a source of great joy to him, and he and Cecil had cemented a friendship and remained on cordial terms. Cecil, like Thomas, Princess Elizabeth, and others, had resumed the outward practice of Catholicism, though inwardly they still sympathized with the Protestant cause.

"Aye, Caius, we are getting on," lamented Thomas one afternoon. "Richard goes to Cambridge next year."

"Nay! 'Tis hardly possible," rejoined Caius, startled.

"Marry, 'tis near twenty-five years gone since we were students there," Thomas reminded him with a smile.

"Aye, so 'tis," said Caius. Thoughtfully, he sipped his cup of mead, then suddenly remarked, "'Tis good your son will study there. I have plans there, too."

At Thomas's inquiring look Caius confided, "I have petitioned the queen and king consort for a license to re-endow Gonville in my name."

"Marry, 'tis so?" Thomas was surprised and delighted to hear that.

"Well, an' have I anything else to do with my fortune?" asked Caius, who had never married. "Cecil agrees 'tis a fine idea."

"And I too," said Thomas warmly. "I wish you good fortune with it, for doubtless it will be a benefit to Cambridge and all England."

A week later, New Year 1556, Thomas carefully dressed himself in his finest clothes, his new white linen shirt sporting a wide, pleated linen collar in the latest fashion for gentlemen. That morning, his barber had come and carefully trimmed his reddish brown locks and close-cut, pointed beard, which were beginning to show traces of grey. Thomas stared at his reflection in the glass. Taller than average, he was slender and aristocratic looking, and cut a fashionable figure in his black trunk hose and close-fitting, fur-trimmed silk doublet. His black hat, which had been made for him in Antwerp, was flat at the crown, and decorated with silk braid and a soft black feather. He buckled on his sword and dagger. As he reached up to fasten the short black cloak his valet had just draped over his shoulders, the bright stones in the rings on his fingers flashed, reflecting the only color adorning his person. With a final glance, he judged himself ready. Today was the day he'd attend the New Year audience with the queen, accompanied by his friend and benefactor, Sir John Leigh.

Thomas took with him a bolt of fine Holland cloth enclosed in a beautiful black Florentine leather case, bound and fastened with fine silver, which would be his New Year's gift to the queen. The forty-year-old Mary and her attendants were decked out in stately fashion and elaborate jewels for this annual ritual. Mary wore a heavily embroidered and jeweled gown of dark blue. A pleated white ruff peeked out at the demure high collar, and a matching little flat cap, embroidered with dark blue sapphires and pearls, was set atop her head. Her brown hair had been drawn back and simply dressed. Her face appeared serene and composed, but beneath the powder a sickly pallor showed, and her eyes were dark-ringed and sad.

Thomas swept Her Majesty a deep and courtly bow, then knelt to proffer his gift, which at the queen's nod was accepted by a herald. Thomas rose and stepped back, and Sir John moved forward to present his gift—a beautiful primer covered in purple velvet that Thomas had also brought from Antwerp. Thomas was then called forward again, and, kneeling, received from the queen the gift of a gilt jug that weighed more than a pound—a gift of much greater value and significance than was usually bestowed upon one of his modest rank—along with confirmation of the gift of the other lands she had previously indicated were to be his. Sir John Leigh also received a gilt jug from the queen, but his weighed a mere fifteen ounces, Thomas noted with satisfaction, as the herald announced the gifts aloud and the lord high treasurer's clerk recorded them.

With such generous rewards, the queen publicly confirmed her friendly disposition toward Thomas Gresham and his work on her behalf. Thomas was almost overwhelmed at receiving open marks of such high favor from the Catholic queen. Sir John, too, was delighted and amused by the queen's clever device of show-

ing him that his advice about Gresham had been of great worth
to her. Thomas placed the prized gilt jug in a position of honor
in the dining hall.

But he found that others had worked against him, behind the
queen's back. During his long absence in Spain, Paulet and Gardiner had been quick to seize their opportunity. They had finally
succeeded in convincing the privy council to delegate most of Gresham's official duties in Antwerp to their own chosen minions. By
March 1556, when Thomas returned to Antwerp, they had managed virtually to wrest the position of royal agent away from him,
and place their own people in charge of the queen's finances abroad.

Thomas was furious when he discovered that, but he had too
much pride and common sense to approach the queen over it. He
hoped that Mary would see for herself what had occurred, and
take steps to reverse it, but the queen was preoccupied with destroying heretics, and grieving for her absent husband. She took little
notice of what had happened in Antwerp, or if she did, she let it
pass without comment.

"Marry, and so let them have it," Thomas said disgustedly to
Richard Clough. "'Tis time I gave attention to mine own affairs
and lands. If it please Her Majesty and the lord high treasurer to
let others mishandle the good I've done her, so be it."

In truth, he was almost glad to be out of the royal position.
He certainly didn't want the issue of his religious beliefs brought
to the fore, especially not now, when the queen's rage against the
Protestants knew no bounds. In that respect, Gardiner and Paulet
had begun openly to tweak the queen about having one who was
known to be a former Protestant represent their Catholic
Majesties—particularly now that Charles V had abdicated and
made her husband the Holy Roman Emperor.

Thomas knew that Mary held him in high personal regard,
and Philip respected him for the great good he had done the treasury of England in the two years he had served them, and he felt
confident that they could not be turned against him by Paulet and
Gardiner. He had done very well for them, as the accounting would
show. He had handled more than £425,522 for Mary in loans and

bills of exchange and had gained for her by his own efforts, according to his final accounting, profit of £11,422.[23]

Though he rankled at the lack of appreciation shown for his efforts, for the next two years Thomas was content to turn his full attention back to his own business as a merchant adventurer. He still divided his time sailing from England to the Low Countries and back. Although deprived of the cachet of royal agent, he nevertheless prospered greatly at private enterprise during that period, as did all the merchant adventurers. Few in number, they held a powerful monopoly over the commerce of the country. Their fleet of more than fifty merchant ships, manned by the best sailors in the realm, still sailed the traditional twice yearly trading voyages to the Low Countries—at Michaelmas and Whitsuntide. In their holds they bore cloth and goods worth more than £800,000 a year in trade.[24] On one journey alone, Thomas shipped 4,500 western kerseys of the best sort, which, he noted in his journal with satisfaction, "sold with great profit to the Italians at Antwerp."

In October 1556, his beloved uncle John died in an epidemic of pestilence that struck London with ferocity. Sir John Gresham left some eleven children by two wives—his first wife, Mary, who had died in 1538 when Thomas was but nineteen years old, and his second wife, Catherine. Thomas found his uncle had appointed "my well-beloved nephew Thomas," conjointly with his trusted friends Sir Rowland Hill and Sir Andrew Judd, as overseers of his will.

Sir John Gresham's funeral, like his brother Sir Richard's before him, was an event of great and solemn ceremony, and Thomas had the sad task of arranging the details of his uncle's burial, as he had his father's. Since the day of Sir John's interment would be St. Andrew's Day, a holy day on which no meat could be eaten, Thomas arranged for a lavish fish dinner to follow the obsequies. The Church of St. Michael Basshishaw, and the streets along the processional route leading to it, were hung with great lengths of black drapery. Sir John's bier was preceded by one hundred poor mourners dressed all in black and lit by sixty great torches. He was buried with his standard and pennon of arms, and his armor of Damascus steel, its plumed helmet carried in honor in the procession, as was the custom. He left to the Mercers' Company a little over £13 "for them to have a feast, desiring that after dinner they will have my soul in remembrance with their prayers." It was with heavy heart and deep emotion that Thomas bade farewell to his uncle, benefactor of Holt Grammar School in Norfolk and many other charities, who had been his mentor and mainstay all of his life. For if he had loved any man on this earth besides his father, it was his venerable uncle John.[25]

Returning to Antwerp, Thomas purchased a large mansion on Long New Street, just outside the confines of the city, and settled in. He hoped that having a fine new home would entice his wife to join him from time to time, but Anne still refused to set foot out of England. However, others were happy to journey to the Continent, and he enjoyed the visits and friendship of many of the social and financial luminaries of Antwerp, as well as of his friends William Cecil, Sir John Leigh, and Dr. John Caius, all of whom came to Antwerp for various reasons and were house guests of Thomas while there.

He also brought into his social circle in Antwerp several prominent artists and poets, for Thomas was a man of taste and sensibility who, like many of his contemporaries, held the arts in high esteem. Relieved of the need to write letters about finance and foreign intelligence to the queen and council, he even found time to try his hand at writing a verse or two now and then.

He had learned a great deal about contemporary art and artists from the Florentine merchants he encountered in Antwerp, who always sang the highest praises for the works of their countrymen Michelangelo, Raphael, and the brilliant Leonardo da Vinci. Thomas, on his sojourns to Bruges, had seen the beautiful marble statue of the Madonna and Child carved by Michelangelo. The Mouscrons, a wealthy family of merchants from Bruges, had commissioned the statue over a half century ago and brought it to Bruges to grace their chapel in the Cathedral of Our Lady there. The sculpture of the serene madonna and her robust toddler was so breathtakingly beautiful, one could stare at it, mesmerized at the lifelike quality of the figures, for hours. Thomas hoped one day to journey to Italy and see other sculptures this man had produced, which the Florentines had told him were greater and more beautiful even than the Bruges Madonna. This he could scarcely credit.

Thomas was personally acquainted with several artists whose work he much admired. One was Sir Antonio More, whom he commissioned to paint several portraits of him. He was also a patron of the poet Churchyard.

On his solitary visits to Antwerp, Gresham had the occasion to entertain many of the brilliant and prominent people who had fled Catholic England to seek asylum on the Continent. He remained fast social friends with financiers like the Fuggers and the brothers Schetz, and among the guests he welcomed to his stately home were writers John Foxe and Richard Verstegan, and the eminent geographer Ortelius.[26]

In England, during the summer and fall months, Thomas and his family went on progress, as the practice was, to his various estates and manors, spending a few weeks at each. That way, their home on Lombard Street could be cleaned, swept of the dirty, vermin-filled rushes on the floors, and aired and washed down during their absence. Traveling to his many estates gave Thomas the opportunity to look them over, order repairs and refurbishment as needed, and tour the factories and mills which he had erected on the grounds of some of his estates. His summer progress made him realize with satisfaction how successful and wealthy a landowner he had become, for in England a man's claim to fortune and prominence lay in the land he owned and the rents he gained from it.

Late that summer he saw his son Richard off to Cambridge, and began to think about his daughter Anne's future as well. Though she was barely four, he insisted they soon hire a good tutor for her. Thomas had recently read the sonnets of Vittoria Colonna, a gentlewoman of Italy. She was rumored to have been Michelangelo's great love. Thomas had heard stories in Antwerp about her husband, a brave military commander who had died leading the forces of Emperor Charles V at Pavia.[27] Thomas had great admiration for her poetry, as he did for all educated women who had the eloquence to express their thoughts and ideas. He hoped his daughter would have that same ability one day.

Anne disagreed with him. "Your ideas will make her foolish, headstrong, and good for nothing except dreaming. The girl must learn needlework and management of a fine home, and simple book work only." Thomas ignored his wife's grumbling, for he fully intended that his daughter would have every advantage his fortune could provide and would one day make a good match, perhaps even with someone of the nobility. To do that, she must have attributes that would overcome the legal barrier of the circumstances of her birth. With the rich dowry he would provide for her, such ambitions were not beyond reach.

As Thomas enriched himself and expanded his knowledge during his hiatus from service to the crown, King Philip heedlessly squandered on war the thousands of pounds Thomas had managed to save the treasury by his astute dealings. In 1557 Philip graced England with a rare visit. Queen Mary, ecstatic, welcomed him with open arms and gave him everything his heart desired, including unfettered access to her treasury for his war with France. As soon as he had secured a new infusion of money, he was off again.

Following Philip's visit, England's finances quickly deteriorated to the point where the queen had no choice but to call Thomas Gresham back to help her. Money was flowing out of the treasury in great rushing rivers to keep Philip supplied with weapons and men. At once, £100,000 had to be borrowed. The proposed moneylender was to be Chemany, and he had offered the money through German Scioll, husband of Cicely Gresham Scioll. Cicely was Thomas's cousin, a daughter of his uncle John.

Queen Mary hoped that Thomas Gresham's experience and influence would help bring the desperately needed loan to pass, and that since Gresham was a kinsman, Scioll would not perceive his entry into the negotiations as a slight on his own abilities.

The queen also longed for more frequent news of her husband, and she knew she could count on Thomas Gresham to provide it for her, and keep his counsel about it, as he had done for her in the past. And so she had prevailed with Gardiner and Paulet, and reappointed Thomas to Antwerp.

Thomas read the queen's instructions with a small smile of triumph, for she had allowed a palliative note to creep into the verbiage, obviously seeking his goodwill again, when she could have simply ordered him to go.

> The said Gresham shall then with all diligence repair to Antwerp again, working according to his accustomed good diligence and wisdom, both for the speedy receipt to our use of the said £100,000 argent bargained for by Scioll, and for the borrowing of £100,000 more for one year, at such favorable interest as he may, foreseeing that he exceed not to charge us with more than fourteen at the uttermost, for the interest of every hundred, besides brokerage. Wherein, the better service he shall do us, the better shall he give us cause to have good consideration of him. The said Gresham shall have a diet [salary] of twenty shillings a day, to begin the first of this present March, and also an allowance of four clerks, every of them at sixteen pence by the day. He shall pay himself out of moneys as shall come into his hands for the prices of any provisions, or for the charges at all times of posting of himself and his servants, and for the charges of sending any messengers either to our dearest lord and husband or to us, our council, or otherwise for our service. Allowance shall also be made to him for the hire of such houses as he shall think necessary for the sure keeping of our treasure, powder and other munitions, and for the charges of carriage and sending of same by land, fresh water, or seas. His oath shall be the only proof required for the audit of his accounts.[28]

Thomas's favorite factor and good friend Richard Clough was delighted to see his employer return to Flanders as official agent for the crown. He enjoyed the city more when Mr. Gresham was in residence, for his master brought excitement and intrigue with him when doing business for the crown. Clough was a rather taciturn Welshman, completely devoted and unswervingly loyal to Thomas Gresham. He was a thorough and dependable business-man with a fine eye for detail—just the kind of man Thomas Gresham needed to handle his business in his absence and to be his righthand man when he was in Antwerp.

Young and strong and a bachelor, Clough could devote the time required to serve Gresham and oversee his complex affairs in Antwerp. He was not averse to taking on dangerous assignments for his employer, or to putting himself in harm's way, on occasion. This quality made him invaluable to Thomas, especially in the matter of procuring and transmitting intelligence for the crown.

Thomas Gresham trusted Richard Clough completely, and Clough proved himself more than worthy of such trust. Thomas considered his factor a friend and companion as well as an employee, and he saw to it that Clough was suitably rewarded with a good wage, frequent praise, and substantial additional fees and commissions for the extra services he rendered to Thomas Gresham and to the crown.

From March until June 1557, Gresham was in Flanders, work-ing with Clough to secure the required loans and procure mili-tary supplies he had been commissioned to purchase: 3500 hagbuts, 1000 pistolets, 500 pounds of gunpowder, 100,000 pounds of salt-peter, 3000 corselets, 2000 morions, 3000 iron caps, 8000 lances.[29] England had no standing army, but relied upon trainbands—cit-izens between eighteen and sixty were required to be trained in martial arts and be ready to come to the sovereign's aid when needed. She had to count on hired mercenaries from other coun-tries for additional troops.

Queen Mary's Parliament had just passed an act requiring all English landowners to provide equipment for Philip's army in his war against France, assessed according to wealth. A landowner with £1000 or more a year income from property was to provide sixteen horses, four corselets, forty Almayn rivets, thirty longbows, thirty sheaves of arrows, thirty steel caps, twenty halberds, twenty hagbuts (arquebuses or hacquebuttes) and twenty morions (visor-less helmets). The poorest landowner, with perhaps only £5 of income a year, need only supply one coat of armor, one longbow, one sheaf of arrows, and one steel cap.[30]

Among those landowning nobles who raised a troop to go and fight with Philip was Robert Dudley, youngest son of the hapless duke of Northumberland, and a childhood friend of Princess Elizabeth. Dudley, who had been too young to be drawn into the plot against Mary, had been spared his father's, and his brother Guilford's, fate. He was young, handsome, ambitious, and strong-minded, and looking for an avenue by which he might return to favor with the crown.[31]

The press of his duties for the queen and Philip in Flanders was such that Thomas scarcely had time to sleep, let alone write letters back home. His very life and favor with the queen depended on his doing a good job for her, and to that end he devoted every waking hour. Boxoll, Queen Mary's principal secretary, who was friendly to Gresham, wrote him on 6 April and reminded him that he had not yet written the queen and council to say whether or not he had delivered the letters they sent with him to King Philip. "Knowing that you look for some advertisement from hence at my hands, I have thought good to advise you that you shall do well, in all your great affairs, from time to time, to repair to the King's Highness, taking orders at his hands (if he will give you any) or at the least making him privy to what you are ordered to do. Whereby you shall better accomplish your mission, and find more help and favor in doing the same, and thus fare you heartily well."

Gresham knew that was a hint from Boxoll that he should get word to Mary about her husband, and quickly, if he wanted "help and favor" from her corner. Wearily, he sat down at his desk to write the queen, informing her of his progress to date and giving her news of her husband, saying, "which letters I delivered with my own hands to the King's Majesty at his coming from the Grey Friars of Boytendal, three English miles from Brussels, where he has kept this holy time of Easter and who (thanks be to God!) is in as right good health as Your Majesty's own heart can desire. He commanded me to advertise you with diligence of certain intelligence that he had from Dieppe, in France, which he gave to me in writing, and which writing here enclosed I give you with as much speed as I can."[32] Enclosing the information with his letter, Gresham sent it off posthaste, hand-carried to England by Richard Clough.

Queen Mary, who had retired to her chambers to read the precious note from her husband in private, crumpled it up after hastily scanning it, and cast it angrily into the fire. She slumped back in her chair, staring at the flames, tears sliding slowly down her cheeks.

In early June, exhausted by his labors and alarmed at the amount of debt Philip and Mary were accumulating, Gresham petitioned the queen and council to be allowed to return to England for the summer. "It would be expedient," he advised, "to forbear for a season to borrow any more sums at interest." They grudgingly acceded, and the queen herself wrote Thomas, asking that he advise her when he planned to return, so that she could personally give secret orders to the admiral about his passage, for Thomas would personally carry money, jewels and arms for the queen on the return voyage.

For the next three months, Thomas remained in England, able to attend to his family and his business affairs. He was granted a brief audience with the queen and was concerned at how pale and tired she looked. He felt a pang of sympathy for the lonely ruler, and resolved to send her more frequent news of her husband when he returned to Flanders.

The leaves had barely turned color when Thomas was dispatched to Antwerp to obtain new loans. Mary personally handed him a "token"—a massive gold ring. "Present this to our dearest lord and husband the king," she commanded, and Thomas noted a tone of sad resignation in his sovereign's voice. On 15 October, Thomas delivered the ring to Philip, who was encamped in the county of Egmonde, near Heading. Thomas then wrote the queen from Dunkirk, "The King's Majesty's commissioners, and the French king's, are treating a peace, which I pray God will send. The King's Majesty hopes, very shortly afterward, to be again in England, and he is in right good health (thanks be given to God!)."[33]

The peace Philip sought would come at a terrible price to England, for with it the country not only would be left deep in debt, but would lose Calais, the stronghold on the Continent that the English had held for centuries. That was the news Philip had delivered to his shocked and disconsolate wife in his earlier note. Queen Mary was as inconsolable as her countrymen over the loss. "When I am dead," she declared, her eyes glittering with unshed tears, "and opened, you will find Calais lying in my heart."[34] Her words were sadly prophetic. Thomas headed home to England in mid-November to meet with the council, and had just arrived when, 17 November 1558, Queen Mary I of England died. Like her father before her, she left her country mired in debt, diminished in stature, and racked with religious and political dissent.

6

A Young Man Again

England was at its lowest ebb in centuries. With a hope that transcended despair, Englishmen everywhere turned to a twenty-five-year-old woman to lift them out of the economic, fiscal, and religious quagmire that Queen Mary I and Philip had so wantonly created.

Following the intrigues of Wyatt's rebellion and her release from the terrors of the Tower, Princess Elizabeth had remained in forced "retirement" at Hatfield, a short distance from London. There she had lived fairly quietly, keeping a low profile so as not to raise the ire of her sister or Prince Philip. Now Elizabeth—a cool, calculating, Protestant and the issue of Henry VIII's ill-fated union with Anne Boleyn—was no longer the outsider, the bastard, the rejected, the scorned. On the day Mary I died, Anne Boleyn's daughter became Elizabeth of England—its fortune, its fate, and its future.

Elated, Sir William Cecil, along with some of the prominent Protestant nobles, hastened to Hatfield to pledge their support and loyalty to the new queen. Elizabeth immediately declared that Cecil would be her principal secretary of state, entrusted with handling all matters pertaining to public affairs. Foremost among the nobles who rode out to Hatfield that day to pay her homage was her old childhood companion and friend, Robert Dudley—Northumberland's son—who had served with distinction in Philip's war with France. When he galloped up, a magnificent figure of a courtier on a splendid white steed, Elizabeth greeted him with happy cries, and promptly appointed him Lord Dudley, her master of the horse. Dudley had, at one time, sold some of his properties, and given the money to then Princess Elizabeth, to help bring her out of debt. Ever after, the queen maintained that Dudley had a special claim on her affections.[1]

On the Sunday three days after Mary's death, Elizabeth held her first council meeting at Hatfield, and Thomas Gresham was among those she and Cecil invited to attend her. Thomas studied his new ruler carefully. Elizabeth had inherited Henry's coloring and the Tudor temperament, as well as (or so he'd heard) her father's propensity to a variety of distressing maladies. Small in stature and slight of figure, her pallid complexion was relieved by a wild mane of red-gold hair and a wide streak of exuberant spirit, making her extremely fascinating and attractive to the opposite sex.

However, it was rumored that like her half-sister Mary, Elizabeth suffered from severe menstrual problems, which probably contributed not a little to the ill-tempered outbursts and hysterical fits of rage that frequently afflicted her. Her sporadic and painful monthly cycle was cause for great gossip, especially among the ladies of her inner circle, and of course it was quickly passed on and became common knowledge at court. Some asserted with authority that because of the severity of those problems, Elizabeth Tudor could never hope to bear an heir for England.[2]

Thomas, like his friend Cecil, fervently hoped that such was no more than idle gossip and held no grain of truth. They prayed the new queen's health would be robust, for in her, they firmly believed, rested the salvation of England.

In her calmer moments, Elizabeth maintained a formidable sense of dignity and balance in the conduct of her official duties and activities. She tended to be less discreet in matters involving her personal life. Her emotional immaturity was perhaps a result of her unfortunate childhood, wherein terror was a daily portion in her life. She had lost both her mother and her first love—Thomas Seymour—to the executioner's ax, and had watched many others meet the same fate. She had come perilously close to it herself. Like a fish on a hook, she had been reeled in and out of favor at the whim of every monarch since her mother's death. In her early teenage years she had suffered, and been punished over, the sexual advances of Seymour—a man much older, and very much married. That, too, had left its emotional scars.

Elizabeth Tudor's forebears, and her rocky past, forged her into a woman of extremes in mood and temperament, but also a woman of resolve and steely determination. She had spent her life waiting for her moment in the sun, never sure it would come and now that it had, she grasped the reins of power in England with a firm hand, determined that none, nor the beast of state itself, would wrest them from her grip.

This day, for her first council, Queen Elizabeth was dressed in a magnificently ornamented gown of russet taffeta and fine Flemish lace. A lavish beading of pearls and brilliants drifted like glittering snowflakes across her bodice. Great ropes of pearls cascaded from her neck to her tiny waist, and more pearls, linked by finely wrought gold chain, accented her elaborate hairdo and her beaded satin cap. Her love for pearls, and their significance, were not lost on her audience. Pearls were commonly referred to as the "jewel of virgins." The farthingales holding her skirt out were so wide she had to turn sideways to enter or leave a room. In her hand she held a folded ivory fan which was attached to her waist by a golden cord. Thomas found himself staring at her, mesmerized.

Elizabeth was not unaware that Thomas Gresham had twice been poorly treated by Queen Mary and had been summarily pushed aside by Gardiner and Paulet, only to be recalled to service when her sister had got herself in deep financial trouble and couldn't get out. Cecil had advised Elizabeth, at their private meeting right after Mary's death, to take Gresham into her service and to heed closely his counsel and advice on foreign finances.

Calling him before her now, Elizabeth promised Thomas that if he would accept the post as royal agent for her in Antwerp, she would see to it that he received better treatment. "I will not only keep one ear closed to [others until I] hear you, but if you do me no more service than you did King Edward my late brother, and the queen, my late sister, I will reward you as much and more than ever they did." Bowing low before her, Thomas, though only thirty-eight, declared with fervor, "Your Grace has made of me a young man again, and causes me to enter upon this great charge again with heart and courage." The lovely young queen smiled and extended her hand out to her kneeling subject. A magnificent ruby and diamond ring sparkled on one of her delicate fingers. Thomas reverently took the small hand of his new sovereign in his and kissed it, signifying his fealty and his acceptance of the position she had just offered him.[3]

However, the outlook for Thomas was far from bright. Elizabeth had inherited even greater debt from Mary than her little brother Edward had from their profligate father, Henry VIII. England's debts had soared to £227,000 during Mary's final months—a sum considerably greater than its total annual revenue, which was around £200,000. Elizabeth needed the mind-numbing sum of £300,000 just to cover her immediate needs.[4] Cecil and Thomas and the queen conferred deeply into the night. Some of the money could be raised by stringent internal economy and some would have to come from increased taxation, but the tax burden on English citizens was already extraordinarily heavy. If Elizabeth increased it, it would then be so burdensome she would not be able to look to her subjects, or her merchants, for any voluntary loans. She'd have to look abroad, they concluded, for all additional monies. However, Thomas cautioned her, that would not be easy. Her debt in those quarters was already high, so the moneylenders were not likely to extend further credit to her at the lower interest rates and on the good terms her predecessors had enjoyed under Gresham's stewardship. Elizabeth then decided that instead of raising taxes, she would make stringent economies in her government and decrease her spending, hoping that way to reduce the burden on everyone.[5]

If Thomas Gresham was a workaholic, his friend Sir William Cecil, now royal secretary of state, was double that. He worked continually, rarely stopping for food or rest until his lengthy business affairs were finished each day. He heard prayers at chapel with the queen every morning and again at six and eleven every evening in his own chapel, supped lightly, and slept very little, so great was his devotion to work. A member of Cecil's household remarked one day, "I myself can testify that in four and twenty years I never have seen him half an hour idle." Queen Elizabeth leaned heavily on Cecil from the first—she made almost no decisions without first consulting him, and this extended even to matters concerning her private life.

Thomas Gresham deeply respected and admired his friend William Cecil, and perhaps because they were of a similar nature, Cecil returned that regard. He had complete faith and trust in Thomas's business and financial abilities and in Gresham's unswerving loyalty to the crown and devotion to the overall good of the country, trust which Cecil in turn communicated to Elizabeth. The day after the council meeting at Hatfield, as Thomas sat reflecting with pleasure upon the friendliness with which Elizabeth had treated him, he was suddenly galvanized into action.

Going to his massive carved oak desk that dominated his office at the back of the shop on Lombard Street, he took up his quill to write a long letter to the new queen, a letter he knew his friend Cecil would read and digest before he passed it on to Elizabeth.

Thomas knew this was his first and possibly his only chance to lay a full outline of the problems and possible solutions of England's financial situation before the new stewards of the realm. If he could but give them a complete picture of the financial proceedings that had occurred since the reign of Elizabeth's father, the good and bad decisions made, and the how and why of the effect of those decisions upon the fortunes of the realm; if he could perhaps give some sound financial advice and specific guidelines the queen and her secretary could follow, perhaps she and Cecil would listen to him. If they would, Thomas felt sure he would be able to help them stabilize the country for the present and eventually restore its financial health and strength.

He sat a long time in thought, his mind wandering back over two decades of royal service. Finally, taking up a quill, he began to write. After a few minutes, he got up and began pacing the room again in agitation. Then he went back to writing. He continued that process—pacing and thinking, stopping only for periods of furious scribbling, for two days. Occasionally he'd pause to gulp down some nourishment and drink from the trays his anxious wife brought to him. "Stop a bit, and rest now, or you'll be sick abed before long," urged Anne. Late at night of the second day, the document to the queen was finished. Thomas did not take time to edit or rewrite it much, for he felt time was too pressing. He needed to get this into Her Majesty's hands as quickly as possible. When finished, it extended to a voluminous document of many handwritten pages, and he had used up fourteen quills and two pots of ink. He peered in the dim light to read it one last time:

> The first occasion of the fall of the exchange did grow by the King's Majesty, your late father, in abasing his coin from six ounces fine to three ounces fine [gold]. Whereupon the exchange fell from twenty-six shillings, eight pence to twenty-three shillings, four pence, which was the occasion that all your fine gold went out of this your realm. Secondly, by the reason of his wars, your father fell into great debt in Flanders.[6] For payment thereof, he had to pay it by the exchange rate, and use more of his fine gold for payment of the same. Third, the great freedom given the steelyard and granting of license for the carrying off of your wool and other commodities out of your realm, which is still one of the major points Your Majesty needs to address, that you never again restore the steelyards to such privilege. For they had advantage of five shillings on the hundred over your own merchants, both on imports and exports, and as they are men that depend upon the exchange for pricing their commodities, by such privilege they were able to undercut your own merchants, which, if it had been allowed to continue, in time would have undone your whole realm, and your own merchants.

Gresham then explained to Elizabeth exactly how he had

brought her brother Edward VI out of the deep debt with which King Henry had left him, and how he had worked the exchange, and the merchant adventurers, to accomplish it. He touched on how poorly he then had been treated by Paulet and Winchester during Mary's reign, especially on the issue of valuation of currency. He related the circumstances in which he had given Queen Mary the relative value of foreign coins at her request, but had cautioned and warned her against setting a specific value upon them, which advice Mary and Bishop Gardiner and the Lord High Treasurer Winchester had ignored:

And whatsoever I said in these matters I should not be credited: and against all wisdom, the bishop went and valued the French crown at six shillings fourpence, the pistolett at six shillings tuppence, and the silver rial at sixpence. Whereupon the exchange immediately fell to twenty shillings sixpence and has remained there ever since, and it was at this rate and in this manner that I was then obliged to bring your sister out of debt of the sum of £435,000.[7]

By this it may be plainly seen by Your Highness that the exchange is the thing that eats up all princes, to the complete destruction of their common wealth if it is not substantially looked after, and also likewise is the exchange the chiefest and richest thing above all to restore Your Majesty and your realm to fine gold and silver, and is the means that makes all foreign commodities and your own commodities and foodstuffs good and cheap and keeps your fine gold and silver within your realm.[8]

He then gave Elizabeth, whom he knew had never left England and was innocent of the workings of international finance and foreign exchange, several examples of how that exchange operates, so she would, he hoped, comprehend its importance, and its impact upon her nation's finances:

For example, if at this time the exchange should be at twenty-two shillings, all merchants would seek to bring into your realm fine gold and silver, for if he should deliver it by exchange, he disburses twenty-two shillings Flemish to have twenty shillings sterling, and to bring it in gold and silver he shall make twenty-one shillings fourpence, whereby he saves eight shillings on the pound, which profit, if the exchange should keep at twenty-two shillings, in a few years you would have a wealthy realm. For all men would profit by five pounds per hundred to deliver it by exchange rather than carry it over in money. So consequently, the higher the exchange rises, the more shall Your Majesty and your realm and commonwealth flourish, which is only kept up by art and God's providence, for the coin of this your realm does not correspond in fineness even to ten shillings the pound.

Gresham summarized his lengthy advice into five major economic points:

1. Your Highness has no other way but when time and opportunity serve, to bring your base money into fine of eleven ounces fine, and so gold after the rate.
2. Not to restore the steelyard to their usurped privileges.
3. To grant as few licenses [trade monopolies] as you can.
4. To take up as little foreign debt as possible.
5. To keep your credit good, especially with your own merchants, for it is they who must stand by you in all events in your need.[9]

Satisfied that he had done the best he could, he raced to close the letter, his quill scratching rapidly across the page as he scribbled out, with great flourishes in his letters, the acceptable closing formula of profound and flattering avowals of faith and humility and willingness to serve. Within the hour, the document was on its way to Elizabeth at a fast gallop.

Sir William Cecil, like Thomas Gresham, was basically temperate of mind and action, and wise enough to keep his own counsel about most things. Tall, fair, and heavily set, with pink cheeks and a pleasing manner, those around him rarely saw Cecil in other than good humor. He strived to separate his business, domestic, and social affairs, a trait for which he was much admired. Born and raised in Burghley, in Northamptonshire, the new lord secretary possessed a personality of contradictions. He was a man of action, who also loved to sit quietly and read undisturbed; seldom was he without a book or not reading petitions that needed attention. He gave equal time to weighty matters and trivial ones that piqued his curiosity. He was a lofty diplomat and statesman who could also putter in his garden like a simple farmer.

Gresham, recognizing the crushing workload Cecil had inherited with his new position, assigned Richard Candeler to wait upon Sir William Cecil every morning at six o'clock to receive any orders he might have for Gresham to handle that day. Anne Gresham was pleased that Queen Elizabeth had returned to her husband some of the recognition he deserved, but was not happy about the appointment of her husband as royal agent in Flanders again, for it meant that his extended absences from home would not only continue, but no doubt increase. Anne grumbled sharply about it. "Methinks you would have served your family better to leave well enough alone and keep to your own business." They already had more than enough money and estates to keep them. "What else you need with this, I cannot imagine." She remained adamant that she would not return to Antwerp with him.

Thomas paid her no heed. How could he resist a summons so charmingly issued by his sovereign? The prospect of serving his country again in an official capacity, the royal cachet, and the power of the inner circle were too seductive to resist.

Within less than a fortnight of Queen Mary's death, Thomas was aboard ship and sailing toward Antwerp. It was urgent that he reassure the moneylenders that Elizabeth fully intended to honor all the bonds and outstanding obligations of her late sister. He also needed to be there so his presence might instill confidence that the royal transition in England was proceeding smoothly and thus keep the exchange from falling into panic over Mary's death and high debt load.

Meanwhile, England was as rife with rumor and gossip as ever. As soon as Queen Elizabeth—attractive, powerful, outgoing, and still virgin—ascended the throne, the court raged with speculation about marriage possibilities. It stemmed from more than just a need for topics of idle gossip to while away the evenings. Since King Edward's death, the succession had been uppermost in everyone's mind. Now Catherine, younger sister of Lady Jane Grey, was the heiress presumptive. However, the Catholics disputed that.

As it had since Henry VIII, religion seethed at the core of the succession question. The Catholic Scots refused to recognize Elizabeth's legitimacy as queen, despite Henry's Act of Succession. They claimed the crown of England belonged on the head of Mary queen of Scots, the wife of Francis II of France, and a staunch Catholic. The succession of Lady Catherine Grey might ensure continued Protestant rule, but she was rather an empty-headed twit and had not as yet married. The crown on the head of Mary queen of Scots would place power back in the hands of the Catholics and put England under the yoke of France—a prospect viewed with great alarm by the English populace.

In point of fact, the English had always viewed the idea of a female sovereign with alarm. Now, not only did they have an unmarried queen again, but none except women as heirs or claimants to the English throne! As Mary Tudor had proved and Mary queen of Scots portended, a queen's marriage could easily make England vassal to another country. Those fears were soon fueled anew, when Philip of Spain began paying court to his dead wife's sister.

Cecil felt it was imperative that Elizabeth marry, and soon, and produce a prince for England. However, that was something she seemed little inclined to do. From the first day of her reign, dashing Robert Dudley had had the inside track to Elizabeth, and although he was married, Elizabeth did little to conceal her deep affection for him. That he was married to a gentlewoman, Lady Amy Robsart, precluded any discussion of a marriage alliance. Elizabeth, for whatever reasons, had stated more than once that she preferred to remain unmarried. However, her lack of discretion in her attentions to Dudley disturbed Cecil, and he attempted, without much success, to quell the wildest rumors about them. Elizabeth was of little help on that.[10]

On Sunday, 15 January 1559, three months after the death of Mary I, Elizabeth Tudor, robed in crimson with a cape of ermine, a small cap of cloth of gold studded with diamonds and pearls perched atop her elaborately coiffed head, rode to Westminster Abbey on horseback, in a long coronation procession similar to those of her brother and sister before her, where she was officially crowned Elizabeth I, queen of England. Since all bishops in the realm were still Catholic bishops, of necessity the ceremony followed Catholic doctrine, a cause for great uneasiness in the Protestant faction. But to Elizabeth, it was of small consequence. "Let me show myself to God thankful, and to men merciful," she said, smiling.[11]

Shortly after Elizabeth was crowned queen of England, the last of the triumvirate of powerful European sovereigns of her father's time, Charles V, died and was buried with great and solemn ceremony in Brussels. Richard Clough, in Brussels on an errand for his master Thomas Gresham, chanced upon the funeral procession, and later described it at great length and in minute detail in a voluminous letter to Gresham: "From the court of the Palace to St. Gudule's Church, the street was laid with black cloth on both sides, and along those black drapes walked three thousand officials and burghers of the town, each carrying a wax torch bearing the Emperor's arms upon them. The church was all hung with black cloth and in the center was a hearse covered in cloth of gold."

Clough described for his master the thousands of candle-carrying attendants, and the "two hundred poor men dressed in black, all carrying lighted torches" that surrounded the bier. After more regiments, floats, and other depictions of the emperor's power, came "one horse covered with cloth of gold to the ground, and out to the sides like a gentlewoman's farthingales, whereon were embroidered in gold and jewels the Emperor's arms, and this horse represented the emperor."

Thomas could scarcely credit this tale of a procession of such splendor and majesty, and such cost as to be hardly imaginable. But as Clough's tale of the emperor's funeral procession continued on for pages, Thomas read with growing amazement and disbelief, stopping briefly when he saw the name "King Philip, the Emperor's son." Yes, Philip the plunderer, Philip the warrior, now Philip the king of many lands, Thomas thought wryly. He'd soon be trying to get his hands on England again, too, for to have a Protestant queen succeed his late wife would rankle Philip no end. Though Thomas personally doubted Elizabeth would consider Philip's suit seriously, he knew that conquering England—one way or another—was a challenge the warlike Philip would not be able to resist. Sighing, he returned his attention to Clough's letter.

"The Marquis D'Aghilar carried the Emperor's scepter, the duke of Villahermosa his sword, pointed down, the prince of Orange the globe, and Don Antonio of Toledo carried the crown imperial, with its great jewels. And after them came the King's Majesty Philip, dressed all in black, in a long robe, with a mourning hood over his head. . . . And thus went the procession to the church. When the burial service was done, the prince of Orange went to the hearse and struck with the hand upon the Emperor's chest, proclaiming, 'He is dead.' Then there was silence for awhile, and he struck the chest again and said, 'He shall remain dead.' And then he waited yet again, and struck the third time and said, 'He is dead, and there is another risen up in his place greater than ever he was.'"

Thomas, familiar with the city of Brussels, could picture the procession exactly in his mind, so well had his factor described it. Clough concluded: "This was the order of the burial of the Emperor. It was sure a sight worth going a hundred miles to see!" Gresham, smiling at that, sent Clough's letter to Cecil, with a note saying, "My servant is very long and tedious in his writing, but this may interest you."[12] Later, he privately cautioned Cecil, "We must assure that Her Majesty keeps a careful eye on King Philip. I like him not, nor his warlike ways, and we can ill afford a fight with him right now. Nor do we want him as king. But Her Majesty must prepare herself to deal with Philip one day."

A few weeks later Gresham was back in Antwerp to finance, refinance, and reduce wherever possible the kingdom's debts, relieved that at last he had a ruler who believed the same tenets as he did and who might even be counted upon to practice some national thrift where finances were concerned. It would, he reflected, make his arduous task a simpler one. However, at the moment he had an immediate and thorny problem to address. To Cecil he wrote: "It may please Your Honor to understand that Her Majesty has some £65,000 in payments due April and May. So for the payment thereof, and for keeping the exchange up to where we want it, Her Majesty has no other recourse than to call on her merchant adventurers, wherein I do know they will stand right stoutly by her in the matter."

Thomas then explained to the queen in a letter he enclosed addressed to her, exactly how to use her merchant adventurers to achieve her purposes: "This matter must be kept secret, and wait until their ships are laden and water-borne and their books of inventory made. And once all water-borne, then make a stay of the whole fleet, that none shall depart until further the Queen's Majesty's pleasure be known. Then demand to see their books and you will know best how to proceed. But however you bargain with them you should not come lower than to have for every pound sterling twenty-two shillings Flemish, but I trust that ere they have finished shipping it will be at twenty-two shillings sixpence, and Your Majesty is cautioned to remember, whatever bargain they conclude, that their money is paid in value money [otherwise termed permission money], for the queen is bound to pay her debts in value money, which should not be forgotten, and if not, it may cost the queen three or four pounds on the hundred."[13] Elizabeth followed Gresham's instructions from the beginning, for he lifted the burden of foreign finance from her slim shoulders, and allowed her to attend to other matters pressing her.

The English people adored their queen and she returned their regard. Her people were always uppermost in her mind. She already had several serious suitors for her hand and Dudley to dance attendance on her every whim at court. King Philip, when he heard rumors that Elizabeth's female problems were such that she might not easily bear a child, began to distance himself from the match, but left his cousin the Archduke Charles in the running. The king of Sweden had begun to advance the first feelers, and the German duke of Saxony was a contender for the hand of the English queen. The French Catholics had laid their money down on Mary queen of Scots, but the nobles of the dissident French Huguenots, knowing Elizabeth was a Protestant, began to cast about for a suitor among their ranks. Elizabeth the girl-woman loved all the attention she was getting. Elizabeth the shrewd queen preferred to retain power herself, and not share it with a husband.[14]

Following Gresham's letter, and mindful of his advice, Elizabeth in the first year of her reign paid strict attention to her finances and began to consider what Gresham had advised her about recoinage. Elizabeth was the only one of Henry VIII's children who had inherited some of their grandfather Henry VII's thriftiness in money matters. She realized, as her father and her half-sister and -brother had not, that great power lay in financial solvency, and in that burning ambition her desires meshed with those of Cecil and Gresham, who became two of her closest advisers.

For England, the linkage of this triumvirate of thrifty financial managers was a stroke of happy fortune. To save money in the face of staggering expense is a project daunting to any financial manager. For those three it was not only a desire, but an absolute requirement, if the realm were to survive. In her first six months as queen, Elizabeth slashed expenses at court to the bone, sparing no one and nothing, including herself. Whereas Mary's expenses in the final six months of her reign had amounted to some £267,000, Elizabeth's were only £108,000 and she was determined they would drop even lower. She exerted rigid economy in her own spending, and enthusiastically welcomed gifts to her from foreign governments and her own nobility—gifts of jewels, clothes, and hospitality.[15]

Notwithstanding her stringent economies, Elizabeth brought gaiety back to the English court. The queen was young and quite vain, she adored beautiful gowns and jewels, and she liked to dance and give parties and masked balls.

In December 1559, Thomas returned home to Lombard Street, as was his habit, to spend the Christmas and New Year holidays with his wife and family. Richard would be home from Cambridge, he hoped, and Thomas looked forward to seeing his fifteen-year-old son again, and to spending time with his wife and daughter. Little Anne at nearly six already knew her letters and could memorize rhymes with amazing agility. With Richard away at school, and soon to go into apprenticeship, Anne doted overmuch on the daughter, but the child didn't seem to be spoiled in spite of the attention lavished on her.

Anne and her older brother Richard looked forward to Christmas with the usual happy anticipation of youngsters. Their mother was more reserved, but planned a suitable celebration. She had invited her sister Jane and her husband Sir Nicholas Bacon to join them. They would be coming to London a few days early, and would stay the holiday with the Greshams.

No one in the family, including Thomas himself, was prepared for the proclamation and invitation which arrived 10 December from Queen Elizabeth I, borne by a royal footman. At Elizabeth's hands, Thomas Gresham's greatest personal dream was about to become reality. On 22 December, with his family in attendance, Thomas again knelt solemnly before Queen Elizabeth. This time she smilingly touched his shoulder with the ceremonial sword, designating him "Sir Thomas Gresham, knight." A rush of pride filled his breast at her words, and he bowed low to hide the tears that came unbidden to his eyes on receiving such a great honor and reward at her hand. His father, his uncle, and his older brother had all been rewarded with knighthood, but he, in a life devoted to loyal service to the crown, had not had such from either of Henry's two successors, even after years of faithfully serving them. "We would have you represent us as our ambassador to the court of the regent in the Netherlands upon your return to Flanders," the queen informed him. "Rise, Sir Thomas."

He had knelt a tradesman—he arose a knight of England, Her Majesty's ambassador to the court of the Netherlands.[16] Sir Thomas Gresham swept Her Majesty a low bow of gratitude, and, looking up, favored her with one of his own rare and brilliant smiles, which lit his somber eyes, crinkling them at the edges. Thomas was transformed into a very handsome man when he smiled that dazzling smile. Queen Elizabeth smiled back at him, aware that by that simple act she had just won the renowned financier's complete and heartfelt devotion. In truth, in knighting him she had gained not only Sir Thomas Gresham's business acuity, but complete access to his personal fortune, at her whim and command. Thomas bowed his way back to rejoin his wife.

Anne smiled radiantly for the first time in a week as she laid her hand proudly upon the arm of her new knight and allowed him to escort her out, the family following in their wake. At last, she was on a social par with her sister Lady Jane Bacon, and her sister-in-law Lady Christiana Thynne, Anne thought smugly. Now she could entertain a brilliant match for their son Richard, and for Anne, too. Doors that had been closed to Mrs. Gresham, mercer's wife, would now swing wide to admit Lady Gresham, wife of Sir Thomas, the Queen's royal ambassador to the Netherlands. Yes, Anne Ferneley Read Gresham had something to smile about at last. She had reached the station in life for which she had longed these many years.

"Marry, now we'll have to move from Lombard Street," she remarked as they rode slowly home. "A house with a shop is hardly suitable for a knight ambassador." Thomas could not help but agree. As a merchant and banker, his home on Lombard Street, though a stately manse, rose above a shop, as did those of all tradesmen-bankers. In his profession as a trader, Thomas dealt not only in cloth and goods at his many warehouses, and in shipping with his ships, but out of the shop below his home on Lombard Street he handled bonds and loans and gold bullion, and sold and traded chains, coins, and other valuable objects. To keep a shop was considered unfitting to the dignity of a knight of the realm, and much as Thomas loved Lombard Street and his shop with the family grasshopper crest swinging above it, he knew they'd have to give it up, and move.

Lombard Street, named for the Italian merchants and money-lenders who had come to England and established a foothold in London in the early thirteenth century, was the hub of finance and commerce for England.[17] Thomas would hate to leave it, but he resolved to turn his attention to that problem immediately after Christmas. From the happy look on Anne's face and the new light of love for him he saw reflected in her eyes, this would be one of their most festive holidays. Thomas smiled, and patted his wife's hand reassuringly. "You'll have your new house, an' a fine one 'twill be," he promised.

In the days preceding his return to Antwerp, from whence he would proceed to Brussels to present his credentials to the regent, he and Anne discussed various locations for their new home, and even visited several possible sites. Thomas pored over plans and drawings with his brother-in-law John Thynne, and with Cecil, for both were avid builders, and men of excellent taste.

Finally, Thomas settled on a large tract of land on Bishops-gate Street, near the center of London, as the site for his new mansion. From the spot, he could see St. Paul's and St. Mary's, and he could still walk to Lombard Street if he'd a mind to. The house he planned would be enormous, taking up almost an entire block. It would be constructed of brick and stone and marble, and boast several floors with scores of rooms on each wing. A spacious central courtyard within, and gardens all around it would set the house off properly. Soon, workmen were swarming over the site. Thomas had already written Richard Clough in Antwerp, asking him to begin procuring and shipping special materials from Flanders. The mansion would take a year or two to con-struct, but when finished it would be a home suitable to Sir Thomas Gresham, wealthy landowner, knight of the realm, royal ambassador to the Netherlands. They would call it Gresham House.

Shortly after New Year 1560, Sir Thomas was again on the high seas, bound for Flanders to take up his new role for the queen. The Lady Anne was content this time to remain behind in England, for she, with John Eliot and John Thynne, would oversee and ensure that construction on Gresham House continued during her husband's absence.

7

The Knight-Ambassador

*I*n her chamber at Hampton Court, Queen Elizabeth lay abed with a fever. She was already being pressured from all sides, with never a moment's rest. Cecil and the council were like dogs at her heels. Mary queen of Scots remained a threat, and Elizabeth didn't dare let down her guard lest the Scottish queen begin a move against her. She needed to neutralize Scotland, but in doing so she might gain a declaration of war from France, from Mary's husband, or worse, from Catholic Spain. Elizabeth sighed and turned restlessly, seeking a more comfortable position. One of her ladies in waiting immediately bent above her, bathing her face with a cool cloth. Elizabeth waved her away with impatience. "Leave us," she commanded weakly, "We would sleep now." The lady obediently withdrew to the other side of the enormous chamber. But sleep would not come to soothe the queen. The tiny figure in the great carved bed tossed and fretted. Who knew better than she, she reflected, that England was not financially sound enough at the moment, nor well enough equipped, to wage full-scale war against a larger nation?

The council was demanding, too, that she decide on a marriage alliance, hoping that way to avert or delay war. Hmmph! The detested subject of marriage was becoming more tiresome each day. Her ministers urged a marriage with Don Carlos of Spain to cement England's relationship with that country, and preclude a Spanish alliance by the Scottish queen, who had been rumored as eager to marry Don Carlos. But to marry Carlos, Elizabeth would have to profess Catholicism, and this she knew she could never do again.[1] On the other hand, Parliament wanted the Protestant succession ensured by a child from her. She wasn't sure she could accomplish that, either. Sighing in frustration, she finally drifted into troubled, dream-filled sleep.

The situation in Scotland was the first military crisis with which Queen Elizabeth had been forced to deal following her coronation. Scotland was ruled by Mary of Guise, who was the mother of, and acting as regent for, the absent Mary queen of Scots. Like her daughter the queen, Mary of Guise was a devout Catholic. When Elizabeth succeeded to the English throne, the Protestants in Scotland were emboldened to launch an uprising against the aging regent. They hoped to oust both Catholicism and the French from Scottish soil. They called on Elizabeth of England for help.

The English queen, recognizing their need, but also aware of her dire financial straits, felt that not a shilling or a soldier could be spared for the Scottish cause, but Cecil knew that England must seize this opportunity, no matter the cost. If they let it go by, there was far greater danger to Elizabeth's crown. He recommended that England help first with money, then with arms, and only in the last resort by sending troops.[2]

When Elizabeth stubbornly resisted, Cecil shocked her by tendering his resignation. "I will serve Your Majesty in any capacity she requires, but as minister I cannot continue if Your Grace will not act." That spurred Elizabeth to decision,[3] and in late December, she dispatched fourteen warships to the Firth of Forth with orders to destroy any French shipping bringing reinforcements or munitions to the Scottish regent. In January of 1560, Admiral Winter destroyed several French ships, and soon afterward most of the rest of the French fleet was lost to stormy weather. There was no longer a threat to England by sea from the French.

By March, Thomas Gresham was at his post in Antwerp. His country's situation, he knew, was most tenuous at this opening of a new decade. From the moment he stepped ashore in Flanders, he was ensnared by the complexities of his dual role. He was royal ambassador to the regent's court in the Lowlands, with all the official duties and responsibilities of that demanding post. In addition, because the queen felt she could trust no other to manage her finances abroad, he was obliged to remain her royal agent in Antwerp. That added additional burdens to his fully packed agenda. Actually, Elizabeth had gone so far as to task him with a third, less defined role—that of royal merchant, or for lack of a better term, royal smuggler.

Elizabeth had pressed upon Sir Thomas her urgent need for him somehow to procure and ship munitions and military supplies to England. She entrusted that task solely to him. She had cautioned him that it was to be done with the greatest secrecy, and to accomplish it, Thomas knew that he and his factor, Richard Clough, would have to put their very lives on the line every day. His instructions were to communicate only with the queen herself or Secretary Cecil on the matter.

In March, following her naval victory, Elizabeth sent an English army across the border into Scotland to lay siege to the French stronghold at Leith. Her ground troops were soundly defeated and she turned in fury on Cecil. Cecil said dolefully, "I have had such a torment herein with the Queen's Majesty, as an ague has not in five fits so much abated."[4]

During those first months, Sir Thomas Gresham ignored all else and bent his full effort to procuring arms and shipping them, for the situation in Scotland looked very grim for England. He feared that Spain, or France, or the Holy Roman Emperor—or all of them—might at any moment declare war on England to defend Catholicism in Scotland. Those disquieting rumors grew in Antwerp, and England's creditworthiness suffered. No one wanted to risk backing the beleaguered English queen. Sir Thomas begged Cecil to send him reliable news from the Scottish front that he could use to counter the damage being done, for not only were the rumors themselves adversely affecting the queen's credit, but her delay in payment of her debts so that she could use money in the Scottish campaign was making it almost impossible for him to borrow any money for her in Flanders.

The atmosphere Thomas had encountered on his arrival in Antwerp was tense, almost mutinous. The English merchants feared their goods and ships might at any moment be seized and impounded by King Philip, or by the Flemish moneylenders, because the queen was behind on her debts. They blamed Gresham for the precarious position they found themselves in. "I can scarce show my face in town these days," Thomas complained to his friend Jasper Schetz as they lunched one afternoon in early April.

He had taken Schetz into his confidence and now sought his help. Though appointed official factor to King Philip, Jasper Schetz was no friend to the Spanish king, and he resented Philip's cruel dominance of Flanders. He promised, for a goodly fee, to spy for the English—to give Thomas all the clandestine information and assistance he could, even though by doing so he would be placing his life in as much peril as Sir Thomas.

Later that day, in his study, thinking about the laws he had been compelled to break to accomplish his missions over the past years, Thomas chuckled ruefully. His was virtually the only intelligence network abroad upon which the English crown could rely. For the sake of the crown and England, Thomas was willing to swallow all scruples, corrupt any and all sources he could, bribe anyone who might be trusted to spy for him, or bring him valuable intelligence, or assist him to accomplish his purposes.

Without a qualm, and with Jasper Schetz's help, he boldly smuggled out the arms Elizabeth sorely needed to defend herself and England. Even in his youthful dreams of high adventure, Thomas had never imagined he would be called upon to do such things, but now all was at stake, and he did not hesitate over scruples.

"The rumor these days about me is that I'm here to rob the Antwerp merchants of all their fine silver and gold," Thomas wrote Cecil that night, "and because of that, I assure you, I am almost afraid to go out, except during the hours of the bourse, when they are all elsewise occupied. I'm told the Spanish and Italian merchants will try to petition the regent against me."[5] Thomas assured

Cecil and the queen that he and his spies would keep careful watch on any troop movements of the French or the Spaniards.

Meanwhile, Philip of Spain, was facing a serious dilemma. He had remained neutral in the Scottish contretemps thus far, because he still had thoughts of espousing Elizabeth and did not wish to alienate that cause. However, he was being sorely pressed by his allies to move against Elizabeth and to quell the rebellion in Scotland before the Protestants gained another stronghold there. Philip also knew that if he stood by and allowed the French in Scotland to suppress the rebels and win the victory, the French might gain control of Scotland, then England, and thus the seas between England and Europe, controlling all shipping. That would be disastrous for Spain.

As for his duties, Thomas was well aware there would be no easy passport from Philip for him as there had been under Queen Mary. With Philip more likely to become an enemy than an ally, England's only choice was to smuggle out the arms Elizabeth and Cecil needed.

Sir Thomas, Cecil, and Queen Elizabeth devised a system of code, designating on their shipping lists certain war supplies as "velvets," others as "damasks," still others as "sateens."[6]

Thomas, with the full knowledge of Cecil and the queen, also undertook the delicate and difficult task of bribing the customs officials at Antwerp. It would require heavy bribes, for if caught they faced certain death by execution, as did he. But soon his network was in place, and he was shipping munitions to England as fast as he could procure them. "I beg you," he implored the queen, "to keep this thing as secret as possible, for if it should be known or perceived in Flanders, my life and all my goods will be forfeited. Also, you must order Mr. Blomefield to maintain the greatest secrecy in the receiving of the fine corn powder that I shall ship daily and of everything else I shall send. I beg also that nothing of what I send be processed through the custom house, whereby any knave or searcher might learn of what I'm sending you."[7]

Nevertheless, hard as Thomas worked, with his life on the line at every moment, gold from the New World was enriching Philip faster than ever, and providing him a war chest greater than England could hope to match. Like many of his colleagues, Sir Thomas wished that England, too, could find a way to establish its own source of wealth in that far-off continent. But Elizabeth felt she could spare neither ships nor money for exploration ventures to the New World as yet.

"Letters have come from Seville," Gresham wrote Cecil early in April, "saying that eight ships from the Indies have arrived at Cadiz, laden with four millions in fine gold and silver, and that King Philip's share is at least one million. They expect four more ships soon, and I wish, for my part, it were all in the Queen's Majesty's coffers, or in the Exchequer." On 18 April, he wrote again, for in Flanders his spies had told him Philip was preparing to ally with France to subdue the Scots, and perhaps seize Scotland. The threat presented to England raised the hairs on Gresham's neck. But he also saw evidence that the Flemish bankers and populace favored the English cause, not Philip's, and that heartened him. "The proceedings of King Philip are not liked here. I pray God turns all things to the best."

Thomas had not yet had a chance to present his credentials to the regent as Her Majesty's ambassador. Cecil wrote him in May, concerned about a force of Spanish troops reported remaining in Flanders, when they should long before have departed for Spain. Sir Thomas penned a quick reply: "The soldiers wait for their wages. They say here that the regent is coming to pay them and send them off and also to appoint new governors of this town. I shall learn more in time and will notify you. I have not yet met with the regent and will not until I have some occasion that affords me access to her, nor likewise the bishop of Arras."[8]

Thomas stepped up his efforts to ship munitions to England, and finally, frustrated, begged the queen and council to allow him to ship more than the £3000 limit on any one ship. After that, the situation in Antwerp had become too dangerous, and Thomas was obliged to ship out of Hamburg in Germany, to escape any notice that shipping such great quantities of arms and war supplies from Antwerp or Amsterdam to England might engender. He rarely slept without a pistol under his pillow and set two guards to watch his door at all times.

Soon he encountered a grave shortage of gunpowder in the Low Countries, and he could not procure enough to serve England's needs. He wrote Cecil again, "The Queen's Majesty would do well to set up three or four mills for making powder there, for the service of Her Highness if the wars continue, or if a breach of friendship should happen between Her Majesty and King Philip."[9]

His request to ship more on each ship was granted by the queen by return post. "Communicate with none other than the queen, myself, or Sir Thomas Parry on these matters," Cecil told him. Thomas in his turn implored them to exercise greater caution. "Your Honors must treat arriving supplies with better security and allow no one to be about when these shipments are opened, else my life and Clough's are forfeit and the same for our other trusted assistants in this." It was a difficult, harrowing time for all concerned, but most of all for Sir Thomas Gresham, whose life was in constant danger.

Fate then smiled on Elizabeth and England. The regent of Scotland fell terminally ill, and the French developed problems on another front. They could no longer afford to fight the rebellion in Scotland, and agreed to treat with England. In May, Cecil left England for Scotland to negotiate the peace treaty.

However, the English still had Spain, and Philip, to concern them, particularly the body of Spanish foot soldiers who remained garrisoned in Flanders, right across the sea from England. When Philip returned to Spain in June, leaving the duchess of Parma once more as regent for him in Flanders, the Flemish people were assured that Philip's troops would be withdrawn within four months. Thereafter, whenever Thomas had a message to send to Cecil, he included accounts of any troop and ship movements in and out of Flanders, and to and from France, Zealand, and Holland.

The secrecy with which these bulletins, and the financing and shipping of smuggled arms, were necessarily conducted soon aroused suspicion and internal jealousy at the top levels of Elizabeth's court. Thomas's old nemesis, Paulet, the marquess of Winchester, resurfaced. Winchester was jealous of Gresham's new rank and outraged that a mere commoner was enjoying a position of privileged communication with the queen and the secretary. Moreover, it was communication to which he, the chief financial officer of the kingdom, was not privy. Suspicious, furious, he began hurling accusations of fiscal mismanagement against Sir Thomas Gresham. He demanded that the council call Gresham to account for some £40,000 which Winchester claimed had been misappropriated, complaining loudly that Sir Thomas was using his position to enrich himself at the expense of the state. With Cecil away, and the queen preoccupied with other matters, Winchester had an open forum in the council, with none to gainsay him.[10]

That news soon reached Sir Thomas at Antwerp. He trembled with outrage upon hearing that such charges were being leveled against him at court, especially since he could not at this critical juncture return to England to challenge Winchester. The lord treasurer was still a wily and dangerous enemy and was in a position where he could easily win others to his side. How could they accuse him of "enriching" himself at the expense of the state? He ticked off the benefices his position as royal agent offered: He earned a diet of 20 shillings a day—not even one gold sovereign—and his expenses were paid, so the cost of his daily life in Antwerp was more or less supported by the crown, leaving his personal trading and rent earnings untouched for his living expenses. But then, if he weren't working for the crown, he wouldn't be required to reside in Antwerp—he could live comfortably with his family at his London mansion.

True, he had an annual entertainment allowance of about £25—a generous sum—but he usually spent more, and that came out of his own pocket and was rarely reimbursed. He was allowed to charge the crown a brokerage fee of half a percent on the loans he negotiated, but that usually went to pay fees and bribes, and when he could collect it—which was seldom—there was always the risk of the exchange, which could either cost him heavily or make him a small profit. He had asked frequently, without success, for an audit of his accounts, and he suspected Winchester was blocking that. Only with a signed audit could he collect from the crown what was owed him. As was the case now, the crown was more often in his debt than the reverse.

Winchester of course was not privy to the actions for which Thomas was obliged to use some of the money funneled to him by the crown, or else pay out of his own pocket, if he were to accomplish his orders, or maintain the realm abreast of international intelligence. And what of the bribes he was required to offer in the queen's behalf? And the risk of his own life every day? They accounted not that he often loaned money from his personal funds to nobles at court, and to the crown itself; that he cheerfully did them difficult and costly favors when asked; that he waited patiently for months—years at times—for repayment of his expenses. And all without interest on his money.

True, Elizabeth's predecessors had rewarded him handsomely, with manors and lands for his services, but others had been likewise rewarded, and far better than he, for doing far less, and seldom at risk of their lives.

But Thomas was stung most by the injustice of Winchester's vicious attack on his honesty and his reputation. For the first time in his life, he felt completely disheartened, ready to quit the royal service and return to being a private citizen. The council's demands upon him were often unreasonable, and then they were ready at his back to believe the worst of him.

Angry as he was, Thomas knew in his heart that Elizabeth and Cecil both trusted him and were counting on him, and he couldn't walk away after all Cecil had done for him. Not that he thought the queen would allow him to walk away—she wouldn't even spare him time away from his duties for a visit home to his wife and family! No, he'd have to defend himself in absentia, while Winchester was free to continue his vicious lies at will. That thought made him even more dejected.

Slowly, Thomas rose, feeling old and weary, though he was but forty-one and known to all as a man of great vigor. Going to his desk, he sat and composed a long and bitter letter to the queen's treasurer Parry. Cecil, away in Scotland, would be unable to aid him in this. Parry was the only other person at court with whom Sir Thomas was authorized to communicate, so he addressed the letter to him. "I assure you, I have not so much as £300 of the queen's money at my disposal—much less £40,000—and if Cecil were not at this moment in Scotland on the queen's business he could be called upon immediately to bear witness to that."

He launched into a rebuttal of Winchester's charges: "I do perceive that the lord treasurer is offended because he is not privy to all my doings, but I cannot make him that, withal, for I was commanded by the Queen's Majesty to make no man privy to them but you and Mr. Secretary. This is the third time that my lord treasurer has served me thus: once in King Edward's time and once in Queen Mary's time, and when his lordship came to see the state of my accounts, he found the crown rather in my debt than the other way around. And I assure Your Honor, in my faith and poor honesty, it shall come out the same again now." Thomas suddenly threw down his quill in fury, spattering ink across the desk top; then he reluctantly picked it up again and signed the letter with a flourish. Calling a servant, he dispatched him to the post "in as much haste as the fastest horse can make!" The man ran for his horse. He had never seen his master so upset.

Agonized, not knowing what lies Winchester might be spreading, or what plots he might be hatching against him in England, realizing the lord treasurer would have the queen's ear now, with Cecil away and he unable to present himself to Elizabeth in his own defense, Gresham fell into deep gloom. He scarcely ate or slept, was irascible with friends and servants alike, and stomped about his large home on Long New Street with a scowl on his face, his eyes dark with unspoken fury. For days, he locked himself away in his study, reading or writing until the last candle of the evening sputtered and died. For the first time the servants could ever remember, the master did not go daily to the bourse, nor would he receive his factor, Richard Clough, and his friend Jasper Schetz when they called at the house. His friends became very concerned.

Twice more that same week Thomas wrote to Parry, pouring out his anguish at how his reputation was being tarnished at Winchester's hands. "It is a heavy care that so honorable a man as my lord treasurer would inform the sovereign with half a tale to the discredit or undoing of any man, and especially him that might be absent and unable to answer for himself. As I have already written you, this is the third time that my lord treasurer has done this to me. However, I can only call to remembrance the faithful promise made to me by the Queen's Majesty at Hatfield: whatsoever Her Majesty is informed of me in my absence, I trust in God that according to her promise, she will keep one ear shut to hear me, until it pleases Her Highness to allow me to come home and present my accounts, which is the only thing that comforts me and which I beg to be allowed to do."[11]

Parry intervened with the council on Gresham's behalf, for he knew that what Gresham was doing was secret and that by the queen's express order. Parry also knew that the lord treasurer's charge was false, but he could not openly challenge the powerful marquess of Winchester. That would be foolhardy. Cecil and the queen were apprised of the problem, and with their subtle help, the lord treasurer was gently calmed and the gossip abated. "I have been so well entertained at your estate, that if you were but a few years younger, I'd choose to marry you above all others," the queen said gaily to the aging treasurer one evening, cooling herself with an ivory fan. Disarmed, Winchester preened, looking around to be sure others had heard. They had. "We trust you understand, milord, what great respect we hold for your high office. We are sure you trust us equally in our other offices." Elizabeth smiled silkily. Winchester knew she was referring to Gresham. "Of course, Your Majesty," he agreed at once, bowing to kiss the queen's hand. "Your Grace has wisdom and reason, as always."

Thus it all blew past, to Thomas's relief. Soon he began once again to go out on his daily errands, made his visits to the bourse, and resumed his normal routine, which gladdened the hearts of his friends and his household staff. Nevertheless, in his heart he harbored great bitterness toward Winchester, who although he desisted in his more spurious charges for fear of angering the queen, continued to bedevil Thomas in other ways whenever he could. Using his royal office as treasurer, he continually postponed audit and payment of Sir Thomas's accounts. But Thomas had been distracted from Winchester, finally, by other, more pressing, matters.

One of his wharf spies passed a message to Clough: "This day, eight new Spanish ships arrived." Thomas went to the docks to see for himself. "They are for transporting Philip's troops out of Antwerp and into Zealand, I'm told," Schetz informed him later that evening. Thomas immediately set the spies to watch those ships carefully, lest they change destination and head for Scotland or England. He wrote to Parry, "The Spaniards are still in their garrisons, but word here is that they'll soon depart. The eight ships are still in readiness to receive them."

A few days later, Schetz again came to visit him. As they walked in Thomas's courtyard garden, away from prying eyes and ears, Schetz said quietly, "I have it from reliable sources that the soldiers will go directly back to Spain, and the ships will there be armed for some other use, one not involving England or Scotland. More than this I do not know for the moment."

A few days later, Gresham was given his first official audience with the regent, who had Granvelle, the bishop of Arras, close by. "An insolent and imperious man who, though despised by all, governs the regent and the council here," Thomas reported to Cecil.

Despite Schetz's reassurances that England was out of danger from Philip for the moment, Sir Thomas and Cecil believed that England was ill prepared on her own ground either to wage or to defend herself in war. She had become too dependent on foreign states for her military resources and supplies. Sir Thomas strongly urged Cecil and the queen to establish manufacture of armaments within England and to strengthen and guard the Royal Navy.

Following his official meeting with the regent, he wrote Cecil and warned him, "We do not know how Philip will proceed against the Queen's Majesty and the realm. It would be most convenient for the Queen's Majesty to make all her ships in readiness within the realm, and to suffer no mariners to leave the realm for any reason." A little later, Gresham was able to reassure Cecil he didn't think Philip would start anything in the near future but cautioned, "Nevertheless, it is good to expect the worst and to trust no word. For my part, I have let it be known that the Queen's Majesty has two hundred ships in readiness, all well armed." Though nothing was further from the truth, Gresham knew from experience how quickly rumors became "fact" in Antwerp.[12]

His official duties were not Sir Thomas's only concerns in those early months. Like any friend abroad with access to exotic goods, he was continually pestered, by this English courtier or that, to procure some special or scarce item and ship it home. One day, he found himself official custodian of a valuable stallion. The horse was being transported by ship from Turkey to England, and when the ship docked in Antwerp the horse was taken off and given over to Sir Thomas's care, by order of Dudley, the queen's master of the horse.

Queen Elizabeth was an accomplished horsewoman, and adored fast horses "which she spares not to try as fast as they can go," lamented Cecil.[13] Dudley had ordered the magnificent stallion as a surprise gift for the queen. Sir Thomas learned that he was expected to see to its welfare until another ship could be readied to transport it on the final leg of its journey to England. Thomas was happy for the opportunity to render the queen's favorite this small service, for with Winchester as an enemy, Thomas was in need of any powerful allies he could cultivate.

However, there was a complication—the horse was delivered in Antwerp sick, and worse, seemed to be lame. Sir Thomas was terrified lest the rare and valuable beast expire while in his charge. He and Richard Clough were forced to begin the tenuous project of nursing it back to health. Thomas and Clough visited the horse daily, to be sure no harm would come to it. Finally, after a month or so of care, the animal was on the mend. It would make a swift and complete recovery, according to the horseflesh specialist Sir Thomas had engaged to care for the beast. The groom had nothing but extravagant praise for the horse, informing Sir Thomas it was one of the finest he'd ever seen. Thomas was able at last to write Parry to "please inform Lord Dudley that Her Majesty's

Turkey horse has begun to mend in foot and body, and he is doubt-less one of the finest horses in all Christendom, and runs the best."[14] Dudley was delighted to learn the stallion had almost recovered. He urged Sir Thomas to get the horse shipped over to England as quickly as possible. Thomas made every effort to comply, for he thought accompanying something so valuable as the queen's new stallion might provide the excuse he needed to gain a longed-for trip home to England.

Thomas had been accustomed to traveling back and forth to England almost at will, often more than forty times a year, but this time months had passed with no prospect of a voyage home. A few weeks later, he sent the news to Parry that "the Queen's Majesty's Turkey horse now waxes a very fair beast, and with the Queen's Majesty's leave, I do intend to bring it home myself. I thank you also for the genteel entertainment you gave to my poor wife, who I well know bothers you daily about my coming home—such is the fondness of women!" He waited, hoping that would arouse Parry's sympathy and move the queen to bring him home, but much to his disappointment, that permission did not come.

Cecil was no different from the others when it came to request-ing little favors of Sir Thomas. There was always a "wish list" in his communications. He desired a clock he'd heard about, and some silk hose for himself and his wife, similar to those Gresham had bestowed upon King Edward. But Thomas could hardly sup-ply Lady Cecil with silk hose unless he first sent some to the queen, for Elizabeth had recently declared, "I like silk stockings so well, because they are pleasant, fine, and delicate, that henceforth I will wear no more cloth stockings."[15] Silk hose were still a rare and valuable item—difficult for even a man with Sir Thomas's trad-ing connections to procure.

A few weeks later, one of Thomas's wharf spies knocked qui-etly at the scullery door and was admitted. "Philip's troops are boarded and gone, south, away from England. They head for Spain, I'm told." Thomas at last had understanding of Schetz's earlier terse comment. The spy had more to add. "The Turks have attacked King Philip's naval base, in Tunis, and he has rushed with all his ships and men to Turkey." Thomas rejoiced at the news. Attacking England would be out of the question for Philip, at least for the foreseeable future. Thomas paid the man well for his service and rushed to write a dispatch to Cecil and the queen.

By June, Thomas was able to assure Cecil with certainty that the Spanish threat had been removed completely from the English doorstep—his spies had brought him news of Philip's great defeat at Tripoli, in which "he lost thirty galleys, and twenty-five great ships, and all the rest of the galleys burned. The saying here is that the duke of Medina Celi did forsake all his galleys and took to a fort that he had constructed, with all his men, and he is provisioned for four months. It is rumored that the Turks' power is such they will take it by famine or otherwise. Sir, this loss is greater than can be known here, and is little lamented over by Philip's subjects here, what with his religion and his government. And now they are saying that King Philip has more need to seek help himself than come to the aid of the French king, because the Turk is so strong upon him, and most of his galleys and ships are taken or lost. Therefore, sir, the Queen's Majesty need not fear King Philip's proceedings for this year."

He then went on to detail the status of munitions ready for shipping to England, using the agreed-upon codes designating the wares by using names of fabrics: "The ships wherein the Queen's Majesty's velvets and crimson satins are, are still here by the reason that the wind is completely against them. I will ship no more until this adventure is past, having in readiness twenty pieces of velvet more to be shipped."[16] The next day, he was able to give more news of Philip's disastrous defeat. "Verily the loss is so great, that K.P. shall not be able to recover in four years such a power of ships and galleys together."

By late July 1560 Cecil was back in London with the signed Treaty of Edinburgh, and with it he had secured three major concessions in Queen Elizabeth's favor: (1) Mary queen of Scots would relinquish her claim to the crown of England, (2) Elizabeth's title would be recognized by the Scots and French, and (3) the French would withdraw their forces from Scotland. All this the representatives of the French and Scottish governments had agreed to.

England's prestige abroad rose at the signing of the treaty, and Thomas Gresham reaped its benefits almost immediately on the money market in Antwerp.[17]

But in France, Mary queen of Scots refused to ratify the Treaty of Edinburgh, and she stubbornly refused to relinquish her claim that the crown of England was rightfully hers. Angry at Mary's recalcitrance, Elizabeth took her rage out on Cecil again. Upon his return to London in what he thought would be triumph, the queen instead berated him for not demanding more practical concessions from the French—like money, or the return of Calais to her. Cecil sighed in despair. His was not an easy task.

The summer passed slowly in Antwerp, seeming longer and more humid than usual. Lately, Sir Thomas's thoughts had been much with his family. The attacks on his character that the lord treasurer had mounted, though abated for the moment, served only to emphasize and heighten his sense of loneliness, and his need to be in England. Since Ghislaine's death, he had not sought another mistress, though there were certainly ample opportunities for him to form a romantic alliance in Antwerp. He had enjoyed the company of many a comely young woman at the banquets to which he was constantly invited, and he always took pains to respond as gently and gallantly as any courtier to their arch looks and idle chit-chat, but his desire for a love affair, or even a sexual liaison, had passed with Ghislaine's death. All his energies were channeled into his work.

Now, he found it was his wife's companionship he missed and desired more than anything else. Now and then he wished Anne were there to talk with about his worries—or even to berate him. He was not overly concerned for his family's ordinary comforts during this longer-than-usual absence, for he knew his factor John Eliot and his family would look to their needs, and he had provided ample funds for that.

But with her husband absent, Anne was unable to enjoy her exalted state as the wife of a knight of the realm, and she let Thomas know about it in her letters to him. Certainly, little comfort arrived for him these days from the home front. But Anne, he knew, was not amiss in her complaints.

Antwerp was not as staid as England, where women were rarely invited about without their husbands along to escort them. Thomas knew the months of separation were longer and more difficult for his wife than for him. His heart went out to her. He had received no encouragement from Parry or Cecil regarding the possibility of making a trip back to England. At one point, he dared a hint to the queen herself, hoping it would move her to have sympathy for him and order him home for a visit. "I shall most humbly beseech Your Highness to be a comfort unto my poor wife in this my long absence in the service of Your Majesty."[18] On Cecil's request, Lady Cecil then saw to it that Lady Anne Gresham was invited to some evening entertainments "in the long absence of your dear husband, Sir Thomas, who remains ever abroad in the service of Her Majesty," read the invitation. In gratitude, Thomas sent Lady Cecil small gifts whenever a ship sailed. He endeavored to render whatever personal services he could to those who were thoughtful of his wife and family.

That summer, too, two monumental tasks for the queen had suddenly fallen upon Sir Thomas's broad shoulders. Elizabeth had decided to heed his advice and undertake a recoinage in England to stabilize the currency. Since it was he who had suggested it, Sir Thomas was charged with negotiating the project. "Tomorrow I send Daniel Wolstat to confer with you," he wrote Parry on 7 July, "if it is still the queen's pleasure to refine all her Highness' base money. He is an honest man, to whom I am much beholden." At about the same time, several of the queen's major debts, totaling £150,000, were coming due in August, and she didn't have enough money in her treasury to pay them. Thomas had anticipated that, having been in delicate negotiations since early May for a loan of £75,000 from a German noble, Count Mansfield of Saxony. The count sent his negotiator Hans Keck to Gresham. After long deliberations, Gresham sent Keck to England, along with his factor Richard Clough, to negotiate directly with Cecil and the council. Then Clough returned to Antwerp, and Gresham sent him on into Saxony, where negotiations for the loan continued. Finally, it was settled that the money would be delivered to Sir Thomas in Antwerp by 15 August for one year at 10 percent. The security would be the usual bond from the queen and the City of London.

Sir Thomas then advised the queen to use only £25,000 to liquidate part of the debt of £150,000. A payment of £25,000 out of the expected £75,000 loan would satisfy her creditors, and she would have the balance of £50,000 in fine silver and gold for her use for other needs. "Even though the payment seems small considering the size of the debt," he told her, "it will be well spoken of everywhere in the world, for that Her Majesty, even in wartime, does make payment on her debts, when King Philip, the French king and the king of Portugal in peace time pay nothing, which has caused money for loans here to be so scarce as has never been seen before. Therefore, at this moment, a payment of £25,000 equally divided among the Queen's creditors will do more good to Her Highness' credit than the whole sum of £25,000 is worth, and by this means too, her debts are lessened and likewise the interest on them."[19]

But to Thomas's great distress and embarrassment, the money from the duke of Saxony never came through. He learned then that it was to come from repayment of a loan by the count to the city of Antwerp, and the city did not pay. As he had done once before in King Edward's time, Sir Thomas was forced to recommend that the queen resort to wringing the money she needed out of her merchant adventurers. The queen was on her summer progress, staying at Basing in Hampshire as a guest of Thomas's nemesis, Winchester.

The lord treasurer's grand country mansion was one of the great estates Elizabeth especially enjoyed visiting. It was one of her economies to stay at the homes of various nobles and knights while on progress, instead of in her own castles. That way, her host had to pay the food and lodging costs for the queen and her enormous train of followers, as well as give her costly gifts in gratitude for having her grace their homes. Thus the considerable cost of her keep during that period of progress—which amounted to at least one fourth of the year—did not come out of her distressed treasury. Elizabeth knew how to save a farthing wherever she could.[20]

Elizabeth was still young, and had always been high-spirited. She couldn't escape into hunting and jousting and sport as her father and brother had, and all too often the weighty affairs of state pressed down upon her slim shoulders with no respite, so she loved to play pranks and plant seeds of gossip for amusement whenever she could. But no matter her high spirits, her cares were never distant from her side. From Basing, the queen wrote official letters to Sir Thomas and to Mr. John Fitzwilliams, governor of the Merchant Adventurers, about her current financial pinch. In her letter to Sir Thomas, she expressed her displeasure that the English merchants, who were to have been prevented from sailing from England with their wares until they came up with the money she wanted (as he had advised her to do), had somehow been allowed to sail. Elizabeth therefore commanded Sir Thomas and Fitzwilliams to secure the money, or bonded promise of the loan, from the merchants upon their arrival at Antwerp, prior to allowing them to display their merchandise for sale on the next "show day."

That she was angry that the lord treasurer had failed her and had not followed orders was evident in her letters, and that she was determined to have the money she needed from the Merchant Adventurers and the staplers upon their dockage in Antwerp was demonstrated by the veiled threats in her 28 August letter to Thomas:

> Trusty and well-beloved we greet you well. So it is, by negligence of such in whom the trust was reposed, they [the merchants] be departed and no bargain concluded. In which manner our treasurer of England has by his letters from London seemed not to allow the payment of our debts by your means, but rather to have the debt of November put over to March, which We cannot allow. Nevertheless, we mean to have him come to Windsor to us by next Sat-

urday. Meanwhile, we thought it necessary to let you know, and also send word to Fitzwilliams, that before any show day, we must be furnished this loan of £60,000 Flemish— 30,000 'fore the 15th of this November, and another 30,000 the 15th of March next. And while we require that the merchants deliver us the money at the rate of 25 shillings Flemish for 20 shillings sterling, because we know not how things may be accomplished there, we leave it to your discretion to get it at somewhere between 23 shillings 4 pence and 25 shillings. We further command you to tell the governor [Fitzwilliams] that if this Our reasonable request is not granted immediately, we shall be obliged to see other means that will perchance be more hurtful to the company [of Merchant Adventurers]. Such we would be sorry perforce to resort to, but so indeed We must and would do. We write this in haste, fearing that to wait longer would make these letters arrive too late, since we are informed the show day may come the 4th or 5th of September.

To Fitzwilliams she wrote, after substantially the same commands she had given Gresham:

Herein we assure ourselves of your conformity, considering how much it touches upon our reputation and honor, and how it shall be beneficial to our realm to be out of debt there, which we most earnestly intend. And if you will take into consideration that the younger merchants, that have more need to use their money over there to buy things, and return home with goods from those parts, than the elder and richer, who may be more easily assessed, and with the greater sums—we think that thus the burden shall be easier and service to us more quickly accomplished. Our factor and agent there (Sir Thomas Gresham) can best inform you how necessary it is that this our request be granted, and that we may not, without great dishonor and discredit, have it denied, therefore believe what he tells you, without us enlarging further upon the matter.[21]

Sir Thomas met with Fitzwilliams, whom he had known for a long time, and between them the deal was concluded, without too much difficulty, at an exchange rate of slightly lower than the queen anticipated—22 shillings sixpence to the pound sterling—but not one she couldn't live with. With it, she got a promissory note from the Merchant Adventurers, with Sir Thomas required to put up, at interest, whatever the merchants couldn't come up with through sales on show day. The staplers pledged their required £13,000. The queen then agreed to squeeze from the treasury enough to make £100,000—which would liquidate two-thirds of the debt—and the lord treasurer arranged that the remaining £50,000 would be "put over" (renegotiated) with a due date of August 1562.

Winchester had tried to sink him again, Thomas realized, but this time the queen herself had caught it, and reprimanded the treasurer. He wouldn't try that again. These latest dealings with the Merchant Adventurers brought to Thomas's mind thoughts of his brother, whom he had barely known. John had died suddenly, at only forty. The news of his brother's death had not reached Sir Thomas until months afterward. Poor John! An adventurer and risk-taker, he had squandered or ventured and lost most of his fortune, and there had been little left for his widow Frances and their only daughter, Elizabeth. Thomas felt fortunate that he could at least look forward to his own son Richard soon becoming a merchant adventurer in the family tradition. His brother had died without a son to carry on after him.

Thomas was concerned for his brother's family, and considered John's paltry financial state a disgrace, especially for one who had not long before been left in such prosperous circumstances by their father, Sir Richard. Upon receiving the news of his brother's estate, Sir Thomas had immediately bestowed upon Lady Frances a generous annual income of £133, for herself and her daughter, out of his own funds.[22]

Now, having resolved the latest problem with the queen's debts, and with the recoinage project proceeding in reasonably good order, Thomas was able to turn his attention again to shipping the queen's Turkish horse to Dudley, sending along with it a young colt as a gift for Cecil. Sir Thomas Parry had also written to ask him to find a small iron chest for the queen, "a little chest with a little key." Elizabeth's hands, about which she was quite vain, were tiny and delicate, and she could not turn the big, heavy keys normally provided with large iron storage chests. Thomas wrote back to advise Parry that he had shipped the queen's horse, and in the letter he enclosed the smallest key he could find. "I have sent you the key of the fairest chest to be found in the city of Antwerp and hope it is not too big. But if it is, and the Queen's Majesty would have a smaller one, I pray you let me know the size, and I shall have a chest and key made to her purpose. I'd be happy to deliver it to Her Grace in person." He hinted that because months had passed and he had not received permission from the queen to return home. Cecil had also requested that Thomas ship him any unusual plants or trees that his friend thought might be suitable for his garden, for Cecil loved his gardens and was always seeking new and rare items to plant in them.[23]

In late September, Thomas received a letter from Anne with news of a shocking scandal at Elizabeth's court: Amy Robsart, wife of Lord Robert Dudley, had been found dead at the foot of a staircase at their country estate, her neck broken. The news of her suspicious death rocked all of Europe. It was widely assumed that Dudley had somehow had his wife killed to free him to marry Queen Elizabeth, though he denied it vehemently. In the ensuing uproar, the queen was forced to send her favorite away from court while the matter was investigated. Thomas was saddened on hearing of the scandal, for he liked Dudley, and he did not believe the young man capable of having ordered the cold-blooded murder of his wife.

Dudley was cleared at the inquest. The verdict was that the Lady Dudley's death had been purely accidental.[24] However, a cloud of suspicion continued to hang over Dudley, and court gossip claimed that it removed him from the list of possible husbands for the queen. However, he remained Elizabeth's obvious favorite.

She had apparently shelved the Archduke Charles, King Philip's cousin, as a marriage candidate, and Cecil was urging her to consider the prince of Sweden, a match that would find more favor with the Protestants.

It was also in that month that the recoinage of the English money was accomplished, after many months of work by Daniel Wolstat and his assistants. On 27 September, the value of base coins was reduced and on the twenty-ninth a royal proclamation to that effect was issued. Although the immediate effect of the move, which had been kept a deep secret, was to diminish the fortunes of many, in time it served to augment them, and the treasury of England as well, by strengthening of the exchange rate of the pound.[25] Barely a week after he received the good news about the recoinage, disaster struck Sir Thomas.

Thomas often rode out from Antwerp to other towns and cities in Flanders, sometimes accompanied by Clough, or another of his agents, to meet personally with his various agents and spies, so that he could keep Cecil and the queen posted on developing events in the Low Countries. Aside from the crown's ambassadors, Sir Thomas Gresham's vast network of paid spies and informants in Europe—from Spain and Tunis in the south to as far north as Sweden—was the only intelligence organization the queen of England had at her disposal. Sir Thomas knew there were many who might scornfully disapprove of his willingness to bribe those who brought him information or pay those who served his needs in smuggling arms, but he knew the well-being of his queen and country depended upon their receiving those goods, and that information, as quickly as humanly possible. To get what they needed, when they needed it, payment of bribes was essential, and that involved risks. Sir Thomas willingly placed his own life at risk to pursue gathering information and to smuggle those needed military supplies for the crown.

It was on one such errand, riding to a meeting with a spy who had sent word that he had important information, that Sir Thomas and his factor Richard Clough were bent as they set out for Brussels that morning in October 1560. The countryside of Flanders was quiet, and there was a slight tinge of onrushing winter in the crisp autumn air. They spurred their horses to a canter, then a gallop. As Thomas negotiated a sharp turn in the road, a noise that sounded like a shot rang out. Startled, his mount stumbled. Thomas jerked hard on the reins, and vaguely heard Clough's cry of warning, but it was too late—he and the horse were falling. His foot caught in the stirrup and Thomas slammed heavily to the ground. The beast, neighing in fright, loomed above him and instinctively, desperately, Thomas tried to twist himself out of its way. The strong smell of the sweating animal filled his nostrils and he felt the heat of its body. Then a searing pain arched through him and he heard the sickening sound of his ensnared leg snapping as the horse's full weight crashed down upon him. His head clapped hard against the earth and he knew no more.

He awoke lying on a rude pallet in a dim, earthen-floored farmhouse. He started up in surprise, and his body was immediately engulfed in flames that scorched him with such fiery pain that he screamed aloud. He could not comprehend what was happening to him. Was he being burned at the stake? Roasted on a spit? Sweat beaded on his brow and ran into his eyes. An old woman appeared in the blurred periphery of his vision, staring down at him. She seemed to be saying something to him, but there was such a roaring in his ears that he couldn't hear her. Mercifully, he lost consciousness again.

Hours passed. Then a sudden excruciating wave of pain, worse than anything he had ever known or imagined, jarred him back to consciousness. He cried out in anguish and his eyes flew open wide in fear, but when he tried to rise, struggling to escape the torment, he saw Richard Clough bending over him, tears streaming, holding him down. "What? What has passed?" he gasped out hoarsely.

"Hist, now, hold still, sir, rest easy." Clough gripped him firmly. "You've broke yer leg, you're hurt bad. I've fetched you a doctor from Antwerp, he be here now, tending you, and milord Schetz follows fast with conveyance for you. Hold now, you'll be all right soon. Here, drink of this." Gently, Clough held a bottle to

Thomas's lips, and Thomas gulped the liquid, hoping for deliverance from the hot pain that would not release him from its grip. The old woman stood by, wringing her hands in her dark skirts, a deep sadness in her eyes, as the doctor worked to bind and stabilize his leg. Thomas bit his lip until the blood ran, but could not suppress the shrieks, moans, and groans that the doctor's ministrations wrung from him, sweat pouring from his brow. He drank more, greedily, whenever Clough held the bottle to his lips. Occasionally, the doctor barked an order, which Clough and the woman leaped to obey. Thomas fainted again.

By the time Schetz arrived with a wagon piled with furs and linens to transport Thomas back to Antwerp, Clough had the patient thoroughly drunk, and the doctor had the leg straightened and bound as best he could for the journey. Nonetheless, Thomas howled in agony as they lifted him, wrapped and cushioned in thick fur robes, into the wagon to begin the slow, torturous return to Antwerp. Richard Clough pressed a few coins into the workworn, wrinkled hands of the old woman, and they were away.

When they reached the city, Jasper Schetz insisted that his friend be taken to be tended to in his mansion, where several of Antwerp's best doctors awaited him. He posted guards at the doors. They did not know what had startled the horses, or even if there had been a shot, or if so, whence it had come. But for now, they could only concentrate on his injuries, which were serious.

"Send for Dr. John Caius, from London," Thomas muttered to Clough, but he knew that was a futile hope. Whatever had to be done, must be done now. There wasn't time, he knew, to wait for word to get to London and for the distinguished physician to make the journey to Antwerp—even if he could. Thomas would just have to trust in the physicians Schetz had summoned to look after him.

Miraculously, he survived, and his badly bruised body and horribly fractured leg slowly mended. The scrupulous attention of the doctors averted suppuration of his wound where the bone had splintered and broken through the surface of the skin. The queen and Cecil sent anxious messages inquiring after his well-being.

Anne volunteered to come to Antwerp to look after him while he convalesced, but Thomas sent word back that he was mending, and bade her remain in London with little Anne. He feared that if his family came to Antwerp, he would never receive the queen's permission to return to London, and now more than ever, he sorely wanted to go home. He had been nearly nine months in Flanders without once returning to England. Even more months would pass before he'd be recovered enough to attempt to board a ship and travel.

The mystery of what had actually happened that day tormented him. "I was so concerned with you, I didn't even see what might have happened," said Clough ruefully. "You're lucky it's no worse." Thomas, lying there in pain, unable to move his leg, did not feel at all fortunate. Was someone after him? Unlikely that Winchester's long arm could have reached this far. Tucker? Thomas doubted he'd try anything so risky as assassination. Tucker was a loud-mouth, but basically a coward. "You'll have to have a better care in future," Clough said, unnecessarily. Future? Thomas thought bitterly. What future? Certainly he would not be galloping around the countryside anytime soon, and he was not at all sure he'd recover enough to be able to do anything.

Slowly, painfully, he healed. Quietly, Clough and Schetz used all their contacts, all their influence to try to find out if anyone had followed him that day, but turned up nothing. Thomas continued to mend, but his leg was horribly twisted; walking was nearly impossible.[26]

Cecil sent Thomas tidbits of news and court gossip as he slowly mended. Their mutual friend John Caius now well situated as primary physician to the queen, and president of the College of Physicians in London. He had elaborate plans for Gonville Court at Cambridge and the establishment of the College of Gonville and Caius there, for which Mary had given Caius the charter in 1557. Since Caius had never married and had no heirs, he had decided to devote his fortune and his life to Cambridge and the college bearing his name.[27]

Although he was delighted to hear the good news about his

old friend, Thomas was discouraged and dejected at his own future prospects. His Antwerp physicians had confirmed his fears: his leg had been broken in a very severe and complicated way. In time, he would be able to ride again and would walk and get about, but he would always be lame. He would walk painfully, and with a pronounced limp, for the rest of his days.

8

Bittersweet Fruits

Four more long months passed. Then, in late February 1561, Sir Thomas received the coveted permission from the queen allowing him to return to England. "We trust," she wrote him, "that after the prolongation of this February debt your leg will be able to carry you on shipboard, to return to us, where both for your recovery and for intelligence of your doings, we shall be glad to see you."[1] Thomas read the queen's brief letter over again, a smile lighting his face, his eyes misting with joy over the royal passport it contained. He could return to England! He had been a full year away. His leg had now healed as much as it was likely to, and he was ready and eager to undertake the long, difficult journey over land by horse to Dunkirk, then by ship across to Dover, and on to London.

Three weeks later, limping painfully down the gangplank, forced to lean on a helpful sailor for assistance, Sir Thomas finally stepped ashore on English soil again. Home in London, he marveled at how Gresham House had begun to emerge from the bare ground on Bishopsgate Street. Designed in the Flemish style, of brick and timber, it would have graceful, colonnaded arcades all around at ground level. From the upper story, its rooms would overlook a spacious interior courtyard and gardens. The construction of the house gave Sir Thomas a sense of quiet pride and joy, and he made his way there almost every day to supervise its progress. He was pleased that his cousin Cicely Scioll, would be their neighbor. Her husband German Scioll had bought Crosby Place, the vast mansion directly opposite.

Thomas continued to mend once he recovered from his arduous journey home, and soon he felt as fit again as before, though his limp was still very pronounced and he needed the aid of a stick to walk. That sorely distressed him, for he was a strong, proud man, quick to move and quick to his horse. It was difficult to adjust to this new restriction on his movements.

Little Anne had sprung up in his absence. She had become a prim and proper young miss under her mother's stern tutelage. She'd start to run to greet him when he returned from Bishopsgate Street, and then she'd hear her mother's quiet reproof. She'd stop short, blushing, and drop a quick curtsey, her skirts pooling in a sea of pale grey about her, her white ruff bobbing, and a few dark curls springing loose from under her cap. Suddenly subdued and ladylike, she'd go quietly to her place beside her mother and pretend to be absorbed in doing careful stitchery on her embroidery frame. Now and then, however, he'd catch a certain light gleaming from her eye, and a tiny dimple of amusement would quiver at the corner of her mouth. That never failed to cheer and reassure him. Young Anne's spirit was being tamed, but not broken. She was the darling of his life.

As for his wife, the Lady Anne welcomed him home and made suitable fuss over his injuries, secretly hoping they would keep him more confined, but the frost that had settled between them over the past several years had thickened during this last long separation—a cool, icy barrier that neither was inclined to work to breach. They drifted into a routine of quiet courtesy, like two old friends residing together, but there was no spark, no intimacy left to their union. When they talked together, it was of family and household business: of the allowance and future of seventeen-year-old Richard as a merchant adventurer; of the education of their eight-year-old daughter, about which Sir Thomas remained adamant.[2] Occasionally, they trifled with the latest gossip at court. But more and more, the details of the building and furnishing of Gresham House claimed their daily attention. Neither happy nor unhappy, they remained calm and outwardly content. The days and weeks flew by.

Thomas was pleased when Cecil visited him once or twice and once he even accompanied Thomas to Bishopsgate Street to inspect the progress being made on Gresham House. They meandered through the area where the gardens would go, and Cecil gave him advice on what trees and plants would grow best there. "Ah, Thomas, you are fortunate that you are much away in Antwerp," Cecil sighed, stopping at one corner of the garden plot, away from prying eyes or ears. "Betimes I wish to be there in your place."

"How so?" His curiosity aroused, Thomas looked keenly at his friend.

"Her Majesty vexes me sorely, for to aid her be like to harness yon wind. She has the quality for greatness in a prince, yet in a trice can show the caprice of a vain and headstrong maid."

Sensing his friend needed nothing so much as to talk, Thomas made no comment, but continued to walk slowly along by Cecil's side on the far side of the lot.

"Her Majesty turns not her head to marriage nor cares about the succession, nor will she take measures for her safety. Yea, methinks 'twould be fine to be away like you, Thomas, for time to think and to read without this contentious, licentious court about me to distraction, for they give no man any peace."

Thomas knew well the weight of Cecil's duties and responsibilities, and he had heard the rumors of how the queen, though shrewd and tough as any politician, would have fits and tantrums with her closest ministers, even to the point of smacking them or throwing her slippers at them. She dangled Robert Dudley before them like a pet hound, but did not marry him. She accepted, even encouraged, suits from foreign princes, but would sign no marriage contract and ended up sending them packing. No one, it seemed, escaped her sarcastic wit or her razor tongue. Thomas counted himself fortunate that he had never borne the brunt of such from his sovereign, but Cecil seemed able to take his burdens in stride. The queen's endless progresses, with her enormous court of followers, her ministers, and her household, were enough to wear out the strongest man. "But," Cecil acknowledged, "she knows the need for the common folk to look upon her in all her glory, for she taxes them sorely." 'Twas true, Thomas agreed.

The queen, like her father, understood that her people needed to see her if they were to follow her, hence her frequent and prolonged progresses to various castles throughout her realm. She also knew, almost instinctively, that she needed to command strict obedience from them and to regulate their lives in every detail if she were to keep them under control. The common people, whose lives were for the most part dreary and colorless, loved a good show and depended on their sovereign to provide it. Save the nobility, every person in England was required to toil from dawn to dusk for his keep, and beggars and vagabonds were little tolerated. The lives of the average people were largely devoid of entertainment, except for church-sanctioned events. But they could speculate and gossip about affairs at court, and they could count on glimpsing their beautiful ruler and her glittering train once a year as she proceeded, arrayed in silks and adorned with jewels beyond imagining, attended by throngs of courtiers, through their quiet neck of the woods. Though he was rarely praised and had thus far not been appreciably rewarded for the enormous amount of work he did for the crown, Sir Thomas realized, upon reflection on the enormity of Cecil's job, what a small cog he was in the whole business of the kingdom.

The queen's court was huge, numbering roughly a thousand people. Intricate in its conception and nature, it was elaborately organized down to the smallest detail of who, by right of birth or station, had the honor of being there to hand Her Majesty everything from her fan to her sanitary wipes. Life at court was rife with intrigue and petty jealousies, gossip and rumor-mongering, accusations and declarations, as everyone jockeyed for a better position and more access to the dazzling pinnacle of power at the top—the queen herself. The four most powerful ministers around her were the lord chamberlain, the lord steward, the lord treasurer, and the lord secretary, in that order. From their hands fell all the plums of political patronage, and through them came all petitions for rewards from the queen's largesse. Above stairs, the lord chamberlain was perhaps the most powerful of all, for he attended directly to the queen's person and those who were about her, and it was he who organized and directed the elaborate ceremonial that attended her every moment.

Below stairs, the lord steward ruled supreme, for he was in charge of the queen's household. He appointed and directed all the servants of the palaces, and had authority over everything from the scullery maids to the royal food taster, to the keeping of the queen's jewels, to the grooms of the stables. The lord treasurer held the purse strings. The secretary of state—Cecil's thankless job—was the go-between politically for the queen, the lord treasurer, her privy council, and the parliamentary and judicial arms of government. He was also at times the queen's liaison with the archbishop and the church, though normally the archbishop had access denied all others, as the ruler's personal confessor.

Though not perceived by the nobility to be as powerful as the lord chamberlain, the lord secretary was an awesome position, for it afforded unlimited access to all others, including the queen. Conversely, it allowed all those personages unlimited access to him as well, Thomas realized. And thereby hung Cecil's continual vexation, for it was impossible to please so many varied, self-centered, petulant, demanding personages. However, it was his responsibility to keep the web of government tightly woven and see to it that it was perceived as such abroad. It was also his responsibility to keep Elizabeth happy, a task at which he was more successful than most. Whatever her other shortcomings might be, in her choice of those who would assist her to rule, the queen had been inordinately clever for one so young. Her ministers and advisers were men of wisdom, prudence, loyalty, and unbounded energy. They held the well-being of England above personal ambition.

Wherever the queen happened to be was the center of the English universe. To her court came everything and everyone of importance, whether suitors for her hand in marriage, delegates from foreign rulers, or merely those who cherished or chased wealth, power and renown. Therefore, to be sent from court in disgrace was the worst punishment imaginable in a world where a single word of praise from the queen could bring rewards beyond a man's dreams and a reward given by the queen's own hand was as manna from the Almighty. Since such rewards were marks of status and approbation, Thomas again wondered when his own promised reward might be forthcoming from Her Majesty. But he said nothing to Cecil about it.[3]

At his first audience with the queen after his return to England, Her Majesty received him graciously and expressed tender and sincere concern for his health. With the interest of a keen horsewoman, she insisted he describe to her in detail the circumstances of his accident. Then the talk turned to other subjects. "We thank you for the care of our Turkey horse." Elizabeth bestowed him with a smile. "He is said to be fair and fleet, and is the pride of our stables, our master of the horse tells us. We shall ride him one day soon and see for ourselves how swift he goes." Above all, Elizabeth proclaimed herself happy to have him once again in England. "We welcome you again to our presence. You have served us well, and we pray daily for your full recovery." Sir Thomas bowed deeply in acknowledgment of such a rare high compliment from Her Majesty, but she gave him no reward of land or other tangible goods for his service, and at that he was much surprised, and not a little chagrined.

Early in August, he petitioned Cecil, as he had several times before, to "review and pass on my account." Thomas knew it was only a matter of time before the queen would require him to leave England again for Antwerp, and he wanted his accounts reviewed and the money the crown owed him paid to him before that happened. But Cecil did not move on the review and audit of Sir Thomas's account. The crown owed Gresham considerable money he had advanced for expenses, and while he knew that Elizabeth was stalling payment to all her creditors, Thomas was surprised to find she was now apparently doing so even on relatively minor bills such as his. By not auditing his account, she would not be obliged to pay him. Nor would she be required to part with rewards. That Elizabeth was reluctant to part with any money or possessions of the crown had already become legend throughout the realm. Her initial economies had turned into virtual parsimony, and many likened her in that respect to her grandfather, Henry VII. Though she was in looks and spirit more like her father, Elizabeth had not inherited his open hand with the treasury. Cecil and the other ministers had to wring money from her, even for necessities.

Thomas hoped he could stay in England this time long enough to make considerable progress toward the completion of Gresham House, but that was not to be. By mid-August of 1561, with his accounts still not settled by Cecil and the lord treasurer, he was once more on the high seas bound for Antwerp. The queen wished him to make payment on her debts with the other £30,000 the merchant adventurers and staplers had loaned her.

As Thomas sat in a special chair he had caused to be rigged and fastened on deck for him to take the air, he looked out at the rolling blue sea and thought about his son Richard, who was at this moment on another of the family's ships, serving his apprenticeship. He had spent little time with his son in the past two or three years. He had lost his only brother, and he had no nephews following along soon. Thomas looked forward eagerly to the day his son would join him in the family trading business, for it was a great responsibility which continued to grow by leaps and bounds. He sorely needed another pair of able and trustworthy hands to steer the family enterprises while he attended to his official duties for the crown. Thomas counted himself lucky to have such a fine son to take the reins when he grew tired of holding them.

His wife, too, had much to bear, with him gone so much of the time. She would not countenance even the suggestion of returning with him to Antwerp, no matter how often he asked. "Nay, not for so much as a visit to that land would I quit England again," she declared. In all, she was a good and dutiful wife, if at times very vexing to a man. This time, Anne had bid him farewell without emotion or complaint. Not only had her mien become more sober, he thought, but she had relinquished all color and gaiety in her dress as well. Of late, Anne affected the sober black and white garb of the more conservative Protestants in England, a fashion that had become popular among the ladies and gentlemen of London and those at Elizabeth's court, too. Now Thomas's customary black garb was the height of fashion, a thought that brought him a wry smile of amusement. The queen's fondness for pearls had also set the fashion in jewels worn by the ladies, for his wife wanted no jewels of him of late except those fashioned with pearls. Well, he would send some fine pearls to her, and to his daughter, too, as soon as he reached Antwerp.

Settled once again into his house on Long New Street, Gresham wrote Cecil to notify him of his safe arrival and bring him up to date on what was happening on the Continent. "Most humbly desiring you to have in your remembrance the passing of my account when Her Majesty comes thither to Enfield on her summer progress, considering the great charge and burden that lays upon me and mine." His concern was that he be repaid at the higher exchange rate at which he had paid out the expense, "for," he complained, "if I'm rated at twenty-two shillings sixpence the pound, as the auditor informs me he has done, I stand to personally lose over five hundred pounds in the repayment of my expenses."[4]

Once again, in addition to paying and renegotiating England's loans abroad, Sir Thomas found himself in the business of procuring and shipping arms to England. Several shiploads had been held up in Germany by agents of the king of Denmark and the duke of Brunswick, who, it was rumored, were plotting war against Sweden. The king of Sweden was still pressing his suit of marriage to Queen Elizabeth, so the embargo by Denmark and Germany on shipment of arms to England was understandable. Thomas was also again occupied with supplying Cecil and the queen with what intelligence he could gather.

Social life in Antwerp, which Thomas had always enjoyed, was at a standstill. "There isn't anything going on here," he complained to Jasper Schetz after a week, "except a lot of drinking and betting over the competition for the Land Jewel. It's a foolish throwing around of time and money, if you ask me."

"Money, for certain," replied Schetz. "They've put more than £100,000 into it already, I've heard."

The Land Jewel was to be a competition between cities in Flanders for a prize in rhetoric, and was a great event, accompanied by parades, pageants, and a series of elimination contests. Competition between the cities, and groups within the cities, was fierce. The final winner would receive the Land Jewel, a large sterling silver cup of great value—Clough had been told reliably that it was worth at least £65,000. Everyone was in a fever, wagering on their favorites to win, and there were frequent fistfights in the streets over who had the better man, or which city would win.[5]

Rumors and gossip flew about in Antwerp faster than the birds that roosted in the eaves of the bourse. First it was said that the king of Sweden was disposed now to marry the daughter of the king of Poland. Then the word was that the kings of Sweden, Poland, and Denmark, together with the dukes of Saxony, Landgrave, and various others were forming an alliance to fight against Ivan of Muscovia. Then the talk was that the king of Sweden was going to travel to England soon, to make one final attempt to convince the elusive Elizabeth to marry.

All this Sir Thomas duly reported to Cecil: "Now, the saying is that the Council of Trent goes forward, but it is thought nothing will be concluded. Also, the king of Spain is demanding a gift, or subsidy of money from these states toward payment of his debts, and they [the Flemish] have said they will grant him nothing unless the Inquisition is stopped, and that they don't want this land bothered with these new bishops in religious matters. The saying is ever strong that the king of Sweden will come to England."

A few days later, Gresham wrote again to Cecil: "The saying here still is that the king of Sweden for certain comes to England, with a great navy to the number of one hundred sails of ships and brings with him two million dollars, at least. However, you probably have better news of this from your ambassadors than I have here. There is also news of a great earthquake in the realm of Naples, that has overthrown many towns and castles, and in which great numbers have perished. Today, my friend Sir John Leigh, whom I most humbly commend to you, as he does himself, arrived here, and will, with God's leave, go home to England by the end of the month."

It was September before Thomas could manage to get the arms that had been detained at Hamburg released and shipped to England. He sent them on two ships, the *Martin Stateman* and the *Christopher of Dittmarche*. In writing Cecil to inform him about the shipments, Thomas felt compelled to express again his concern about the gossip, still strong in Antwerp, of the king of Sweden and his hundred ships, "that the Queen's Majesty would suffer such a number of ships to come into her realm, if the Queen's Majesty and he should not part friends. . . ."

Also, the treasury was now causing him financial distress in other areas—his large bills of exchange were not being paid, and he suspected the delay was due to his old enemy the lord treasurer. "Please, if you will, take it up with my lord treasurer," he implored Cecil, "to pay my bills of exchange, for the preserving of my good name and credit, which does concern me a lot, for as of the 25th of this month [September] not a penny has been paid. I thank you in advance for any good you can do me in that matter, and I await only the new bonds you have dispatched, and upon the recovery of the old ones, I do intend, with the Queen's Majesty's leave, to come home."[6]

Sir Thomas was not the only one with thoughts of home. The still young and recently widowed Mary Stuart, queen of Scots, was headed home from France to Scotland. The House of Valois, like the rest of France, was in political and religious turmoil, and sunk into bankruptcy by the excesses of the French court and its wars. The dukes of Guise were plotting to take the throne of France from the Valois. With her husband the king dead, there was nothing left for Mary in France. She requested passport to travel through England on her way home, but Elizabeth, at Cecil's prompting, denied it to the Catholic queen. She could not allow Mary to travel leisurely across England to Scotland, rousing the passions of the Catholic faction in England—especially those who firmly believed in the Scottish queen's claim to Elizabeth's crown.

Upon reaching Scotland by sea, Queen Mary found her position there decidedly tenuous. She was a Catholic queen in a country that had gone Protestant in her absence. She settled in and began her quest to wrest control of her country out of the hands of the Protestants. Now, two attractive, marriageable queens—one widowed, one virgin—held sway over the kingdoms of the Isles. They were both enticing marriage bait for all the ambitious princes of Europe, but Elizabeth would prove more clever than Mary in playing at that game.[7]

That Christmas, Thomas was again in London, supervising the progress of Gresham House. On New Year's Day, he and Anne went with Sir John Leigh to court to present their New Year gifts to the queen. Sir Thomas, leaning on his walking stick, bowed as best he could and offered Her Majesty £10 in fine gold angels (coins) encased in a black silk bag with silver trim. Elizabeth, resplendent in pale grey silk, with a wide, lacy ruff, her neck and bodice garlanded with the familiar ropes of pearls, graciously thanked him, for no gift pleased her better than money. In turn, she presented him a finely shaped gilt jug with a hinged cover, weighing twenty-four ounces. Then Lady Anne, dropping a deep curtsey, offered the queen a pretty silver box filled with sweets, and received a token gift of a Spanish fan and a compliment from the queen in return. Stepping forward after Anne, Sir John Leigh gallantly presented Her Majesty with a large, intricately carved and gilded wooden box, containing combs, looking glasses, and glass balls for dressing her hair. The queen, delighted as a child with his gift, gave Sir John a jug similar to the one given to Sir Thomas.[8]

Leaving the palace, Leigh remarked casually to Thomas, "I hear 'twas Spinola who won the cup for gifts to the queen this year." Benedick Spinola, scion of a wealthy Genovese merchant family, had given Her Majesty the most extravagant gift of all—an entire bolt of expensive purple velvet cloth from the finest weavers in Italy. "He seeks to make reparation, no doubt," added Leigh, "for his confession, taken only last week by the secretary, that he has stolen thousands in avoided customs fees on the goods he has shipped in the name of others, misusing Her Majesty's license to him."[9] Thomas's ears perked up. "God's truth?" he asked. For this touched on a subject to which Thomas had given much thought lately.

Thomas was always on the lookout for ways to improve the international trading system or to save the crown money. On his two most recent sojourns in London, he had made it a point to go down to the custom houses to watch how they operated. Now, after hearing what Sir John Leigh had to say about Spinola—the same confirmed by Cecil a few days later—Thomas wondered how the customs system in London measured up against the one in use in Antwerp.

Immediately after Christmas he wrote to Richard Clough in Antwerp, asking him to send complete information on the customs system in Flanders. He was surprised not only at the alacrity with which Clough responded to his request, but also at the intelligence his factor passed along about corruption, which Clough swore was running rampant in the London customs system:

> Sir, I'm glad you asked for this information, and I hope it can be used to the queen's advantage, for here they talk of nothing else except how easy it is to deceive the queen's customs officials.
>
> They say the queen's custom collections depend on five or six searchers, all of whom are known to be men that will accept bribes. If Her Majesty would check on this, and spend but two or three thousand pounds now to correct the matter, she will save at least five thousand pounds a year thereafter. There are many ways that custom is stolen in London, probably more in one month in London than here in Antwerp in a whole year. One of the ways used is when the merchants have the goods at home in their houses, they have to wait sometimes up to ten days to get a searcher to come and oversee the opening of the goods. And then he comes only if he is paid a bribe. And if anyone asks them why they demand bribes, they say they are

paid pitifully small wages, which they cannot live on. So they steal. Better it would be if the matter were rendered so that men could be paid the wage they should be. And of course if a merchant is left with a pack of silks in his house, and has to wait eight days for the customs man to come, considering the heavy duty he has to pay on silk, it is not unusual for him to take out the silk and put other material, less costly, in there. The customs searcher would say no, for the goods have the seal upon them. But the one who makes the searcher's seal can also make another, and merchants are not as simple as people think they are. And what a further shame it is to us Englishmen, that considering what a great city London is, they have not found the means to make a bourse but must walk around in the rain, more like peddlers than merchants, while in this country and most others, when people must meet to do business, they have a place to meet for that purpose![10]

Reading Clough's letter again, Thomas was suddenly reminded of his father, and his father's lifelong dream of building a bourse in London. As Clough had pointed out, nothing had been done to improve conditions for tradesmen in London since his father had addressed pleadings for a site for the bourse in Lombard Street to King Henry and Lord Cromwell back in 1538. More than twenty-three years had passed since that day, and while all three of King Henry's children had come to sit upon England's throne, his own father's dream was no closer to being realized now than it was then. Limping to the door of his shop, Thomas stepped out and looked around him, up along the length of narrow Lombard Street. The stench of cooked cabbages, garbage, and offal rose harshly in his nostrils, and the sights and sounds of the City, like its smells, immediately assaulted his other senses. Hammers pounded in the next street, metal pots clanged and clinked, wagon wheels creaked, horses' hooves rang against the cobblestones, their drivers cursing and shouting and wielding the whip. It was midday, and throngs of people were out. Everywhere rose the cries of the streetsellers: "Sweeep, chimney sweep! Fine Seville oranges! Lemons for milady! Ripe Hartychokes, riiipe! Pies, yer hot mutton, yer hot apple, try me pies!"[11]

Thomas saw small groups of men gathered farther down Lombard Street, in pairs and threes, talking together, occasionally passing documents back and forth. Now and then, some would step into the public house to cement a deal over a pint. Others stopped a seller to buy a pie or an orange. Yes, England had come a long way in these twenty-three years, but her merchants in London still made their deals in the open street, without shelter from the elements, as they had in his father's time, and in his father's before him. Thomas hoped he could change that before it became Richard's turn.

Suddenly little Anne appeared and took his hand, bringing him his walking stick. "'Tis time to sup, papa. Come, I'll take you up."

He looked down at her, and smiled. "Soon you'll have a finer house than this to sup in, miss."

"Finer than this house, papa?"

"Yea, my pretty little maid, much finer. A pretty house for a pretty maid, and pretty dresses too, for you are the granddaughter of Sir Richard Gresham, once lord mayor of this entire city." He swept his arm in a half circle, encompassing everything in sight. Anne's eyes widened.

"'Tis so, papa?"

"Yes, child, so you are, and your fair new home grows even now, by yon tower." Her father pointed toward Bishopsgate Street. "We'll go there and see it on the morrow."

Then he turned and followed her inside, muttering as if to himself, "Yea, 'twere much still to be done." When the child stopped and looked up at him questioningly, he signaled with his stick for her to precede him up the stairs. "Marry, mistress Anne, there is much still to be done, so we must haste now ... to sup."

March of 1562 found Sir Thomas on one of Her Majesty's warships, this time with an escort of four caravels, bound for Antwerp. He was, as usual, to pay some of the queen's bonds and renew others, but this time he was tasked with personally carrying four cases of gold sovereigns with him to satisfy certain of the queen's creditors. Ordinarily, this would have given Thomas scant concern, but with his injured leg he was less sure of his physical prowess than before, and there were many thieves and vagabonds who plied this route. He had hired two strong bodyguards to accompany him.

During the crossing, a great storm came up, and for a while Thomas feared the ship, and he, would not weather it. The wind howled and moaned in fierce gusts, driving mountainous foaming waves before it. The wooden hull of the ship creaked so loudly it seemed to be crying out in anguish each time a wave crashed against it. Thomas, confined below decks, heard a great crack as a mast broke, and there were shouts and screams above as shrouds of wet canvas crashed to the deck. The officers screamed out orders, and the crew gamely tried to follow them, but it was touch and go. Two men were lost overboard and quickly vanished from sight in the churning seas. They lost sight of their escort. Finally, when hope seemed gone, and Thomas was sure he was condemned to die in the foaming fury of the sea, they outran it, and the following morning the beleaguered ship, with its weary and frightened crew and passenger, sailed into the harbor and tied up at Dunkirk. Hours later, three of the caravels showed up. The fourth had gone down in the storm.

Thomas decided it would be safer to leave the ships there, where they could make speedier return to England, and proceed overland to Antwerp. Two armed sailors were assigned to go with him. He procured a wagon for the cases of coins, and with four heavily armed guards keeping careful lookout, they made their way on horseback as swiftly as they could across the countryside of Flanders to Bruges, where they spent the night. As he dined at the quiet hostel, down one of the narrow streets near the Church of Our Lady, he thought of Ghislaine, smiling warmly at the memories of the happy times he'd spent with her in their house along the canal.

After dinner, he walked slowly there. As he crossed the bridge over the canal, he stopped. Cold moonlight glistened on the water, and in the shadows on the bank two swans and a duck nestled close under the boughs of a drooping tree. A cold wind blew off the water. Thomas shivered. Leaning heavily on his gnarled stick, he continued on, until he stood before the door of the house that had once been theirs. Standing there, he could imagine her face at the window, her smile of welcome. So much had happened, so much had changed since those days. Thomas spoke silently to her ghost, "Our daughter is beautiful—like you—she'd make you proud. And I—I'm old and ugly now, a poor old cripple. The lusty, vigorous man you knew here has gone." A single, hot tear of loss and self-pity slid down his cheek, startling him. Furtively, he wiped it away, embarrassed. Abruptly, he turned from the house and resolutely stepped along away from it, his stick rapping smartly against the stones. Soon, he reached his rooms. The guards had become anxious, and were glad to see him return. The next morning he was up early and they trotted off with their precious cargo, finally reaching Antwerp on 15 March.

Events in Antwerp were closely tied to the religious war that was raging in France between the followers of the duc de Guise, staunchly Catholic, and the prince de Condé, and his Protestant Huguenots. England and Flanders paid close attention to the struggle, for the safety of both countries was staked on the eventual outcome. Philip was openly assisting the duc de Guise, and Elizabeth began making plans to send help to Condé and the Huguenots.

Two weeks later, Thomas wrote Cecil that he would return to London shortly. "With the Queen's leave I will call myself to account again, trusting that now Her Majesty will bless me with her royal gift for my service in such sort as her late brother King Edward and her late sister Queen Mary did. The gossip here is that the Queen's Majesty will have war with Monsieur de Guise and ally with the prince de Condé, and they write out of Germany that on the 7 September the Emperor's son Maximilian shall be crowned king of Bohemia in the city of Sprague."

On 22 April he submitted a brief of his accounts to the crown, "for three whole years and 159 days," including, in the final itemization of just over £3646: "An iron chest with small key, £20; charge of a Turkey horse, £10; riding and posting charges, £1627; house-hire £200; Diet and necessaries, £1819." Hoping at last to be reimbursed and to spend the rest of the year at home in England, he left Antwerp.[12]

But in less than six months he was back in Antwerp, his accounts with the crown still unsettled, for the queen needed more money to finance her aid to the Huguenots, and was not ready to pay him. In fact, she needed to borrow funds. However, Sir Thomas did not to find things in good order in the Low Countries, and even his friend Jasper Schetz could not help him this time. "For there comes such news out of France daily that no man knows what to say or do," Schetz remarked, sadly. Fearing that England might be caught short of arms again, Thomas wrote Cecil:

> If Monsieur de Guise and the papists should win the upper hand, let Her Majesty make her reckoning they will go after her for religion's sake! Which has made getting credit here so difficult this pen cannot write you how much so. However, they say here that now is the time for England to recover those areas we have lost of late in France, or even better pieces. Being assured that Her Majesty has provisions of men, munitions and armor to do it withal. However, if I were to be able to persuade with Her Highness, I would wish her to be provided with three or four hundred thousand pounds of saltpeter more, for all possibilities, for I know she has enough brimstone to make twenty hundred thousand weights of saltpeter, and I know she hasn't more than four hundred thousand weight of clean saltpeter in her stores. Be assured, it is only that which she might lack if war should chance to come, and we should take care to foresee it in time, because as you know our forces and ships are nothing without powder. And, as Your Honor knows, no supplies will be allowed to pass out of the King of Spain's dominions. Also, I trust you have enough bow staves. As Your Honor knows, Bremen and

Hamburg are the places we must ship from and it must be brought from the land of Bohemia, where the best is to be had, and that is no simple feat.[13]

Up to then, Thomas had managed to manipulate the queen's debt load abroad so well that credit had been easy to obtain for Queen Elizabeth at only 10 percent interest, where other rulers had difficulty getting money at upward of 14 percent. Therefore, Elizabeth had financed her battle in Scotland with relative ease. Now the crisis in France, and especially the rumor that Elizabeth was poised to send troops to help the Protestants, shriveled her credit prospects. "I will assure you, here is the greatest scarcity of money that has ever been seen or heard of, and I am unable to negotiate loans for even the smallest amounts," Sir Thomas was forced to inform Cecil. The queen's debt, due to be paid in Flanders in August 1562, was more than £64,500.

Thomas found himself unable to negotiate with any of the moneylenders, for they were certain that Elizabeth faced war in the near future. If the duke of Guise won in France, they reasoned, then all the Catholic nations would immediately go to war against Elizabeth to drive Protestantism from England and Scotland, whether she helped the French Protestants or not. Elizabeth's position was the most precarious it had been since she came to the throne. "Whereupon," Sir Thomas wrote Cecil, "there are here such great doubts cast upon our estate that the credit of the Queen's Majesty and the whole nation is at a stay, and glad is that man who may count himself quit of an Englishman's bill!"

But it was not just war, credit, and supplies with which Sir Thomas had to contend that summer in Antwerp. The arrival of another charge to his door made for an invigorating change of routine from his lonely and frustrating duties for the crown. Cecil had begged Sir Thomas to come to his aid in regard to his son, young Thomas Cecil, who was traveling to increase his education, and was presently in Paris with his tutor, Wyndebank. Thomas Cecil was causing his father grief through what Cecil perceived as wanton and derelict behavior.

Cecil was furious in a way Thomas had never seen him. His son, he claimed, was spending his time and money in gambling, carousing, and other foolish pursuits. Cecil upbraided young Thomas and his tutor by letter, but also asked Sir Thomas to see to it that they did not run out of funds while over in Europe. The tutor had written Cecil: "Sir, I humbly beseech you that in your letters to your son Mr. Thomas you remind him not to lose the commodity of the morning for his profit. We received, the 9th of this present, a bill of credit for three hundred dollars from Mr. Gresham's man at Antwerp. I pray God we may bestow them [the dollars] well. As yesterday being the 9th, my lord ambassador went to court [in Paris] and presented Mr. Thomas."[14]

Before long Cecil, at his wits' end with his son's antics, begged Sir Thomas to intervene. Sir Thomas invited tutor Wyndebank and his charge to come to Antwerp for a visit, so that he could observe Cecil's son firsthand and decide for himself about the young man's comportment. Once they were settled in as his house guests, Thomas observed Cecil's son carefully. He found Thomas Cecil to be civil, polite and apparently advancing with his lessons. His behavioral peccadilloes amounted to little more than the juices of a young man with too much leisure time and too much money at his command. The gambling, wenching, drinking, and sport that the elder Cecil so detested in his son were normal pursuits of the young gentry of Thomas Cecil's age.

Sir Thomas was careful to question Thomas Cecil closely about his interests and his studies, slipping from French to Latin to Greek as they talked. Young Cecil followed his host's linguistic turns with amazing alacrity and seemed eager to share his adventures and his knowledge with Sir Thomas, whom he had known since early childhood. Withal, Thomas Cecil would be a fine man one day, when he had more maturity to him. This Thomas was the same age as his own son Richard, and he'd be proud if his son were this learned, though assuredly he'd hope not so taken by the vicissitudes of life. However, an apprentice in the merchant adventurers had little money, and certainly no time to spend on frivolity. In that, his Richard was better served than Cecil's son. Nevertheless, this young man had good character. Better he spend some time visiting other countries and learning more, than return home to disgrace, and his father's certain wrath. Perhaps if he lingered awhile in Europe, he'd have enough of whoring and drinking and gambling before he returned to England and his father's inevitable retribution, decided Sir Thomas.

Sir Thomas wrote and advised Cecil not to worry overly much about his son. "Your son has grown taller, and has used his time well, for he speaks very good French, and is as full of civility and virtue as your heart could desire. You'd do well to let him travel more while here, and to that purpose you would do well to ship three horses to them here, for horseflesh here is expensive and hard to come by, and I'll be happy to provide a guide to go along with them on their travels to see that they come to no harm." Since Sir Thomas had no further need of the bodyguards who had traveled with him from England, and as one of the bodyguards was a man well acquainted with the Continent, he decided he would send him on with young Cecil and Wyndebank.

At the end of August, Thomas saw them off, and sat down to write Cecil. "I have dispatched your son and Mr. Wyndebank, and given them £50 in their purse and £50 more at credit for them to receive when they wish, until I hear further from you. I shall take care to furnish them with anything they might need, and I thank you for entrusting me with the care of your son, whom I will look after as I would my own son. Be assured, that as of this writing, you have as handsome and virtuous a son as you could wish for. I assure you, while he was here, and for all he saw in this town, I did not see him spend one penny in waste, and he was careful in his writing and in all other things that would please you. You do not need to send any horses, for I have procured them at good price."[15]

But soon Cecil's attention, and Sir Thomas's, was distracted from the minor peccadilloes of young Thomas Cecil. In October 1562, with Cecil beset with complex problems abroad and the foreign debt risen to £280,000, with no available means to pay it, Queen Elizabeth fell gravely ill. Physicians were summoned, but even the eminent Dr. Caius could not put a sure diagnosis to the source of her high fevers. Dr. Burcot, a renowned German doctor, was called in to consult. He took one look at the feverish queen and, although there were no recognizable outward symptoms of such, he declared, "It's the pox." Elizabeth was so outraged at that awful pronouncement she ordered the doctor out. He left in a rage, insulted. For five days more the queen's fevers continued unabated, with no visible spots or other usual signs of smallpox. Finally, her doctors sent for Secretary Cecil. "My lord, we do not expect Her Majesty to live out this night." The privy council gathered immediately to debate the succession: Would it be Lord Hunsdon, who claimed he was a descendant of the Plantagenets? Or the Lady Catherine Grey, sister to the hapless Queen Jane? Elizabeth had banished Catherine to the tower for marrying and having a son without her permission. No one dared even whisper the name Mary queen of Scots.[16] Elizabeth rallied briefly from her stupor when the privy council gathered round her bed. Seeing them all there, she realized she was near death. Weakly, she recommended her young cousin Lord Hunsdon to them, and asked the lords to be good to him. "Milords, I beg you pledge you will make Robert Dudley protector, with an annual income of £20,000. And give also his servant, Tamworth, who sleeps in his room, £500 a year." Then, as if someone had spoken the question aloud, the queen rallied again and declared distractedly, "before God, though I love Lord Robert dearly, nothing amiss ever passed 'twixt us." At that, Cecil rushed to the queen's side to soothe her, shooing the others away, and he quietly promised her that the council would do all as she had directed.

Meanwhile, Cecil and Caius, conferring together, had dispatched messengers by fast horse to Dr. Burcot, who had refused to return to treat the queen. "He shall be brought hence on pain of death!" a furious Cecil ordered. A few hours later, Burcot appeared, at sword's point. Quickly, he examined the nearly comatose queen. "Almost too late, my liege," he muttered to her. Wrapping Elizabeth from head to foot in a length of cloth, he directed that her maids put her down close to the fire to sweat, leaving only her head and one of her hands out of the wrappings. Then he gave her a bottle, from which he ordered her to drink.

"Drink as much as you can," he urged, "all of it, if you like." Elizabeth, now awake and sweating profusely from the heat of the fire, drank thirstily from the bottle. Soon they saw red spots coming out on her hand. "Aha!" declared the doctor triumphantly, holding her hand up before her bleary eyes. "What is this?" cried Elizabeth fearfully. "'Tis the pox, Milady Queen, as I told you 'twould be," Burcot answered mildly. "Better to have it out, on the hands and face, than in the heart, where it kills the body." Elizabeth, with a great cry, fainted away.

Fortunately, the queen had only a mild case, and eventually the scabs on her face and hands went away, leaving her virtually unblemished. In gratitude, Elizabeth granted Dr. Burcot a great tract of land and gave him the gold spurs that had belonged to her grandfather, Henry VII. Unfortunately, Lady Mary Sidney, Robert Dudley's lovely sister, one of Elizabeth's ladies in waiting who had staunchly nursed the queen back to health, was not so fortunate. She caught the pox and was horribly disfigured by it.[17]

After that fright, Cecil, the privy council, and Parliament determined that the queen must marry and have children, and as soon as possible. They began once more to search for a suitable political match, and this time they looked to the French Protestants for a possible candidate.

In February 1563 the Catholic duc de Guise was assassinated, and a peace reasonably favorable to the Protestant cause was signed in March. The English returned LeHavre to the French, though they did not regain Calais in exchange, as Elizabeth had hoped. England and France were at peace again, and that was what mattered most.

But there was another, unanticipated and terrible result of that war. In August, a killing fever broke out ferociously in London. It had been brought back to England by the soldiers garrisoned at LeHavre, and it spread like a terrible poison throughout England. The queen and her court quickly fled to the countryside. Sir Thomas took his family to Intwood. It was said that more than a thousand people were dying every week in London alone. In truth, the pestilence visited upon the people of London that autumn was threefold—they suffered from the killing fever, from lack of money, and from a shortage of food. All trading in London had halted. Stores were shuttered and Lombard Street was deserted, for those who had not bolted to the country to escape the fever were afraid even to speak to another person, for fear of catching it.[18]

By October 1563, Sir Thomas was obliged to set out for Antwerp directly from Intwood, for the queen's debts had not been paid, and the moneylenders were threatening the wholesale arrest of English merchants and seizure of all English ships and goods in Flanders. Sir Thomas was more concerned at the damage to the queen's credit—credit he had worked for years to build. He told Cecil he would go and try to resolve the problem. When Cecil protested that there was still great danger from the fever, Thomas shrugged it off, "I must go, for it will be better for us if I am there and they see me."

When he reached Antwerp, he found that not only had Elizabeth not the money to pay her debts, she had gone so far as to reduce his paltry salary as well. In truth, the queen was treating Sir Thomas no worse than her ministers and other officials, for they were not being paid either, but on hearing this latest turn of events, Sir Thomas felt most aggrieved. "Methinks the Queen's Majesty deals very hardly and extremely with me," he complained to Jasper Schetz. Then he sat down and wrote Cecil another letter listing all the services he had performed for the queen in the five years he had served her, reminding them that even his lameness was a result of trying better to serve Her Majesty's needs. Cecil understood just how his friend Sir Thomas felt, but there was little he could do, for he was working even harder for the queen than Sir Thomas, and receiving just as little in return. Elizabeth was cleverly tapping and draining the personal fortunes of all the ministers, ambassadors, and agents who worked for her, for they not only had to cover their own expenses, they then had to wait—not knowing how long it would be—in hopes she might see fit to reimburse them for their loans to the crown.[19]

But worse was yet to come. On New Year's Day 1564 Sir Thomas headed for Zealand with Sir Thomas Cotton, again accompanied by four of Her Majesty's warships, for he was carrying gold bullion with which to pay two of the queen's more obstreperous lenders, Broketrope and Ratzsavi. Once in Zealand, he made his treacherous way overland by heavily guarded wagon to Antwerp. The two bankers refused to accept payment in bullion—they wanted coin. Thomas was obliged to pay out of his own pocket to have the bullion melted down and made into coin. Frustration at the difficulty and cost of accomplishing even the simplest task for Elizabeth began to overwhelm him.

In Antwerp, the regent had issued a proclamation that, for fear of importing the plague—but Sir Thomas surmised there was probably a more political reason behind it—no English ships would be allowed to dock there, and no English cloths or wools could be imported to Flanders. Worse, now when English and Spanish ships encountered one another at sea, there were brash acts of piracy, wherein the stronger ship and crew boarded and plundered the weaker.

The regent then went a step further—she prohibited the exportation to England of the merchandise on which the English merchants had already paid export duties. Gresham and the other English merchants were outraged. Thomas fumed to Schetz, "We were told that such goods as be intended for England, being shipped *before* the proclamation, should pass; but now even that proves untrue, for she [the regent] will not let pass nothing."[20]

Thomas grunted in frustration, pacing with his quick, crooked gait up and down the halls of his house in Long New Street. This was a devilish turn of affairs! England and Flanders were not at war. The people of Flanders wanted to buy English goods, and the people of England wanted goods from the Low Countries. Yet, the regent had suddenly placed an embargo on all trade between the two countries. The devil take her! They'd simply move the seat of commerce elsewhere. The merchants would not be denied their opportunities to trade their goods. If Flanders didn't want them, they'd go somewhere else.

That afternoon, he called Richard Clough to him, and they consulted at length about other possibilities for the merchant adventurers. Clough recommended against Embden and Hamburg, favoring instead Hull or York. Thomas wrote Cecil requesting further advice.

The matter was still being debated, and the Flemish people were just beginning to feel the nasty bite of the regent's rash decision, when at the end of January 1564, Sir Thomas received word to return on the next available ship. Something was gravely amiss. He hastened home as fast as horse and ship could carry him. A grave-faced John Eliot was there to greet him when he entered the hall on Lombard Street. Eliot drew his master gently into the parlor. "Sir, 'tis a terrible thing I have to tell you. Richard, your son, has died of the fever."

Thomas stared at his factor blankly. "What! My son you say? Richard?" He shook his head. "Nay, 'tis not possible! 'Tis a mistake ... he's but a young man, you must be mistaken."

"No, sir...." Sadness filled Eliot's eyes. Then his cousin Cicely appeared, and stretched her arms out to him, "Oh, Thomas ..." she began, tears springing to her eyes. But he turned away from her, unable to comprehend the enormity of the news he had just been given. His only son Richard, that strapping lad, so strong, so healthy, so full of life, dead? No, it could not be!

Frozen with disbelief, he stood there unable to speak, his mind racing. This could not be. Not his son, upon whom he had pinned all his hopes and dreams for the future! God would not be that cruel to him. Gone at only twenty? Impossible! Yet the house was dark, and all in it were in mourning clothes. The rooms were draped in black. "Anne? Anne!" he called loudly. Where was his wife? She alone could release him from this band of iron that had suddenly wrapped his chest and held him prisoner. She would tell him nothing was amiss. Richard would be home soon. "Mistress Gresham!" he called, desperation clawing at his throat.

"Your lady wife is in her bed," his cousin informed him softly. "She sleeps, God be praised. 'Tis a terrible grief to her poor heart to lose Richard."

"The fever, curse it," said Eliot. "Nineteen on his ship died of't. Almost none 'scaped."

With a great cry of anguish, Thomas smashed his walking stick against the doorframe. The fever! Curse the fever! He leaned his head against the wall and pounded the bare wood of the doorframe with his fist until his hand bled.

"Come, sir, sit and rest a bit, now. The lad's to be buried on the morrow." Anne, he learned, had been taken to his sister Christiana by her governess.

Sir Thomas and Lady Anne buried their only son at St. Helen's Church on a cold, blustery winter's day. Afterward Sir Thomas could not bear to return to Lombard Street, but instead took his wife to stay awhile at their manor house at Osterley, a quiet country residence in Middlesex, about ten miles from London. There were no memories of Richard at Osterley, for he had never been there. It was there that the broken parents settled for a spell to deal as best they could with their grief and loss.

And it was from there several days later that Sir Thomas at last roused himself from grief enough to pen a few lines, his writing barely legible, to his friend Cecil in London: "From my poor, melancholy house at Osterley." He tried to tell Cecil how he felt, but the words simply wouldn't come.[21] All the honor, wealth, and rank of the realm which it had been his good fortune to attain had come to naught. His greatest hopes were blighted by the loss of his only son, a loss that his heart could barely sustain.

Thomas laid down his quill, and turned to regard his wife. Anne was wrapped in a black woolen shawl, as she had been for days now. She sat utterly still, staring out at the frozen fields, and the bleak January sky. She neither cried nor spoke. During these past days, her face had frozen into a mask of sadness, her sallow complexion heightened by the black gown and hood of deepest mourning, that shrouded her grief. Thomas went over and laid his hand gently upon her shoulder. She reached up and put her hand over his. Neither spoke. Then Thomas turned and limped out, in search of a servant to carry his letter to Cecil in London. He did not know it then, but more than twenty thousand had died of the fever that took his only son.

9

For the Glory of England

For the next year and a half, Sir Thomas remained in England. Richard Clough handled matters in Antwerp for him, writing frequent letters and keeping him abreast of the religious turmoil fomenting in the Flemish city. Because money was so tight as a result of the unrest there, the queen had to resort to financing her needs through sale of crown lands and by raising parliamentary subsidies.[1]

Sir Thomas, realizing that matters on the Continent would only worsen, counseled Her Majesty to turn inward for her financial needs and to try to free the crown as quickly as possible from dependence upon foreign loans.

Gresham House was finally completed, and it was breathtaking. A rambling edifice, it was a spacious home, nearly a palace, of a size and magnificence that Anne Gresham had hardly dared imagine. "There is no finer house in all of London," she said, in a rare compliment to her husband. Sir Thomas moved them into it from Lombard Street, but his joy in the beauty of that great house had dimmed considerably with Richard's death. Fortunately, their son lay close by in St. Helen's, and Sir Thomas and Lady Anne went often to visit his final resting place. The completion at last of Gresham House—his dream home—had lost its significance. Now, it seemed huge and empty to him.

Broken in body and spirit, Thomas divided his time between Gresham House and Osterley. That autumn, in the last burst of brilliant orange and gold that heralded grey winter, his soul at last turned and began to heal. He sat deep in thought. He was a man who had everything material in life, but little to leave to mark his success as a man. His daughter Anne would have a fine dowry, but her sons, if she had sons, would bear another name, and not his. And the circumstances of her birth would preclude them from being his legal heirs. He thought long and hard, and after a while, he came to a decision: he would build his father's bourse for London. He'd build the exchange his father had dreamed of, and it would be a bourse fitting to the memory of both his father and his son—and to himself, too, and the Gresham name. He arose with new energy and set about planning the project.

He reviewed his idea with Cecil and John Thynne. They were enthusiastic, pleased to see him vital and smiling once again. Then, his plans ready, he approached the lord mayor and aldermen of London. "Your honors," he told them in January, "I have here a formal design and proposal for the construction of an exchange, in the City of London, at my own charge and expense. You need only provide the site of land upon which to build it, and I will do the rest."

Murmurs of shock, surprise, and approval ran through the room. Sir Thomas, they knew, was extremely wealthy, but this—it was a generous gift indeed from one person, and would cost him a fortune. The City representatives were delighted, and quick to accept his offer. A general subscription was opened by the court of aldermen in March, whereby the public might donate to purchase the land on which to build the exchange.

With the tender of his proposal to the City, and its acceptance, Sir Thomas was revitalized. He had conceived his monument—a project that would require his full attention, a project to which he could devote his considerable energies for the next few years.[2] And why not? The queen had not bestowed upon him any tangible reward for his services—in fact, the crown still owed him a considerable sum which remained unpaid, including upward of £1000 he had loaned out of his own pocket to subsidize several of the queen's ambassadors.[3]

By 1565 the diligence of Sir Thomas and Secretary Cecil had brought the queen's foreign debt down to barely £17,000, the lowest achieved by any of the Tudor rulers.[4] Sir Thomas had also succeeded in securing for Elizabeth a far greater asset—her credit abroad was impeccable. Her reputation for almost always paying her debts on time, and, more important, for always meeting the interest payments, had put her in a better position to raise funds than any other ruler in Europe. England was experiencing new prosperity—a tenuous one, perhaps, but prosperity had been so far from their grasp for so long, it seemed almost a dream.

With the munitions Sir Thomas had procured and shipped from Antwerp, and his constant caution to Elizabeth to keep her ships and navy well maintained and provisioned, England had become materially strong in both military and naval fortifications. The recoinage and currency reform Sir Thomas had accomplished had restored solvency to the currency and confidence to the merchants. Elizabeth's stringent economies, undertaken initially from dire need but continued out of habit or nature, had proved that the government not only could continue, but would run more efficiently if fed less money. Bloated bureaucracies were stripped to the bone; every expenditure was examined and re-examined before being approved.

Labor legislation that had been passed in 1563 was finally beginning to show results, and opportunity now existed for expansion of industry. Sir Thomas ordered paper, oil, and corn mills constructed at Osterley, on his vast estates there. The paper mill was a new venture, for there was none like it in England.[5]

With so many projects going at home now, Thomas lost interest in journeying back and forth to Antwerp. He was forty-six, and continuous travel for so many years had exacted its toll on his leg injury and his general health. Besides, Antwerp had little these days to entice him. The queen's ambassadors and agents were still trying to convince the regent to restore reasonable trade agreements between England and the Low Countries, but the duchess was interested more in restoring Catholicism to supremacy than in protecting the lucrative commercial base Flanders had enjoyed for so long.

At home, the thirty-two-year-old Queen Elizabeth had come no closer to marriage—her country's only hope for a Tudor heir. She had raised Robert Dudley to the exalted title of earl of Leicester, tickling him playfully on the neck in full view of the scandalized court and the clutch of foreign ambassadors who attended the lavish investment ceremony. Cecil was upset at that, but dared not complain. He was certain that Elizabeth's indiscreet behavior with Dudley was minimizing her chance for an important political match with a foreign prince. Nevertheless, to his surprise, in February 1565 the French ambassador came forward with a formal proposal for the marriage of the young Valois king to Elizabeth of England. The king's mother, Queen Regent Catherine de Medici, informed Elizabeth, "We would be pleased if our dearly beloved sister queen would marry our son and become a daughter to us. You would find," her message assured, "both in the body and mind of the king that which would please you."

Elizabeth, still smarting from the ruthless queen regent's defeat of the English troops supporting the French Huguenots at LeHavre, was nonetheless flattered by the proposal and well aware of the benefits that a marital alliance with France might afford her. However, she had no intention of marrying the seventeen-year-old French king, a devout Catholic, and making England a pawn for the conniving Catherine de Medici. For a while, though, she kept Cecil, the French ambassador, and the grasping queen mother of France dangling, filled with hope.[6]

Thomas listened sympathetically to Cecil's laments about the queen's marriage dilemma, but in truth he was beset with work and his own problems and could little appreciate the queen's love affairs.

In April, his beloved stepmother Lady Isabella died, leaving him to execute her will and handle her financial estate. Along with numerous valuable articles, jewels and properties, Thomas inherited some cherished family heirlooms—a finely worked counterpane with imagery of grasshoppers, and two oriental carpets bearing the family golden grasshopper crest. These he removed to Gresham House, to be proudly displayed there. The kind-hearted Lady Isabella had left a significant charitable bequest to the poor of her parish in London: she designated that the rents from certain properties she owned on Lad Lane, as well as from her home on Milk Street—which she left to the Mercers' Company—would be collected by the Mercers and distributed to those poor parishioners each year.[7] After the stately obsequies for his stepmother, whom he had loved as the only mother he had ever known, Sir Thomas turned his attention back to the building of his exchange.

Meanwhile, still hopeful for a Tudor heir from their queen, London buzzed with speculation about when and whom Elizabeth might marry. It was gossip of which they never tired. Though he was always in Cecil's confidence on the subject, Sir Thomas rarely discussed the queen's marriage prospects with anyone, even in idle chit-chat. His wife and close friends could not draw him into discussion on that subject any more than they could about other rumors they had heard about government affairs. Sir Thomas was as closemouthed as he had been as a youth. And because of it, Thomas remained the one person in whom Cecil could confide his frustrations without fear that they would go any further. Sir Thomas listened carefully, but said little. He was a good sounding board for Cecil.

The king of France and the Archduke Charles were still pressing their suits for Elizabeth's hand, Cecil informed him. Both would be Catholic liaisons, which Parliament feared—and the king of Sweden had not bowed out, either. But Dudley still had Elizabeth's affections, if not her hand, and earlier in the year it had been rumored that some of Her Majesty's suitors might bolt and turn their suits to the widowed and very eligible Mary queen of Scots. At that, Elizabeth had coyly suggested that Dudley himself be advanced as a suitor to the Scottish queen. Indeed, if at heart Elizabeth had no intention of marrying, as seemed the case, it would be a political coup, Cecil acknowledged to Sir Thomas. What better insider to have as king of Scotland than Elizabeth's own dearest friend, Robert Dudley?

But Mary of Scotland had her own plans. She had set her heart on marrying the tall, handsome young Lord Darnley, a power in the Catholic faction in England. When they became aware of this, Cecil's government rushed to dangle a tantalizing bait before Mary: if she would desist from her pursuit of Darnley and marry either Dudley, earl of Leicester, or the duke of Arundel, they would allow an act of Parliament that would designate her heiress presumptive to the English crown. But Mary of Scotland, like Mary of England before her, foolishly allowed infatuation to override political prudence. Without the consent of Parliament or the Protestant lords, she married Darnley and proclaimed him king of Scotland. Soon, she was expecting an heir.

Elizabeth, bitterly angry that Dudley had not succeeded in winning Mary's hand, quarreled with him. This falling-out between the queen and her favorite, Leicester, had a profound emotional effect on Elizabeth. The queen's mercurial temperament swung to even greater extremes, and fits of laughter gave way to fits of anger, followed by fits of tears. To deal with the queen required all the patience at Cecil's command during those waning months of 1565.

Eventually Elizabeth and Leicester reconciled. Shortly afterward, Dudley came to Cecil and told him he felt sure the queen was going to make up her mind at last to marry him. He requested that Cecil break off all other marriage negotiations in progress. Cecil thanked Leicester kindly, committed to nothing, and went off to think about it. Though Cecil desperately wanted, as he said, "for someone to come and lay hands on her to her contentation," he wasn't convinced that Robert Dudley, earl of Leicester, should be that someone.[8] Parliament, meanwhile, had issued what almost amounted to an ultimatum: The queen must marry, and produce an heir for England.

Sitting at his desk cluttered with papers, Cecil sighed and shook his head. The Catholic Scottish alliance loomed menacingly at the border, the king of Sweden was slipping through the net, and with the queen's open flirtation with Leicester, success of either

238

the Spanish or the French suits did not look promising. Europe was running out of princes to propose for the queen's hand. All in all, prospects for an heir for England looked bleak indeed.[10]

When 1566 dawned, with the queen no closer to marriage than before, Sir Thomas was fully occupied with his bourse. He loved the City of London, and its citizens did not fail him, either. More than seven hundred of them had come forward to subscribe to buy the land needed for the exchange. With the building of Gresham House, and now the exchange, Sir Thomas seemed to have kicked off a building frenzy all over London.

The nobility were abandoning their imposing country manors and flocking to take up residence in the stately mansions they were having built in or near London. So many great estates in the far countryside were falling into disrepair that in the streets and pubs of London, Sir Thomas and his cohorts began hearing popular ballads sung about it:

> Great men by flocks there be flown to London-ward
> Houses where music was wont for to ring
> Nothing but bats and owlets do sing, Welladay,
> Houses where pleasures once did abound
> Nought but a dog and a shepherd is found ...
> Places where Christmas revels did keep
> Is now become habitations for sheep.[10]

The abandonment of their palatial country properties was the result of several factors: the tantalizing lure of London, where the heart of government and seat of power remained most of the year; the spiraling cost of upkeep of vast country estates; and of course Queen Elizabeth's celebrated tightness and her penchant for descending upon her noblemen's country estates with her entire retinue when she went on progress. The cost of appropriately entertaining the queen and her entourage for an extended visit was enough to bankrupt even a wealthy man.

During that time, Sir Thomas was not the only one complaining to Cecil and the lord treasurer about the state of his finances—particularly about not being reimbursed or rewarded for labors on behalf of the crown. Cecil himself was feeling the pinch, as were others who served Her Majesty. "I am driven in service here into such lack of fortune as I never expected," Cecil lamented. "I am forced to sell my office in the Court of Common Pleas, which was the mainstay of my living. I cannot carve for myself, but if I might avoid the court, and service, I should recover my losses." Lord Montague, too, wrote Cecil that year, "I beseech you, Sir, to procure me the payment of my diets, which shall not come, be assured, before I need them." And Sir William Pickering was forced to write several pleading letters in order to recover his expenses from the queen.[11]

Back in 1563, when Sir Thomas was still in Antwerp and imploring that the lord treasurer pay him what was due him, Sir Thomas Smith, assigned an urgent mission for the queen but given no funds to accomplish it, had asked Cecil if his expenses in Flanders could be paid to him by Sir Thomas out of crown funds there. Cecil had replied sadly, "Sir Thomas Gresham, in truth, has not a penny of the queen's money in his hands, nor has commission to take up [borrow] any, but has due to him more than we be ready to pay." Now, three years later, even though the queen's debts had diminished considerably, Sir Thomas's accounts had not yet been audited or settled. He was beginning to despair of ever being paid what was owed him.

He was distracted from those concerns, however, when he learned that the site had been acquired for the exchange. A number of old houses, and the land they sat upon on Cornhill, along Bread Street, and in alleys like Swan Alley, which opened onto Cornhill, were gradually acquired by the City of London for a total cost of £3737. The houses and structures were then sold for £478 to contractors who readily agreed to tear them down and haul the debris away. The salvaged materials would bring the contractors a tidy profit on resale. Title to the land was kept by the aldermen, in the name of the citizenry of London. The aldermen then made formal presentation of the cleared site "To Sir Thomas Gresham, knight, thereupon to build a bourse, or place for merchants to assemble in, at his own proper charges."[12]

On 7 June 1566, with a sense of excitement he hadn't felt since childhood, Sir Thomas ceremoniously laid the cornerstone of his exchange. A crowd of citizens had awaited his arrival at the site since dawn. He was accompanied by several aldermen of the City of London and a small group of nobles and friends. After he had set the first stone, each official and noble came up and ceremoniously placed a gold coin upon it. Then the workmen came and took up the gold pieces, dividing them among themselves, and promptly set to work. The crowd, which included many of the merchants of Lombard Street and as many of the merchant adventurers as were present in London, applauded and cheered. And in that manner, the exchange of London, his father's fondest dream, was officially begun.[13]

Sir Thomas showed his guests around the site. Its general design was Flemish, modeled after the bourse in Antwerp, he informed them. "It will be four-sided, with rectangular buildings, beginning here, and going all 'round there, and there, and back to here," Sir Thomas gestured expansively with one hand and his walking stick to encompass the area planned for the building. Now and then he'd point with his walking stick to mark something for them. "'Twill be in height three stories, here, but two only on the interior courtyard, and the roof shall be steep pitched. Here be the main entrance, and above, there," the stick designated a dot somewhere in the blue June sky, "shall be a bell tower, exactly as the bourse in Antwerp, and the bell therein shall ring out weekdays at noonday and at six of the clock, when 'tis time for the merchants to assemble."

The group murmured in wonder at the size and scope of the building their host and his walking stick were describing in the summer air. His deep blue eyes sparkled and his voice vibrated with an enthusiasm they had rarely seen in this normally taciturn man. "Here, in the inner courtyard, will be cloistered walkways to shelter our merchants from the elements whilst they conduct their business, an' inside—along there—will be halls and rooms aplenty for their pleasure. We'll adorn them with statues of Her Majesty and the great merchants of England for them to look upon." Then he smiled widely, and his eyes almost twinkled. "Yea, an' there will be shops aplenty too, above and along here"—once more the stick described a long arcade—"where your wives and ladies may buy their fill of exotic trinkets from beyond the seas, gentlemen, or take sweets of an afternoon." Then he chuckled aloud at their astounded looks and appreciative nods.

Shrewd tradesman that he was, Sir Thomas had foreseen that shops offering rare and beautiful goods would lure the rich and the acquisitive in swarms. The profits he'd reap from renting out those shops to tradesmen and selling them goods his ships brought would not only repay him for some of his outlay on the building, but also defray the maintenance expense of the exchange once it was open.

Once the cornerstone was laid, it fell on Richard Clough's broad, capable shoulders to do the compiling, purchasing, and shipping of the enormous amounts of material that Sir Thomas needed to complete such an immense building project. Timber and brick would come from England—the timber from Sir Thomas's estate at Ringshall, in Suffolk, which had dense woodlands. Slate, paving stones, wainscot, and glass would come from Flanders and Amsterdam.

Later that summer of 1566, Thomas received orders from the queen. He was to proceed to Flanders on the queen's business once again. She wanted him to prolong the loan of £32,000 due 20 August and borrow £20,000 more.[14] It was a dangerous undertaking, for the Protestants were objecting to Philip's detested Inquisition with savage uprisings, and it was worth a man's life to be out on the streets with money or bills of exchange.

Clough had been writing him weekly of the "marvelous stirs" that were taking place in Flanders: "For so far as I can perceive, the Protestants do more than they are allowed to do, because they want to see if the papists will begin against them, which if they do, I predict they will all go to wreck. For if bloodshed begins, then the whole stir will begin. God be merciful to them, and to us all! For if they do begin, it will be a bloody time." Even the regent had become quite alarmed, Clough reported, "She pretends to be sick, has sent all her jewels and gold to Cologne, and would be gladly gone there herself."

On 21 August a shaken Clough reported a terrible uprising in Antwerp.

> All the churches, chapels, and houses of religion have been utterly destroyed and nothing left whole within them, but all are broken and gone. Especially Our Lady Church, which was the costliest church in Europe, they broke up the choir and tore all the books, and then took the statue of Our Lady, which had just been carried about the town last Sunday, and utterly defaced her and her chapel.
>
> When they had done, I went, with the crowd of more than ten thousand strong, into the churches, and coming into Our Lady Church, it looked like a hell, for there were over one thousand torches there burning and such noise as if heaven and earth were crashing together, with images being torn down, and costly works, and damage so great that a man could not walk through the church. And so they spoiled upwards of twenty-five or thirty churches before three o'clock in the morning. There is no looting, for if they find gold or silver in chalices or crosses, they break and deface them, then surrender them up to the head officer by weight. One of their group did hide something of the value of four or five shillings, and right there they caused a gallows to be built and hung him, saying, "we come not to steal, but to spoil those things that are against God."[15]

Clough was concerned that Sir Thomas might attempt to prolong the queen's bonds, which he felt was not a wise course in such turbulent political climate. Perhaps enervated by what he had witnessed that night, he was uncharacteristically outspoken to Sir Thomas about it. "I have always heard say that there can be no more plague than when God takes away a man's wisdom, and in this point you do much forget yourself. As also I do see that you do bring over new bonds for prolongation of the debt, and here do I find no man willing to prolong, unless it be one or two."

Sir Thomas was relatively unperturbed about the danger. "Well, I do intend to do the queen's business," he replied when he got there. "The only reason I delayed in London awhile longer is that I needed to send the lord treasurer £2000, which is to be paid, for the most part, to the hungry Irishmen. I never saw men so greedy of the receipt of money! So I paid my lord treasurer the whole sum of the £2000, and kept none of it for my needs in Antwerp."[16]

Sir Thomas immediately began the touchy business of negotiating the loan of £20,000 for the queen, which he found to be the most difficult trial ever. "The recent occurrences have panicked one and all here, and daily the wealthiest merchants flee," he told Cecil. He was shocked and saddened by what was happening in Antwerp. That once beautiful city was being systematically reduced to a heap of rubble by destructive mobs doing their dirty work on the coattails of the Protestant reformers, and it was worth a man's life to go abroad in the streets, even in daylight.

The Fuggers and the Schetz brothers could not help him with funds, and Sir Thomas, after much difficulty, negotiated the funds from some German moneylenders, who demanded the personal signatures of many of the nobles and officials of Queen Elizabeth's court, in addition to her royal bonds, before they would give him any money.

When he wrote to request the additional personal bonds the Germans required, Sir Thomas cautioned Cecil, "Remember that the year of our Lord changes here in Antwerp at Christmas, and with us at Easter, therefore you must make the bonds to pay in the payments of the cold-marte, anno 1567—which payments end the last of February next coming: which point in no wise may not be forgotten." At a minimum, Gresham informed him, the Germans would require the bonds of Sir Nicholas Bacon, the lord keeper of the privy seal; the duke of Norfolk; Dudley, earl of Leicester; Secretary Cecil; and W. Haward; E. Rogers; F. Knolles; and W. Mildmaie. "All these must be had, for otherwise they will not lend to us. You would do well also to send to the earl of Pembroke and the Lord Marques and the lord treasurer for their signatures, too. I am anxious to get this from these Germans, the Welsers, for

I've never been able to get them in as lenders to us, until now. They're men of great name and fame throughout all Europe, whom I met during my negotiations for the money for Queen Mary in Spain twelve years ago, and I've been working on them ever since, without success. So pay good heed to this, for if we don't get the money from them, we shall not get it."

A week later, he had accomplished his mission:

> I have spoken with the Queen's Majesty's creditors for the prolonging of the other £32,000, with whom I have had much ado; but now (thanks be to God!) I am at a point of agreement with them. So I have delivered them the new bonds to consider, and upon the receipt of the old ones, I intend, with the queen's leave, to depart this town. Here there is no more money to be had at any price, and with my sudden departure from here I shall give the bourse and all the merchants here to understand that we have no more need of their money, and that I have contented all the creditors, which is good for us right now. I have conferred with all the money men here in one way or another, especially all those with whom I was wont to deal—the Fuggers, Schetz, Paules Van Dall, Rellinger, Lixall, even the heirs of Lazarus Tucker, and many more, and could not borrow a penny from any of them, because they are so deep in with their prince, and so indebted here they are borrowing whatever they can themselves to pay their interest and preserve their credit. So, I will not further molest you with what a scarcity of money there is here now, nor what I have had to do to get this money. I am only glad, in this miserable time, that I have accomplished the things Her Highness sent me here for ... and this week, I do intend to banquet the Queen's Majesty's creditors, both new and old.[17]

Sir Thomas didn't want to remain a day longer in Antwerp than required. He and Clough had instigated strong security precautions immediately upon his arrival in Antwerp, and Clough had made sure that he and his home were well guarded during his sojourn there. For his own part, Thomas ventured abroad on the streets as little as possible.

But he was convinced that he needed to stay long enough to give a show of strength and fearlessness to the moneylenders and keep the queen in good graces in their minds. To that end, he hosted a lavish banquet at his home the following week, to which he invited the most powerful moneylenders, distinguished nobles, and cultural lights of Antwerp. It was one of the glittering evenings for which Sir Thomas Gresham was justly famous, and he enjoyed himself immensely, although Clough looked around nervously all evening, expecting at any moment that a pistol shot would ring out and his master would fall over dead. However, the evening passed without untoward incident.

Then, with expenses of building the exchange facing him, still chafing that the queen and the lord high treasurer refused to square his accounts and pay him what they owed him, Thomas could not resist the impulse, however risky, to tweak Her Majesty about her promised reward to him if he did her good service. He had done far more for Elizabeth than for either of her predecessors and had received nothing in return. Using a request she had made of him as his excuse for writing her, he dared address Her Majesty personally on the subject:

> In consideration whereof, and for the other great services which I have done Your Highness for the space of these eight years, I trust now in my old days Your Majesty will have like consideration of my services as King Edward and Queen Mary, your late brother and sister had, whom I had not served but two years apiece, yet they gave me between them £300 land a year, to me and my heirs forever.
>
> Other I have not to molest Your Highness withal, but as yet I cannot find any horse or sword that Your Highness will like, but for your headpieces of silk, I shall bring you those rollers that you shall like. Also, on the 4th of this month [September] the prince of Orange [governor of the town of Antwerp] sent for me to dine with him, and he

entertained me well, and he demanded of the health of Your Majesty and he himself talked to me of all the proceedings of this town, and what a dangerous piece of work it was, and in this discourse he said, "the king would not be content with our doings," which causes me to think this matter is not yet ended, but likely to come to great mischief, and specially if the king of Spain gets the upper hand. The prince also asked me "whether or not our nation was minded to depart this town or not?" I told him "I heard of no such matter." And at dinner he carved for me, with his own hand, and in the midst of dinner, he drank a carouse to the Queen's Majesty, which carouse the princess, his wife, and all the rest joined in. And then one of our lenders to whom we owe a good bit of money, Giles Hoffman, who is a devout Protestant, asked me, "How think you, Mister Gresham, forasmuch as the Queen's Majesty and her realm is of this religion, think you that she'll give us aid, as she did in France, for the religion's sake?" To that I asked him if he had requested any help of Her Majesty? He said he could not tell me. I said, "I am no counselor, nor do I deal in such great matters."[18]

Thomas, disturbed by all that he saw and heard in Flanders, knew that his letter would be read by Elizabeth and would intrigue her. He was loath to see England drawn into the religious controversy boiling there, as she had been at LeHavre with the Huguenots, having come out of that contretemps with nothing except more debt, and the raging pestilence that had claimed his son and so many others. The next day, he wrote to Cecil:

I like nothing here of these proceedings; therefore Your Honor shall do very well in time to consider some other realm and place for the commerce of our commodities that are made in our realm, whereby Her Majesty's realm may remain in peace and quiet, which is one of the most important things your honor could do right now, considering how this country now stands, which is ready

247

to cut one another's throats for matters of religion. For after the prince did banquet me, one Giles Hoffman, to whom the Queen's Majesty owes a good bit of money, came to me and said, "How think you, Mister Gresham, for as much as the Queen's Majesty and her realm is of this religion—think you that she gives aid to our noblemen, as she did in France for the religion's sake?" To that, by reply, I asked him whether the noblemen have demanded help of Her Majesty. He said he could not say. Whereby I replied that I am not a minister of Her Majesty and do not deal with such great matters. But look you well to this problem, sir, for I fear it will bedevil Her Grace in months to come.[19]

Thomas had especially enjoyed inciting the prince of Orange to drink at that banquet, and while in his cups the prince revealed contempt for the edict of Emperor Maximilian II, that it would mean death for any German to bear arms against Philip, king of Spain and the Low Countries. The Protestant prince of Orange openly sneered. "Not only the Germans will take arms for us in our cause," he shouted loudly, pounding the table angrily for emphasis, "but the Danes, the Swedes, and many others will not be found wanting!" Sir Thomas wasted no time in communicating this intelligence to Cecil.

Shortly after that, at Cecil's urging, Sir Thomas returned the hospitality in his queen's behalf by inviting the prince and princess of Orange to a formal banquet at his home. He took special care with the arrangements, and though all the society in Antwerp longed for an invitation, Sir Thomas decided to keep the guests that night to a select few. It was an intimate, glamorous evening, for Sir Thomas made sure that the hospitality of the queen of England was of a caliber and quality to be not only remarked upon that night, but long remembered by those in attendance. On the crest of that success, he returned to England.

While Elizabeth personally favored the cause of the prince of Orange, she wisely heeded the counsel of Sir Thomas and Cecil and maintained the appearance of neutrality. Above all, she did not want to bring the wrath of France and Spain down upon her. Her treasury was just beginning to show signs of regaining health, as were the subjects of her realm, and she needed time to nurture this burgeoning prosperity so that it could flower.

When Sir Thomas reached England, the foundation of the exchange was already completed and covered with slate, and the workmen were ready to begin work on the main building. He spent the remainder of the year occupied with his favorite project, paying meticulous attention to every detail of its design and construction.

Lady Anne had tackled the monumental task of properly furnishing Gresham House and refurbishing Osterley. Sir Thomas, pleased to see his wife busy and active again, gave her a free hand and a lavish allowance. For reasons Thomas could never understand, among all the properties he acquired or had inherited—which were numerous—Anne Gresham disliked his father's country estate at Intwood almost as much as he himself loved it. Nor did she much fancy their enormous country manors at Ringshall and Mayfield in Sussex, or Westacre in Norfolk. The urbane atmosphere of Osterley and Gresham House was more to Anne's liking. Both properties were so large they required a considerable expenditure of her time, not to mention Sir Thomas's fortune, in order to furnish and decorate them in a manner that appropriately reflected the Greshams' high social status. Young Anne often accompanied her mother on shopping excursions to buy furnishings for the two residences, and Sir Thomas ordered his factors to be sure that the two ladies had ample funds and credit enough everywhere to purchase whatever might take their fancy.

Thomas was pleased to see color returning to his wife's complexion, though she still wore unrelieved black from head to foot. It gladdened his heart too, to see the sad look begin to pass from his daughter's eyes and her cheerful, dimpled smile come back to her lips. It had been a brutal two years for all of them. Richard was sorely missed. They longed for his sudden and unexpected visits—never to happen again. Thomas grieved for lost opportunity—for he had never really gotten to know his son—and for the loss of his only heir.

The Lady Anne did not hesitate to make shopping demands on Richard Clough now that her husband was no longer in Antwerp to procure special items for her. She ordered many things for her households, and jewelry for herself and her daughter. That year, she decided she wanted another pearl. She wasn't sure she could trust Clough to select just the right one for her, and sent several letters nagging him to be sure it was "a fair jewel, and large." Clough, stung and insulted, did not answer her directly but remarked to Sir Thomas, "I hope that my lady likes well what I send her, hoping it is come safely into her hands, for touching the pearl, it shall be good, else I would not buy it.[20] She doesn't seem to trust me much, but you know, sir, I have bought fairer jewels than this for members of Her Majesty's court, with never a complaint from them." Thomas was obliged now to call upon Clough to render his friends and patrons the purchasing favors that up to then he had handled himself when abroad. The tasks that evolved to Clough were many and complicated, and his workdays were long.

The year passed quickly, and autumn found Sir Thomas and his wife once more in residence at Gresham House and ready to begin the season of entertaining. Sir Thomas contemplated his wife across the wide table that sparkled with silver in the candle-light. Though her hair was beginning to streak with gray and her deep blue eyes had dulled with sorrow and no longer held their youthful sparkle, Anne Gresham was still a fine-looking woman when she condescended to don her best and grace his table. He held his wife in affection in his heart. He knew all too well that she had endured many trials over the years, often without him by her side, and this last great blow, the loss of their son, had also fallen upon her while he was away. He felt a pang of deep guilt.

One guest that fall was the earl of Sussex, who was scheduled to undertake an embassy to Vienna on behalf of Queen Elizabeth early in the New Year. Elizabeth was seriously considering the suit of Archduke Charles, brother of Emperor Maximilian II of Austria. Mary queen of Scots and Lord Darnley had triumphantly produced a son and successor, Prince James, and Elizabeth had suddenly felt the sting of her own lack of an heir to succeed her. "The Queen of Scots is mother of a fair son, while I am barren stock!" she had exclaimed in dismay, upon hearing the news.

Sussex wanted to make a strong impression at the emperor's court in Vienna, for the nobles of England were anxious that this latest marriage prospect for their queen be brought to speedy fruition. He importuned Sir Thomas to procure for him a large quantity of "fair pearls" to adorn his official regalia. Thomas passed the order on to Clough, who wrote back a few weeks later, "As for the pearls for my lord of Sussex, I cannot find in this town as many as my lord would have, and to match with his, for his are very fair. And in some places where I have in the past found two hundred or three hundred like them, I cannot now find twenty that he would like. I have asked brokers to seek out more, and if any are to be had around here, I will so write you in my next. I have also received the sapphire, which has been very ill handled, notwithstanding, I have caused it to be set again, but it has not been delivered to me."[21] Pearls, now the rage not only at Elizabeth's court but at all the courts in Europe since her accession, had become scarce and expensive.

Then Sir Thomas learned to his amazement that he had become the agent not only for selection of court jewels, but for transmitting sensitive correspondence as well. All the secret and important Continental dispatches going back and forth between royal dignitaries and ambassadors were suddenly being transmitted and received through him, sometimes via Richard Clough in Antwerp. Gresham's influence at court, and his popularity with many of the highest ranking nobles on both sides of the water who knew they could count on him to arrange safe transport of documents and valuables without exposing or losing them, had suddenly made him the natural conduit of choice for such messages.

It was through Sir Thomas personally that every communication from the earl of Sussex passed during his embassy to Vienna—official notes between Sussex and the queen's government as well as social correspondence between the earl and his private friends. John Fitzwilliams, governor of the Merchant Adventurers in Antwerp, communicated with Cecil via Gresham. Letters between Lord Pembroke and his son were routed via Gresham and Clough, as were letters from the queen's ambassador in Spain, Mr. Maig; the letters of Sir N. Throckmorton; and letters to the earl of Pembroke and Lord Lumley from Lord Arundel and Mr. Herbert in Italy. "Now I'm their private post," grumbled Sir Thomas to Lady Anne one morning as yet another packet of letters was delivered to him. Since many of these communications concerned the marriage prospects of Queen Elizabeth, it was most critical to everyone involved that no other eyes be privy to them than those for whom the missives were intended. Cecil had assured them they could place complete trust in Sir Thomas Gresham and his factor, Richard Clough.

In December of 1566, the powerful Catholic duke of Norfolk invited himself to Gresham House, much to Sir Thomas's surprise. He wondered what the duke might want of him. The house was festively decorated, and a great feast prepared in the duke's honor. Dressed in a green gown set off by delicate, creamy lace, her dark hair tucked under an embroidered hood, with a simple cross set in pearls gracing her bosom, young Anne Gresham curtseyed to the duke upon his arrival and presented him with a gift of a fine gold medallion from her father. The duke thanked her with grave courtesy, and complimented Sir Thomas on his charming daughter. "Be careful of the young bloods at court," he cautioned. Sir Thomas beamed. Anne was already showing signs of the loveliness that womanhood would bring to her coltish frame. Though Sir Thomas was curious, and even a little apprehensive, about what the duke might wish to discuss at dinner, his lordship was most jovial and raised no issues of controversy. He seemed only to want to enjoy himself with Sir Thomas, whose hospitality was beginning to gain the renown in London that it had long known in Antwerp. Political matters were not broached.

Though he had been invited to join them that evening, Cecil had been plagued with gout, and the cares of government played havoc with his digestion. Regretfully, he declined. Later, Sir

Thomas met with him at Cecil's home. "I wish your health had permitted you to be there—for it was a fine evening with His Grace, and your presence would have been a great comfort to me," Sir Thomas remarked.

"Ah, and I wish I could have availed myself of your table too, for there are not many evenings of leisure to distract me in these trying days. Her Majesty's foolish attachment to Leicester brings little comfort to my life of late." Cecil was relieved to learn that the evening had passed on a purely social note, and that nothing of great import had occurred or been said. However, he was concerned about the duke of Norfolk's leanings, given the continual foment created by Mary queen of Scots, and wished the duke might have tipped his hand a bit to Sir Thomas on that evening.

The holidays passed uneventfully, and on New Year's Day 1567, a radiant Queen Elizabeth, at the peak of womanhood and conscious of the power and magnetism she possessed, presided in state as her subjects came to lavish her with gifts of fabulous cloths, jewels, plates, jugs, cups of precious metal, purses filled with gold and silver, hair ornaments and other rare and exotic items. She received them all graciously and reveled in the knowledge that she was one of the most sought-after women, not to mention one of the most powerful rulers, in the world. She looked magnificent in a gown fashioned from the merchant Spinola's gift of purple velvet which had been richly embroidered with silver and studded with pearls and precious stones. The next day, word flew from the French ambassador to the Spanish ambassador that Lord Leicester had slept with Her Majesty on New Year's night. Cecil took to his bed again with a burning ague.[22]

In the ensuing months, Cecil had enough on his plate to keep him in severe indigestion. In February, the burghers of the Reformed church in Antwerp wrote formal letters to Cecil and Sir Thomas, begging them to intercede with the queen for her help with "the fearful desolation that has befallen our country." Cecil they addressed in English, but to Sir Thomas they wrote in the more familiar French, saying, "Since you yourself have seen what is happening here, and since you also have, by God's providence, such favor and authority with Her Majesty, we address this our petition to you."[23]

If he and Cecil would but intercede with Queen Elizabeth on their behalf, they implored, the ruin with which the Low Countries seemed threatened might be averted, and King Philip might be brought to accede to their request for freedom of religious worship without molestation. Thomas could only shake his head in sadness at what had happened in that once prosperous country. Shortly thereafter, the queen dispatched him to Flanders as her emissary. He was to tell them that she would not openly intervene in the internal problems in Flanders. "I gave Marcus Pirus, one of the chief Burghers, your answer," he told the queen, "and upon that he asked me, out of friendship, to tell him whether or not, if he and his friends go to England, whether they might live in quietness and safety there. I said *yes*, that there were many come over already for reasons of religion. So if this religion has not good success here, I assure you the most of all this town will move into England."[24]

Gresham also knew that while Protestants were fleeing Flanders for safer havens in England and Germany, Catholic supporters were leaving England and settling in the Low Countries, where they continued to agitate against Queen Elizabeth and her Protestant rule. "Here be many papist knaves of our nation," he wrote to Cecil, "and especially a villain friar that has so unreverently preached against the Queen's Majesty that if the dog ventures forth into the streets we shall see to it that he be well beaten up!"

Sir Thomas was host to the earl of Sussex in Antwerp. Sussex was en route to Vienna once again, and Sir Thomas feasted him well and loaned him £3000, for, as he reported to Cecil, "My lord has need of great sums, over and above his diets, for which I have furnished him this sum." Thomas hoped the queen would reimburse him for his loan to Sussex when he returned to England, for it was no small amount he had advanced.

Sir Thomas had barely set foot back in England when Richard Clough wrote requesting permission to take time off from his duties in Flanders to make an extended visit to his native Wales.

Sir Thomas, surprised, replied that he preferred that Clough remain in Flanders "until you have dispatched all provision of stone for the Bourse." Nevertheless, Clough left for Wales, leaving John Worrall in charge of Gresham's affairs in Antwerp. Sir Thomas was taken aback by that, since in all the years he'd known him, Clough had never before done anything against his employer's wishes, let alone disobey a direct request. But he was mollified, and vastly pleased, when he finally learned the reason: Clough had hastened to Wales to claim a bride.

Thomas was amazed to learn that, because Clough had not talked about a woman, let alone a prospective bride, even though they'd been together daily in Antwerp recently. He had chattered about local affairs without cease, and his letters to Sir Thomas went on for pages and pages about ceremonies and politics and business, but Clough was closemouthed as a clam about his own personal life.

However, Clough indeed had gone to Wales to marry, and he married exceedingly well. His bride was Katherine of Berain, the only daughter of a distant relative of Henry VIII. Clough and Katherine had grown up together, and Clough had always had an eye for her, but her father had betrothed her to another, and Clough, disappointed, had remained a bachelor. Then, news had come to him in Antwerp that Katherine's husband, Sir John Salisbury, had died. The letter also warned him that another was already poised to pay suit to the young widow. On hearing that, Clough had rushed to Wales, determined he would not lose his Katherine again. He had brashly proposed to her as he escorted her into the church to attend her husband's funeral. Three weeks later, Katherine Salisbury and Richard Clough were wed.

After the nuptials, the newlyweds traveled to London to visit Sir Thomas and his wife at Gresham House, for Clough was anxious to mend his fences with Sir Thomas, whom he feared might be angry at him for leaving Antwerp as he did.[25]

Sir Thomas and Lady Anne welcomed the newlyweds to Gresham House, and during their brief stay, the men became even closer. Anne was cordial and friendly to Clough's bride, which surprised Sir Thomas, since Anne normally had nothing to do with his employees or their families. But Clough knew well why Sir Thomas's wife, who had never treated him with anything but distant contempt, and whom he personally disliked, had put herself out more than usual for them—it was Katherine's tie to the royal bloodline that had won the Lady Gresham's regard.

In Clough's absence, John Worrall had handled the dispatch of three ships laden with stone that had been cut for the exchange. In short order, more ships were traversing the sea with building supplies, for when Cecil saw the marvelous marble and slate Sir Thomas was importing for his exchange, he ordered some stone and other supplies for his mansion at Burghley as well. By spring, Clough was back in Antwerp, and with his factor there to assist him, Sir Thomas could then proceed with commissioning the statue of Queen Elizabeth that was to adorn the place of honor in the interior of the exchange. Many of the huge statues that were to be placed in and around the exchange had already been carved in England, but Queen Elizabeth's, which was to be the principal statue, Sir Thomas commissioned from Antwerp. He shipped several of the other statues over to Clough for the artist to use as models of style. "I have received the statues you wrote of," Clough wrote a few weeks later, "in which style I will cause the queen's Majesty's to be made, and will send the others back to you as soon as it is done."

Meanwhile, Cecil was enjoying no respite from his gout and digestive upsets. Queen Elizabeth continued to skirt marriage, and the antics of Mary queen of Scots to the north had increased alarmingly. Darnley, the Scottish queen's husband, had died in a mysterious explosion. Everyone believed it was a plot hatched by the henchmen surrounding Lord Bothwell, the Scottish queen's current lover. Queen Mary, whose passions, it was rumored, ran high, had become enamored of the handsome young Bothwell after her husband, Lord Darnley, turned out to be little more than an alcoholic and a wastrel. Unfortunately, she had allowed her romantic nature, and her infatuation with Bothwell, to overrule good sense. Barely two months after the murder of her husband Darnley, Mary

defied her lords and married Bothwell, the man the Scots suspected had arranged her husband's death. With that marriage, all
Scotland rose up in outrage. "Burn the whore!" screamed her subjects. Murder they might tolerate, impropriety never.[26]

The Protestant lords of Scotland, encouraged by this latest
turn of public sentiment against the queen, promptly revolted.
They captured and imprisoned Mary queen of Scots in Lochleven
Castle. Queen Elizabeth's attention was once again diverted to the
ominous events across her northern border.

Meanwhile, the earl of Sussex had returned from Vienna with
high hopes, but the unfortunate religious accommodations
demanded for marriage between Archduke Charles and Elizabeth
were such that she declared, "I cannot, in conscience, accept."
Negotiations were broken off, and shortly thereafter the archduke
married the daughter of the duke of Bavaria. Elizabeth was too
upset by the events in Scotland and the threat they represented to
her anointed supremacy and the integrity of the crown, to be
affected by something so insignificant as the loss of another suitor.

Although Elizabeth approved when the Protestant council in
Scotland curtailed Queen Mary's powers, she was nevertheless a
devout royalist, and she strongly disapproved of any nation daring to rise up and imprison its sovereign. Elizabeth took Mary's
imprisonment by her subjects as a personal affront to the power
of a queen. She was even angrier when the council forced Mary
to abdicate in favor of her baby son, who was crowned James VI
of Scotland, and given over to his Protestant uncle as regent. But
Elizabeth's worries would only increase. Aided and abetted by
Catholic sympathizers, Mary escaped from Lochleven Castle and
fled across the border into England, where she begged Elizabeth
for protection.

There followed several months of protracted investigations,
inquiries, and meetings by Parliament and Elizabeth's privy council. By her foolish actions, Mary had lost not only her rights to the
Scottish throne, but all hope of succession to the English throne.
Her brother was confirmed as regent for her son, and he returned
to Scotland in triumph. Mary was accorded asylum in England

and resided in grand style at Tutbury Castle in Staffordshire. She was surrounded by her own ladies and gentlemen, and lived under the kindly guardianship of the earl of Shrewsbury. Nonetheless, she was a virtual prisoner of Elizabeth, and a resentful and restive one at that. The duke of Norfolk began making solicitous calls on her, and that was cause for immediate concern at Elizabeth's court. Cecil confided to Sir Thomas that it would have been better for England if Mary had been found guilty of treason and executed, for he was convinced that as long as the Stuart queen remained alive, Queen Elizabeth's crown would never be secure. But Elizabeth could not countenance executing her rival queen, for she remembered well the fate of her own mother and eschewed the death sentence for Mary. She did not want to embrace a precedent that her own enemies might use against her one day.[27]

In August, Cecil and his wife at last found time for some leisure, and they took it at Gresham House with Sir Thomas and his wife. Thomas saw to it they were well and merrily feasted and entertained, in such manner as would chase all thoughts and cares from his friend's mind, at least for the space of one brief day. Cecil was suitably impressed by Gresham House, and on the tour Thomas gave him, he took careful note of certain architectural and garden details he would later incorporate into his own houses.

The exchange was going up rapidly. Sir Thomas could scarcely wait to see it finished and open, filled with merchants and citizens and people in the shops. In December, he notified Cecil that the chief architect Henryke would be leaving again after the holidays, to procure more materials overseas. "Would you like your gate set up before his departure or after his return?" Henryke was at that time also working on Cecil's estate at Burghley. "When he has returned will be soon enough," replied Cecil.

The situation in the Low Countries continued to deteriorate, especially after the regent retired and the feared and hated Duke D'Alva was named as her replacement. Alva immediately instigated harsh edicts and reforms against the Protestants, ordering them tortured and executed at will. Refugees fled the Low Countries by the shipload, flooding into England. Cecil was alarmed at this sudden influx of humanity, and wrote to the lord mayor of London, attempting to discern just how many foreigners had been arriving in the City. "The Queen's Majesty being given to understand that the number of strangers coming into the realm out of France, Flanders, and other countries do daily abound and increase, in such sort as Her Highness thinks that her realm shall be overcharged with so great a multitude, especially those reported to be unsavory types, as with such multitudes it couldn't be otherwise."[28] There was also a concern that the immigrants might bring and spread pestilence among the populace of London. As a result, the lord mayor of London issued a proclamation: Strangers would henceforth not be allowed to tarry in London more than a day and a night. But of course there were always distinguished exceptions to that rule.

In Flanders, the prince of Orange rose up against the Duke of Alva with a force of more than twenty-eight thousand men, but could make no progress against the trained Spanish forces of the hated duke, and was finally forced to disband. He managed to evade capture, or his fate most certainly would have been sealed.

Then in the autumn of 1568, the French Cardinal Chastillon, once a powerful Catholic bishop, but now one of the strongest supporters of the Protestant Huguenots in France, came to England unannounced, seeking political and religious sanctuary. His flight to England created an international stir.

Lord Cobham, constable of Dover and lord warden of the ports, received the cardinal, and sent an urgent message to Cecil asking for news of what accommodation and reception would be accorded Chastillon on his arrival in London. Cecil and the queen conferred and agreed that Sir Thomas Gresham, and Gresham House, would be appropriate to receive this distinguished refugee, since the bishop of London was indisposed and could not himself act as host. The queen, seeking to avoid an international incident, absented herself from the capital, using the Scottish situation as her excuse.

Thomas hurried to put his house in readiness to receive the cardinal, sending servants and employees scurrying in haste through the streets and markets of London to procure appropriate victuals and wines and appointments for his eminent guest. It was an honor of the highest order for the Greshams to be asked to render this service to Her Majesty. At ten o'clock the night of 11 September, a messenger galloped up to Gresham House, his lathered horse panting and snorting, to deliver a packet of official letters and relay a message to Sir Thomas. "My lord cardinal voyages Sunday morning towards Gravesend, where he means to spend the night. The next morning he leaves for London, by water. Mayhap 'twould be meet to bring a horse for my lord's saddle, should he think to ride."[29]

Less than an hour later, Sir Thomas dispatched his own messenger by fast horse to Cecil: "I have made my house in readiness to receive him with as great hospitality as shall lie in my power to do. Here is the letter from Mr. Kingsmill and a letter to my lord of Leicester and one also to Your Honor, and tomorrow I will go and meet him (God willing) on the road, beyond Gravesend. This messenger departed me at 11 o'clock at night, the 11th of September, 1568."

As Sir Thomas watched the horseman gallop away, he couldn't help wondering what this latest evidence of the state of persecution of the Protestants in Europe would mean for the future of English trade abroad. All-out war between the papists and the Protestants loomed even larger. Sighing, he turned abruptly and limped back inside, his walking stick thumping in mournful cadence on the stairs. The household, with the exception of his personal servants and one scullery maid, had been long abed, but the master still had hours of work to do. There would be little sleep for him this night, and the morrow would be another long and tiring day.

The cardinal, with his extensive retinue, arrived by decorated boat at Tower Wharf the next night, and Sir Thomas, in full knight's regalia, was there to receive him. He was flanked by a considerable train of city officials and important citizens, including the lord mayor and aldermen of London, and the governors of the

Merchant Adventurers and Staplers. After greeting the cardinal, they all rode in stately procession along Cheapside to Gresham House on Bishopsgate Street. The residents were agog at all the sudden activity, and crowds of curious Londoners stood vigil to see what exciting events might take place around Gresham House. They were not disappointed.

Not a half hour later, a herald in royal livery galloped up to deliver a message. The major-domo entered the silk- hung drawing room to whisper in Sir Thomas's ear that the French ambassador, Bochetel de la Forêt, was en route to Gresham House to present his personal compliments to Cardinal Chastillon. Sir Thomas and a flustered Lady Anne immediately made ready to receive this second unexpected and very distinguished guest. Servants were dispatched in every direction. Young Anne was quickly brushed and primped to make her curtsey to the ambassador upon his arrival. Lady Anne rushed to her chamber, where her maids repaired her coiffure, reworked her toilette, and adorned her with pearls and her laciest headgear. Kitchen servants set about renewing the supply of refreshments in the huge dining hall. Sir Thomas, meanwhile, remained outwardly unperturbed by all the excitement that had suddenly descended upon his house. He chatted affably with Chastillon and his other guests, plying them with sweetmeats, dried fruits, ale, and a new, exotic beverage served in silver cups—chocolate—topped with frothy cream.

Ambassador de la Forêt arrived with his entourage and found his hosts and their accommodations so pleasant he elected to remain and take dinner with Sir Thomas and the cardinal. Sir Thomas Gresham's reputation for dispensing the finest food and wine at his table had not gone unnoticed at court, and the French ambassador longed for a good Continental repast. Presided over by Sir Thomas and his two ladies and served by an army of servants, this feast exceeded even those Sir Thomas had provided for the queen's creditors in Antwerp, for he was representing his sovereign on her own soil, and he was determined that the French visitors to Gresham House would know that England was a sophisticated power and a country to be respected.

The next morning the crowds began their vigil before dawn outside the huge gates of Gresham House, and at about eight of the clock they were rewarded, for Sir Thomas and the cardinal, with a large following, emerged on brightly caparisoned horses, with appropriate pennons flying, and passed out of the gates of Gresham House and down the road to begin a stately progress about London.

Fortunately, it was one of those rare, clear autumn mornings. London was bathed in tawny light, and her buildings seemed hewn from gold and copper. Chastillon and Sir Thomas were outfitted in Venetian breeches and hose, with soft leather leggings for riding, and both sported short cloaks with high, stiff collars—the newest fashion for gentlemen. They were armed with long rapiers slung at their sides. The cardinal's high-crowned hat was embellished with lavish plumes, but Sir Thomas still favored his smaller black headpiece—though he had conceded to fashion on this day by adding a silvery grey and white feather fastened in place by a jeweled clip of brilliants and rubies. His wide, pleated white ruff emphasized his dark beard and gave him a very distinguished air, and the crowds murmured in admiration as the brightly colored procession, with Sir Thomas and Chastillon at its head, passed.

Their first stop was the French Huguenot church, where Chastillon heard brief services in his honor. Then they rode slowly up to Cornhill, past gawking crowds that lined the streets on both sides. There they dismounted, and Sir Thomas conducted the cardinal and his followers around the nearly completed exchange, explaining its functions and his plans for it. Remounting, they proceeded to St. Paul's, in the heart of London, where they attended another brief religious service. Then they returned to Gresham House for a copious noonday meal. They were joined there by Secretary Cecil, Ambassador de la Forêt, Sir Nicholas Bacon, several members of the court, the lord mayor, and some high-ranking city officials and clergy whom Cecil and Sir Thomas had invited. Cecil took that opportunity to present the queen's official welcome to Chastillon and inform him that Her Majesty was most anxious to entertain him at court immediately upon her return to London.

The Greshams were obliged to host the cardinal and all the attendant retinue, hangers-on, officials, and guests for a full week before Queen Elizabeth finally summoned Chastillon to court and extended him her royal hospitality. Elizabeth gave the cardinal Sion House for his residence, a sure sign that he was high in Her Majesty's favor. That only served further to rankle the Catholic faction in England, for Chastillon had been excommunicated by the pope and stripped of his rank of cardinal by the church.

This latest sign of the queen's esteem for the Greshams was not lost on London society, and Sir Thomas and Lady Anne were soon deluged with invitations to all the finest banquets and entertainments in the city. Sir Nicholas Bacon, who had noted that his niece, Anne Gresham, had matured, mentioned to Sir Thomas that they should meet soon to discuss a possible future match between Anne and his son Nathaniel. Sir Thomas was pleased and flattered at the prospect that his Anne might marry into the Bacon family. "We shall be most happy to entertain any proposal from your distinguished family on our daughter's behalf," he murmured gallantly, with a courteous bow to Sir Nicholas. Then he hurried off to tell his wife. If it came about, it would be a match that superseded their greatest hopes for their daughter, given the delicate circumstances of her birth.

However, Sir Thomas's attention was soon drawn from such matters to focus once more on Flanders. Incensed at Elizabeth's open welcome of Chastillon, and with knowledge from his spies that Sir Thomas Gresham, a merchant, had been the cardinal's host and refuge, the Duke D'Alva retaliated by harassing English merchants in Flanders. He quickly sent word, advising the English merchants to move their base of operations from Antwerp before they came to harm at Alva's hands.

The Merchant Adventurers tried moving their commerce center to Embden for the time being, but the lure and convenience of Antwerp kept drawing them back there. Inconveniences, interdictions, brawls, reprisals, edicts—all the elements of a major conflagration were present. They needed only a spark to ignite them.

In England itself, the powerful dukes of Northumberland and Norfolk remained strongly on the Catholic side, sympathetic to Mary queen of Scots, and they were more determined than ever now to remove the strongly Protestant Cecil from his position of influence with Queen Elizabeth. If they could topple Cecil, they reasoned, it would be easy to push Elizabeth aside and place Mary on the throne, thereby returning Catholicism to England.

To that end, the duke of Norfolk began working to enlist the help of Dudley, earl of Leicester, in his cause. Dudley, though he did not agree with the idea of overthrowing Elizabeth, was not averse to toppling Cecil, who he believed had thwarted his aims with Elizabeth. Cecil soon detected the first waves of resistance against him, but kept it from the queen. She had problems enough already, he felt.

Though he strongly respected Leicester and the power he continued to wield with the queen, and he knew the duke of Norfolk was one of the most powerful nobles in the realm, Sir Thomas remained staunchly in William Cecil's camp. With such a formidable force ranged against him, Cecil could have stepped down, taking the easy way out, but he stood his ground firmly against Norfolk, the new duke of Northumberland, and the others. He would not see England, and his work of ten years to bring her back to prosperity, destroyed at the hands of unskilled traitors, delivered up on a platter to Catholic Spain and Mary queen of Scots.

Though he had allies in friends like Sir Thomas and Sir Nicholas Bacon, and his strongest support came from the queen herself, Cecil stood virtually alone in this latest crisis, because now most of the countries of Europe, not to mention the highest nobles in his own land, were aligned against him. Soon, with Leicester ceaselessly at her ear, even the queen was being pulled one way and another. Cecil had been right all along—while Mary of Scotland lived, able to rally support to her cause, Elizabeth's crown would never be firmly fixed on her head.[30]

December brought the spark that would ignite passions on all sides. Early in the month, a half-dozen Spanish barques and pinnaces, laden with treasure reportedly intended for the Duke D'Alva to pay his troops, were chased by the French men-of-war of the Protestant prince of Condé. The heavily laden Spanish ships, caught far out in the sea (Channel), were outmanned and out-gunned by the French and raced for a safe harbor. They came in at Plymouth and Southampton in England and beseeched safe haven. The Condé's ships withdrew and awaited Elizabeth's move.

A dispute immediately arose. The Spanish captains claimed the treasure was Spain's, sent from King Philip to the duke of Alva. Others argued it belonged to Italian and English merchants and had been "appropriated" by D'Alva, who was sending it to Philip. Cardinal Chastillon avowed to Cecil that much of the cargo belonged to Genovese merchants, from whom D'Alva had forcibly taken it. Since its true ownership was clouded, it was a most tempt-ing prize for the English treasury. The French, fearful Elizabeth might give it back to the Spaniards, threatened to come into the English harbor to wrest it away. Tempers on both sides of the water were at boiling point.

An enormous year-end gift had fallen into the hands of Eliz-abeth of England—if she decided to keep it. A report informed her that on one ship alone there were no fewer than fifty-nine cof-fers, each containing twenty thousand Spanish reales.[31] The other ships were equally charged with Spanish coin. Bills of lading or letters of factorage which could give some clue to the origin of the treasure were nowhere to be found. Various ambassadors and the privy council hastily assembled to confer about what to do about the ships and their treasure. Cecil sought advice from his friend Sir Thomas Gresham, on behalf of the merchants, as to what course of action should be taken. Sir Thomas advised, "stay Her Majesty's hand, sir, on these matters, and bide her time awhile," he advised. He'd try to find out through his spy network who the rightful owners were. Cecil agreed that was a good idea.

As 1568 drew to a close, though he had ostensibly retired from his duties as the queen's agent in Flanders and as her ambassador to the Low Countries, Sir Thomas was more active in govern-ment service than ever. He not only was deeply involved with Cecil's political problems, the queen's diplomatic affairs, and her finances at home, but had become virtually an ambassador-at-large for Cecil and the privy council, tasked with receiving foreign dignitaries and arranging and conducting diplomatic meetings. In addition, he had become the wealthiest and most powerful merchant in all England, and was the most sought after for financial counsel.

He was known as a man of passion and action rather than a man of study and theory,[32] and while his bold schemes sometimes went awry, he remained by nature an inveterate gambler with a sharp killer instinct—the two indispensable qualities of a successful entrepreneur.

Sir Thomas ended the exceptionally busy year—his fiftieth—with achievement of his greatest dream. On 22 December, on the ninth anniversary of his knighthood at the hand of Queen Elizabeth, Sir Thomas, surrounded by a host of family members, employees, friends, nobles, and City officials, proudly opened his bourse—the completed Exchange of London.[33] In those tense days, it was a welcome respite of celebration, pomp and ceremony to herald the Christmas season. The advent of its own exchange was a boon to London, to all England in fact, and the people turned out in throngs to celebrate with Sir Thomas and to admire their City's most beautiful new structure.

Balanced on the tip of the weather vane atop the magnificent bell tower, a great golden grasshopper soared grandly above the colonnaded arcades, the polished marble halls, the magnificent statues, and the lush gardens below, its wings vibrating as the bell beneath them tolled out the joyous news of the new exchange. The tiny insect, emblem of the Greshams for centuries, had leapt far and high from its humble origins in the grasslands of Norfolk. However, its fate and future, like those of Protestantism and Elizabeth Tudor's crown, now quivered in a delicate and precarious balance atop a high and lonely perch.

10

To Leave His Mark

ifteen sixty-nine arrived in a thick cloak of ice and snow that concealed for a brief period the flames of resentment and the plots and counterplots set to boil beneath its calm, icy surface. As the freezing winds blew in off the Thames, whistling around the turrets of the Tower and searching out chinks in every building, the poor of London huddled over their meager fires; the unfortunate froze and were carted off to await burial at the first thaw; the rich and prosperous sat wrapped in warm robes before roaring fires—hatching diabolical schemes.

Norfolk, Northumberland, Arundel, Leicester, Mary—names that had rung with solemn tones down through the annals of English history—all plotted for their own glory and fortune the overthrow of Elizabeth the queen, and her secretary, Cecil. Mary queen of Scots had written the Spanish ambassador, "Tell your master [King Philip] that if he will help me, I shall be queen of England in three months, and mass shall be said again all over the kingdom."[1]

Queen Elizabeth had clung tenaciously to her crown for a decade, and her philosophy did not hold with religious persecution. She had already seen far too much of that in her lifetime. She tolerated the Catholic faction, provided they did not encourage open revolt against her authority. Cecil at fifty was still the queen's right hand and together with Sir Thomas Gresham's expert financial advice and assistance, they had brought a stability to the government that had not existed since before Henry VIII.[2]

Sir Thomas, home at Gresham House, was dressed and ready to go out on this the first day of a new year. He was smiling and happy, for his exchange was open and he had received permission from Cecil to present his daughter Anne, who would shortly reach her sixteenth birthday, to the queen at the New Year ceremonies. He missed having his friend Sir John Leigh to accompany them, as had been their custom for so many years, but the aging Sir John had died peacefully at sixty-four. Sir Thomas missed him and his wise counsel, very much.

Finally, the ladies were ready, and they set off. His daughter Anne was gowned in grey silk with accents of deep blue, her deep blue cloak trimmed in grey fur. He nodded and smiled approvingly when she presented herself at the foot of the stairs and, with a shy smile, swept him a practiced curtsey. In the great hall of the palace, though obviously nervous, Anne did not misstep as she made her curtsey to the queen and presented Elizabeth with a gift of a satin box of finely wrought lace handkerchiefs. Her Majesty thanked her graciously and commented to Sir Thomas and Lady Anne, "Your daughter is a fair jewel of a maid." At that, Anne blushed and smiled, sparking the interest of the company of nobles surrounding the queen. The freshness of youth bloomed in her complexion. Her appearance with her parents on this occasion had been carefully planned by Sir Thomas and Sir Nicholas Bacon to catch the notice of all the assembled lords and ladies—but one in particular. Among the courtiers attending that morning was twenty-four-year-old Nathaniel Bacon, son of Sir Nicholas.

Nathaniel took pains to observe mistress Anne Gresham rather more closely than the others as she made her curtsey to the queen. His father had recently informed him that he thought Anne would be a most suitable and well-dowered bride for him. Though most believed they were first cousins, Nathaniel knew Anne was not his aunt's real daughter but her ward, and therefore not of any blood relation to him. Being older, he remembered little of her except as a shy, gangly child at her father's knee or hiding behind her mother's wide skirts on his occasional visits to their home. Now, however, it was an extremely composed young damsel he saw making her obeisance to the queen, one who sparked his interest. Wealth and comeliness rarely ran together. He himself made no claim to handsomeness of appearance, but he was bright and capable and had a good future. He hoped she also had some wits about her. But at this moment, hearing the interested murmurs of the young nobles about him, Nathaniel decided to press his suit for mistress Gresham's hand at once, before someone else made a move to claim her.

Later, in reviewing high points of the day, Cecil remarked to the lord keeper about Sir Thomas's daughter. "Your niece, is she not?" he asked Bacon. "Yea, her mother is sister to my wife," replied Sir Nicholas evasively, though both knew of Anne's parentage. "Well, an' Sir Thomas had best keep a watch about him on that one," remarked Cecil, "lest she be carried off sooner by one of these young bloods at court."

"The mistress Anne is yet young," countered Bacon with feigned indifference, for his son had already approached him, after seeing Anne at court that morning. "Well, with Sir Thomas for her father, an' the rich dowry she'll hold, she'll marry well enough and soon enough too, I trust," said Cecil. "Yea, God's truth, an' I hope 'twill be with my own Nathaniel," revealed Bacon, deciding to let Cecil in on the news. They'd need the queen's approval, after all, for the marriage, and they might need Cecil's help with any technicalities. "Marry! 'Tis so?" Cecil was delighted that the children of two of his favorite friends might make a match, and an advantageous one for both.

The Bacons were an old and highly respected family, as were the Greshams. He assured the lord keeper that he would help smooth the way for the nuptials to proceed without incident, if and when Bacon and Sir Thomas reached a satisfactory agreement.

"I am honored by your generous offer on behalf of my daughter." Sir Thomas concealed the deep emotion he felt as he responded to Sir Nicholas when that worthy came to him with his son's formal proposal for Anne's hand in marriage. "As you know

I favor this match. And rest assured, my daughter's dowry, as you surely must know, will not be lacking." Sir Nicholas nodded gravely, and thanking Sir Thomas, took his leave. The only remaining child of Sir Thomas would come to his son extremely well dowered, that he knew. That her husband-to-be was a kinsman, so to speak, would mean an even better sum. It would be a fine match for both sides, and fortunately the two young people involved seemed not averse to it. As he rode home, he remembered the fateful outcome of the ill-timed and ill-fated match of Northumberland's son to Suffolk's daughter, the Lady Jane Grey.

Pray to God that this match would be a fortuitous one. They were fortunate that this represented only the merging of families, not of royal pretenders.

The Lady Anne was delighted at the prospect of their daughter marrying her nephew and gave immediate and enthusiastic assent to the match. Anne, when informed of Nathaniel's proposal agreed to entertain Nathaniel Bacon as a formal suitor for her hand. And so the two began their sanctioned courtship while their fathers worked out the details of the marriage agreement and petitioned the queen for permission for the two to marry.

Happy wedding thoughts were quickly overshadowed, as animosity between the Catholics and the Protestants in England continued to fester. Dr. John Caius, open in his Catholic leanings during Mary's reign, had not changed his outspoken viewpoint when Elizabeth succeeded to the throne. He had retained his position as Elizabeth's chief physician only because the queen liked him personally and respected him professionally, and because of his close friendship with Cecil and Sir Thomas. However, with a new rupture between the Catholics and Protestants a virtual certainty, even such an eminent physician as John Caius could not escape the consequences of openly favoring the Catholic cause. He was summarily dismissed from his post as the queen's chief physician. Fortunately, no further sanctions were taken against him, and he retained his standing in his profession and his post at Cambridge University.[3] Nevertheless, Sir Thomas was concerned. "I beseech you, Kees, keep your religious position to the back in your work, lest you find yourself 'pon Tower Hill, 'stead of at the colleges." But the religious uproar was only beginning.

Late in January, Cecil received an urgent message, brought by messenger from Gresham House. Sir Thomas had just received word "from Richard Clough that the Duke D'Alva has arrested all English ships, confiscated all English goods, and all English-men have been thrown into prisons in Flanders."[4] The duke was still smarting over the incarceration of his treasure and his ships by the English.

The Merchant Adventurers and Staplers, outraged, immedi-ately addressed strident protests to the queen, demanding that the Spanish ships and their crews receive the same treatment the Duke D'Alva was showing Englishmen abroad. Further, they demanded "that a proclamation be made by the Queen's Majesty's authority forthwith, for the avoiding of collateral bargains, transports, and contracts hereafter to be made."[5]

Elizabeth, furious at this treatment of her merchants, promptly had the Spanish ambassador and the captains and crews of the cap-tured Spanish ships arrested. Then she issued a proclamation embargoing all English trade with Flanders and breaking off rela-tions with Philip of Spain.

D'Alva, realizing too late he had made a serious tactical blun-der, quickly dispatched his agent, Dassondeville, to England, to negotiate with Queen Elizabeth and her council about the trea-sure. Dassondeville was lodged by the English at Crosby Place, across from Gresham House. Crosby Place was now owned by alderman Bond, who had purchased it from German Scioll. Dassondeville requested that, prior to addressing his lord's mes-sage to the privy council, he be allowed to confer with the impris-oned Spanish ambassador. The queen and Cecil assigned the delicate task of bringing the two together and overseeing their conference to Sir Thomas. Gresham House and its occupants and staff were once again thrown into a frenzy of preparation to receive important visitors and host tense high-level meetings.

After the meeting between Dassondeville and the Spanish ambassador on 12 February, Thomas reported the results to Cecil in private. "In truth, Dassondeville has no orders from the duke but to demand that we give back the treasure, nor could the Spanish ambassador advise aught else. So that's their whole case."

Meanwhile, the Spanish treasure had been secretly brought to London and deposited in the Tower vaults for safekeeping, out of reach of any fleet sent to reclaim it. On 22 February, Cecil and Sir Walter Mildmaie conferred with Dassondeville at Gresham House, but nothing was resolved. The queen promised to return the treasure only if the duke agreed to release and fully indemnify all her subjects being held by D'Alva in Flanders. Further, they would have to agree to ratify the ancient treaty and alliance between the crown of England and the House of Burgundy.[6] On 8 March, Duke D'Alva's dejected emissary left to return to Flanders with these newest terms.

Sir Thomas was glad for a brief respite, for he still had important family matters to attend to. The queen had blessed the joining of their two families, and he and Sir Nicholas were to meet in a few days and settle the marriage contract. He needed time to formalize the dowry he would bestow on his daughter and to wrestle with some of the touchy problems this wedding might entail, given that Anne was "base-born," and not legal issue of his marriage to his wife. He sat late in his study, carefully drawing up Anne's dower document. He had to settle upon her now everything he wished to go to his beloved daughter and any children she might have, for he knew that by English law, even though she was his only living child, Anne and her children could not be his legal heirs.

When he had finished, he was certain it would please his daughter and more than satisfy Nathaniel Bacon's family, for Sir Thomas had bestowed upon Anne estates and lands in Norfolk and Kent that would produce an income of nearly £300 a year in rents, in addition to their real property value.[7] She would also go to her husband with a magnificent trousseau, suitable to her father's station in life—trunks full of gowns and lingerie, chests full of hand-embroidered linens and carefully worked tapestries, personal jewels, valuable silver, a full set of silver spoons ornamented with their new family crest, and many other valuable art objects for the home of the newlyweds.

The ladies were already in a fever of planning, for the wedding was to take place in September, barely six months hence. The details of the dowry completed, Sir Thomas sat back, as memories of Bruges flashed through his mind. It was hard for him to believe that their daughter was of marriageable age. Had it been all that long ago? He hadn't been back to Bruges in years. For a brief moment he wished that he could send Anne and Nathaniel there on a honeymoon trip so that Anne could come to know her birthplace, but the political situation now made that impossible. Just as well—it would only bring his wife's wrath down upon him.

He and Sir Nicholas amiably concluded the marriage negotiations in mid-March, setting the wedding date for 10 September 1569. Then in late March, word came to Sir Thomas that Richard Clough had been arrested by the French at Dieppe, as he was trying to leave Flanders with important letters for Queen Elizabeth.

Clough, charged as a traitor, was "to be delivered up to the Duke D'Alva, bound hand and foot, for his pleasure." At that news, Sir Thomas fell into a great rage. "My horse!" he ordered. Mounting up, he set out for Burghley House at a fast gallop, risking life and limb.

Cecil, too, was furious when he learned not only what the French had done, but worse, what they were threatening to do. He and the queen were well aware of the invaluable services Clough had rendered them. He also knew that the French were probably still smarting at Elizabeth's high-handed refusal of the suit of the French king.

However, the queen could not allow them to use Clough to show their displeasure. Cecil immediately dispatched a strong message to the French: "A very great insult has been given Her Most Gracious Majesty at Dieppe in the arrest and detention of her subject Richard Clough, agent of her factor, Sir Thomas Gresham. This has displeased the queen more deeply than her secretary can express."[8]

The possibility of creating an incident that might draw them into a war between Spain and England was not what the French desired. When they received the secretary's strong note, they immediately released Clough. Sir Thomas directed that Clough be safely returned, with his family, directly from France to England.

Sir Thomas then turned his attention back to helping Cecil and the queen decide what to do about the Spanish treasure still lying in the Tower vaults. Since trade relations with Flanders had been broken off, and neither side would give in, an uneasy truce had settled in between England and Spain, each awaiting the other's first move.

Antwerp was no longer feasible for trading, so Elizabeth opted to send her fleet of cloth merchants, heavily protected by a fleet of warships, to Hamburg instead. In Flanders, the Duke D'Alva was making war preparations against the Protestants there, and fierce pirates freely roamed the sea between the countries. The prince of Orange continually beseeched Elizabeth's help to arm his Protestant troops to fight back against Alva, as did various Protestant movements in Germany. A religious war on the Continent seemed inevitable.

At first, it was thought that Sir Thomas should accompany the cloth fleet, but he had his daughter's upcoming wedding to attend to, and his injured leg had begun to cause him difficulty, so Clough, who was familiar with Hamburg, went in his stead. The Hamburg venture was successful, and given the situation in Flanders, the merchants decided that Hamburg would be their new base for English trading abroad. Clough was offered the position as deputy of the Merchant Adventurers in Hamburg, and accepted the commission. It was with great emotion and sadness that Sir Thomas bid farewell to his loyal factor and his family. For with this new appointment, Clough would be leaving Gresham's employ, and would thereafter seek his own fortunes.

Queen Elizabeth's reputation abroad was solid and rising, and her affairs there seemed finally to be coming under control, but her situation at her own court was not salutary. The queen was nonplused—she was suddenly experiencing difficulty in assembling her own council to consider pressing matters of state. Even Dudley was acting strangely, and had absented himself from her presence of late, claiming to have some vague indisposition.

Then, on Ash Wednesday, without warning, they all appeared at the queen's apartments just before supper. Elizabeth, surprised at this unexpected attendance upon her, couldn't resist remarking in an acerbic aside to Cecil, "Such honor surprises us—we've had such difficulty of late in finding our lords assembled at our council table." However, she could not conceal a pleasurable blush at seeing Dudley and enjoying his attention and company once more. Elizabeth, as always, was vain and capricious where Leicester was concerned.

Dudley bent his knee before Elizabeth. "Madame, I speak not for myself but for the thoughts of all your subjects when I say Your Most Gracious Majesty must take measures against the lord secretary and his party, for they will be the downfall of all England!"

Even the doting Elizabeth could not suppress a gasp at this audacity. Cecil, astonished at such a bold and public attack upon him, paled, and sweat broke out upon his brow, but the queen suddenly showed herself to be her father's daughter and every inch the absolute monarch. Stepping back from him, she shouted at Dudley in fury. "What! You dare make accusation against our secretary? You dare claim to speak for OUR SUBJECTS?" Her voice rose nearly to a shriek. The other lords paled and began to murmur in concern. Then, taking heart, they stepped up and agreed with Dudley, voicing their objections to Cecil.

Outraged, and finally perceiving them to be joined in a plot against her, the queen curtly and summarily dismissed them. "Out, all of you. Leave us at once! Only our loyal secretary shall remain at our side." Terrified, the lords made a hurried exit.

When they were gone, Cecil, with a heavy heart, having hoped to spare Elizabeth this grief, revealed to the queen the rumors circulating about a plot by Norfolk and the Catholics to overthrow him, and her with him, and place the crown with Mary queen of Scots.[9] On hearing that, Elizabeth's rage was so terrible she flushed deep red, then went deathly pale. "Thank you for alerting me to this danger. You have served me well in this and shall be rewarded. Leave me now that I may think upon things, and we shall meet on the morrow to counteract this menace."

A few days later Dudley, who now realized how the wind was blowing with the queen, decided to save himself by betraying his fellow conspirators. Realizing that the queen had intelligence of their motives, he threw himself on her mercy and confessed the full details of Norfolk's plan to marry Mary queen of Scots, free her, then seize the throne of England. Elizabeth, in a cold rage, ordered that Norfolk come to her "Immediately!" Though he tried desperately to avoid answering her summons, Norfolk knew he was exposed and trapped. Four days later he appeared before her, and Elizabeth ordered him arrested at once and committed to the Tower prison. Then she appointed a special council of Cecil, Sir Nicholas Bacon, the duke of Northampton, and several others whom she trusted, and told them to question Norfolk. That accomplished, the queen took to her bed, distraught and sickened by this latest turn of events.[10]

As these frightening matters were being untangled at court, the Greshams suddenly found themselves the unwilling guardians, at the queen's express order, of the youngest sister of the unfortunate Lady Jane Grey. Lady Mary Grey had been a lady in waiting to Elizabeth and was herself a distant pretender to Elizabeth's crown. Like her older sister Catherine, she had secretly entered into a marriage with the sergeant porter of the queen's household, without permission of the queen or her advisers. Marriage by anyone of royal blood without permission of the queen and Parliament was strictly forbidden. "The offense is very great," Cecil had informed Sir Thomas when Lady Mary's folly was discovered. Lady Mary's marriage was an even greater offense in Queen Elizabeth's eyes, because any male offspring produced by her cousins could become key in the royal succession.

As punishment, Elizabeth had separated the newlyweds, imprisoned the sergeant porter in the Tower, and stripped Lady Mary of all her lands and possessions, committing her to "protective custody." Several court nobles had already served as guardians of

Lady Mary, and each had quickly begged free of it. It now became Sir Thomas's turn, or rather his misfortune, to be designated the unhappy young woman's "protective custodian"—in effect, her jailer. Some "favors" of the queen were more punishment than reward.[11]

"What! We cannot be saddled with this burden, not now, when there is so much to do for our daughter's wedding!" Lady Anne wailed in outrage when Thomas brought her the news. However, there was little they could do except petition for relief through Cecil. The custody of Lady Mary was not only a personal imposition on them, but a financial burden, too. Lady Mary came to them in impecunious straits, with no arrangements for her keep, and Sir Thomas was forced to make outlay for her basic needs and comforts from his own pocket.

Nor was she a pleasant person to have in the household. She grieved for her husband and her freedom, and complained continually. Sir Thomas dared not address the queen and petition her directly to remove Lady Mary, for Elizabeth had more than enough pressing matters with which to contend. They would just have to accept the arrangement for the moment, Sir Thomas advised his angry wife. That advice did not endear him further to her.

By late spring, the prince of Orange, desperate to gain funds for the Protestant cause on the Continent, offered Queen Elizabeth the fabulous jewels and priceless art objects of the queen of Navarre, who had put them up as collateral for a loan to help the Protestant cause abroad. The prince's agents arrived in London in August, and by his order went immediately to Sir Thomas Gresham and asked him to negotiate a deal with Queen Elizabeth for them.

Sir Thomas ordered the jewels and treasure carried to Queen Elizabeth at Richmond, where she was in residence, and she gasped in wonder on seeing them, so magnificent were the pieces. A sultan's ransom in great rubies, diamonds, and emeralds tumbled in glittering disarray from silken pouches. Satin covers were slid carefully aside to reveal exquisite vases, enameled gold boxes and other trinkets fashioned of gold, jewels and precious stones. Elizabeth particularly coveted a beautiful gold and agate vase. She sent the treasure off to her goldsmiths, who valued the jewels and objects at £60,000. Sighing with regret, the queen openly declined to advance any money from the English treasury on them. "The jewels are not for our use, and we cannot lend upon them," she announced publicly.

Then she turned to Sir Thomas. "We desire to speak with you and Mr. Secretary in private about the next sailing of our merchants, and of the markets across seas," she said, for the ears of others. "You may walk a way with us." She signaled for all the rest, except Cecil, to remain behind.

Gresham, Cecil, and the queen strolled slowly down the wide path, Elizabeth's small hand resting lightly upon the portly Cecil's outstretched arm, the two men relegated to walking on the grass on each side of the path, in order to accommodate the queen's wide skirts. Out of earshot of curious onlookers, they held private council about the jewels. "We would have you spirit the jewels to safekeeping," Elizabeth told Sir Thomas, "and try to raise some monies on them from the merchants, if you can." But, she cautioned, she would never entertain that it was by her wish or through her authority. Sir Thomas nodded his understanding of the queen's difficult orders, knowing he had little choice in the matter, and when he had bowed and taken his leave, he shook his head and sighed in exasperation. It was already common knowledge that the queen of Navarre's treasure had arrived in England. Keeping this business quiet, let alone secret, would be nigh to impossible.

Barely two days after the meeting at Richmond, the French ambassador wrote home: "Her Majesty positively declares that she will lend nothing on the queen of Navarre's jewels; which declaration is made to satisfy you, Majesty, and certainly her own counselors. But Sir Thomas Gresham is secretly using all diligence to find £30,000 in London to loan against the jewels for their [the Protestant's] cause. And so it is that the supplies for the aid of Rochelle, both here and in Germany, are obtained on the queen's credit, but without the privity or consent of either herself or her council, and often in direct opposition to both, being conducted with such a degree of secrecy, that it gives me the greatest trouble to detect. Her Majesty further assures me that she never saw the jewels, and she believes they have been taken to Germany by the Hamburg fleet, but I would wager they are still in the keeping of Sir Thomas Gresham, principal merchant of London."[12]

Cecil, in truth, was still in a quandary over what to do about the treasure from the Spanish ships, and the queen of Navarre's fortune in jewels only added to his worries. He decided to leave that problem to Sir Thomas.

The treasure was another matter. To give it back to Spain would be to enrich and strengthen an adversary, to keep it might mark England as an aggressor against that same adversary. All nations seemed to be arming for war. At bottom it was a question of Protestant interests against Catholic interests, and predictably, advocates were lining up on their respective sides.

Summer came, and the fever of wedding preparations continued at Gresham House. And, the biggest question: Would the queen grace them with her presence? Sir Nicholas Bacon arranged for ecclesiastical dispensation for the posting of the marriage banns however, whenever, and in whatever church they wished. The dispensation authorized the groom, if he wished, publicly to declare the banns verbally, rather than in writing, and they would be honored.[13] Anne's wedding dress had been designed and the dressmakers were working hard to complete it by September. There were endless fittings and discussions.

Lady Anne sent urgent messages abroad to Richard Clough to procure more pearls, of good quality, to embellish her daughter's gown. The Gresham factors were set to the task of procuring and shipping to London the quantities of rare wines and victuals that would be provided by Sir Thomas and Lady Anne for their guests at the wedding feast, and hundreds of invitations were hand-delivered by liveried grooms.

In mid-August, Sir Thomas believed he had gathered enough reliable evidence to prove that the treasure from the Spanish ships had been confiscated—pirated, really—from Italian merchants by the Spaniards. He immediately conveyed this intelligence to Cecil and the queen, giving them some further advice on how he thought they might safely handle the matter: "Now, sir, seeing that this money in the Tower does belong to merchants, I would wish the Queen's Majesty to put it to use for some profit to her, and to mint it into her own coin whereby she would gain £3000 or £4000 and enrich her realm with so much fine silver. And for the repayment of it [to the merchants] Her Highness may pay it by way of exchange, much to her profit. Also, Her Majesty may, if she wishes, take it up [borrow it] from the said merchants at interest, on the usual bonds, for a year or two, which I think they will be glad to do, and so with that Her Majesty can pay her debts here and in Flanders, to the great credit of Her Majesty throughout all Christendom."[14]

Cecil shook his head in wonder upon hearing that. No one but his friend Gresham could have hatched such an audacious, and advantageous, plan! He hastened to put it before Her Majesty. The queen was pleased. She had not foreseen that such an easy and profitable way might be found to move her out of her dilemma. She was grateful to Sir Thomas and to Cecil, and agreed to act upon their suggestion. By the first of September, the treasure was being secretly reminted into English coin. Later, as the queen needed money, she could sell the other objects that had been confiscated from the Spanish fleet—plates, jugs, vases, and other precious objects.

Feeling safely in the queen's grace, and Cecil's, Sir Thomas again begged Cecil to intercede for him in the matter of Lady Mary Grey. "Please give my regards to the earl of Leicester and may it please you both to have my suit in mind for the removal of my Lady Mary Grey."

The queen's special council had held their deliberations on the actions of the duke of Norfolk, and they now approached Elizabeth warily to recommend clemency for the duke. At her look of astonishment, Cecil hastened to give reasons. "The queen of Scots is, and always shall be, a dangerous person to your estate." He advised Elizabeth that if she would only marry, keep Mary imprisoned, and refuse to permit Mary to divorce her husband Bothwell so that she would not be free to marry another, the problem would go away. "We do not find the duke's actions to be treasonable under the law," he concluded.

Elizabeth, however, smelled a deeper danger. She knew that if she did not move quickly and harshly to snuff this move against her, her crown would never again be safe. That Cecil and her other counselors did not see Norfolk's action as treasonous threw her into a fit of hysterical anger. Pale and agitated, she stormed up and down in her chamber. Her ladies hovered in a far corner. They knew better than to draw close when Her Majesty was in such a mood as this. Anything might fly. Elizabeth railed angrily at Cecil and the others, her delicate hands upraised, tears glittering. That the head of her own nobility had been in league with the queen of Scots against her was insupportable! Couldn't they see that? Couldn't they understand what a threat this was to her crown, to all of them, to the realm itself? Elizabeth abruptly stopped and drew herself up in front of them, her eyes blazing in fevered fury out of a face gone suddenly white as snow. Cecil, concerned, fell to one knee before her, his head bowed. The others quickly followed. "Pray, calm yourself, Majesty," Cecil urged quietly, " 'Tis naught to upset Your Grace so."

"Indeed! I shall have Norfolk's head off, by my own authority!" The queen then fell to the floor in a faint. Cecil, alarmed, lunged to catch Her Majesty as her ladies, crying out in fear, rushed to her aid.

The court was in disarray, the lord keeper Bacon was distracted by heavy duties of state, Sir Thomas was concerned about Cecil's fate in all this, and before they knew it, Anne and Nathaniel's wedding day was upon them. The queen regretfully declined to attend. However, Secretary Cecil and his wife, and Dudley, earl of Leicester, were prominent among the assemblage of important guests.

The heavily embroidered pale yellow silk cloth for Anne's wedding gown had come from Paris, the lace for her veil had been handmade in Bruges at Sir Thomas's request and smuggled to them by Jasper Schetz. Sir Thomas had also ordered some magnificent jewels for his daughter to wear for her wedding day. Anne was a radiant if nervous bride, and Nathaniel awaited his bride attired stylishly in russet-colored velvet and creamy lace. Afterward, the feasting, music and revelry lasted long into the evening.

But for the queen, at Windsor, there was no peace or revelry in those days. In November, the Catholic rebellion broke out into the open, but the queen and Cecil had wisely moved the Scottish queen in secret to Warwickshire. When the rebels reached Tutbury to release their Mary, they came up empty-handed. Elizabeth's troops, under the command of Lord Admiral Clinton, Lord Warwick, and the dukes of Hunsdon and Sussex, soon routed the Catholics.

The two rebel leaders, Northumberland and Westmoreland, together with their wives who had ridden beside them, were driven in retreat across the border into Scotland. They had thought they'd be returning to London in the triumphant procession of the new Catholic queen of England, but instead they found themselves outlaws in hiding. The Catholic rebellion in England was effectively extinguished.

It was in the aftermath of that incident that Elizabeth's rage knew no bounds. She was livid that the rebels had dared to plot against her and openly oppose her authority; she resented the drain on her treasury caused by having to raise and send troops to crush the rebellion; and she was frustrated to learn that by law she could not seize the property of the outlaw rebels in reprisal—the crown could get them only if the owners stood trial and were convicted of treason. Elizabeth took the whole affair as a personal insult. "They shall be punished!" she declared. The poorer rebels, who had nothing to forfeit except their lives, she ordered summarily executed. The wealthy nobles who were within reach, including Norfolk, were clapped into the Tower to await trial and sentencing. But again—perhaps remembering her own mother's fate—although she decreed death to the hundreds who participated in the rebellion, Elizabeth still could not bring herself to order the execution of Mary queen of Scots.[15] At that, Cecil had another attack of ague.

Sir Thomas had been busy for the queen on other fronts throughout this latest domestic crisis. Elizabeth, deciding to help the Protestants on the Continent, had tasked Sir Thomas with single-handedly wringing a large loan from the merchants for the secret use of the Protestants in Germany and the Low Countries. He had also been able to convince the queen to sequester the bulk of the profits made from the latest cloth fleets in Germany, and keep it there, to strengthen her credit abroad and have collateral in place for her uses whenever she needed it.

The French ambassador, Fenelon, wrote home worriedly that of the estimated value of the recent English trading, which he figured to be around £750,000, "less than a third will return to England."[16] That much money available to the Protestant cause on the Continent represented a serious threat to all Catholic rulers. None of them had credit left with the moneylenders. Elizabeth's foreign credit, on the other hand, was at its zenith. This placed Sir Thomas high in Queen Elizabeth's esteem and personal affection, for in the ten years of her reign, she had seen firsthand the truth of what Sir Thomas had advised her at the very beginning: an imperiled treasury—and corresponding loss of credit—meant loss of independence and power for any ruler.

Elizabeth's scrupulous attention to her finances from the start had kept her from that fate. "I know for certain," Gresham told Cecil, "that the duke of Alva is more troubled with the Queen's Majesty's great credit and with the sale of Her Highness's commodities at Hamburg than he is with anything else, and quakes with fear."

Sir Thomas had never favored incurring foreign debt. "I would wish that the Queen's Majesty in this time should not use any strangers, but rather go to her own merchants for money, whereby the duke of Alva, and all other princes, may see what a prince of power she is."

Sir Thomas succeeded in negotiating loans for the queen from the English merchants (even managing to override a veto at one point by enlisting help from Cecil and the council to rebuke the merchants who refused), and as the loans were promptly repaid, at interest, and the confidence of the merchants was gained, they were more willing to make further loans upon demand.[17] Their sovereign returned their trust by not squandering the money they loaned. Thus, following Gresham's advice, Elizabeth managed to establish credit with her own bankers, right there in England, for when she needed funds. And the merchants found they could profit from the crown's repayment at interest. The renting of money in England was no longer frowned upon, and Sir Thomas heard no accusations of "foul usury" from anyone any more.

Elizabeth continued to maintain personal vigil over her treasury, examining the expenditures of her officials, and studying their accounts, income, and properties assiduously. Little or nothing escaped the queen's watchful eye where finances were concerned.[18] She was also aware that Sir Thomas Gresham's generous gesture in establishing an exchange in London would prove financially beneficial to her realm, especially now that Antwerp was lost to them as a trade center.

The new decade dawned, and with it came a slight political thaw for Elizabeth. England had kept its tenuous hold on a Protestant kingdom with a growing economy, it had maintained profitable trade routes with Europe, and a wary truce had been maneuvered with Philip and the Catholic rulers of Europe.

Then, in February 1570, Pope Pius V, from his Vatican throne, hurled a lightning bolt at Elizabeth of England. Frustrated by the failure of Mary queen of Scots to gain the English throne for the Catholic cause in Europe, he decided to step in. He issued a papal bull, summarily excommunicating "Elizabeth, the pretended queen of England and all those heretics adhering to her." The papal bull went on to encourage sedition, and virtually commanded open treason against the English ruler, stating that "the nobles, subjects, people, and others shall not dare to obey her or any of her laws, directions, or commands, binding under the same curse those who do anything to the contrary." King Philip of Spain and the French regent Catherine de Medici both received the papal order with groans of dismay, for neither had been consulted about it, and neither wanted to be placed in a position of being required by it to declare and wage war with the English queen.

With his action, the pope had forcibly placed all Catholics in Europe in direct opposition to Elizabeth—including the Catholics in England, Scotland, Ireland, and Wales. Bishop Jewel answered for Elizabeth. He denounced the position Pope Pius had taken, and reaffirmed the rock of the regard of the English for their monarch. "God gave us Queen Elizabeth and with her gave us peace, and so long a peace as England has seldom seen before."[19]

The English people were stung with outrage at the audacity of the pope, and rallied round their queen. The ultimate result was positive for Elizabeth as far as her own country was concerned, for it had given her a new and unexpected solidarity, and support, from the English populace. The pope's objective, which was divisiveness, had failed miserably.

Seizing her advantage, Elizabeth had Norfolk beheaded for his part in the Catholic rebellion, showing the Catholics once and for all her disdain for Mary queen of Scots, the pope, and their pretensions to her crown. Norfolk's execution sent a strong and unmistakable signal across the waves to Europe and Rome.

At about that same time, a messenger speeding in the other direction, from Europe to England, brought Sir Thomas sad and shocking news. Richard Clough had died suddenly in Hamburg of an unspecified illness. Sir Thomas's closest associate and friend was gone, and at barely forty years of age. In trying to absorb the shock of that news, Sir Thomas recalled that Clough had written him not long before, complaining of not feeling well. "I have such a pain in my head that I have not slept one wink of all this night.... I am not able more to write, having not slept six hours in twelve days and nights," he had written.

Sir Thomas at once sent to Hamburg for further details. Though prominent doctors had attended him in his final weeks, he learned, they had been unable to save Clough. Death had claimed him quickly. Clough left his grieving widow Katherine with two infant daughters—little Anne was but two, and the baby Mary barely a year old. Sir Thomas was also surprised to learn that his former factor had left two older children by mistresses before his marriage—a son Richard and a daughter Winifred. Clough had indeed been a deeply private person about his personal life, Sir Thomas realized, for as well as he thought he knew Clough, he had never heard a word about the existence of the older children, until this moment.

In his will, Clough left his lands to his widow, but everything else "I do freely give to my said master, Sir Thomas Gresham, all my movable goods to do his pleasure therewith, and refer it to his will whether that he will suffer my wife and children to enjoy them, or no. Oh my master, do unto my poor wife and children as you would I should do to yours if you were in the same case, for they have no father to trust unto but you; and thus I bid you and my gracious lady farewell, till it please God to send us a merry meeting."[20]

Upon reading those words, Sir Thomas laid his head down upon the polished oak of his desk and wept bitter tears for his closest friend and companion of nearly twenty years. For weeks afterward, he went about with a heavy heart, but he looked after the widow Clough and the children and their affairs as Clough would have wished. He returned all the holdings Clough left to him to the family, providing in addition a home and an annual income for the widow and paying off all of Clough's debts, from his own purse.

The Lady Mary Grey continued to plague Sir Thomas's household with her pitiful presence, and he continued to beg for relief almost weekly. He told Cecil toward the end of the year, "I pray you to set your good hand to the removing of her, for my wife would like to ride into Norfolk to see our daughter, soon to have a child, and her own dear old mother, who is now fourscore and ten years of age and a very weak woman, not likely to live much longer."[21]

Cecil promised to do what he could. However, relief from the charge was not soon forthcoming, for no one else would take her in. The holidays brought the welcome news to the Greshams that their daughter Anne, who had gone up to the Bacon family seat at Norfolk with her husband, had been safely delivered of a little daughter, Anne Bacon. Tears sprang to Sir Thomas's eyes upon receiving the news of his first grandchild. William Read, Anne's son from her first marriage, had already presented them with grandchildren, but little Anne Bacon was his first grandchild of his own blood, and he rejoiced in her.

The new year thus began on a high note for Sir Thomas. It also arrived with good portents for him and Cecil in regard to the queen's favor. On New Year's Day 1571, as he and Lady Anne presented their gifts (£10 each in gold coins), Sir Thomas learned that the queen intended to pay a visit soon to both Gresham House and his new exchange. He was overwhelmed by such an honor and immediately set about making arrangements for Her Majesty's visit.

As a boon for such an auspicious occasion and to make the exchange as attractive as possible to the royal eye, Sir Thomas gave the merchants in the upper galleries free rent for the year and directed his own factors to procure all manner of exotic goods from near and far to provision the shops. The milliners and haberdashers displayed not only their traditional hats, clothes, and tailoring, but also bird cages, shoehorns, and intricately worked lanterns. There were apothecaries, armorers, booksellers, and goldsmith shops "as plenteously stored with all kinds of rich wares and fine commodities as any great place in Europe. Even foreign princes send to here to be sure of finding the best items available," Sir Thomas boasted to Cecil with glee. The queen would see it all. Since night would fall early at that time of year, he ordered thousands of beeswax candles and torches installed, to illuminate the exchange for her visit.

For two weeks, Sir Thomas made twice daily visits to the exchange, limping painfully along the full length of the upper galleries personally to inspect the premises and see that all was in order. When he returned home, exhausted but still full of plans and directions, the servants at Gresham House were driven nearly to distraction with the preparations he ordered there for the queen's visit to his residence.

Dressmakers arrived at Gresham House daily, and Lady Anne went out in the afternoons and shopped nonstop. Even Lady Mary Grey was caught up in the excitement. She hoped that perhaps the queen, upon seeing her, would decide to relent and free her. Sir Thomas fervently shared that hope and willingly opened his purse for a new dress for the Lady Mary for the occasion, as well as for splendid new dresses for his wife.

Her Majesty had decreed she would not only visit Gresham House, but also stay and sup with her favorite financial adviser and his family. Rare and exotic foods were brought in to be personally inspected by Sir Thomas and his chef, together with the queen's own chef and taster. The vast scullery and kitchen at Gresham House was kept in a fever of activity. Dishes were prepared, tasted, commented upon. Finally a menu was selected. The chef sweated over its preparation and presentation, screaming orders at his battalion of assistants, banging kettles and rapping sluggards smartly with his cooking implements. His responsibility was staggering, for Her Majesty's retinue numbered in the hundreds. But Gresham House was enormous, and there was ample room to accommodate them all.

On 23 January, with great fanfare, the queen made her slow, stately progress into London, attended by all her nobility. Huge crowds of Londoners had gathered to see their queen, and lusty cheers rose on all sides as she passed by—smiling, nodding, and waving, her slim white hands encased in dark leather gloves. The bells of St. Margaret's and Westminster rang out joyously. Dressed in white silk, with accents of cloth of gold, her cloak of black and gold lavishly trimmed in white ermine and fastened with great gold chains of office, the queen entered the City by the Temple Bar, proceeded along Fleet Street, down Cheapside, and along the north side of the exchange to Bishopsgate Street, thence into the courtyard of Gresham House. There she was welcomed by a band of musicians, a fanfare of trumpets, and ushered by her bowing host and hostess into "our poor and humble house, so honored by Your Majesty's exalted presence." Sir Thomas hoped, too, that the sight of her cousin Lady Mary Grey would move the queen to take pity on them all and remove her from their household.

Queen Elizabeth thoroughly enjoyed Sir Thomas Gresham's

hospitality and the sumptuous dinner he offered, and was in high spirits as he escorted her and her party to Cornhill to visit the exchange. Once more the bells of the City rang out to announce Her Majesty's presence, and the bells of the exchange tolled continually as she made her progress toward it. Once again the crowds lined the streets to gawk at, and cheer for, their beloved queen. Many had remained standing out in the bitter January cold the entire time she was in Gresham House, just to catch a glimpse of her when she came their way again.

The queen's party entered the exchange on the south side, and she insisted upon being taken on a full tour of the building and the shops, exclaiming with approval over the magnificent statue of her in the central position of honor. Upstairs, at the shops, she murmured in womanly pleasure at the rich and unusual wares displayed in them. Sir Thomas gallantly presented several of the most exquisite items to the queen as mementos of her visit, and she smiled and graciously thanked him. Then, turning to her lord chamberlain, Elizabeth whispered an order, whereupon her heralds were summoned and a fanfare of silver trumpets sounded. A hush fell. Then the chief herald called out, "Hear ye! Hear ye! This bourse is henceforth, by command of Her Most Gracious Majesty the Queen Elizabeth, proclaimed the Royal Exchange of England, to be henceforth so designated and called, and not otherwise!"

At that solemn proclamation, Thomas felt a thrill rush along his arms, and his heart swelled with pride until he thought it would burst. He wished his father could have been here to see this day! Tears sprang unbidden to his eyes, but he hid them with a low bow of thanks to the queen who had bestowed him with such honor. It was a moment to be forever remembered.

Then he turned. "Warm ale, for Her Majesty and for all!" he commanded. "We shall drink a carouse to our Most Gracious Sovereign for this honor!" The ale was brought, and Sir Thomas raised his cup, "To Our Gracious Majesty's health and long life, and to the Royal Exchange, long may they both stand for England!" A lusty cheer went up, as all echoed and drank the toast. Later, the rumor flew through the streets of London that Sir Thomas had purchased the most expensive pearl in the goldsmith's shop that night and had crushed it in his cup to drink to the queen. A poet wrote:

> Here fifteen hundred pounds at one clap goes!
> Instead of sugar, Gresham drinks the pearl
> Unto his queen and mistress: pledge it lords![22]

But that was mere fantasy on the part of the public and the poet, engendered perhaps by the legends of Cleopatra. Even one so wealthy as Sir Thomas would not have countenanced such an extravagant gesture as the deliberate destruction of a costly jewel.

The very next month, Elizabeth, still in a rare giving mood, handed Cecil his promised reward for his long and loyal service to her: she raised him to the peerage, creating a new title and naming him baron of Burghley. Though he knew that of course Cecil would have preferred something more tangible from the hand of the queen, like lands or money, Sir Thomas was delighted at his friend's great honor. The investiture ceremony would be a memorable one. He enjoined Lady Anne to purchase a new gown, the finest available, for the ceremony that would invest Cecil as a peer of the realm.

On 25 February they stood with the rest of the court in the hushed silence of the Presence Chamber of Westminster. A strong current of excitement arched through the room when the heralds announced Her Majesty. The queen entered, attired in a splendid gown embroidered all over in gold thread, with a great lacy ruff of sheerest white lawn standing out from her bodice. Huge amethysts and diamonds dangled from gold chains, winking amidst her customary waist-length ropes of pearls. Her russet hair was caught back in a net of golden mesh, and a diadem of rubies and diamonds flashed upon her head.

The heralds' trumpets outside sounded another fanfare, and the great double doors swung open. The heralds entered, marching two by two. They were followed by the garter-king-at-arms, who carried in his hands the charter of the creation of the barony.

After him marched Lord Hunsdon, who bore across his out-stretched arms the new baron's scarlet-trimmed cloak of office.

Then came Cecil himself, his white hair and beard and pale pink skin a sharp contrast to his raiment of rich black velvet embroidered with gold. A finely pleated white ruff framed his face and more ruffles showed at the edges of his sleeves. A great diamond and pearl brooch adorned his doublet and another of rubies and pearls attached to his sleeve. Ironically, he was escorted on one side by the splendidly attired earl of Leicester (who barely a year before had demanded his removal from office) and on the other by Lord Cobham. Approaching the queen, they made deep bows, and the lord chamberlain solemnly handed the charter, written in Latin, to the queen, who in turn gave it to her Latin secretary to read aloud. At the proper moment, the queen took the cloak from Lord Hunsdon and placed it gently around Cecil's shoulders. "We pronounce you Lord William Cecil, Baron of Burghley," she said, patting his shoulder lightly and giving him an affectionate smile. "Rise, Lord Burghley." Then she handed him his charter. As the procession filed solemnly from the chamber, the assembled ladies swept into deep curtseys and the gentlemen bowed low when the queen and the new Lord Burghley passed.

A great celebration feast had been laid in the hall. There Cecil's title was proclaimed to the assemblage by the heralds. They made a ceremonial bow and withdrew, crying "largesse, largesse, largesse!" Outside, they distributed purses of alms from the new baron to the poor. Sir Thomas and his family were seated with Sir Nicholas Bacon and his family. Anne and Nathaniel were with them. They were staying with the Bacons during this visit, which was not far from Gresham House. Sir Thomas had at last had a chance to become acquainted with his new and charming little granddaughter, Anne, to his great delight. The sisters Lady Anne and Lady Jane, grandmothers to the babe, spent their days cooing over her lavishly decorated cradle-bed, and ordering tiny gowns and robes for her.

After they had dined, he found a moment to approach and congratulate the new Lord Burghley, and make his bow to the queen, thanking her again for the honored visit recently bestowed upon his family and the Royal Exchange.

When all the excitement died down, Cecil wrote his friend Nicholas White, "My style is Lord of Burghley, if you mean to know it for your writing, and if you want to write truly, the poorest lord in England." For as with Sir Thomas, the queen had been lavish with praise, and scarce with tangible rewards for her new baron. From then on, he preferred to be addressed as William Burghley, rather than Cecil, though it would be by the latter name that he would always be better known to his friends.

Cecil gave a great sigh, remembering the outlay Sir Thomas had made for his daughter Anne's wedding to Nathaniel Bacon the previous year. "Yea, 'tis naught but a father's cost and worry to be plagued with a daughter," he lamented to Sir Nicholas. The marriage of his own daughter Anne to the earl of Oxford was approaching. His Anne, too, was barely sixteen, a sweet and placid girl who would make Oxford a fine wife. The nuptials would take place at Westminster Abbey in December. Cecil, always a frugal man, groaned inwardly at the outlay of funds his daughter's marriage would require. The poor Baron Burghley would be even poorer after that day's feasting!

In September, the Lady Mary Grey's husband, the sergeant porter, died, and Sir Thomas thought that might signal the quittance of his custodianship of the poor widow, "who takes her husband's death right grievously," he informed Cecil. "Seeing that God has taken away the occasion of Her Majesty's just displeasure, perhaps you can aid me to see an end to my suit for the removing of her, to give my wife and me some peace in our advancing age." Cecil promised to do what he could, but could offer his friend no assurance of immediate relief.[23]

Though only fifty-two, Sir Thomas felt like an old man now. Like Cecil, he suffered badly from gout, and his injured leg continued to plague him. Fragments of bone were working their way out, and he was forced to consult a surgeon to relieve him. The pain was constant and unrelenting, especially in winter, and although he endeavored to ignore it and keep to his heavy schedule, at times it was almost impossible for him even to get up and limp along, even using his stout walking stick for support.

He had long since abandoned his frequent and rigorous trips to the Continent on the queen's business, though he still went across on rare occasions, on matters of great importance to the crown which the queen wanted him to handle personally.

At Christmas that year, the Greshams attended the glittering wedding of Lord Burghley's daughter Anne to the earl of Oxford. Cecil seemed pleased enough about the match, but Sir Thomas did not like Oxford, who seemed to him to be rather dissolute, and he'd heard he was a gambler. He counted himself fortunate that his Anne had found a good husband in Nathaniel Bacon, who watched Anne's money carefully and squandered nothing.

When New Year 1572 arrived, Sir Thomas was laid up with the problems in his leg, and he summoned a famous surgeon from the north country to attend to it. "I have returned Derek the surgeon home again," he told Cecil. "He has brought my leg to better ease now that the bones have come out, and he says that it will be healed very shortly. With the leave of God I'll be with you again next Sunday." In March, his lifelong enemy Paulet, marquess of Winchester, died, but Sir Thomas was in such great pain with his leg, he could scarcely celebrate the relief he felt at hearing that news. It served to remind him, though, that his account with the crown was as yet not settled, for Paulet had continued blocking him at every turn. He had never lost hope that one day he'd see Gresham's downfall.

Nearly five years had passed since the last settlement of his accounts with the crown. He decided he'd press Cecil about it as soon as his leg was well enough to go and visit with him. But then that winter, Cecil fell seriously ill. The faithful lord secretary, the cares of whose office had taken such great toll on him in recent years, hovered near death, and Sir Thomas, unmindful of his leg, joined the queen at Cecil's bedside.

Sir Thomas consoled the queen, and Cecil's distraught wife and family, as best he could and quietly saw to Burghley's financial and personal needs throughout the crisis. Fortunately, after a week or so, Cecil rallied, and by late April was well enough to attend the ceremony wherein the grateful queen installed him with the order of the garter.

In June, the queen raised Cecil to lord treasurer, the office left open by Winchester's death. Sir Thomas was pleased at this latest honor accorded to the hard-working Cecil and hoped that the new office would bring some respite to him. The queen did not slight Sir Thomas, either. She instructed the lord mayor of London, Sir Lionel Duckett, to consult with a board of directors, to which she named Sir Thomas Gresham as "a person of great trust, wisdom, and experience," to advise Duckett on matters of jurisdiction and administration of the City.[24] So in that way, though again there was no tangible reward, the queen again showed her favor to her two closest financial advisers.

That summer the queen relented, and the Lady Mary Grey, who had been in the care of the Greshams for more than three years, was finally removed from their household and allowed to establish her own residence. The pain in his leg was beginning to abate somewhat, and Sir Thomas rejoiced over the Lady Mary's departure, and the lifting of the dark cloud her presence had placed over his household for those years.

Cecil visited them, and informed Thomas that negotiations were again in progress for a marriage alliance for the queen. This time the suitor was the French duc D'Alençon, and for a change, Cecil said, everything seemed to be proceeding well. They were almost at a point of resolution.

Thomas was pleased. Hopes for Elizabeth to settle into a marriage and perhaps produce an heir for England seemed this time to be a possibility. Then, in September, news reached England of a great massacre of Protestants in Paris on St. Bartholomew's Day. Crowds of Huguenots had gathered to witness the wedding of young King Henry of Navarre to the French king's sister, Marguerite of Valois.

"Hundreds of Protestants were killed. Everyone is up in arms over this," Cecil informed Sir Thomas sadly, "and the people are crying out for revenge against the Catholics, and here they want the head of Mary queen of Scots."

Burghley wrote the earl of Shrewsbury on 7 September, "None of any name of the religion is left living but such as fled and escaped their pursuers . . . their flames may come hither and into Scotland, for such cruelties have large scopes. God save our gracious queen, who now assembles as many of her council that may come to consult what is to be done for some surety. The French ambassador came yesterday to Oxford, but the Queen's Majesty is not hasty to hear any of them. All men now cry out against your prisoner Mary queen of Scots."[25]

Shortly after Cecil brought them the tragic news of the St. Bartholomew's Day massacre, which effectively ended any possibility for a liaison between Queen Elizabeth and the French duke, the Greshams left for Mayfield, in Kent, the most splendid of all of Sir Thomas's residences. It was a favorite with Lady Anne, and Sir Thomas, pleased that she liked it, spent over £5000 on lavish interior appointments for it. Mayfield had become the talk of the court, and Queen Elizabeth decided that on her next progress, in the summer of 1573, she would pay a visit to Sir Thomas there. The Greshams hastened there now to make any repairs or refurbishment needed in preparation for the queen's visit.

The queen and her considerable entourage would be at Mayfield for a three-day visit. The surrounding countryside was thrilled at the prospect of a royal visit, and by early summer that year, Mayfield had been polished and spruced up, its parks and paths cleaned, clipped, and swept, its balustrades scrubbed and polished. The queen's chamber had been cleaned and recleaned, inspected and reinspected to ensure that Her Majesty's every comfort would be anticipated.

As the day neared, musicians were brought in from London, and players, mimes and entertainers were engaged by Sir Thomas to stage pageants and games for the queen's amusement. The chefs ordered great quantities of game and fowl to be roasted and served, and all manner of delicacies were prepared in the kitchens. Mayfield was immense, its parks and gardens were vast and magnificent, and the estate, like Osterley, could easily accommodate the queen on her summer progress. Finally the great day came, and Elizabeth arrived at Mayfield, making her way through cheering crowds along the way. She enjoyed her stay there so much that she informed Sir Thomas she intended to make a visit to Osterley soon, as well.

Shortly after the queen's visit, Sir Thomas returned to London, where he and Cecil were shocked to learn that their friend John Caius had died. Following Caius's dismissal as a court physician, Sir Thomas had seen little of his friend, except when Caius came to London, for the eminent doctor had moved to Cambridge to devote his days to the building of his college at Cambridge University, where he had pursued writing down the vast knowledge of disease he had gained over the years. While at Cambridge, he was able to maintain his standing in his profession and was elected president of the College of Physicians in London for the ninth time in 1571.

But Caius's relationships at Cambridge were touchy and often acerbic, for many of the fellows feared he might attempt to restore Catholic doctrine to the college, and they were determined that would not happen. There were many confrontations between Caius and the fellows, and he had difficulty maintaining his authority over them. Caius's retaliations against them were at times so vicious and vitriolic, Sir Thomas became alarmed. "For now they dispute but with words and anger, but have some care, Kees my friend," Sir Thomas had cautioned him earlier, "lest they waylay you one day with staves and knives." Saddened, worn out, and deeply discouraged at what he saw happening to his religion and the discipline at his beloved college, Caius simply lost his will to live, and expired on 29 July at age sixty-two. Sir Thomas and Cecil attended his funeral and deeply mourned the loss of their brilliant but decidedly eccentric friend.[26]

Within the space of but a few weeks, they felt the loss of Caius and his professional expertise even more. In September, Lord Burghley and his wife were forced to flee Burghley House and seek refuge at Gresham House, for the sweating sickness had struck especially fiercely in their area of London. Cecil could not at that time leave the city to escape it. Sir Thomas welcomed them warmly and enjoyed the few days he was able to spend with them. He and Cecil were both feeling their age, suffering aches and pains of body and heart. They sat before the fire in Sir Thomas's study and talked for many hours. Cecil was not unmindful of the assistance Thomas had given him on many occasions, not only with his son Thomas, but also with his impossible son-in-law, the earl of Oxford. He confided to Sir Thomas that he had refused a match for his other daughter Elizabeth with the son of the earl of Shrewsbury, fearing it might be perceived as favoring the cause of Mary queen of Scots.[27]

In November, Sir Thomas's niece and sole remaining legal heir, Lady Elizabeth Neville, the only child of his long-deceased brother John, was visiting him at Gresham House, when she was suddenly taken ill. It was the malignant fever. Despite all Sir Thomas's efforts, they could not save her, and on 7 November, she died, leaving six young children and a very distraught husband. Their oldest child, Elizabeth, was barely twelve, the eldest son Henry—known as "Harry" —who would now become the Gresham heir, was only ten. The others were two, three, four, and five. Sir Thomas, deeply fond of his niece, grieved terribly. He felt then that his family had somehow been cursed. If only Caius had been alive, he was convinced, he would have somehow saved her. Seeing the body of his poor dead niece, so young, so frail, Sir Thomas broke down and wept. His brother's only child, like his own Richard, had been swept from life in her prime, claimed by the relentless fever that snuffed out the lives of so many in London every year.

Then, rousing himself and taking charge as usual, he had his niece's body transported to Billingbere in Waltham Lawrence, where he did his utmost to console her grieving husband Sir Henry, and supervised matters as she was buried there on a cold, rainy November day.[28]

At fifty-five, Sir Thomas was weary, and sunk in despair. Except for his daughter Anne and his two little granddaughters Anne and

Elizabeth, there was naught that brought joy to his heart any more. He was plagued with gout, he suffered unremitting pain in his twisted leg, and he was fast losing his eyesight. He had drastically reduced his participation in Elizabeth's government, and finally, in 1574, he begged the queen and Cecil to allow him to retire. In the sixteen years he had tirelessly served Queen Elizabeth—far longer and far better than he had served any of her predecessors—she had not given him a single tangible reward, despite her fervent promise to him on that memorable day at Hatfield, when she assumed the throne of England.

Now Sir Thomas had little use for the queen's ear, nor for more land, or royal rewards. With whom would he share the joys of such honor? To whom could he leave such rewards? He already had more than enough land and money for his wife's lifelong needs. Anne and her daughters were well provided for, and the Bacons were handsomely situated in their own right. His granddaughters would lack for nothing. But he had no legal male heir of his blood to whom he could leave his own vast fortune.

In preparation for full retirement from government service, Sir Thomas once again submitted his accounts to the treasury for settlement. Despite his frequent pleas to Cecil, they had gone unaudited for more than eleven years. Now, at last, the government functionaries took up the resolution of his accounts. At first, he was only mildly annoyed when they engaged him in a back-and-forth harangue over minor sums. His claim for salary for the four clerks allowed him by Mary, then Elizabeth, was struck down, and he was told he would be allowed for only two. His claim for £1125 for journeys and boat hire back and forth to the Low Countries over eleven years was struck out and arbitrarily reduced to £500. Rent allowance for his mansion in Antwerp, claimed at just over £666 for eleven years was reduced to £300, without explanation. And so it went. When he handed in his accounts, Gresham claimed Elizabeth's treasury owed him close to £11,000, which included interest for eleven years on the money, and an allowance for change in exchange rates. However, when the crown's accountants finished making their adjustments and disallowances, the scales had tilted the other way, and the claim was that Sir Thomas owed the royal treasury more than £10,000. He'd have to pay in cash immediately to settle his account with the government, or face disgrace.[29]

Upon hearing that, Sir Thomas was thrown into a towering rage. This was too much, the absolute last straw! Not only had he received no reward from the crown, but decades of risking his life, opening his purse, and ignoring his own lucrative trading business in favor of the crown's interests had now come down to haggling over his twenty shilling diet, and other accounts to which he had been given absolute access by the rulers who appointed him. Preposterous! What did these bureaucrats know of the financial machinations he had worked for the queen and Cecil, the secret deals, the quiet loans and private allowances he had unobtrusively obtained for Her Majesty, often using his own funds and credit on her behalf? What did they know of the demands made upon his finances, the losses he sustained, the expenses and loans he could not reveal, but could only reclaim as best he could within those very accounts that the accountants were rejecting willy-nilly?

Now, with the figures on the official treasury account sheets staring him relentlessly in the face, the damage was done, the die cast. Certainly, this claim that he owed Queen Elizabeth's treasury £10,000 would do him severe damage financially if it were pressed. It was no small amount of cash to produce, even to a man as rich as Sir Thomas Gresham. Worse, it could ruin him—by destroying the fine reputation he had worked so long and hard to build. Anger again boiled up in him. He would not stand for such insult. But how to avert it? Boldly, he hatched his plan.

Seeking out the chief accountant, Sir Thomas requested the unofficial duplicate copy of the audit report that showed him to be in debt to the crown. The unsuspecting accountant was happy to oblige. He was going away on holiday for the weekend, he told Sir Thomas, and would not be working on the account until his return, so he had no need of the duplicate, and Sir Thomas was welcome to have it for his review.

Mounting up, document in hand, Sir Thomas set out at a gallop for Kenilworth, where the queen and her court were staying. When he arrived there he went immediately in search of Robert Dudley, the earl of Leicester. "By your leave, milord, I would a moment with you. I come on a matter of great urgency on which I seek your counsel." Curious, and noting the tone of urgency in the old knight's voice, Dudley quickly excused himself from the others, and he and Sir Thomas walked a short distance away. Gresham showed him the account. "I beg Your Grace to intercede for me with Her Majesty on this affair, lest I be ruined afore one and all." Dudley nodded, for after scanning the document he was as shocked as Sir Thomas at the size of the bottom line. He also felt a clutch of fear, for he owed Sir Thomas money, as did many of the other nobles, and if this went forward, Sir Thomas might demand payment from them in order to clear his accounts.

Leicester sent for Burghley. The treasurer greeted Sir Thomas with pleasure. "What brings you forth to Richmond, my friend?" Sir Thomas showed him the account. Burghley had seen some of the earlier manipulations and had attempted to constrain the functionaries in their zeal. Now he studied it carefully, then gave a start of surprise, his expression showing open amazement when his eye lit upon the final figure. He knew now without a doubt why his friend had ridden in such haste to Kenilworth.

Forthwith, they begged audience with the queen, and were shortly ushered into her presence. Elizabeth was seated in the long gallery on a bench strewn with cushions, enjoying the late afternoon air. At forty, she was no longer the bright and shining damsel she had been at Hatfield. Age was starting to exact its toll. She was delighted to see three of her favorite gentlemen approaching, and they stopped and bowed deeply before her. She smiled at Burghley, held out a jeweled hand imperiously for Leicester to draw near her, and greeted Sir Thomas cordially.

Going close, Leicester whispered in Her Majesty's ear for a moment, then without further ado handed her the accounting scroll. Elizabeth slowly unrolled it and carefully studied it. Her eyes widened when she came to the final figures. She, who watched every farthing that was paid out and every shilling that came into her treasury, knew that Sir Thomas could not possibly owe such a sum to the crown. The group there all knew the real truth—that the crown's account with Sir Thomas was decidedly different from what showed on this document. For the barest instant, Elizabeth the penurious was tempted. After all, Sir Thomas Gresham was very rich—he had estates and land, factories and mills, ships and shops and warehouses full of goods. The three men knew she could simply demand he pay this enormous sum, and he would have no choice except to pay it or forfeit his lands, and possibly even his life.

Elizabeth regarded her loyal agent, who had served her with singular devotion since her first moment as queen. Sir Thomas Gresham had advised her wisely and bargained well for her. He had smuggled for her, manipulated for her, spied for her, risked his reputation, and his very life for her. With his help, her crown had remained secure and her treasury intact.

He had much, this merchant prince ... but he had lost much also. Like the queen herself, he had achieved great things, but had no heir to follow in his steps. She asked him what he sought of her. Sir Thomas bowed again, deeply, then looked earnestly at the queen. Their eyes locked in understanding, and he spoke out boldly. "I seek naught but justice and your pardon, Majesty, and Your Grace's leave to retire to the peace of my old years."

The queen turned to Leicester. "I say grant this knight his boon, Your Grace," he said. Then looking at Burghley, the queen again arched her brow in question. He nodded. Satisfied, she turned back to Sir Thomas. "Then be it ordered done, by my hand," she commanded, handing the document to the lord treasurer. "Your account with the crown is hereby counted fully cleared." Sir Thomas, relieved beyond measure, favored Her Majesty with one of his rare and radiant smiles. "Your Majesty has made me a young man again," he said, repeating the phrase he had uttered to her at Hatfield so long ago, when she had declared him her royal agent.

As the three left to have quittance of the account ratified by the signatures of the council, the queen permitted herself a small, triumphant smile. Elizabeth had won it both ways. She had managed to reward the most canny financier in the realm without spending a penny, and had won admiration and gratitude for the granting of a boon that was not a favor at all, but a debt of honor she clearly owed Sir Thomas Gresham.[30]

As the calendar turned over into 1575, Sir Thomas took stock of his situation. He had survived countless dangers, international intrigues, and the tumultuous upheavals of four reigns. He had grown weary of pain, and indeed, if the truth be known, weary of life. He had resolved his account with the crown, though many still murmured he had duped the queen. Sir Thomas gave a short laugh. They should only know who had duped whom! Now there remained his lands and his considerable fortune. To what good might he turn them?

Others had also taken an interest in that, for it had not escaped notice in England that perhaps the wealthiest and most powerful merchant in the realm was left with only a nephew as heir. The colleges at Cambridge began a lobbying campaign to get Sir Thomas to leave the bulk of his fortune to endow a school there. When he did not immediately consent to the proposal, they approached Cecil's wife, Lady Burghley, asking her to appeal to Sir Thomas on their behalf. They intimated that at one time he had promised that he would give £500 to the college.

However, much as he loved Cambridge and revered the education he had received there, Sir Thomas had other ideas for an educational endowment. His first and greatest love was his home base—the City of London. Cambridge had plenty of public schools and colleges; in London there was none deserving of mention.

As spring began to deck itself out in a riot of birds and blossoms, Sir Thomas tackled the arduous task of putting his complex business and personal affairs in order. He'd sit for hours in his reading room at Gresham House, studying documents and writing. He'd walk the grounds of Osterley deep in thought.

By June, he had made some important decisions. Sitting at his massive desk he took pen in hand and began writing his new will. First, Lady Anne Gresham was to enjoy Gresham House and the rents from the Royal Exchange for the rest of her life, if she survived him. From those and other properties, she would receive a clear annual income of at least £2400.[31]

His twelve-year-old grand niece Elizabeth Neville, the oldest of his late niece's children, would receive £100 a year from the date of her marriage. His other grand nieces of his brother's daughter, the same, if they did not marry before age fifteen. His grand nephew "Harry" at age twenty, £100, and the same to any of Harry's male heirs. His niece Elizabeth's widower Henry Neville would, upon Sir Thomas's death, assume the duties of wardship for young Harry as to the manors of Mayfield and Wardhurst, with all their factories, lands, and appurtenances thereto, until his great nephew came of age to assume his inheritance. If Harry did not live to majority, or died without male heirs, then Wardhurst and Mayfield would go to the other male heirs of his niece Elizabeth Neville: Edward, Francis, and William.

His quill scratched slowly, laboriously across the pages, where once it had flown swiftly, and with eloquence. As to his wife, Dame Anne Gresham, to whom he had left all his London properties, plus Intwood in Norfolk, and his estate at Osterley: Upon her death, his London properties, including the Royal Exchange and Gresham House, would become the property of the Corporation of London and the Mercers' Company, jointly, to administer and fund Gresham College, which would be endowed and situated in Gresham House.

Pausing to think again, Sir Thomas began a fresh sheet, giving detailed specifics for the endowment and administration of the college that would bear the Gresham name:

1. Seven professors, nominated by the administering groups, would be endowed, and they would receive an honorarium of £50 each per annum, to be taken from the profits from the rents of the Royal Exchange shops.[32]
2. The professors were "to lecture successively, one each day of the week, on the seven sciences of divinity, astronomy, music, geometry, law, medicine, and rhetoric."
3. The professors should all be unmarried men who would live

in separate apartments created for them in the halls of
Gresham House.

That completed, Sir Thomas went on to make further
bequests—one to the eight almshouses he had erected in the parish
of St. Peter-in-the-Poor, immediately behind Gresham House in
Bishopsgate Street. The Mercers' Company was amply provided
with funds to maintain the buildings and to feed, house, and edu-
cate the tenants for generations to come. He left funds for the
Mercers' Company to entertain its members with banquets four
times a year. He then made provisions for his other properties and
gave explicit instructions and details for how his funeral was to be
conducted. He wrote out bequests to all his loyal employees and
servants, apprentices, other nieces and nephews, cousins and rel-
atives as he felt appropriate.

He had carefully considered it, but in the end decided to leave
nothing to Cambridge University—kings, queens, nobles, and
other wealthy and learned men like Dr. John Caius had already
made handsome bequests there, and others to come would continue to see to its needs. Sir Thomas preferred instead that after
his demise and after the death of Lady Anne, all available Gresham
monies and annuities should accrue to the benefit of Gresham
College and the maintenance of the poor of London. He made
his wife the sole executor of his will. Lady Anne Gresham was free
to dispose of Osterley, Intwood and her numerous other estates,
lands, and possessions not otherwise designated by Sir Thomas,
as she pleased upon her death.

I, the said Sir Thomas Gresham," he concluded, "have
written this will with mine own hand ... and have set my
seal with the grasshopper, this 5th day of June, in the seventeenth year of the reign of our sovereign lady Queen
Elizabeth, in the year of our Lord 1575.[33]

He returned his pen to the inkstand and heaved a great sigh
of relief. The task of directing the distribution of his fortune and
property was done. It had taken a mere eight sheets of foolscap to

dispose of the accomplishments of a lifetime. But with the building of the Royal Exchange and the founding of Gresham College for the City of London, he was satisfied that the dream he had nurtured since that afternoon in the garden of Intwood so many years ago had been realized. Fate had determined that he would leave no sons or grandsons to follow him, but he would depart having left his mark, and that of the golden grasshopper, upon England.

11

Postscript

Sir Thomas Gresham lived only four years after devising his will. He retired, dividing his time between his favorite country estates at Osterley and Mayfield, and Gresham House in London. In May of 1576, Queen Elizabeth made her promised visit to Osterley at the beginning of her summer progress, and Sir Thomas and Lady Anne received and entertained Her Majesty in customary splendor. Sir Thomas Churchyard was commissioned to write a pageant for Queen Elizabeth's visit. When the queen arrived, she was much taken with Osterley, but remarked to Sir Thomas that she found the entrance courtyard much too large. "'Twould appear more handsome if 'twere divided, with a wall in the middle," she remarked.[1]

That night, after the dinner and the entertainments were concluded and the queen and her court had retired for the night, workmen summoned by Sir Thomas arrived at Osterley and spent the night quietly transforming the courtyard. Thus it was that when Her Majesty awoke the next morning, she found the courtyard of Osterley completely rebuilt, exactly as she had suggested. She clapped her hands and laughed in delight when she saw what had been done while she slept. Those around her commented they were not sure whether it was from sheer vanity at having her whim and fancy served at such great cost and effort by her host, or from pleasure at seeing the recommended architectural change in the property.[2]

Sir Thomas Gresham died suddenly of a seizure, probably a stroke, on 21 November 1579, at age sixty, at Gresham House. He was buried with all the solemn ritual and pageantry he loved. Queen Elizabeth cried openly when informed of his passing. His funeral procession was of a splendor seldom seen in those days and was rumored to have cost more than £800, over twice what was spent on funerals of the high nobility. Two hundred poor men and women, all clothed in black gowns, followed his body to its final resting place. His helmet was borne in procession on a satin cushion and ceremoniously placed upon his bier. The five chief mourners assigned to him as a knight of the realm were Sir Henry Neville, his cousin William Gresham, his son-in-law Nathaniel Bacon, and his friends William Killigrewe and Edmond Hogan. The queen, as a mark of esteem, sent her king of arms and heralds to preside over and direct the obsequies. Richard Clough, had he been present, would have smiled a secret smile of recognition, for much of the pageantry attending Sir Thomas Gresham's funeral was as he himself had described the funeral of Charles V, the Holy Roman Emperor, in his letter to Sir Thomas long ago.[3]

Lady Anne Ferneley Read Gresham survived her husband by seventeen years, spending her summers at Intwood and Osterley and her winters in London at Gresham House. She enjoyed the company of her children and grandchildren—those of her adopted daughter Anne and Nathaniel Bacon and of William, her surviving son from her first marriage to William Read. Though Sir Thomas had provided more than handsomely for her, she twice tried to sue to overturn the terms of his will, not wishing the London properties to go to public use upon her death.[4] She refused to build the steeple at St. Helen's Church, as her husband had promised the parishioners he would do. She allowed the Royal Exchange to fall into a sad state of decay, to the point where she was formally rebuked by the council and threatened with the queen's displeasure if she did not comply with the terms of her late husband's will and fix it up and maintain it. She was forced, reluctantly, to comply. She ordered a huge brick barn to be constructed at Intwood, destroying the esthetic beauty of the place—some said out of spite because Sir Thomas had earlier forbidden her to build it. She died 15 December 1596 and is buried with Sir Thomas and their son Richard in the Church of St. Helen's, Bishopsgate, London.[5] That church was, at the time of this writing, closed for renovation and repair.

Lady Anne left all of her properties from her first marriage and also those she inherited from Sir Thomas Gresham to her eldest son by her first marriage, William Read, who was fifty-eight years old at the time of his mother's death.

The only known oil portrait of Lady Anne Gresham still in existence, by Sir Antonio More, hangs next to that of Sir Thomas in the Rijksmuseum in Amsterdam. An engraving of that portrait of her hangs at Titsey Place, near Oxted, in Surrey.

Nothing factual is known about the birth of Sir Thomas's beloved daughter Anne, whose dower property from her father assured her of a yearly income of £280 from her marriage in 1569 to Nathaniel Bacon, until her death.[6] Her mother was said to be a woman of Bruges, and was described by ancient genealogists variously as Thomas Gresham's mistress, his concubine, and once even as his first wife, though there is no evidence he was ever married more than once. We know only that she was brought up in her father's household, named for Sir Thomas's wife, Anne, and was well educated by her father. Anne Gresham Bacon lies buried with her husband Nathaniel Bacon in his tomb in the church at Stiffkey, in Norfolk.[7] She and Nathaniel had no sons, but they did sire three daughters: Anne, Elizabeth, and Winifred Bacon. The eldest daughter Anne married Sir John Townsend, knight, of Raynham in the county of Norfolk, and from them are descended the marquess of Townsend and the present earl of Sydney. Elizabeth Bacon married Sir Thomas Knevet, knight, of Ashwellthorpe in Norfolk, and Winifred married Sir Robert Gawdy, knight, of Clayton in Norfolk. None of the sources we consulted gave the date of Anne Gresham Bacon's death, nor is it recorded on her tomb. Nathaniel took a second wife, Dorothy Hopton Smith, a widow, by whom he had no children. Dorothy is also buried in his tomb in Stiffkey. Nathaniel Bacon "lived in great reputation" until his death at seventy-seven years of age, in 1622.

The eminent physician Dr. John Caius (Sir Thomas's friend "Kees"), for whom Gonville and Caius College at Cambridge is named, spent his last years amid controversy at Cambridge. He compiled his *Annals* of the College, and later a *History of the University*, which was purported to be "a distraction from his harassed and dejected feelings" in those final years. Dr. Caius's records and descriptions of the symptoms of the sweating sickness are still the definitive account of that disease, and his medical writings remain some of the most important ever produced in England.[8]

Mary Stuart, queen of Scots, remained Queen Elizabeth's prisoner for more than seventeen years, with the earl of Shrewsbury as her reluctant jailer for most of that time. She was finally ordered beheaded at the Tower of London in 1587 for continual plotting against the crown of England. It is said that Queen Elizabeth cried for weeks after signing the order for Mary's execution, and even Cecil was afraid to approach her for days after the sentence had been carried out.[9] Her execution resulted in the attack on England by the Spanish Armada of Philip of Spain the following year.

Sir Thomas's friend William Cecil, Lord Burghley, lived to great old age, serving Queen Elizabeth I to his last breath in 1598. In his final days, his mind was "troubled that he could not work on peace for his country, for which he earnestly labored and most desired ... seeking to leave peace, as he had long kept it."[10]

His portrait, along with one of his friend Sir Thomas Gresham, hangs next to that of Queen Elizabeth I in the National Portrait Gallery in London. Cecil's granddaughter Mildred eventually married Sir Thomas Read, son of William Read, Lady Anne Gresham's son by her first marriage. Thus the Cecils eventually became holders, through marriage, of several of Sir Thomas Gresham's great manors.

The threat of a marriage between Queen Elizabeth I and Robert Dudley, earl of Leicester, which Cecil feared for so many years, was removed in 1579, the year Sir Thomas died, when

Leicester married Lettice Knollys, daughter of Sir Francis Knollys and widow of the earl of Essex. However, the queen continued her strong attachment to Dudley until his death in August of 1588. Across his final letter to her, which survives among the state papers, is written in Elizabeth's own hand, "His last letter."[11] Few in England mourned his passing, and he left no heirs.

Queen Elizabeth I, though courted by many, remained unmarried and childless. She reigned long and well, dying in 1603 at the age of sixty-nine, and with England's "virgin queen"—the last heir of Henry VIII—died the Tudor dynasty. It is largely through the tireless efforts of Sir Thomas Gresham in smuggling arms to England and exhorting Queen Elizabeth to maintain financial independence, begin manufacturing her own arms, and maintain her navy ever at readiness that Elizabeth was able, in 1588, to mount a naval force strong enough to defeat the Spanish Armada and keep England free from Spanish domination.[12]

King James of Scotland, the Protestant son of Catholic Mary queen of Scots, succeeded Elizabeth I. With his accession as James I of England, the Stuart dynasty at last gained its English crown.

The magnificent Royal Exchange built by Sir Thomas Gresham was destroyed in the Great Fire of London in 1666. Curiously, only the statue of Sir Thomas Gresham remained intact following the conflagration. All of the statues of the kings and queens of England since the Norman Conquest were completely destroyed. Burgon quotes a writer of the time who described it thus:

> When the fire was entered, how quickly did it run around the galleries, filling them with flames; then, descending the stairs, compasseth the walks, giving forth flaming vollies, and filling the court with sheets of fire! By and by, the kings fell all down upon their faces and the greater part of the stone building after them (the founder's statue alone remaining) with such a noise as was dreadful and astonishing.[13]

The Royal Exchange was rebuilt, only to be destroyed again

by fire in 1838. Queen Victoria in 1844 moved the Royal Exchange to its location at the northern end of the seven-way intersection at Cheapside. It has little to do with the Royal Exchange Sir Thomas created for England.

A copy of Sir Thomas's *Book of Days,* as well as his will and some old engravings of the Royal Exchange, are kept in the Guildhall Library at the Guildhall in London, as are many books and documents of that period. Other books and documents pertinent to the sixteenth century and the life of Sir Thomas are maintained in the British Library and the British Museum, as well as most public libraries, and are listed in the bibliography that follows.

It was not until after Anne Ferneley Read Gresham's death that Gresham College became a reality. Gresham House—then Gresham College—escaped the Great Fire, and it was there that the Corporation of London took refuge and kept its offices afterward. Sir Thomas's great mansion was also used as the first site of the Royal Society.

Sadly, the college that he envisioned, founded and generously endowed, which had the potential to become a great university in London, did not fare well under the joint stewardship of the City of London and the Mercers' Company, which became the joint owners of Sir Thomas Gresham's great London properties, and the rents and income they generated, following Dame Anne Gresham's death. Initially, the administrators took their duties seriously and appointed eminent professors from Oxford and Cambridge, including the great architect of London, Sir Christopher Wren, to the seven chairs. The Gresham professors became "a distinguished body of men."

However, as early as the mid-1600s complaints of mismanagement of Sir Thomas Gresham's bequest by the City and the Mercers' were lodged. In the ensuing century, the City fathers and the Mercers' allowed Gresham House and Gresham College to sink slowly into ruin. The City property upon which the college was situated had become so valuable it became politically expedient for them to sell Gresham House to the crown, which could later tear the neglected building down and sell the real estate at a lucrative profit. That was done by act of Parliament in 1767.[14]

The Gresham lectures thereafter were given in an obscure room at the Royal Exchange until, in 1841, another Gresham College, quite different from the one envisioned by its wealthy founder, was established on the corner of Gresham and Basinghall Streets in London.

Perhaps had the City fathers and the Mercers' Company been as visionary as their benefactors, and exercised more fiduciary caution in their stewardship of the considerable assets left to them by the Greshams, Gresham College would now be a great and thriving university in the center of London, the residual wealth of its properties engendering more than enough to support it and the students who would have thronged to it. It would have been infinitely better, in retrospect, had Sir Thomas and his stepmother Lady Isabella left the residual of their properties in London to Cambridge University, where doubtless the monies would have been better managed, and might still be providing the quality education in the Gresham name that Sir Thomas envisioned as his family's enduring legacy to the country he loved and served so well.

The portrait of the young Sir Thomas Gresham, painted for the occasion of his wedding in 1544 and described earlier, hangs in the Mercers' Company, Fishmonger Lane, London, as do several other portraits of him done in later years. There are also numerous documents and accounts written by Sir Thomas Gresham in the archives there, but they are not made readily available to the public. A vestige of Gresham College still exists in London, supervised by the Mercers' Company.

The descendants of the Greshams are numerous and illustrious. In addition to the aforementioned earl of Sydney, the duke of Sutherland, earl of Granville (descended from Sir John Gresham, Sir Thomas's uncle), Lord Braybrooke (descended from Elizabeth Gresham and Sir Henry Neville), the marquis of Stafford, the late marquis of Bath (descended from Christiana Gresham and Sir John Thynne of Longleat), and many Leveson-Gowers in England are present-century offspring of the Gresham dynasty.

Many Greshams, Grishams, and Grissoms in America, too,

are Gresham descendants. Two Gresham progeny immigrated to Virginia and Maryland in the 1600s.

A portrait believed to be of Sir Thomas's father, Sir Richard Gresham, hangs at Longleat in Wilts, once the home of Christiana Gresham Thynne, Sir Thomas's sister.

Sir Thomas's uncle, the merchant adventurer Sir John Gresham, loved his country manor, Titsey Place, in Titsey Park near Oxted and Limpsfield in Surrey, England. On his death, it was bequeathed to his eldest son, William, and has remained in possession of the Gresham line ever since. Thomas Christopher Gresham Leveson-Gower (last of the Titsey line of Greshams) died in 1990, without heirs.

The manor house, bequeathed to Titsey Foundation, has been refurbished and should now be open to the public for pre-arranged visitation. Set in a lovely park about an hour by train from London, Titsey Place manor house, though small, contains some magnificent sixteenth-, seventeenth-, and eighteenth-century portraits, mantelpieces, and furnishings. It contains several oil portraits of Sir Thomas Gresham, including a duplicate of the Antonio More seated portrait (which the family claims is the original) as well as the aforementioned engraving of Lady Anne Gresham.

The manor also contains interesting portraits of other members of the Gresham family, and Sir Thomas's intricate double wedding ring and a sixteenth-century silver poesy ring. Of particular interest is a splendid portrait of twin girls, about age four, of the Elizabethan period. The identity of the artist, and of the twins, is unknown, but it is believed to be a Flemish painting of that period and was no doubt the property of Sir Thomas Gresham at one time. Leveson-Gower left the property in trust "for the preservation for the public benefit of the property known as the Titsey Estate." The trust governing Titsey Place is administered by the firm of Strutt & Parker, London.[15]

A distinguished economist wrote about Sir Thomas in 1949: "Perhaps Gresham should be hailed as a prophet. His analysis fits conditions as they exist today even better than those which obtained in the sixteenth century. Gresham was keenly aware of England's position as a debtor nation. . . . He therefore urged the government to throw off these shackles by liquidating the foreign debt and urged it to promote English trade by taking aggressive measures against foreign competition. By these means Gresham expected England to secure a favorable balance of trade and to become a creditor nation. Once in this position, she would be able to recover 'her old riches' and 'her wonted honor.' "[16]

The truth contained in the maxims of Sir Thomas Gresham, financial genius of the Renaissance, holds as strongly today, as we stand as a fragile planet, deeply in debt, on the threshold of the twenty-first century, as it did in the tumult of religious dissension, global exploration, and mercantile expansion of the sixteenth century in which he lived.

Appendix

Excerpts from the Pen of Sir Thomas Gresham.

The first occasion of the fall of the exchange did grow by the Kinges Majesty, (Henry VIII) in abasinge his quoyne ffrome vi ounces fine to iii (3) ounces fine. Whereuppon the exchainge fell ffrome xxvi s. viiid. (26 shillings, 8 pence) to xxiii s. iv d. (23 shillings 4 pence) which was the occasion that all your ffine goold was convayed ought of this your realme.

> *Excerpts from a letter from Thomas Gresham to Queen Elizabeth I, in 1559, found among Lord Burghley's (Sir William Cecil's) papers*

The exchainge is the thinge that eatts ought all princes, to the wholl destruction of ther comon well, if itt be nott substantially loked unto; so likewise the exchainge is the cheffest and riches thinge only above all other, to restore your Majestie and your realme to fine gowld and sillvar, and is the meane thatt makes all forraine comoditties and your owne comodites . . . good cheapp, and likewise keeps your fine golde and sillvar within your realme.

So consequently the higar the exchainge riseth, the more shall your Majestie and your reallme and common well florrish . . .

> *Sir Thomas Gresham to Queen Elizabeth I, 1559*

To be playne with your Grace.... if there be not some other ways takyn for payment of his Majesty's detts but to force men (his creditors).... to prolong them, I say to you the end thereof shall neyther be honnorable nor profitable to his Highness....

Thomas Gresham to Northumberland, August 1552; Reign of King Edward VI

... Fourthly, to come in as small debt as you can beyond seas ...

... Fifthly, to keep your credit; and specially with your own merchants, for it is they who must stand by you at all events in your necessity....

Thomas Gresham to Queen Elizabeth I, 1559

... It dothe not only take away the living of your merchants, but in process of time, the few number of (foreign) retailers will eat out all the merchants within our realme, and it will also be a meanes to bring our commodities out of repute, and make foreign commodities in high repute.

Gresham to the Duke of Northumberland, 1553

Note: Parenthetical notes ours.

Endnotes

Chapter 1

1. Michaelmas falls on 29 September; Whitsuntide, or Pentecost, on the seventh Sunday after Easter, or seven weeks after Passover—normally in May or June. *Catholic Encyclopedia*.
2. The Field of Cloth of Gold is described in many works; e.g., Hackett, *Henry the Eighth*, pp. 110–17; Bowle, *Henry VIII*; Bogaert et Passeron, *Les Lettres Francaises, Seizieme Siecle*, illus. p. 8; Ridley, *The History of England*, p. 131. Names of Gresham's ships came from *Dictionary of National Biography*, p. 582.
3. *Dictionary of National Biography*, p. 582.
4. See Burgon, *Sir Thomas Gresham*, vol. 1, pp. 7–8. "Gresham" is the ancient word for "grasslands"—and the Gresham family came from the grasslands of Norfolk. Hence their name, and the grasshopper as their emblem.
5. See Hackett, *Henry the Eighth*, p. 125.
6. Bessie Blount, a maid in waiting, had borne Henry VIII a son out of wedlock—Henry Fitzroy, Duke of Richmond, who died at an early age. Queen Catherine's only male child was stillborn. However, those two boys proved Henry VIII capable of fathering a male heir.
7. Details of Henry VIII's reign are based primarily upon accounts in Hackett and Bowle. Other sources, such as Stowe's *Chronicles;* Trevelyan, *A Shortened History of England*; Ridley, *The History of England*; and *Dictionary of National Biography* were also consulted.
8. Equivalent today to approximately £750,000 or $1.35 million U.S.
9. See Hackett, *Henry the Eighth*, p. 196.
10. Value of rich furnishings and silver plate in a palace like Hampton Court or York Place could exceed £150,000, which today would equal £75 million, or $135 million U.S.

Chapter 2

1. Considering the amount it represented (£750,000 or $1.35 million), one is not surprised that Henry was very interested.

2. Hackett, *Henry the Eighth*, pp. 199, 211. Bowle, *Henry VIII*, pp. 155–56. That Richard Gresham was custodian of part of those funds is detailed in Burgon, *Sir Thomas Gresham*, vol. 1, p. 23. Bowle says most of the funds were held by a priest, p. 156.

3. Bowle, *Henry VIII*, p. 163. The word "marry" as it was used then was a common exclamation of surprise or anger, and usually meant: really, indeed, or forsooth. *Webster's New Universal Dictionary, 1986.*

4. The yale is apparently a mythical animal, believed capable of moving its horns independently of one another. Descriptions of Tudor era Cambridge are from Grant, *Cambridge*, pp. 66–98.

5. Ridley, *The Tudor Age*, p. 50.

6. The discussion of Caius, and the Cambridge days, is based upon Venn, *Biographical History of Gonville and Caius College*, vol. III, pp. 30–32; and Brooke, *A History of Gonville and Caius College*, chap. 4.

7. Bowle, *Henry VIII*, p. 165.

8. Ibid., p. 171.

9. Ibid., pp. 178–79.

10. *Dictionary of National Biography*, p. 583.

11. Ibid., p. 583. Value of £2000 today: approx. £1 million, or $1.8 million U.S.

12. Ibid., p. 583.

13. Bowle, *Henry VIII*, p. 205.

14. *Dictionary*, p. 583.

15. Chapman, *The Last Tudor King: A Study of Edward VI*, p. 29. Discussion of the death of Queen Jane is based on Hackett, *Henry the Eighth*, pp. 310–11.

16. Williams, *The Cardinal and the Secretary*, p. 204.

17. Quotations from Richard Gresham's correspondence are from Burgon, *Sir Thomas Gresham*, vol. 1, pp. 13–30. *Note:* Wherever extensive letters and documents are quoted in this work, the authors have taken the liberty of modernizing the language somewhat, condensing them, or editing for clarity as they felt necessary, without, it is hoped, sacrificing any of the meaning, flavor, or intent of the original. Those wishing to read the letter or document in the original sixteenth-century verbiage, or in its entirety, are encouraged to consult the sources cited. Most quotations of Gresham correspondence are from Burgon, *Sir Thomas Gresham*.

18. Ibid., vol. 1, pp. 26–28; see also Salter, *Sir Thomas Gresham*, p. 25. John Gresham, Richard's brother, also succeeded in having the lunatic asylum at Bethlehem ("Bedlam") restored to its former use. Salter, p. 26.

19. £2000 equals £1 million or $1.8 million.

20. Burgon, *Sir Thomas Gresham*, vol. 1, pp. 32–33. The offer of £1000 would represent an investment by Sir Richard equivalent to about half a mil-

lion pounds in today's money, or nearly $1 million of his own funds—a very substantial amount in those times.

21. *Dictionary*, p. 583.

22. Hackett, *Henry the Eighth*, p. 398.

23. The remaining ring is now at Sir John Gresham's ancient country manor, Titsey Place, in Titsey Park, near Oxted and Limpsfield in Surrey, England. Titsey Place has been refurbished, and can be visited by special arrangement. The grounds are open to the public.

24. Burgon, *Sir Thomas Gresham*, vol. 1, p. 50, attributes this famous canvas to Holbein, but Scharfe, *Dictionary*, p. 595, assigned it to Geralamo da Treviso. In a recent publication, Doolittle, in *The Mercers' Company*, Plate I, facing p. 40, claims that the painting was probably done in Flanders, and recent research suggests it may be the work of William Scrots. The painting is owned by the Mercers' Company, Fishmonger Lane, London, and hangs in its hall, but is not on display to the public.

25. Hackett, *Henry the Eighth*, p. 393.

26. See Ridley, *The Tudor Age*, pp. 336–45.

27. Henry Fitzroy, born 1518, died at age 18 in 1536, unmarried and without heirs. In any case, he could not have succeeded to the throne due to the "bar sinister"—he was born out of wedlock while Henry was still legally married to Queen Catherine.

Chapter 3

1. Burgon, *Sir Thomas Gresham*, vol. 1, app. IV, p. 461. This represents today over £1 billion, or $1.8 billion, much of which King Henry had borrowed at interest rates of 12% to 14%.

2. Ibid., p. 61. £1.2 million sterling then represents about half a billion pounds now, or nearly $1 billion. It is believed that at that period, and from the staggering wealth of that family, came the widely used colloquial term "a rich Fokker," to denote a man of considerable wealth and prominence. In usage for centuries, the term later became corrupted to an even more colorful significance, and this colloquial epithet is still used in the twentieth century. Ibid., p. 61, note i.

3. Burgon, *Sir Thomas Gresham*, vol. 1, pp. 70–76.

4. See Ridley, *The Tudor Age*, illus., pp. 70–71.

5. Chapman, *The Last Tudor King*, p. 82.

6. The name comes from the beam, or yard, called a "steel," used to weigh goods, like hemp or linen, imported into London. The unit of currency was called "easterling," from which the term "sterling" might have been derived. The "steelyard" was located on the Thames, near London Bridge, on the site that is presently Cannon Street Station. Sir Thomas Gresham's own steelyard weighing instrument is shown in a photograph in Doolittle, *The Mercers' Company: 1579–1959*, p. 29.

7. Chapman, *The Last Tudor King*, p. 88.
8. Ibid., pp. 88–93. It was observed then that Edward's handing over of the tribute to a lesser personage caused some offense to the city officials. That was thought to be prophetic that the realm might also be too heavy for the child king to handle.
9. Ibid., pp. 94–95.
10. Jenkins, *Elizabeth the Great*, p. 26.
11. Ibid., p. 31.
12. Sir Richard Gresham left his widow Isabella an annual income of £282, equivalent to about £141,000 or $250,000 today. His eldest son John received £188 annually, and Thomas Gresham was left an annual stipend of about £95—equivalent to £47,500 a year, or $85,500. Among his many properties, in addition to Intwood, Bethnal Green, and Hoxne Abbey— referred to in the text—were: in Yorkshire, the sites of DeFontibus Abbey and the priories and lands of Nun Kelynge and Swinhey; Aldeburgh; Swinton Grange and Lownde; in Suffolk, the manors and lands of Ring-shall, including lands in Charles, Rokelles, Rawlyns, Battesford, Combes, Wattesham and Barking; in Norfolk, Keswick, including lands in Sward-ston, Cryngleford and Dunston; and Hardwick, including lands in Shel-ton, Throp, Threton, Stratton, Waghton, Pullam, Marie Starston, Harleston, Henney and Alberowe. Many of the above-mentioned prop-erties were designated by Sir Richard to pass to his younger son, Thomas Gresham, upon Dame Isabella's death. Others were to go to his elder son, Sir John Gresham. See Leveson-Gower, *Genealogy of the Family of Gresham*, will of Sir Richard Gresham, knight, pp. 65–76; also Burgon, *Sir Thomas Gresham*, vol. 1, pp. 43, 460.
13. Burgon, *Sir Thomas Gresham*, vol. 1, pp. 100–101.
14. Equivalent to £20 million a year, or $36 million U.S.
15. Burgon, *Sir Thomas Gresham*, vol. 1, pp. 63–65.
16. Chapman, *The Last Tudor King*, p. 207.
17. Ibid., p. 209.
18. Burgon, *Sir Thomas Gresham*, vol. 1, p. 64.
19. This custom is comparable, on a smaller scale, to the custom of impos-ing "points," or additional interest, on a borrower to secure or renew a loan.
20. Burgon, *Sir Thomas Gresham*, vol. 1, p. 101.

Chapter 4

1. See Burgon, *Sir Thomas Gresham*, vol. 1, pp. 57; 80–82.
2. Ibid., p. 82.
3. Ibid., pp. 82–83.
4. Chapman, *The Last Tudor King*, pp. 210–13.
5. Ibid., p. 213.

6. Ibid., p. 216.
7. Ibid., p. 218.
8. Burgon, *Sir Thomas Gresham*, vol. 1, pp. 107–9.
9. What Sir Thomas Gresham served at his banquet is not recorded, but was likely as described here. Description of a typical banquet of the time is taken from Ridley, *The Tudor Age*, pp. 196–217. Forks were unknown then, and more than two or three knives at table were unusual. Meat was cut with a knife, which was usually shared, and eaten with the fingers. Spoons—finely wrought silver ones for the wealthy—were used for soups, creamy foods, and puddings. The potato had not yet come to the European continent.
10. The banquet painting of Sir Thomas Gresham was probably a large and important work. The authors were unable to trace it, but hope it still exists, perhaps in a private collection somewhere. The last known record of it is in an inventory of the countess of Leicester's belongings at Essex House in 1596. It was valued at that time at £5 (today £2500 or $4500), which attests to its probable large size and great worth. See Burgon, *Sir Thomas Gresham*, vol. 1, p. 85 and app., p. 462.
11. Ibid., p. 85. We disagree with Burgon's conclusion that the bill was for a single banquet. We believe from the wording of the account, which covers March through July, that the £26 was for general entertainment expenses during that period, and might have included other dinners or entertainments as well. £102 for out-of-pocket expenses equals approximately £51,000 or $92,000. The £106,000 repaid on the king's account during the first eighteen months of Gresham's tenure is equivalent to about £53 million, or $94.5 million.
12. Ibid., pp. 86–94. The letter to Northumberland is extremely long and detailed. The highlights have been presented here. The authors have, in most instances, put Gresham's, and his correspondents' words into logical sequence and more modern English, hopefully retaining some of the flavor of the period, so that the reader will not be distracted by the language and can better analyze the character and motivation of the writer or writers.
13. Ibid., p. 108.
14. Ibid., p. 111.
15. Chapman, *The Last Tudor King*, p. 257.
16. Ibid., p. 260.
17. Ibid.
18. Later named the plague.
19. A number of sources record this unique gift. It was the rarity, rather than the value, that made it a spectacular offering. "Gresham's gift constitutes the earliest mention of that article of dress in this country," says Burgon. *Sir Thomas Gresham*, vol. 1, p. 110.
20. Equivalent today to £2 million or $3.6 million.

21. Burgon, *Sir Thomas Gresham*, app. VII, p. 463. This long pleading has been summarized, and the language modernized, by the authors.
22. "Edward's chief concern was religion, after that came the currency. His best adviser, Sir Thomas Gresham, was something of a financial genius, for between 1551 and 1553 he had managed to raise the national credit abroad by playing the exchange, so that the value of the pound in Antwerp had risen from 16 shillings to 22 shillings." Chapman, *The Last Tudor King*, p. 269. See also Burgon, vol. 1, pp. 97–100.
23. Burgon, vol. 1, p. 99.
24. Turton, *Builders of England's Glory*, pp. 209–216. See also Chapman, *The Last Tudor King*, p. 276. The Lady Jane Grey was heir presumptive after her mother, the Lady Mary. The Tudor line, in all branches, was desperately short of males.
25. Chapman, *The Last Tudor King*, p. 276; Turton, *Builders of England's Glory*, p. 210.
26. Turton, *Builders of England's Glory*, p. 210.
27. Burgon, *Sir Thomas Gresham*, vol. 1, p. 111. See also Chapman, *The Last Tudor King*, p. 269.
28. *Dictionary of National Biography*, p. 507.

Chapter 5

1. Turton, *Builders of England's Glory*, pp. 211–12.
2. Ibid., p. 214.
3. Ibid., pp. 216–17.
4. Read, *Lord Burghley and Queen Elizabeth*, p. 101.
5. Burgon, *Sir Thomas Gresham*, vol. 1, pp. 122–24.
6. About £200 million, or $360 million. The interest amounted to about £20 million, or $36 million, a year.
7. Burgon, *Sir Thomas Gresham*, vol. 1, pp. 115–20 for verbatim text of the letter. £1.5 million would equal about £750 million today, or over $1.25 billion.
8. Ibid., pp. 134–35. Condensed and modernized here.
9. Durant, *The Reformation*, p. 832.
10. Burgon, *Sir Thomas Gresham*, pp. 127–39. For full text of the queen's commission and instructions to Gresham, see Burgon, vol. 1, app. X, p. 471.
11. Ibid., pp. 141–42. Reworded for clarity. Economist Allan Meltzer, of Carnegie-Mellon University, says, "The reigning orthodoxy of the time was mercantilism. Countries did not want to lose their gold, and often sought to make their exports cheap, even if it meant low wages and low standards of living for the populace. Mercantilists believed nations should accumulate gold as wealth, so they were eager to import, and reluctant to export, gold." (Letter to the authors, August 1993.)

12. Ibid., p. 145.

13. Ibid., app. XIV, p. 477. The ducat was worth about 14 shillings 6 pence then; 320,000 gold ducats would have equaled about £232,000 then. Today, Gresham's 320,000 ducats would be the equivalent of about £116 million, or $210 million.

14. Salter, *Sir Thomas Gresham*, p. 67. "The merchants themselves got paid their outstanding accounts at the big fairs, the institutions which, by old tradition, served as the clearing-houses and settling places of international commerce." The French gold crown was worth approximately 6 shillings 8 pence then; the emperor's rial of fine gold, 11 shillings. Burgon, *Sir Thomas Gresham*, vol. 1, app. XIV, p. 477.

15. Worth £2.5 million per ship, or $4.5 million.

16. Burgon, *Sir Thomas Gresham*, vol. 1, p. 152.

17. Ibid., pp. 168–69.

18. Turton, *Builders of England's Glory*, p. 224.

19. This was one of the first corporations, or companies formed under the modern principle of shareholders and director, although those terms were not used in the 1550s. See Salter, *Sir Thomas Gresham*, p. 74; Burgon, *Sir Thomas Gresham*, vol. 1, pp. 370–72; Southgate, *English Economic History*, pp. 78–79.

20. *Dictionary of National Biography*, p. 588. £200 was equivalent to £100,000 or $180,000 in added annual income, besides the actual real estate value of the lands given him.

21. The queen's debt level had dropped to £74.2 million ($133.7 million), considerably less than at the beginning of her reign. See Burgon, *Sir Thomas Gresham*, vol. 1, note "a," p. 182.

22. Ibid., pp. 182–84.

23. Thomas Gresham had handled today's equivalent of £213 million pounds ($383 million) for Queen Mary as of that date, and had brought her treasury a profit of about £5.7 million ($10.2 million). The full accounting of monies handled by him during her reign is presented (all figures in Roman numerals) in Burgon, *Sir Thomas Gresham*, vol. 1, app. XIII, p. 476. We have converted the numbers to Arabic ciphers for the reader's convenience.

24. A present-day worth of £400 million ($720 million).

25. A brief description of Sir John Gresham is given in Burgon, *Sir Thomas Gresham*, vol. 1, pp. 11–21.

26. Ibid., vol. 1, pp. 202–4.

27. Durant, *The Renaissance*, pp. 584–85.

28. Burgon, *Sir Thomas Gresham*, vol. 1, pp. 191–94.

29. Ibid., p. 194, note "m."

30. Ridley, *The Tudor Age*, p. 303.

31. Two of Northumberland's four sons—Dudley's brothers—had died earlier. Guilford Dudley, husband of Queen Jane Grey, had been beheaded.

Henry accompanied his brother Robert to fight with King Philip, and was killed in battle.

32. Burgon, *Sir Thomas Gresham*, vol.1, pp. 156–57; 194–96. Excerpts condensed, and paraphrased.
33. Burgon, *Sir Thomas Gresham*, vol. 1, p. 201.
34. Prescott, *Mary Tudor*, p. 381.

Chapter 6

1. See Jenkins, *Elizabeth the Great*, p. 64.
2. Ibid., p. 77.
3. Burgon, *Sir Thomas Gresham*, vol. 1, pp. 217–18.
4. Salter, *Sir Thomas Gresham*, pp. 75–76. Value of £227,000 = £113.5 million ($204.3 million). Gross national product of £200,000 then equals £100 million ($180 million) today. £300,000 = £150 million ($270 million) today.
5. Ibid., p. 77.
6. Braudel, in *The Mediterranean World*, vol. II, p. 840, agrees with Gresham's premise on the financial waste caused by war: "War is a waste of money ... The expenses of war crippled states, and many wars were unproductive. The ... costly Irish wars ruined Elizabeth's finances towards the end of her brilliant reign."
7. Equal to about £217 million ($391.5 million).
8. de Roover, in his monograph *Gresham on Foreign Exchange* (pp. 264–65), states, "Gresham believed that England as a debtor nation was the prey of the continental bankers and the victim of the economic policies of foreign powers, especially Spain ... Gresham did not advocate the acquisition of treasure (i.e. gold and silver) for its own sake but for the purpose of gaining power through financial control of the money market. His analysis in this respect is far superior to that of the other early mercantilists ... One should also consider that, in 1559, there was not a single Englishman except Gresham who had any extensive knowledge of the intricacies of the exchange business, or who had enough prestige to deal successfully with the continental bankers ... In the manner of exchange control, for example, he saw clearly what could and what could not be done."
9. The full text of Gresham's letter to Queen Elizabeth is included in Burgon, *Sir Thomas Gresham*, vol. 1, app. XXI, p. 483.
10. Jenkins, *Elizabeth the Great*, pp. 76–78.
11. Ibid., pp. 67–73.
12. This abbreviated version of Clough's letter is presented to give the reader a flavor of the ceremonials of the time. Those interested in Clough's full description of the funeral of Charles V will find it in Burgon, *Sir Thomas Gresham*, vol. 1, pp. 242–57.

13. de Roover, in *Gresham on Foreign Exchange*, (p. 16) states: "Gresham, indeed, appears to be the first who tried, sometimes successfully, to keep up the exchange by manipulating the money market...." Gresham may here be speaking about what is sometimes referred to as "trade coin," that is, payment in coin with a high content of precious metal (value money) rather than the base coinage, which might purport to have the same value but contain less precious metal, and therefore be worth less on foreign exchange.

14. Jenkins, *Elizabeth the Great*, p. 76, describes Elizabeth as "a woman with a genius for authority who thoroughly enjoyed the exercise of power."

15. Ibid., p. 82. £267,000 would be equal today to about £133.5 million or $240.3 million. £108,000= £540,000 or $97.2 million.

16. Burgon, *Sir Thomas Gresham*, vol. 1, pp. 278–79.

17. "In Lombard Street, then, at the sign of *the grasshopper*, dwelt Thomas Gresham; and I beg the reader will not lose any of the respect he may have conceived for him, on being informed he was a banker such as I have described... and a banking house is technically called a shop...." Ibid., p. 284. Burgon tells us that a banker in early times pursued a different trade from that of bankers today. In Elizabethan times, the banker was at once a moneylender, a pawnbroker, a money-scrivener, a goldsmith, and a dealer in bullion. "At the period of Gresham's death, a considerable portion of his wealth was in gold chains," says Burgon. Ibid., vol. 1, p. 281. The earliest bankers were Jews, succeeded by Italians. "To them succeeded the Lombards... (who) obtained a footing in this country about the middle of the thirteenth century, establishing themselves in Lombard-street, making it their business to remit money to their own country by bills of exchange...." Ibid., p. 282.

Chapter 7

1. Jenkins, *Elizabeth the Great*, p. 14.

2. Ridley, *The History of England*, pp. 155–56.

3. "To wait and see how ... others would commit themselves, and then to intervene at the last possible moment, was her method all her life, and it was fully developed in the first year of her reign." Jenkins, *Elizabeth the Great*, p. 80.

4. Ibid., p. 81.

5. Burgon, *Sir Thomas Gresham*, vol. 1, p. 289.

6. Ibid., p. 309, note "n." See also pp. 320–21.

7. A strong type of gunpowder manufactured in corn, and less finely granulated than serpentine powder. Ibid., note "x," p. 288.

8. Preceding discussion from ibid., pp. 291–96. Edited for clarity.

9. This advice to the queen and Cecil was typical of Gresham's caution and concern about England's dependence on foreign arms. It was through

his insistence that England manufacture and provision its own arms, rather than rely on imports, and his constant caution to Elizabeth to maintain her navy and ships always in readiness, that Elizabeth I and England were able to defeat Philip's Spanish Armada, though that didn't happen until 1588, after Sir Thomas Gresham's death.

10. Ibid., p. 328.

11. Ibid., pp. 328–29.

12. The foregoing account is based upon ibid., pp. 290–300. Edited for clarity.

13. Jenkins, *Elizabeth the Great*, p. 83.

14. Burgon, *Sir Thomas Gresham*, p. 300.

15. Ibid., p. 303, quoting Stowe's *Chronicle*, ed. 1631, p. 867. Silk stockings had to be handwoven in those days. Mechanical knitting or weaving of silk stockings was not done until around 1600.

16. Ibid., p. 309. Though Philip's troops still remained when Sir Thomas wrote this letter to Cecil, they soon departed, for they were among the few troops and ships left to him after his defeat by the Turks.

17. Jenkins, *Elizabeth the Great*, pp. 81–82.

18. Burgon, *Sir Thomas Gresham*, vol. 1, p. 306. During this period of Gresham's life, loneliness must have weighed heavily upon him, for he entreated each and every correspondent to look after his "pore wyfe" in his long absence.

19. Ibid., pp. 344–45.

20. Smith, in *The Elizabethan World*, pp. 90–91, notes, "Remembrance was always made easier by the presentation of a well-timed gift. The amount was expected to be commensurate with the favour demanded." And further, "That a political system, based on patronage, gratuities, influence, factionalism, ceremony and queen-worship did not deteriorate into simple jobbery, fawning, corruption, and senseless ritualism was one of the marvels of the Elizabethan age."

21. Burgon, vol 1., pp. 348–53.

22. Ibid., p. 373. This would be equivalent to an income of £66,500 a year today, or $120,000—a very generous gesture, and an indication of what the size of Sir Thomas' personal fortune must have been at that time.

23. Ibid., p. 301.

24. Jenkins, *Elizabeth the Great*, pp. 84–85; Hume, *The Courtships of Queen Elizabeth*, pp. 50, 54, 63, 83. The circumstances surrounding Amy Robsart's death remain shadowy, but her husband Dudley was exonerated of guilt, and the death was officially termed an "accident." It was known that Lady Amy had a disorder of the breast, and in recent times physicians have speculated that she may have had breast cancer which, if left unattended, could have metastasized to the bones of the spine and neck. With those bones rendered extremely fragile by cancer, it is not beyond the realm of possibility that a spontaneous fracture of the neck might

have occurred, causing her fall, and death. However, that is merely one theory, of many, about the mysterious death of Lord Robert Dudley's wife.

25. A number of sources treat this landmark occasion in Elizabethan finance, and most authoritative sources attribute it solely to Gresham's advice to the queen. Burgon, *Sir Thomas Gresham*, vol. 1., p. 360. See also Salter, *Sir Thomas Gresham*, pp. 87, 143–44. Salter comments, "The recoinage seems to have been largely, if not entirely, due to the suggestion of Gresham." See also Trevelyan, *A Shortened History of England*, p. 253.

26. Burgon, *Sir Thomas Gresham*, p. 368. The exact circumstances surrounding Sir Thomas's fall from his horse, which caused his crippling injury, are not known. It is known that at that period he was deeply involved with gathering intelligence for the queen and Cecil, which often took him on extremely dangerous excursions. "There is abundant evidence of his disposition, and the personal exertions he constantly made to accomplish his objects." Ibid., p. 367. And that he had enemies, and worked in secrecy, is also known. "Sometimes he transmitted the letters ... but always with a request that 'for dyvers respects, as soon as the Quene had considered them, they might be burnt'" (from Flanders correspondence, 26 June 1560, containing French intelligence. Ibid., p. 367).

27. Brooke, *A History of Gonville and Caius College*, pp. 62–64.

Chapter 8

1. Burgon, *Sir Thomas Gresham*, p. 368.
2. *Dictionary of National Biography*, p. 595: "This daughter, whose mother is said to have been a native of Bruges, was well-educated by Gresham, and brought up in his family."
3. Description of the court of Elizabeth I is from Smith, *The Elizabethan World*, pp. 81–86.
4. Burgon, *Sir Thomas Gresham*, vol. 1, p. 396.
5. Ibid., pp. 377–87. To give an idea of the enormity of the event, and value of the competition, the Land Jewel Cup at £65,000 then would equal about £32.5 million, or $58.5 million to the winner, or winners—truly a Super Bowl of rhetoric. Clough's full and detailed description of it has been condensed and edited here, for clarity.
6. Ibid., pp. 400–403.
7. See Smith, *The Elizabethan World*, pp. 166–70.
8. Burgon, *Sir Thomas Gresham*, vol. 1, p. 404.
9. Spinola's confession, drawn up by Cecil, was made December 27, 1561. Landsdowne Manuscripts, no.5, art. 48.
10. Burgon, *Sir Thomas Gresham*, vol. 1, pp. 408–9.
11. This glimpse of daily life in Elizabethan London is from Byrne, *Elizabethan Life*, pp. 60–63.

12. Burgon, *Sir Thomas Gresham*, vol. 1, p. 416.

13. Burgon, *Sir Thomas Gresham*, vol. 2, pp. 10–11.

14. An extensive treatment of Cecil's and Sir Thomas's letters pertinent to Cecil's concerns with his son Thomas Cecil, is given in Burgon, *Sir Thomas Gresham*, vol. 1, pp. 420–50.

15. Ibid., p. 425.

16. Jenkins, *Elizabeth the Great*, pp. 97–98; Hume, *The Courtships of Queen Elizabeth*, p. 68.

17. Jenkins, p. 99.

18. Burgon, *Sir Thomas Gresham*, pp. 23–24.

19. Ibid., pp. 29–36. Smith, in *The Elizabethan World*, says, "No Elizabethan official ever received an adequate salary . . ." (p. 90).

20. Ibid., vol. 2, pp. 51–52.

21. The exact cause of the death of young Richard Gresham, Sir Thomas Gresham's only son, in 1564, is not known. He was at that time young— not quite twenty—and presumably healthy, and most likely an apprentice on one of his father's ships, traveling back and forth to the Continent. The plague was then running rampant throughout Europe and the shipping lanes; it is likely that he died of it. As to the extent of Sir Thomas's grief over the loss of his son, Burgon relates, "the bereavement must have been long and severely felt; . . . *this* was the event to which he must have habitually looked back with sorrow; which must have cast the broadest shadow over his declining years; and which, perhaps, even counterbalanced, in his estimation, the splendid results of a life of enterprise." Ibid., vol. 2, pp. 77–78.

Chapter 9

1. Salter, *Sir Thomas Gresham*, p. 83.

2. "The building of the Royal Exchange, for which Gresham provided the funds, was another step toward making London independent of the Antwerp money market." de Roover, *Gresham on Foreign Exchange*, p. 264.

3. Burgon, *Sir Thomas Gresham*, vol. 2, p. 33

4. Salter, *Gresham on Foreign Exchange*, p. 84. £17,000 then = £8.5 million or $15.3 million today.

5. Ibid., p. 84.

6. Jenkins, *Elizabeth the Great*, pp. 122–23.

7. Leveson-Gower, *Genealogy of the Family of Gresham*, "Will of Lady Isabella Gresham," pp. 76–79. The properties she left to charity, in trust for support of the poor of London, were to be administered by the Mercers' Company. As to what eventually happened to them, Burgon, in *Sir Thomas Gresham*, vol. 2, pp. 106–7, quotes the official report, 1820, of the Commissioners for Inquiring into Charities in England and Wales, p. 116, on the bequests of Isabella Gresham: "About the year 1745, the affairs of the Mercers' Company were in a state of embarrassment, and

several of their estates were vested, under the authority of certain acts of parliament, into trustees, for the payment of their creditors. *These houses were included in that settlement."* Those properties, if still held in trust by the Mercers' Company today, as Lady Isabella had intended, would be of incalculable real estate value to the poor of London.

8. Jenkins, *Elizabeth the Great*, p. 120.

9. Ibid., pp. 113–20.

10. Byrne, *Elizabethan Life*, p. 50.

11. "Fees, tips, gratuities and gifts ... made up the difference between official salary and actual income. They were held as legitimate perquisites of office in an age which regarded governmental posts as both public trusts and private sinecures." Smith, *The Elizabethan World*, pp. 90–91.

12. Burgon, *Sir Thomas Gresham*, vol. 2, p. 87. At £3737 cost, the land purchased by the citizens for the site of the exchange was worth about £1.8 million or $3.2 million. Labor cost of £478 = £240,000 or approximately $500,000.

13. Ibid., vol. 2, p. 87.

14. £32,000 then = £16 million, or $28.8 million today. £20,000 = £10 million, or $18 million U.S.

15. Burgon, *Sir Thomas Gresham*, vol. 2, pp. 140–41. Strada, historian of the Low Country wars, gives a much more colorful description of this raid on the churches. Flanders Corr. State Papers Office.

16. Burgon, *Sir Thomas Gresham*, vol. 2, pp. 153–54. £2000 then = £1 million or $1.8 million today.

17. Ibid., p. 158.

18. Ibid., pp. 162–63.

19. Ibid., pp. 155–63.

20. Ibid., p. 179.

21. Ibid., p. 180.

22. See Jenkins, *Elizabeth the Great*, p. 120.

23. Burgon, *Sir Thomas Gresham*, vol. 2, pp. 186–88. We translated and abbreviated the following passage, to give the reader a general idea of the contents and direction of that letter: *"Et ce, d'authant plus, qu vous mesme avez este spectateur du partie des noz affaires, et qu'aussy avez, par la providence de Dieu, acquis tant de faveur et d'authorite, qu'on adjoustera foy comme ausy la Rayson le veut a vostre parolle; ou aultres, qu ne sont de semblable qualite seront, comme gens indignes de foy, meprises. Nous scavons, tres bien, combien de faveur et credit qu'avez ver sa Majeste...."*

24. Salter, *Sir Thomas Gresham*, p. 98.

25. See Burgon, *Sir Thomas Gresham*, vol. 2, pp. 211–15.

26. Smith, *The Elizabethan World*, p. 172.

27. "Elizabeth's strength as a ruler was that she could read the mind of the nation she governed, whereas that of Mary's people was a closed book to her." Morrison, *Mary Queen of Scots*, p. 259.

28. Burgon, *Sir Thomas Gresham*, vol. 2, pp. 266–67. Edited for clarity and brevity.
29. Burgon describes Chastillon's flight to England and his visit and dinner with Sir Thomas Gresham in *Sir Thomas Gresham*, vol. 2, pp. 269–76. The authors added color and life to his sojourn there with details on customs and dining from Ridley, *The Tudor Age*, pp. 200–217. Chocolate was brought to Europe from Mexico by the Spaniards in the early 1500s, and spread throughout Europe soon afterward. Montagné, *Larousse Gastronomique*, p. 271. Drinking of chocolate was a rare novelty, enjoyed only by the very wealthy in England, until the seventeenth century.
30. Read, *Lord Burghley and Queen Elizabeth*, pp. 12–13.
31. Burgon, *Sir Thomas Gresham*, vol. 2, p. 281. Report of Edward Horsey, Capt. of the Isle of Wight, to Cecil, extant in the State Papers. To give some idea of the size of the hoard: 20,000 Spanish reales were equivalent to about £750. Therefore, the treasure of 1.2 million reales in the 59 coffers of silver coin on that Spanish ship alone was worth approximately £45,000 sterling, or £22.5 million ($40.5 million U.S.) in today's money. This does not count the treasure on the other ships, nor the jewels, plate, and other goods on board.
32. de Roover, *Gresham on Foreign Exchange*, p. 276.
33. Burgon, *Sir Thomas Gresham*, vol. 2, p. 345.

Chapter 10

1. Jenkins, *Elizabeth the Great*, p. 147.
2. Rowse, *The England of Elizabeth*, pp. 117, 123. "…. the greatest English financier of the century, the government's constant adviser … Gresham was a remarkable man: a sort of combination of Pierpont Morgan and Keynes in his day…." "Though Gresham was the expert, actual policy was in the hands of Cecil."
3. *Dictionary of National Biography*, p. 674.
4. Domestic Corresp., State Papers Ofc.; Canterbury, 3 January 1569.
5. See Burgon, *Sir Thomas Gresham*, vol. 2, pp. 290–91, and Read, *Lord Burghley and Queen Elizabeth*, p. 18.
6. Fenelon, *Depêches*, vol. 1, p. 194.
7. See Burgon, *Sir Thomas Gresham*, vol. 2, p. 470, footnote "x." Rental income from the properties Sir Thomas settled on his daughter at her marriage would produce a handsome income for Anne and Nathaniel— about £140,300 a year, or $250,000, in today's money.
8. Fenelon, *Depêches*, vol. 1, p. 274.
9. The French ambassador, de la Mothe Fenelon, wrote to the French king, "We behold a set of ambitious, disappointed nobles, conspiring to effect the ruin of Sir William Cecil; having all the while before them a grand ulterior object—the subversion of Protestantism, and the introduction of Popery." See Burgon, *Sir Thomas Gresham*, vol. 2, pp. 293–94.

10. Jenkins, *Elizabeth the Great*, pp. 148–58.

11. The story of Lady Mary Grey is discussed at length in Burgon, *Sir Thomas Gresham*, vol. 2, pp. 387–415.

12. Fenelon, *Depêches*, vol. 1, pp. 140–41. The jewels were valued at what would today be £30 million, or $45.4 million.

13. From Leveson-Gower, *Genealogy of the Family of Gresham*, 1569, 11 Eliz. June 29th. *"Dispensatio fuit cum Nathanieli Bacon filio honorandi viri Nich. I. Bacon militis, Dni. custodis magni sigilli Angliae et Gresham virginis ut ipsi possint solum matrimonium absque bannis tempore prohibito in quacunque ecclesia (sive oratorio) P'donatur quia honorand' viri Nich' I. Bacon Mil. Dni. Custod. Magni Sigilli Angliae Filius."*

14. Burgon, *Sir Thomas Gresham*, pp. 304–6.

15. Information about the rebellion and Elizabeth's actions came from Jenkins, *Elizabeth the Great*, pp. 138–150; Read, *Lord Burghley*, pp. 18–20; Burgon, *Sir Thomas Gresham*, vol. 2, p. 184.

16. Profits from that single trading voyage would represent about £375 million or $675 million. Two-thirds of that remaining on the Continent for the Protestant cause would amount to about £250 million or $450 million, a substantial threat.

17. Burgon, *Sir Thomas Gresham*, vol. 2, pp. 342–44.

18. Jenkins, *Elizabeth the Great*, p. 155.

19. Ibid., p. 158.

20. Burgon, *Sir Thomas Gresham*, vol. 2, pp. 355–75.

21. Ibid., p. 406.

22. This description taken from ibid., pp. 349–54.

23. See Salter, *Sir Thomas Gresham*, pp. 116–18.

24. Burgon, *Sir Thomas Gresham*, vol. 2, p. 427. Others were the archbishop of Canterbury, the bishop of London, Lord Wentworth, Sir Anthony Cook, Sir Thomas Wroth, Sir Owyn Hopton, Dr. Wylson, and Thomas Wilbraham.

25. Read, *Lord Burghley and Queen Elizabeth*, p. 87.

26. See Venn, *Biographical History*, p. 56.

27. Read, *Lord Burghley and Queen Elizabeth*, pp. 149–50.

28. Burgon, *Sir Thomas Gresham*, vol. 2, p. 443. Also Leveson-Gower, *Genealogy of the Family of Gresham*, p. 12.

29. Sir Thomas would have had to produce the equivalent of about £5 million today, or $9 million, in cash, to pay that claim.

30. A great deal has been written about, or speculated about, the handling of this account. Hall, in *Society in the Elizabethan Age*, pp. 63–68 and appendix, gives an exhaustive treatment of the matter. But no concrete evidence of the queen's reasoning, or Gresham's, is given in any of the many writings we perused. It is known that the eleven-year-past-due final accounting of Sir Thomas Gresham's expenses resulted in the treasury's determination that he owed over £10,000 (about £5 million, or

$9 million in today's money) back to the crown. Whether or not that figure was justified, or absolutely correct, is not made precisely clear in any of the documents we researched. Sir Thomas and the crown's accountants differed on numerous items. There were many arbitrary disallowances. Suffice it also to say that the treasury was unaware of many of the secret activities assigned to Sir Thomas by the queen, activities which are documented in his letters, but which he presumably could not reveal openly on an expense account, since we know that not even the lord treasurer, Winchester, was privy to information about Sir Thomas's clandestine activities for the crown during that period in Flanders.

History does record that after some bold (some allege patently deceitful) maneuvering by Sir Thomas, and requests for intervention to his friends on the council, in order to rectify what he felt was an erroneous final tally, Queen Elizabeth I personally pardoned his account, affixing to it her royal seal and counting it squared.

It is difficult for these authors to give credence to the popular notion that Queen Elizabeth I, famed for her penny-pinching economies, her grasping greed, her parsimony, her exploitation of the personal fortunes of her ministers, and her minute control over every farthing in her treasury, simply pardoned without further question the final account of Sir Thomas Gresham. It is hardly credible that a queen capable of ordering the execution of the duke of Norfolk would simply "forgive" the richest man in England such a sum, thereby donating to him an enormous fortune he didn't deserve—out of sheer compassion, or a generous heart. A more likely conclusion is that the crown owed Gresham that amount, and more, and no one knew the truth better than the queen herself. And although we did not dispute use of the word "pardon" (which may have had another connotation in the sixteenth century), that is how we chose to portray the matter in this account.

31. This gives an idea of the extent of Sir Thomas Gresham's fortune. Lady Anne's income would amount to nearly £1.2 million, or $2,150,000 a year, today. And £100 to his grand nieces meant they'd have the equivalent of £50,000 yearly or $90,000 a year each, for life, from their great uncle's estate. His nephew Harry Neville would also inherit a vast fortune in estates and income, as would the Mercers' Company upon Lady Anne's death.

32. Burgon, *Sir Thomas Gresham*, vol. 2, pp. 435–41. The amount specified for the professors of Gresham College was more than Henry VIII had designated for the professors of divinity at Oxford and Cambridge. £50 = today about £25,000 or $45,000 U.S. a year. At the death of Lady Anne Gresham, who survived her husband by some seventeen years, the annual revenues from the Royal Exchange amounted to "a clear yearly value of £751 5s." or the equivalent of more than £375,000 ($675,000

U.S.) today. Those monies, and the property, went to the Mercers'
Company.

33. Ibid., vol. 2, p. 441. A full text of Sir Thomas Gresham's will is contained also in Leveson-Gower, *Genealogy of the Family of Gresham.*

Chapter 11

1. Burgon, *Sir Thomas Gresham*, vol. 2, pp. 447–48.
2. Ibid., p. 441.
3. "Details from Testimoniall of the daye of the death and fun'all of Sr.
Thomas Gresham, Knight," in Leveson-Gower, *Genealogy of the Family of Gresham*, p. 10; see also Burgon, *Sir Thomas Gresham*, vol. 2,
pp. 472–73.
4. Lady Anne's net annual income after Sir Thomas's death was enormous
for any individual in that age, and in addition to the properties, the furnishings and art in the various estates Sir Thomas left her were worth
countless millions.
5. See *Dictionary of National Biography*, pp. 593, 595.
6. An income of net £120,000 a year today, or $250,000, not considering
the values of the properties her father gave her in dowry, which produced those amounts in rent.
7. Leveson-Gower, *Genealogy of the Family of Gresham*, p. 12.
8. *Dictionary of National Biography*, p. 677.
9. Jenkins, *Elizabeth the Great*, pp. 278–79.
10. Read, *Lord Burghley and Queen Elizabeth*, p. 545.
11. Ibid., p. 435.
12. "(Elizabeth) and Cecil were both friends of Sir Thomas Gresham, the
founder of the Royal Exchange. She used him to raise State loans at
home and abroad, and took his advice on financial questions.... Because
she was 'a little Englander,' and an economist ... she laid the sea-foun-
dations of the Empire...." Trevelyan, *A Shortened History of England*,
pp. 253–54.
13. Burgon, *Sir Thomas Gresham*, vol. 2, p. 503, app. XXX.
14. Rowse writes, in *The England of Elizabeth*, pp. 528–29, "It is a thousand
pities that in the unreformed age of George III Gresham College was
virtually confiscated; its site was handed over by the City to the Crown
for a rent of £500 a year. The ultimate value of its site and that of the
Royal Exchange would have been enough in the next age to form a
nucleus for a university in London. As things are, a few lectures are all
that remain today from this noble foundation, so characteristic an expression of the desire of that age for knowledge."
15. From the Trust Deed, dated 26 April 1979. The Leveson-Gower Trust
is designated The Titsey Foundation.
16. de Roover, *Gresham on Foreign Exchange*, pp. 263–65.

Select Bibliography

This is a list of sources used in the research and writing of this life of Sir Thomas Gresham. Readers interested in learning more about the Tudor period might wish to consult the annotated bibliography by Mortimer Levine: *Tudor England 1485–1603* (Cambridge: Cambridge University Press, 1968. Current to 1966). Available in the United States from UMI Out of Print Books on Demand, 300 N. Zeeb Road, Ann Arbor, Michigan 48106.

Bogaert, J. and J. Passeron. *Les Lettres Françaises, Seizième Siècle* Paris: Èditions Magnard, 1958.

Bowle, John. *Henry VIII: A Study of Power in Action.* Boston: Little, Brown and Company, 1964.

Braudel, Fernand. *The Mediterranean and the Mediterranean World in the Age of Philip II.* 2 vols. New York: Harper & Row, 1973.

Brodin, P. and F. Ernst. *La France et Les Français.* New York: Holt, Rinehart and Winston, 1966.

Brooke, C. *A History of Gonville and Caius College.* Cambridge: Cambridge Press, 1905.

Burgon, John W. *The Life and Times of Sir Thomas Gresham.* 2 vols. London: Robert Jennings, 1839.

Byrne, M. St. Clare. *Elizabethan Life in Town and Country.* London: Methuen & Co., 1925.

Catholic Encyclopedia. Chicago: Catholic Press, 1950.

Chapman, Hester W. *The Last Tudor King: A Study of Edward VI.* New York: Macmillan Company, 1959.

Concise Columbia Encyclopedia, The. 2d ed. New York: Columbia University Press, 1989.

Dakes, Caroline.*The Blue Plaque Guide to London.* London: W. W. Norton Co., 1982.

de Roover, Raymond. *Gresham on Foreign Exchange.* Monograph. Boston: Harvard University Press, 1949.

Dictionary of National Biography. Vol. VIII.

Doolittle, Ian. *The Mercers' Company: 1579–1959.* Leeds: W. S. Maney & Son, 1994.

Doty, Richard G. *The Macmillan Encyclopedic Dictionary of Numismatics.* New York: Macmillan Company, 1982.

Durant, Will. *The Story of Civilization.* Vols. 5 & 6. New York: Simon and Schuster, 1953.

Friedman, Milton and Anna J. Schwartz. *A Monetary History of the United States, 1867–1960.* Princeton: Princeton University Press, 1963.

Froude, James A. *Froude's History of England.* Vol. V. New York: Charles Scribner and Company, 1872.

Grant, Michael. *Cambridge.* New York: William Morrow & Company, 1966.

Grun, Bernard. *The Tables of History.* New York: Simon and Schuster, 1975.

Hackett, Francis. *Henry the Eighth.* New York: Horace Liveright, 1929.

Hall, Hubert. *Society in the Elizabethan Age.* London: Swan, Sonnenschein & Co., 1902.

Heilbroner, Robert L. *The Worldly Philosophers.* New York: Simon and Schuster, 1964.

Hume, Martin. *The Courtships of Queen Elizabeth.* Suffolk, Eng.: Richard Clay & Sons, n.d.

Jenkins, Elizabeth. *Elizabeth the Great.* New York: Coward-McCann, 1958.

Leveson-Gower, William. *Genealogy of the Family of Gresham.* London: British Museum Library; Washington: Library of Congress. Unpublished, 1883.

Macleod, Henry Dunning. *The Elements of Political Economy.* London: Longman, Brown, Green, et al., 1858.

Mee, Arthur. *The King's England: The Bank of London.* London: Hadden & Stoughton, n.d.

Montagné, Prosper. *Larousse Gastronomique.* New York: Crown Publishers, 1961.

Morrison, N. Brysson. *Mary Queen of Scots.* London: Vista Books. Longacre Press, 1960.

Morrison, Samuel Eliot. *The European Discovery of America.* London: Oxford University Press, 1974.

Phelps, Brown, E. H. and Sheila V. Hopkins. *Seven Centuries of the Prices of Consumables.* Survey paper, 1956.

Prescott, H.F.M. *Mary Tudor.* New York: Macmillan Company, 1954.

Read, Conyers. *Lord Burghley and Queen Elizabeth.* New York: Alfred A. Knopf, 1960.

_____. *Mr. Secretary Cecil and Queen Elizabeth.* New York: Alfred A. Knopf, 1955.

Richardson, Walter C. *Mary Tudor: The White Queen.* Seattle: University of Washington Press, 1970.

Ridley, Jasper. *The History of England.* New York: Dorset Press, 1981.

_____. *The Tudor Age.* New York: Overlook Press, 1988.

Rowse, A. L. *The England of Elizabeth.* New York: Macmillan Company, 1951.

_____. *The Expansion of Elizabethan England.* New York: St. Martin's Press, 1955.

Salter, F. R. *Sir Thomas Gresham.* London: Leonard Parsons, 1925.

Saunders, Ann. *The Royal Exchange.* London: W. S. Maney and Son, Guardian Royal Exchange, 1991.

Shakespeare, William. *Henry VIII.* New Haven: Yale University Press, 1925.

Smith, Lacey Baldwin. *The Elizabethan World.* Boston: Houghton Mifflin Company, American Heritage Library Ed., 1991.

Southgate, George. *English Economic History.* London: J. M. Dent and Sons, 1934.

Sutherland, C.H.V. *English Coinage: 600–1900.* London: B. T. Batsford, 1973.

Trevelyan, G. M. *The History of England.* London: Longman, 1926.

_____. *A Shortened History of England.* New York: Penguin Group, 1987.

Turton, Godfrey. *Builders of England's Glory.* New York: Doubleday, 1969.

Venn, John, ed. *Biographical History of Gonville and Caius College.* 3 vols. Cambridge: Cambridge Press, 1897–1901.

Waldman, Milton. *The Lady Mary: Biography of Mary Tudor.* New York: Charles Scribner's Sons, 1972.

Ward, John A. *Lives of Professors of Gresham College.* Johnson Reprints.

White, R. J. *Cambridge Life.* London: Eyre & Spottiswoode, 1960.

Williams, Neville. *The Cardinal and the Secretary: Thomas Wolsey and Thomas Cromwell.* New York: Macmillan Company, 1975.

Williamson, James A. *The Tudor Age.* London: Longman, 1953.

Woodward, G.W.O. *Queen Elizabeth I.* London: Pitkin Pictorials, 1975.

Also: In the British Museum and Library manuscript and reading rooms, the authors consulted: the State Papers, Landsdowne Manuscript, Depêches de la Mothe Fenelon, Stowe's original *Chronicles*, Leveson-Gower's *Genealogy* and many other original documents, microfilms, books, portraits and artifacts pertaining to the Tudor period. They also conducted research at the Tower of London, Longleat, the Guildhall Library, Titsey Place, Cambridge; Antwerp and Bruges in Belgium; and the Mercers' Company, London.

About the Authors

PERRY EPLER GRESHAM was President Emeritus and Distinguished Professor of Humanities at Bethany College, Bethany, West Virginia.

Born in California in 1907, he was raised on a ranch in Colorado. Although he dropped out of high school, he later graduated *summa cum laude* from Texas Christian University and received scholarships to the University of Chicago and Columbia University.

Dr. Gresham taught philosophy at Texas Christian University and lectured in philosophy, religion, and political economy at the University of Michigan and University of Washington. He assumed the presidency of Bethany College in 1953.

In addition to being a pre-eminent educator and minister, Gresham was a businessman, journalist, and author. He received seventeen honorary doctorates during his lifetime, as well as numerous other honors and awards. His lectures took him to cities and universities throughout the United States, Canada, Mexico, and Great Britain. His monograph *Think Twice Before You Disparage Capitalism* has been translated into three languages, and has received wide international distribution. He was a trustee of, and lecturer on political economy for, the Foundation for Economic Education. He conducted a seminar on Plato's *Republic* in Athens, Greece, in celebration of the 2400th anniversary of that great philosopher's birth, and a seminar on Adam Smith's *The Wealth of Nations* at St. Andrew's University in Scotland on the occasion of the bicentennial of its publication.

Dr. Gresham was a member of the Mont Pelerin Society, and served as a director of the Chesapeake and Potomac Telephone Company of West Virginia, Cooper Tire and Rubber Company of Findlay, Ohio, and Wesbanco Holding Company of Wheeling, West Virginia, and as a trustee of the John A. Hartford Foundation of New York City. He served two terms as chairman of the North Central Association of Colleges and Universities in the United States. He was also a member for forty years of the Author's Club, London, and the Royal Scottish Automobile Club, Glasgow.

For many years he wrote a syndicated weekly column, "The Old Professor," in the *West Virginia Hillbilly*, and another, "Growing Up in the Ranchland," in Colorado's *Ranchland News*. His book *With Wings as Eagles* (Anna Publishing, 1980), was one of the early treatises on the rewards of aging well. The Greshams have contributed in great measure to the advancement of higher education.

Sadly, Dr. Gresham passed away, a victim of cancer, during the final publication stages of this book. His widow, Aleece Fickling Gresham, resides in Advance, North Carolina.

CAROL JOSE is an author and journalist. She has collaborated on several books, primarily histories. A native of New Jersey, she is a graduate of the University of Central Florida, earning a bachelor's degree in French and a master's degree in business administration. She attended the Defense Language Institute in Monterey, California; has been a teacher of English literature and foreign languages; was a financial analyst and human resources manager for a U.S. Fortune 200 corporation; speaks several languages; and has traveled widely.

She retains honorary life membership on the boards of the American Cancer Society, the Florida College Placement Association, and the National French Honor Society. She is the recipient of the Human Relations in Education Award for the State of Florida, and is a member of the National League of American Pen Women and the Space Coast Writers' Guild.

She writes two weekly columns in *Florida TODAY*, a Gannett newspaper—one on food and cooking, another on trends in dining out—and many of her articles on food, travel, and current issues have appeared in newspapers and magazines.

Ms. Jose currently resides in Indialantic, Florida.

Index